Palgrave Studies in Lived Religion and Societal Challenges

Series Editors
Nancy Ammerman
Religious Research Association
Galva, IL, USA

R. Ruard Ganzevoort
Vrije Universiteit Amsterdam
Amsterdam, The Netherlands

Srdjan Sremac
Vrije Universiteit Amsterdam
Amsterdam, The Netherlands

Palgrave Studies in Lived Religion and Societal Challenges publishes monographs and edited volumes that describe and critically interpret pressing societal issues from a lived religion perspective. Many contemporary societal challenges regard religion, directly or indirectly, and usually religion contributes to the problem as much as it fosters positive outcomes. Topics to be addressed would range from conflicts and (in-)tolerance to building inclusive societies; from urban development and policymaking to new forms of social cohesion; from poverty and injustice to global ecological challenges of the 21th century. While such issues are studied by several disciplines, with different approaches and foci, this series aims to contribute to this field by adding a particular focus on the everyday practices of religious and spiritual actors. Contexts to be studied include, but are not limited to faith communities, educational and health care settings, media, and the public sphere at large. The series has a global scope and is open to studies from all contexts and religious backgrounds. This interdisciplinary series will showcase scholarship from sociology of religion and cultural anthropology, religious studies and theology, history and psychology, law and economy. The defining feature is that religion is approached not as a stable system of official positions, traditions, creeds, and structures but as a fluid and multi-layered practice of what people actually do, experience, think, and share when they appropriate religious repertoires and negotiate their religious performance vis a vis the religious and cultural traditions they draw upon, specifically in the context of dealing with societal challenges.

More information about this series at
http://www.springer.com/series/15215

Michelle Walsh

Violent Trauma, Culture, and Power

An Interdisciplinary Exploration in Lived Religion

Michelle Walsh
School of Social Work
Boston University
Boston, MA
USA

Palgrave Studies in Lived Religion and Societal Challenges
ISBN 978-3-319-82425-3   ISBN 978-3-319-41772-1 (eBook)
DOI 10.1007/978-3-319-41772-1

© The Editor(s) (if applicable) and The Author(s) 2017
Sofcover reprint of the hardcover 1st edition 2017
This work is subject to copyright. All rights are solely and exclusively licensed by the Publisher, whether the whole or part of the material is concerned, specifically the rights of translation, reprinting, reuse of illustrations, recitation, broadcasting, reproduction on microfilms or in any other physical way, and transmission or information storage and retrieval, electronic adaptation, computer software, or by similar or dissimilar methodology now known or hereafter developed.
The use of general descriptive names, registered names, trademarks, service marks, etc. in this publication does not imply, even in the absence of a specific statement, that such names are exempt from the relevant protective laws and regulations and therefore free for general use.
The publisher, the authors and the editors are safe to assume that the advice and information in this book are believed to be true and accurate at the date of publication. Neither the publisher nor the authors or the editors give a warranty, express or implied, with respect to the material contained herein or for any errors or omissions that may have been made. The publisher remains neutral with regard to jurisdictional claims in published maps and institutional affiliations.

Cover image © epa european pressphoto agency b.v. / Alamy Stock Photo

Printed on acid-free paper

This Palgrave Macmillan imprint is published by Springer Nature
The registered company is Springer International Publishing AG
The registered company address is: Gewerbestrasse 11, 6330 Cham, Switzerland

Dedicated to the lives and memories of Moses, Kenny, LeVar, Jaewon, and Evens—as well as all others lost to or impacted by violence in our one precious shared world.

In our continuing moral bonds,
"The dead have a pact with the living."

Lyric from Dr. Ysaÿe M. Barnwell's song "Breaths" ("Breaths" Lyrics By Birago Diop/Musical Setting By Ysaÿe M. Barnwell, Barnwell's Notes Publishing, Inc.)

A Prelude of Lived Experiences

From where do any books arise, even "academic" books? Whether we acknowledge it or not, our lived experiences in the world shape what we study and what we write—and perhaps there is a larger academic "objective truth" and capacity for connection, even sacredness, in acknowledging and taking ownership of this very human reality. Perhaps we should begin to *demand* a detailed preface of lived experiences—the social experiences and identities from which we write—for every academic book published as a matter of ethical accountability within institutional systems of domination. *My* interest in the interdisciplinary exploration of violent trauma evolves out of my own lived experiences with trauma and social identity border crossings, as well as out of specific sociohistorical events.

I grew up as a fourth-generation mid-western American, racialized as white and of Irish, French, German, and Welsh descent. Historical trauma in my family system taught me how trauma leaves its marks, even as the generations seek to resist transmitting it—painful marks as well as marks of survival, resiliency, and strength. I was baptized Catholic, but generally unchurched and without religious language and practices, other than broad cultural and semi-secularized ones until my late young adulthood. I also was the first in my family history to complete a college education through the generosity of financial aid at an elite women's college in the United States, Wellesley College, acquiring the experience of being a "class cultural traveler" in this as well as through additional higher education. My lifeworld journey of meaning-making eventually led me to discovering a Unitarian Universalist (UU) congregation in Newton, MA at age 28 in late 1989. This was my first exposure to being part of a religious community and learning religious concepts and language that were connected to religious practices we engaged in together. This time period also began a different intersection of my life with history. In this intersection with history, a need arose for deepened connection to religious practices that could assist me with the violent trauma to which I was exposed vicariously for many years to come.

In April 1991, two young boys, Charles Copney, Jr., age 11, and Korey Grant, age 15, were killed in a gang related incident in Roxbury, MA. Charles was the youngest such victim during a period of heightened violence in Boston.[1] My particular suburban congregation already was involved in racial and economic justice work,[2] but in the aftermath of Charles' and Korey's murders, my then minister, Reverend Gerry Krick, spontaneously turned his pulpit over to an African-American community activist. At the activist's invitation, members of the First Unitarian Society in Newton began to develop a youth program primarily for African-American families and children in low-income Roxbury. This was the beginning of what would become a weekend youth ministry I led as a lay community minister[3] for nearly 18 years, a youth ministry placed under the UU Urban Ministry a year after its founding. Simultaneously, I entered social work school and worked for many years in urban clinical social work, including eventually as a clinic director and now university educator in the field of social work. It was through a social work school retreat and my initial encounters with stories of violent trauma that I learned to practice as a clinical social worker/UU layperson in the Zen Buddhist tradition of Thich Naht Hanh, particularly the practice of mindfulness in the encounter with suffering.

In the journey of completing this book, I realized how deeply these life identity border crossings and initial professional career choices enculturate and frame the way I view the world and human being in it, such as the interdisciplinary academic lens and language I bring as both an urban clinical social worker and urban minister, as well as a practical theologian by later training. These lens include social work's dual focus on the macro (sociocultural) and micro (clinical) levels of social justice and human ecological development, as well as social work's emphasis on strengths and resiliencies in human development.[4] Ten years after becoming a clinical social worker, I also chose to go to a Methodist seminary and became ordained as a UU clergyperson and community minister, a non-creedal liberal religious tradition with a heavy emphasis on ethical relations and social justice. For contemporary UUs, a central unifying theological role is played in this tradition through: (1) *theological anthropology*, a belief in the finite and contextual nature of human knowledge and capacities in relationship to knowing the divine, as well as an affirmation of several sources for knowing the divine, and (2) *covenantal theology*, a practice of promising to be in relationship with and accountable to each other according to certain ethical principles around shared experiences of and public practices in relationship to the divine.[5] These two core beliefs and practices result in a professed *public theological* respect for the ultimate transcending mystery[6] that underlies all human faith or spiritual quests, including secular quests for truth and justice, even if private beliefs and spiritual practices are quite diverse.[7]

I brought to seminary, as well as to my later practical theological doctoral studies, my eclectic, and perhaps eccentric or "queer," lived experiences of border crossing social identities, spiritual practices, and intellectual disciplines—and still a relative ignorance of the breadth and depth of the language and culture of the Christian tradition. This enculturation into a personally meaningful connection to the Christian tradition came later and continues to evolve as I hold it in tension with the meaningfulness of a Buddhist tradition alongside the meaningfulness of a humanist heritage, inclusive of the secular social sciences—a joyful and "queer" hodgepodge best experienced as "meaning full" in the sacred path of living tradition sources of revelation for a Unitarian Universalist.[8] As I have walked this sacred path, I also have grown more sensitized to the practices through which this particular "queer" religious tradition has held itself together, including through practices of play and experimentation with language and metaphor.[9]

In this sense, I remain truly a practical theologian, equally alongside my social work and ministerial identities, in a "confessional" commitment (understood in a broader metaphorical sense) to my lived religious and spiritual tradition as a UU. If the root metaphoric meaning of "faith" is that in which one grounds one's trust and if the root metaphoric meaning of "to confess" is simply to admit one's adherence to and belief in a faith tradition—a faith tradition that encompasses ethical promises and practices of how to be and act in relation with one another and our broader world rather than being restricted to particular doctrinal beliefs—then *confessional* is indeed what I am. I am *confessional* to this queer contemporary religion called Unitarian Universalism, forged as a consolidation of two different centuries-long Christian traditions in the crucible of the 1960's political upheavals of race, class, gender, sexual orientation, and war. If the term "queer" also is understood in its root metaphoric meaning as "peculiar," "off-center," "strange or eccentric" as judged so by a dominant culture normatively, then indeed Unitarian Universalism is judged as a heretical and queer religion by a dominant Christian culture and Christian institutions of power. Yet I have a sneaking suspicion that it also embodies the larger potential for Christianity when queered—when freed in its faith *practices* to encounter the depths of difference in lived experiences, culture, language, and worldviews among peoples of faith.[10]

My formal and professional education in both fields—social work and the Christian tradition—occurred during my time of praxis with this inner-city youth ministry over nearly two decades with the UU Urban Ministry. As a living praxis, this meant border crossing, translation, and finding mutual relevance and meaning-making in creating connections, both intellectual and pastoral, between graduate school, human service agencies, suburban churches, and community immersions, as well as across borders of race, class, gender, ability, sexual orientations, religion, and exposure to violent trauma. The formative event for this book occurred in the first semester of my doctoral studies when, in September 2006, my African American goddaughter's 17-year-old nephew, Kenny Hall, was shot and killed in Boston, a murder that remains unsolved as of the writing of this book.

It was this tragic event that brought me into more direct contact with the Louis D. Brown Peace Institute, a subject of study in this book, though I had been well aware of their work for many years and had previously experienced the murder of another young adult related to our youth ministry in 1995, Moses Grant. In the month after Kenny's murder, October 2006, our UU urban youth ministries experienced three additional murders within a week's span, murders that impacted on staff and youth, including another young adult related to several of the youth in my ministry, LeVar Jackson. Once again, I referred families to the Peace Institute. During this period, I also felt compelled to take pictures of the spontaneous street memorials that sprang up in the aftermath for both Kenny and LeVar, memorials that I noticed springing up more frequently since the widely covered murder of ten-year-old Trina Persad in 2002.[11]

In the spring of 2007, I was taking an anthropology course for my doctoral program when I mentioned the phenomenon of the street memorials I had been observing and was encouraged by my professor to engage in a pilot study of these spontaneous shrines. My research introduced me to cultural folklorist Jack Santino's international studies of spontaneous shrines and to UU ethicist Sharon Welch's expanded metaphoric understanding of Johann Baptist Metz' Christian use of the phrase "dangerous memories."[12] Both helped me to consider the political performative and prophetic (a Jewish-Christian-Islamic term) protest function of such street memorials alongside their commemorative function. This initial pilot study led to a separate pilot study of the funerals and specialized orders of funeral service developed by the Peace Institute. Then as my prospectus for my dissertation was being written in mid-2010, another young man who had grown up in my youth ministries was shot and killed, Jaewon Martin. The summer after completion of my dissertation, I lost one more from my youth ministry, Evens Archer. The names I share here are not the only male and female young people sacrificed to violence whose stories and lives I knew or came to know and care about over my years in urban ministry and research.

This book thus is threaded with autoethnographic experiences and perspectives and a deep sense of commitment to the families of Boston whose lives have been so deeply intertwined with my own for well over 25 years now. My exposure to the impact of violent trauma has been up close and personal, deepening my own need to lift up the voices of those who have suffered the unspeakable, as well as the voices of those who companion and serve them in the aftermath. This includes those in my own UU denomination who discover that trauma and violence cut across all the lines of race and class and gender, as well as power, privilege, and other oppressions that may otherwise divide us in our sociocultural imaginations and limited institutions and life experiences. There are no neat "objective" lines here—trauma and violence show no respect for our desires for tidiness and control, including the control perhaps that the cultural lens and language of our respective intellectual disciplines might seek to impose. If I can "rattle the self-imposed cages" of our disciplinary boundaries as we seek to learn from and address violent trauma in our larger world, including beyond a US context, then I will feel that I indeed have provided a service to the voices of survivors, and those who serve them, those from my particular studies as well as hopefully others beyond these particular studies.

Boston, MA, USA   Michelle Walsh

Notes

1. See a Frontline documentary, "A Kid Kills," available at http://www.pbs.org/wgbh/pages/frontline/programs/info/1022.html (accessed October 16, 2013).
2. Issues of race and class were brought to light for Boston area congregations when a white suburban man accused a black man of murdering his pregnant wife, but later admitted his own guilt and committed suicide. See https://en.wikipedia.org/wiki/Charles_Stuart_(murderer) (accessed October 16, 2013).
3. In the Unitarian Universalist tradition, community ministry is ministry that occurs beyond the walls of the parish—what some might term the "missionary" ministry of Unitarian Universalism, whether lay or ordained. An early nineteenth-century pioneer in community ministry, Rev. Joseph Tuckerman, was recognized to be an ecumenical pioneer in social work as well by a Catholic priest. See Daniel

T. McColgan, "Joseph Tuckerman: Pioneer in American Social Work" (PhD diss., The Catholic University of America, 1940).
4. A few foundational books and articles in the field of social work illustrating these perspectives include: C. Wright Mills, *The Sociological Imagination* (New York: Oxford University Press, 1959); Urie Bronfenbrenner, ed., *Making Human Beings Human: Bioecological Perspectives on Human Development* (Thousand Oaks, CA: Sage, 2005); and Dennis Saleeby, "Power in The People: Strengths and Hope," *Advances in Social Work*, Vol. 1, No. 2 (Fall 2000): 127–136.
5. The Unitarian Universalist Association was birthed when two historically Christian traditions, Unitarianism and Universalism, consolidated in 1961, initially creating a shared statement of principles in its bylaws and then later adding explicit theological language of "covenant" in a re-covenanting process, first in 1985 and then lastly in 1995. Tracking specifics of these General Assembly processes represent practical theological studies yet to be done for Unitarian Universalism. In the meantime, see Mark W. Harris, *Historical Dictionary of Unitarian Universalism* (Lanham, MD: Scarecrow Press, 2004). The newly formed association was tested in many ways by the social and political turbulence of the 1960s through the various civil rights movements; racism and what would be called "the black empowerment" period; the Vietnam War and the draft; and generally the political empowerment of the voices of and actions by marginalized peoples (youth, women, people of color, gays and lesbians, etc.). See these additional sources for further historical perspectives and their legacy for contemporary struggles of Unitarian Universalists: Warren R. Ross, *The Premise and the Promise: The Story of the Unitarian Universalist Association* (Boston: Skinner House Books, 2001); Leslie Takahashi Morris, Chip Roush, and Leon Spencer, *The Arc of the Universe is Long: Unitarian Universalists, Anti-Racism and the Journey from Calgary* (Boston: Skinner House Books, 2009), as well as other resources listed in the bibliography.
6. See a former UUA president, William F. Schulz, "Our Faith," in *The Unitarian Universalist Pocket Guide*, ed., William G. Sinkford, 4th ed. (Boston: Skinner House Books, 1993/1997/2004), 1–6, in which

he writes that Unitarian Universalists "... *respect the mystery more*. We believe ... that no single religion ... has a monopoly on wisdom; that the answers to the great religious questions change from generation to generation; and that the ultimate truth about God and Creation, death, meaning, and the human spirit cannot be captured in a narrow statement of faith. The mystery itself is always greater than its name ...." This essay on "Our Faith" survived at least three editions since 1993 (until the publication of the most recent pocket guide) as a *written practice* for explaining the Unitarian Universalist faith tradition to a newcomer. See also the Commission on Appraisal, *Engaging Our Theological Diversity* (Boston: Unitarian Universalist Association, 2005) and their *Interdependence: Renewing Congregational Polity* (Boston: Unitarian Universalist Association, 1997) for further history and empirical data on contemporary Unitarian Universalism. There also is a very strong *ecological* orientation within the Unitarian Universalist tradition, beyond its mystical and ethical commitments and its focus on the language of "love." A recent dissertation by a UU scholar tracks historical Transcendentalist contributions to evolving ecotheology possibilities within liberal Christianity, as well as its complicity in manifest destiny. See Sheri M. Prud'homme, "Gleam Of The Infinite Majesty: The Interplay of Manifest Destiny and Ecotheology in Thomas Starr King's Construction of Yosemite as Sacred Text" (PhD diss., Graduate Theological Union, 2015). I also have argued in other settings that contemporary Unitarian Universalist "God-Talk" expands beyond the anthropomorphic through its seventh principle: "the interdependent web of existence"—that this also becomes the tradition's metaphoric "God-Talk" in practice in addition to "mystery" "justice," and "love" and which bears further theological development in and analyses of *practices* within the tradition.

7. When I bring the term "public theology" to bear on Unitarian Universalism as a religious tradition, I am drawing on Bonnie J. Miller-McLemore's definition that public theology "attempts to analyze and influence the wider social order ... Different from civil religion's generic universal appeal, public theology attempts to make a

recognizably valid and self-critical claim for the relevance of specific religious beliefs and practices," in Miller-McLemore, "Pastoral Theology as Public Theology: Revolutions in the 'Fourth Area'," 1370, In *Dictionary of Pastoral Care and Counseling*, edited by Rodney J. Hunter, 1370–1380 (Nashville, TN: Abingdon Press, 1990/2005). For Unitarian Universalists, the term "public theology" applies both to a congregation's particular covenant and to the larger associational covenant between congregations. Unitarian Universalists distinguish in *practice* between the personal faith and practices of individuals and the public faith and practices of a congregation and the larger association or denomination. There is a unification of diverse personal theologies and practices, within any particular congregation, as well as between congregations in the larger association, through profession to a public faith and ethical practices. This public profession emphasizes respect for personal access to the divine and a covenant to ethical principles of shared practice, which then creates an umbrella under which a significant amount of public *prophetic* witness and social justice work may occur. Thus, there is an underlying theology at play from the stance of theological anthropology and ecclesial organization that marks what results as a self-critical "public theology" in shared beliefs and practices for Unitarian Universalists.
8. See www.uua.org (accessed March 2, 2016) for more information generally on the tradition, as well as http://www.uua.org/beliefs (accessed March 2, 2016) for information regarding the tradition's seven ethical principles and six living tradition sources to which its congregations within the Unitarian Universalist Association are bound by covenant.
9. See Unitarian ethicist, theologian, and minister James Luther Adams' early work in this area, "Root Metaphors of Religious Social Thought," in *An Examined Faith: Social Context and Religious Commitment*, 243–255 (1973/1988), edited by George K. Beach (Boston: Beacon Press, 1991), as well as a later series of essays produced in response to a controversy over religious language, Dean Grodzins, ed., *A Language of Reverence* (Chicago: Meadville Lombard Press, 2004). See also Tom Owen-Towle, *Freethinking Mystics With Hands:*

Exploring the Heart of Unitarian Universalism (Boston: Skinner House Books, 1998) and Fredric John Muir, *Heretics' Faith: Vocabulary for Religious Liberals* (Unitarian Universalist Church of Annapolis, MD, 2001).
10. Kathryn Lofton ponders, "A church of the queer may or may not be possible" (p. 203) in her chapter "Everything Queer?" in *Queer Christianities: Lived Religion in Transgressive Forms* (New York: New York University Press, 2015). While she stays within a current association of the term "queer" with homosexuality, she also opens a door to a broader metaphoric interpretation in saying, " . . . Christianity itself was also queer: a tradition simultaneously averse to expressions of homosexuality while also offering multiple scriptural, ritual, and social experiences of self-understanding, self-formation, and revelation as a dissenting subject" (p. 199). See also Rev. Elizabeth M. Edman, *Queer Virtue: What LGBTQ People Know About Life and Love and How It Can Revitalize Christianity* (Boston: Beacon Press, 2016); Pamela Lightsey, *Our Lives Matter: A Womanist Queer Theology* (Eugene, OR: Pickwick Publications, 2015); and Ian Barnard, *Queer Race: Cultural Interventions in the Racial Polities of Queer Theory* (New York: Peter Lang, 2004/2008). However, I stress that I am broadening the metaphoric use of the term "queer" beyond solely its contemporary usage in the BGLTQI context, though it remains inclusive of that context, particularly in attention to the marking of bodies and visceral discomforts raised as well as institutional oppression of bodies. See also Janet R. Jakobsen, "The Body Politic vs. Lesbian Bodies: Publics, Counterpublics, and the Use of Norms," in *Horizons in Feminist Theology: Identity, Tradition and Norms*, 116–136, edited by Rebecca S. Chopp and S.G. Davaney (Minneapolis, MN: Fortress Press, 1997) for hints of intersectionality possibilities in queer theory as well.
11. See http://www.boston.com/yourtown/boston/roxbury/articles/2012/06/01/conflict_of_interestsmemorial_park_is_targeted_for_housing/ (accessed October 16, 2013) and http://archive.boston.com/yourtown/news/dorchester/2013/08/hold_in_dorchester_a_slaying_youth_is_remembered_through_art.html (accessed May 4, 2016).

12. See Jack Santino, *Signs of War and Peace: Social Conflict and the Uses of Symbols in Public in Northern Ireland* (New York: Palgrave MacMillan, 2001) and Jack Santino, ed., *Spontaneous Shrines and the Public Memorialization of Death* (New York: Palgrave MacMillan, 2006), as well as Johann Baptist Metz, *Faith in History and Society: Toward a Practical Fundamental Theology*, trans. J. Matthew Ashley (New York: The Crossroad Publishing Company, 1977/2007) and Sharon D. Welch, *A Feminist Ethic of Risk* (Minneapolis: Fortress Press, 2000, 2nd edition).

Acknowledgments

I am so very grateful for the support of many in the fits and starts labor of love that has been the journey of this book. First, there are no words adequately to thank my families of birth (mom, dad, Kathy, Mike, Judith, Robbie, Harry, Kendra, and Elizabeth) as well as of adoption (Gena, Azariah, Vaughnda Sr., and the entire clan) for all that they have shared with me over the years and all that I have learned from them—their practical support, their emotional support, their love, humor and patience, their sheer grit and fierceness of survival, and their commitments to and dreams of a more just world. Additionally, I have been gifted for many years to know and serve families in Roxbury, Dorchester, and Mattapan, as well as in Unitarian Universalist (UU) congregations, particularly in Quincy and Newton, and to be part of a larger community of professional love, care, and ministry. There also are no words to adequately express all that I have learned and received from you, as well from the survivors, members, staff, and supporters of the Louis D. Brown Peace Institute, UU Trauma Response Ministry, Unitarian Universalist Association (UUA), and Tennessee Valley UU Church who graciously agreed to be part of the original research.

I am grateful to the series editors for their interest in my research, and particularly to Srdjan Sremac for his gentle encouragement and patience along the way. In the shaping of my attention and sensitivity to method and writing in my original research formation, I extend my enduring gratitude to Shelly Rambo and Dale Andrews, who also lived patiently, and hopefully with humor and at least some reward, through an interdisciplinary writing and cross-cultural encounter in their supportive work with me. Many other colleagues and scholars, senior and junior, across disciplines have been foundational to my shaping and are too numerous to mention, though you will find their work liberally referenced throughout this book and its bibliography.

Opportunities to present at, gain feedback from, or network through a variety of conferences and gatherings over several years helped me to hone concepts and understandings of the significance of interdisciplinary explorations for the societal challenge posed by violent trauma. These included presentations at an international conference on Trauma and Spirituality in Belfast in 2011 and a Trauma and Lived Religion conference in Amsterdam in 2015, along with attendance at other 2015 conferences such as the Council on Social Work Education, Jean Baker Miller Summer Intensive Institute, and the Internal Family Systems annual conference. Additional presentations over several years with the American Academy of Religion, as well as with the UU Scholars and the Collegium of Liberal Religious Scholars, were helpful in the early stages of my original research. More recently, presentations at a 2016 transdisciplinary conference on theopoetics and at the 2016 Biennial Association of Practical Theology, as well as at the 2016 Cultural Studies Association, shaped some final thoughts and revisions. Research also needs institutional funding, and I therefore am grateful for several years of financial support received for the original research through Boston University's School of Theology and their Center for Practical Theology, as well as for the major scholarship I received from the Fund for Nurturing UU Scholarship under the Panel on Theological Education.

In all things, family and close friends are foundational to feeling supported—you know who you are and my gratitude is so profoundly heartfelt! Most of all, however, I want to thank my great love, soul mate, and intellectual partner, my husband Rev. Clyde Grubbs, who accompanied me patiently throughout this journey, cooking for me and reassuring me and sharing his wisdom when asked as a person of indigenous heritage. Most particularly, his keen indigenous insight into the challenges posed by a Western Enlightenment scientific heritage has been deeply influential on my thinking. This includes a very recent sermon in which he stated: "one of the weaknesses of the Enlightenment science was to see phenomenon in isolation—breaking complexity down can be helpful, if one doesn't destroy the phenomenon in the process. Sometimes phenomenon cannot be understood except in its relationship with its surroundings." He deepens my understanding of how our Western scientific heritage of simplifying and categorizing can create normative and visceral cultural barriers to a richer embodied and interdependent phenomenological approach in lived religion studies. Through intimate living, daily encounter with our shared love in and commitment to reaching across our own lines of cultural difference, not without struggle and effort but overall with a sense of humor, I have learned so much for which to be grateful for a lifetime.

Contents

A Prelude of Lived Experiences   vii

Acknowledgments   xix

List of Figures   xxv

1   Introduction   1

2   Challenges and Possibilities in Interdisciplinary Encounters   23

3   Two Case Studies by a Researcher Living Between Worlds   51

4   Trauma in a Lived Religion Perspective   87

5   Attending to "Survivors as Experts": Lessons Learned   141

6 Cross-Cultural Encounters in the Research: Lessons
   Learned   193

7 Poetics and Ethics of World/Sense: Cultivating the Lessons   247

A Queer Postlude of Intersections in the Aftermath   289

Bibliography   295

Index   317

List of Figures

Fig. 1.1	Scene from a Boston Street Protest	3
Fig. 3.1	Peace Institute's Seven Principles of Peace	58
Fig. 3.2	TVUUC Partial Exterior Building View	68
Fig. 3.3	TVUUC Sample Exterior Panels	69
Fig. 3.4	Permanent Welcoming Congregation Plaque	70
Fig. 4.1	Spontaneous Street Memorial #1	101
Fig. 4.2	Spontaneous Street Memorial #2	102
Fig. 4.3	Spontaneous Street Memorial #3	103
Fig. 4.4	Public Artistic Memorial—Long Shot	106
Fig. 4.5	Public Artistic Memorial—Close Up	107
Fig. 4.6	Permanent Town Granite Memorial "Touchstone" Handprint	108
Fig. 5.1	Peace Institute survivor's sandplay example	147
Fig. 5.2	Other art by Peace Institute survivors	149
Fig. 5.3	Home altar example	152
Fig. 5.4	Peace Institute funeral order of service, sample resource page	169
Fig. 5.5	Traveling memorial button project	170
Fig. 6.1	TVUUC Linda Lee Kraeger Library Memorial	205
Fig. 6.2	TVUUC Pellet-Marked and Memorialized Door	206
Fig. 6.3	Peace Institute Funeral Order of Service, Sample Pastoral Care Advice Page	216

List of Figures

Fig. 7.1 Intersecting issues at the Mothers' Day Walk for Peace   278
Fig. 7.2 Intersecting issues at a climate change protest   279
Fig. 7.3 Intersecting issues through youth activism and new stories   280

1

Introduction

Violent Trauma and the "Land of the Free, Home of the Brave"

The people of the United States live in one of the most violent nations on earth, according to studies by the Centers for Disease Control and Prevention (CDC). As cited by Deborah Prothrow-Stith and Howard Spivak from CDC reports,[1] the US homicide rate is ten times as high as Western Europe, seventy times as high as Japan, and five times as high as Australia, Canada, and New Zealand. Of 26 industrialized nations, 73 percent of all child homicides occur in the United States. According to research by Adam Lankford presented at the 2015 Annual Meeting of the American Sociological Association, "Despite having only about 5 percent of the world's population, the United States was the attack site for a disproportionate 31 percent of public mass shooters globally from 1966–2012."[2] The year 2012 ended with the extraordinary mass shooting of 20 preschool children and eight adults in Newtown, CT (inclusive of the shooter's mother and his own subsequent suicide).[3] Mass shootings have continued and worsened on a regular basis in the United States, including in school and religious settings.

Parallel to this rise in mass shootings is a rise in visible and documented police violence against black persons in the United States. Observing the international interest expressed by a UK newspaper, *The Guardian*, and their "*The Counted*" database collection of US police shootings, researchers from the Harvard University School of Public Health expressed dismay that it is "startling that we, in the US, must rely on a UK newspaper for systematic timely counts of the number of persons killed by the police."[4] They further argued that such deaths at the hands of the police, as well as killing of police officers, constitute a public health issue for families and communities and require tracking and data collection as such:

> Law-enforcement–related deaths, of both persons killed by law enforcement agents and also law enforcement agents killed in the line of duty, are a public health concern, not solely a criminal justice concern, since these events involve mortality and affect the well-being of the families and communities of the deceased; therefore, law-enforcement–related deaths are public health data, not solely criminal justice data.

The United Nations (UN) also has taken note of the rise in American public violence, including its racial dimensions. In 2014, the UN Committee on the Elimination of Racial Discrimination (CERD) condemned US acts of police brutality and called for a review of the controversial "Stand Your Ground" laws in 22 states,[5] laws that permitted the killer of 17-year-old African American Trayvon Martin to be released on the ground that he killed in self-defense. This pivotal violent trauma spawned the national Black Lives Matter (BLM) movement, founded by three black female activists,[6] in resistance to the larger systemic structures oppressing black people in the United States. This was followed in 2015 by the African American Policy Forum's launching of the social media-based #SayHerName campaign,[7] also as an act of resistance. BLM has grown beyond the US context to make intersectional and international links to the causes and resistances of peoples suffering from violent trauma and colonial oppression, including black immigrants, black transgender people, and Palestinians.[8] While situating itself in the particularities of black oppression, BLM also affirms its solidarity with and

Fig. 1.1 *Scene from a Boston Street Protest.* Marching on the streets of Boston in 2015 for increased funding for jobs for youth and against prioritizing police funding at the expense of jobs, education, health, and housing. Flyer handout states: "This hurts Black youth and youth of color: women, gender-nonconforming, transgender, poor, and queer"

intersectional awareness of the unique cultural and institutional impact of violent trauma on other marginalized and oppressed groups, such as Native Americans and Muslims (Fig. 1.1).[9]

The dominant US' cultural "stock"[10] image of itself, often taught in its public schools, is that it was founded on freedom from violent religious persecution in Europe, with separation of church and state as the rule of law and ample opportunities in the new land for all individuals to advance equally. Yet the "concealed story"[11] is that the United States also is rooted in legally enforced colonial violence and religious oppression through the genocide of indigenous peoples and the transport and enslavement of persons from Africa, including the contemporary emergence of a "New

Jim Crow" through mass incarceration that particularly impacts "America's poorest, brownest, and blackest neighborhoods."[12] Violent trauma at the historical, religious, and institutional core of the United States appears to be unraveling before much of the contemporary world's astonished media eyes. The idealistic stock story lifted up of the United States as "the land of the free and the home of the brave" in a stanza of the US national anthem, "The Star Spangled Banner," is laid bare to have yet another concealed story.

The concealed story is of its author, Francis Scott Key, a man who believed deeply in the racial myths of his day—in the genetic inferiority of African slaves and the God-granted superiority of the American white race to conquer the land.[13] This same culturally and historically embedded violent experience of white supremacy, including its intersectional religious and racial dimensions, plays out in contemporary US national politics when a presidential candidate for election calls not only to build a wall against Mexican migrants but also for a ban on Muslims and later is allowed to banter about a violent apocryphal colonial story of murder of Muslims with virtually no recrimination.[14] With so many variables in the mix of this rising tide of violence, the United States is uniquely situated for lived religion case studies drawing from interdisciplinary perspectives.

The Need for Interdisciplinary Lived Religion Studies of Violent Trauma

Violence experienced by individuals and communities begets trauma—a rupturing of the experience of bodily safety, meaning-making, and communal connections. Bodies, meaning-making systems, and communal relationships are situated in historical, religious, and cultural contexts of institutionalized power when violent trauma occurs, as seen in contemporary racial and religious conflicts in the United States. Such experiences of violent trauma have both sociological and religious impact within communities, disrupting faith beliefs and spiritual practices and resulting in profound human brokenness at both personal and communal levels. Creative meaning-making in the aftermath through new or innovative religious and spiritual responses are structured along cultural and historical dimensions of institutionalized power in communities as well.

Despite the prevalence of violence both in the United States and beyond, it is rare to find an *organized* institutional religious response to trauma that correlates interdisciplinary social scientific understanding of trauma *with* spiritual or religious practices and rituals for personal healing *as well as* for public policy advocacy in the aftermath of such violence. It is even rarer to find interdisciplinary scholarship on what such a religious response might look like or how it might function when organized institutionally.[15] Such potential for disruption of and creative responses by communities urgently calls for an interdisciplinary exploration of clinical, health, educational, public policy, and pastoral prophetic religious and spiritual responses to violent trauma—practices that heal and transform on an individual level as well as on interpersonal, institutional, and sociocultural levels. The United States' violent context is uniquely positioned for such case studies, though, of course, it is not the only potential context internationally for such studies—and lived religion studies are uniquely interdisciplinary by their very nature.

The language of "lived religion" is used in multiple disciplinary contexts, from sociology to history to anthropology to practical theology.[16] Violent trauma as a rupturing force in our world and communities also commands our respective intellectual and professional disciplines, with their respective tools and language, to find new, creative, and innovative ways for speaking to and working with each other if researchers and our different professions are to have practical meaning and responsive impact in the world and for communities in the aftermath of trauma. Lived religion thus is situated as an important field of study for cross-disciplinary explorations of personal and communal embodied and material practices central to the lived experience of rupturing and meaning-making in the aftermath of trauma.

While situated thus, the use of lived religion methods for studying violent trauma also need further mechanisms of translation and correlation *between* the disciplines. Such methods also need to be sensitized to and explicitly acknowledge the intertwining phenomena of culture and power in their use, particularly if a researcher or profession seeks to contribute to an in-depth and richer knowledge base for interdisciplinary purposes. There is a need for a more diverse and larger number of lived religion case studies in which the conceptual and linguistic capacity for describing the culturally unique dimensions of the impact of violent trauma is broadened. This includes the particularities of a community's emerging religious or spiritual practices in the aftermath. Such broadening needs to be inclusive of factors of historical oppression and contemporary power relationships as well. This is a need and ethical mandate regardless of the stance of the lived religion researcher as secular, religious, or theological in commitment, purpose, and professional discipline. Through studies of this nature, we can begin to find the creative, new, and innovative points of interdisciplinary connections that can speak and work together in the ruptured spaces of violent trauma, perhaps even pointing toward the transdisciplinary.[17]

The Louis D. Brown Peace Institute (LDBPI or Peace Institute) in Boston and the Unitarian Universalist Trauma Response Ministry (UUTRM) were two organized trauma ministries in the United States context open for such study, one primarily lay, para-ecclesial,[18] and community based and the other ecclesial and national, at times international, in scope.[19] They each seek to bring together religious, spiritual, and social scientific resources and practices in organized institutional form to assist people experiencing trauma. This book addresses a gap in empirical studies of *organized* religious or spiritual responses to violent trauma by utilizing and expanding upon a lived religion approach. Case studies of these two specific trauma ministries, and their clinical pastoral and prophetic justice responses to violent trauma in the US context, were examined through an interdisciplinary lens with ethnographic and phenomenological approaches. The larger hope is that in offering these two case studies from the United States as a beginning point—researched just prior to the most intense period of rising mass shootings and the emergence of BLM—interest in further interdisciplinary or transdisciplinary lived religion studies of violent trauma across national and religious contexts might be stimulated.

The Trauma Response Ministry Case Studies

As described in my prelude, the auto-ethnographic aspect of my historical immersion in Boston urban ministry as a Unitarian Universalist (UU) for nearly two decades, first as a layperson and clinical social worker and then later as clergy, cannot be escaped in both my access to and the trust extended for the two case studies from which I draw for this book. These case studies encompassed an examination of the prophetic pastoral care practices, themes, and vision of the LDBPI and the UUTRM, respectively.[20] My research at the time was limited in its capacity to engage in a full evaluation of each organized ministry, including the entire scope of survivors served by each ministry in either community or congregational context. Given the relational auto-ethnographic[21] nature of my access to these organized ministries, and the sensitive nature of discussing traumatic experiences, I relied on the leaders of each trauma ministry to refer me to particular people the ministry had served in extending an invitation to be interviewed, ensuring also that anyone interviewed was at least one year away from the initial traumatic event. Thus my research was not evaluative in scope but only a beginning step toward investigating what organized trauma response ministries might look like in practice. This provided an opportunity to lift up the "prophetic pastoral care" practices in which the ministries engaged, drawing on language from the Christian tradition for analysis of the initial research, and the experiences of at least some survivors with the effectiveness of those practices. The research also allowed me to explore and draw upon a more extended range of interdisciplinary conceptual tools for lived religion studies that correlated with the lived experiences and language of the study participants.

The LDBPI serves families in the aftermath of homicide in the greater Boston, Massachusetts region of the United States. I was aware of the work of the LDBPI throughout most of the years of my ministry, though the UU urban youth ministry I led as a layperson began in 1991, and the tragedy leading to the founding of the LDBPI occurred in 1993. In the fall of 2006, as I was beginning my doctoral studies, my personal life intersected with their work more closely when my African American goddaughter's 17-year-old nephew, Kenneth Hall, was shot and killed in what remains an unsolved murder in Boston. Then three more murders related to the UU Urban Ministry's staff and programs occurred in the span of a week only one month later. By the spring of 2007, I was initiating pilot studies of the spontaneous street memorials that were created in the aftermath of Boston area homicides, as well as funeral practices developed by the Peace Institute. This eventually led to a period of formal ethnographic and phenomenological research during 2010–2012—not only with the Peace Institute but also with the UUTRM.

The UUTRM responds to a broader range of traumatic incidents related to UU congregations, and, like many other UUs, I first became aware of their existence when they were given a denominational award in 2007 for their work with congregations impacted by Hurricane Katrina.[22] Then in the summer of 2008, after completing pilot studies related to Boston area violence and the work of the Peace Institute with survivors, I found myself participating, now ordained as a UU clergyperson, in a peace vigil with members of my own Newton, Massachusetts UU congregation. This peace vigil was organized as a solidarity gesture for the Tennessee Valley Unitarian Universalist Church (TVUUC) in Knoxville, TN, in the aftermath of a violent shooting in their sanctuary. The second case study was of the UUTRM's work with this congregation, including aspects and innovative practices of the congregation's and larger Unitarian Universalist Association (UUA)'s own responses to the violence—as reported through the lens of a few key leaders, thus not a full congregational study.[23]

For both of these case studies, I drew upon ethnographic observations, pictures, and field notes; the published materials and documents of the two trauma ministries; and phenomenological interviews with ministry leaders, survivors, and institutional supporters of each ministry for the purpose of triangulation of data.[24] Core demographic differences between these two trauma ministries included that the majority of participants in the LDBPI case study were African American and that survivors and ministry leaders possessed a maximum of a bachelor's degree, while the majority of participants in the UUTRM case study were white and educated to a master's degree and often higher. I interviewed five ministry leaders, five survivors, and five institutional supporters for each trauma ministry—thus 30 interviews overall.

This project also was engaged as an oral history ethnographic and phenomenological study. For each trauma ministry case study, the board of the respective organization gave permission for research to be conducted, and each study participant was given the opportunity to review, add to, or correct their interview transcript and to retain a copy of their transcript for further measures of accountability. To maximize confidentiality due to the very public nature of each ministry, aggregate demographic data was shared using the above three categories of interviewees but was generally not attached to specific individuals. Exceptions included the LDBPI founding ministry leader due to the centrality of her public role in establishing mission and programs, as well as the TVUUC minister and the former UUA president due to the centrality of their public roles in the aftermath of the church shooting. As appropriate also due to the content of material shared, the roles, race, and/or gender of those interviewed were identified at different points in the case study, which may make them more identifiable for those close to the ministries and their lived situations.

Of particular note for the respective case studies, the LDBPI institutional supporters included a mental health clinician, a public health doctor, an anti-oppression consultant, an urban minister, and a city councilor. All LDBPI survivors interviewed were mothers of murdered youth and members of what was called the "Peace Warriors" group at the Peace Institute at that time. (Four of the ministry leaders also were survivors of child or sibling homicide while a fifth ministry leader had experienced another form of traumatic loss of a friend, thus the ministry itself was considered to be survivor-led at the time.) For the UUTRM case study, I gathered data and interviews over the course of one year in 2011, which included travel to the TVUUC for one immersion weekend of interviews and observations as well.

Specifically of the five UU Trauma Response Ministry leaders interviewed, four were direct founders of the UUTRM and all were ordained as UU clergy. The five TVUUC leaders interviewed as survivors included the minister, two former board presidents, a former church administrator, and a former volunteer media coordinator, the latter four being laity at the time of the shooting (though one would go on to become clergy). Three were present in the sanctuary at the time of the shooting while the minister and media coordinator arrived on site the same day in the aftermath. The five institutional supporters at the time interviewed included a former UUA president, a current UUA vice president, a former UUA transitions director, and two current UUA district executives.[25]

Neither case study should be considered a complete case study of all possible dimensions of a trauma ministry's work in a community or with a congregation. Instead, these case studies give glimpses only into the lives of those particular individuals interviewed. These are their *particular* lived experiences in their respective communities with practices that helped or did not help in the aftermath of violent trauma. These included their self-reports of the religious or spiritual dimensions of these practices and their differences in cultural experiences with institutional power, as well as its historical dimensions. Given disparities of race and class in social identities among the study participants, the case studies also yielded opportunities to explore interdisciplinary tools for the study of, and experiences with, culture and power in lived religion. In sharing my findings from these participants, I also share a larger hope for mutual creative and innovative benefit to all academic disciplines drawn from for the case studies in their encounters with each other. My hope is that such encounters witness to the challenges and rewards of interdisciplinary exploratory talk and action for a crucial social issue in our time—understanding and ameliorating violent trauma and its impact. A beginning example of the possible lessons from one such interdisciplinary encounter follows, with others spread throughout this book.

Beginning Stories of Language and Visceral Boundaries Between Disciplines

As a clinical social worker, urban minister, and later ethnographer, I have been engaged in "border crossing" of one nature or another for many decades. Engaging interdisciplinary work for social problems, particularly for highly charged problems such as the impact of violent trauma, entails crossing the lines of respective academic discipline languages and narratives—in effect, the respective cultural worldviews of the different disciplines. Cultural worldviews represent more than surface differences in visible rituals and practices.[26] Cultural worldviews are constructed on lived experiences over time, lived experiences in relationship to the world that are embodied, enlanguaged, and finite in nature, including epistemologically.

Crossing such disciplinary lines of embodied and enlanguaged cultural worldviews can provoke a range of visceral reactions, including exploratory openness, excitement, and curiosity—as well as confusion, anxiety, or discomfort. Experiences of the latter can foster the creation of boundaries around particular phenomenon in a respective discipline's capacity to witness to or understand the phenomena through language, which can be problematic for social issues that require multiple lens in approach for effective problem-solving and amelioration. For example, public health researchers who draw upon transdisciplinary approaches also report experiencing this difficulty. Dr. Sarah Gehlert[27] of the Washington University Brown School of Social Work stated in an interview:

> The hardest part of transdisciplinary work in general is that it literally involves separate cultures ... Disciplines are cultures, and they have their own languages. My favorite example is a half-day meeting that just wasn't going well until we finally discovered that we each defined the term sustainability in different ways. For neuroradiologists, sustainability means two seconds, but for social scientists, it means months or years.

I also encountered examples of these translation challenges, particularly between the humanities and the social sciences, in the course of interviews for the studies illustrated in this book, as well as in the "Spirituality and Social Work" course I have taught for several years on a graduate student level with social workers—and in additional contexts beyond these two. One particular example is the reaction of people trained solely in clinical disciplines—whether as social workers, mental health counselors, or psychiatrists—to the use of the word "prophet" in the title of my practical theological dissertation research when they inquired about it. Associations of this word by secularly trained clinicians have included a mentally unstable or manic person, whether biblical or not, who hallucinates and assumes that title, *or* a lack of any recognition of the word at all by clinicians—as though it was completely from a foreign language, as indeed it is in both respects. There is no association to a language of social justice, or to challenging the power structures of a society, or to contemporary images of someone such as Martin Luther King, Jr. for such secularly trained clinicians, though this understanding and metaphoric imagery is readily available to those trained in Jewish, Christian, and Islamic theological and clerical traditions and language.

On the other hand, someone trained solely in the above religious traditions might be surprised or shocked by such a secular association of a clinician to the word "prophet." The cultural worldviews and lived experiences between such a clinician and a theologian or clergyperson are radically different and not commensurate without further words of translation. This entails introduction minimally to images with which their respective different lived experiences in relation to the world might be understood, drawing from the multivalent capacity of metaphors, a point explored more deeply in the next chapter. Engaging in such encounters and translations is the essence of trust building in cross-disciplinary work, however, and such trust building manifests in and on a plane of visceral reality.

This visceral plane lives in an academic discipline's training in borders and boundaries, borders and boundaries that limit what phenomena can be seen or known and given language. For example, a mental health counselor interviewed, who otherwise I knew to have worked closely with the LDBPI, became very cautious in describing any material that might hint of a religious nature in relation to the work of the Peace Institute staff. She firmly stated, "*I* don't think of their work as ministry," while she did spontaneously offer that there seemed to be "a component of faith" in their work and "I certainly have heard references to prayer and to God." Since I was aware from my ethnographic immersion that the core staff of the Peace Institute at that time were embedded deeply in their respective lay Christian traditions and viewed their work as ministry, the very firm desire of the mental health counselor to draw a clear boundary between her work and their work in the mutual clients they served was striking on a phenomenological basis: "I don't refer people there … *because* I think they are faith-based in the sense of religious affiliation … I don't know what they bring up in conversations about their own views . . . I mean, I can tell you what *we* do here but I don't know . . . what they do." Yet she did refer people to the Peace Institute and recognized, supported, and praised their unique success with survivors in the aftermath of a family homicide. However, she did not delve into and preferred not to reflect upon the religious dimensions of their work. Such boundary drawing then *loses* human phenomenological data as possible experiential truth that the religious dimensions of the Peace Institute's work might have a correlation to their cultural success with survivors from their community.

This type of discomfort with, or even blindness to, the significance of religious or spiritual material in the lives of clients by clinicians is not uncommon in my personal experience as both a clinical supervisor and social work educator in the US context. Some in public health are referring to this academic blindness to religion as "the invisible social determinant," suggesting "religious literacy is a twenty-first-century skill."[28] Clinical intakes rarely inquire about a client's religious or spiritual beliefs or practices, or do so only minimally, with few taking these experiences seriously as rich material with which to engage positively for treatment plans, the one exception often being clinical secular interest in mindfulness practices. Rarer still, in my experience, have I seen religious or spiritual communities or leaders engaged by clinicians in the actual treatment process for a client.

More often than not, a very strict and firm boundary is drawn around this material by clinicians and their agencies, this despite the concern for cultural competency across other dimensions of human experience. Yet more is at stake than simple religious literacy. Our ability to build authentic and empathic connections of relational trust as a foundation for shared action is at stake. This entails being open in an embodied sense to the lived experiences of different worldviews—and this sometimes is risky for its transformative capacity of identity by all involved. This is a risk that ethnographers, and the communities they come from or enter, know only too well. To cross this particular divide between academic disciplines, and the meaning-making phenomena studied by lived religion, means further training and opportunities for engagement—and sitting with, learning from, and writing about the visceral reactions generated.

Engaging interdisciplinary work to study effective practices in the aftermath of violent trauma means engaging fundamental assumptions in our respective academic disciplines. It means being open not only to learning language for different phenomena but also, on an experiential level, to witnessing and allowing oneself to go through embodied reactions to phenomena that may be significantly different from one's lived experiences in the world. Such cross-cultural engagement entails certain risks of possible transformation in the process, including in one's sense of self and identity—risks that can prove fruitful and expansive or painful and confusing. These risks are greatest when power differentials are at play and a subdominant culture needs to learn the language of the dominant culture in order to survive or thrive, sometimes losing entirely its own language and lived experience of the phenomenon.[29] How often do our academic disciplines superimpose our own culturally dominant language and mediated tools for research purposes, limiting thereby our fullest capacity to understand a phenomenon on its own culturally understood terms?

This means that power differentials in the actual act of crossing academic disciplines and engaging in shared research needs ethical attention. The potential fruits of such interdisciplinary and cross-cultural engagements can be an expanded pragmatic capacity for understanding the range of possible meaning-making cultural practices, including spiritual or religious practices, that assist in the aftermath of violent trauma. This also can include a deepened respect for the uniqueness of context and sensitivity for the effect of institutional power in that context. Perhaps in doing so, we all may share more compassionately and empathically in what different religious and spiritual traditions experience as "the something more" of meaning-making, as well as perseverance in the face of the more tragic dimensions of human existence. In this sense, my larger hope is for this book to speak not only to researchers of lived religion and professional religious practitioners but also to any human service and health practitioners, educators, or policy makers concerned to address and ameliorate the impact of violent trauma as we work together toward a world of human, ecological, and planetary well-being and flourishing.

Organization of the Book

Throughout this book, I engage in auto-ethnographic sharing, including beginning each chapter with a personal vignette. In doing so, I situate myself among those in ethnography who experiment with different forms for writing ethnographic research and their lived experiences, including fictional ethnography for some.[30] My beginning chapter vignettes, which are drawn from my lived experiences, function as an invitation for the reader to enter imaginatively into a short story of cultural border crossings, including the crossing of academic and professional cultural disciplines—a story which could be their own story if they too carried the particular social identities and lived experiences of myself or any of the people in these stories. It is thus an invitation for each reader to enter into the characters of the story from their own social locations as possible. Through this technique, I hope to expand the interdisciplinary and cross-cultural lived and felt imagination for just a few moments in perhaps a more visceral and embodied way.

The second chapter focuses on challenges and possibilities in interdisciplinary encounters with a more philosophical vein, including its impact within lived religion studies. Attention is drawn specifically to the body, language, and imagination in different respects, including their role in the social construction of academic truth claims in the context of historical structures of oppression. I seek to preserve the integrity of each discipline's own language by beginning to introduce the power of embodied metaphorical correlation, particularly for lived religion approaches to studying trauma. This chapter is meant to be a more lighthearted and less formal, with a somewhat provocative tone, broad stroke introduction to some key debates that will appeal to those readers in need of such an orientation as ground for my deeper work. The third chapter then moves into a thicker introduction to and description of the two case studies, both historically and programmatically and in their philosophical influences as trauma ministries.

The fourth chapter explores more deeply a lived religion approach to studying trauma, including a wide variety of new or additional interdisciplinary tools and language based on their fit with my experiences of ethnographic immersion in the communities I studied and phenomenological interviews with the participants of the two case studies. I expand here upon the embodied metaphorical correlational method I introduced in the second chapter, and in my previous research, for engaging or bridging interdisciplinary connections, continuing also to point toward transdisciplinary possibilities. In doing so, I also propose an alternative metaphor to "worldview," that of "world/sense" as a more richly embodied metaphor. Finally, I also explore the poetics of material meaning-making in survivor practices as well as theories that assist in illuminating issues of culture and power in survivor practices, bridging in the end back to correlational possibilities for religious and spiritual language in trauma studies.

The fifth and sixth chapters then draw out specific lessons learned from each case study as these bore on attending to survivors as the experts of their own experiences and language, as well as attending to the intercultural encounters between the two different sociocultural contexts as these highlighted the differential impact of culture and power on respective communal meaning-making practices. Finally, the seventh chapter revisits the vision of peace cultivated by each case study ministry and includes sociological recommendations for next steps in light of the lessons learned as well. These recommendations specifically are made for clinical, pastoral, health, and human service care providers; secular and religious educators; social and religious institutions; and theological and religious scholarship. I then situate my work in further emerging interdisciplinary and intersectional connections based on this research. Finally, I end with a queer postlude pointing back to where I began with my prelude and introduction for this US context so troubled by its violent past and increasingly violent present. I turn now to the second chapter.

Notes

1. Deborah Prothrow-Stith and Howard R. Spivak, *Murder Is No Accident: Understanding and Preventing Youth Violence in America* (San Francisco: Jossey-Bass, 2004), 39. Also as reported in 2011 by the CDC: "During 1991-2007, homicide was ranked as one of the top

four leading causes of death each year for persons aged 1-40 years living in the United States... Homicide rates for males are estimated to be approximately 3-4 times higher than that for females ... In addition, minority racial/ethnic children and young adults in the United States are disproportionately affected by homicide." Centers for Disease Control and Prevention, "Homicides—United States, 1999—2007," *Morbidity and Mortality Weekly Report*, Supplements, 60(01), (January 14, 2011): 67.
2. http://www.eurekalert.org/pub_releases/2015-08/asa-uh5081815.php (accessed September 3, 2015).
3. I consciously include the shooter and his mother as they are often excluded in public reports of statistics.
4. http://journals.plos.org/plosmedicine/article?id=10.1371/journal.pmed.1001915 (accessed February 19, 2016).
5. http://www.huffingtonpost.com/2014/08/30/un-police-brutality-stand-your-ground_n_5740734.html (accessed February 20, 2016).
6. http://blacklivesmatter.com/herstory/ (accessed February 16, 2016) and https://medium.com/@patrissemariecullorsbrignac/we-didn-t-start-a-movement-we-started-a-network-90f9b5717668#.noozv8enn (accessed February 23, 2016). See also http://gawker.com/unarmed-people-of-color-killed-by-police-1999-2014-1666672349 (accessed May 7, 2016).
7. http://www.aapf.org/sayhername/ (accessed February 20, 2016).
8. http://mondoweiss.net/2015/01/between-blacklivesmatter-palestine/ (accessed February 20, 2016); http://inthesetimes.com/article/18505/palestinian-lives-matter-too-blm-activists-draw-international-connections (accessed February 20, 2016); http://www.huffingtonpost.com/tia-oso/shared-past-shared-future_b_6622270.html (accessed February 20, 2016); and http://www.dailydot.com/politics/black-lives-matter-queer-trans-issues/ (accessed February 20, 2016).
9. http://www.huffingtonpost.com/david-a-love/brown-lives-matter-muslim_b_6757280.html (accessed February 22, 2016) and http://www.truth-out.org/opinion/item/32896-our-history-and-our-dreams-building-black-and-native-solidarity (accessed February 16, 2016).

10. Language such as "stock story" and "concealed story," as well as "resistance story" and "emerging/transforming story," comes from the narrative work of critical race theorist Lee Anne Bell, *Storytelling for Racial Justice: Connecting Narrative and the Arts in Antiracist Teaching* (New York: Routledge, 2010).
11. Ibid.
12. For quoted phrase, see Heather Ann Thompson, "Inner-City Violence in the Age of Mass Incarceration," http://www.theatlantic.com/national/archive/2014/10/inner-city-violence-in-the-age-of-mass-incarceration/382154/ (accessed June 3, 2016). See also Roxanne Dunbar-Ortiz, *An Indigenous Peoples' History of the United States* (Boston: Beacon Press, 2014); Michael Omi and Howard Winant, *Racial Formation in the United States* (New York: Routledge, 2014, 3rd edition); and Michelle Alexander, *The New Jim Crow: Mass Incarceration in the Age of Colorblindness*, Revised Edition (New York: The New Press, 2012).
13. http://www.theglobalist.com/the-land-of-the-free-and-the-home-of-the-brave/ (accessed February 16, 2016). See also Jefferson Morley, *Snow-Storm in August: The Struggle for American Freedom and Washington's Race Riot of 1835* (New York: First Anchor Books, 2013).
14. http://www.cnn.com/2016/02/19/politics/donald-trump-south-carolina-john-pershing/index.html?eref=rss_politics (accessed February 20, 2016).
15. One significant pastoral care resource contribution, specifically for congregations impacted by trauma, is Jill M. Hudson's *Congregational Trauma: Caring, Coping, & Learning* (The Alban Institute, 1998). Another resource of note for congregational impact in the aftermath of clergy misconduct, including traumatic impact, is Beth Ann Gaede, ed., *When a Congregation is Betrayed: Responding to Clergy Misconduct* (The Alban Institute, 2006).
16. For a few examples of lived religion studies from diverse methodologies, see the works of David D. Hall, ed. *Lived Religion in America: Toward a History of Practice* (Princeton: Princeton University Press, 1997); Robert A. Orsi, *Between Heaven and Earth: The Religious*

Worlds People Make and the Scholars Who Study Them (Princeton: Princeton University Press, 2005); Nancy T. Ammerman, ed., *Everyday Religion: Observing Modern Religious Lives* (Oxford: Oxford University Press, 2007); Meredith B. McGuire, *Lived Religion: Faith and Practice in Everyday Life* (New York: Oxford University Press, 2008); and R.Ruard Ganzevoort, "Forks in the Road when Tracing the Sacred: Practical Theology as Hermeneutics of Lived Religion" (Presidential Address to the Ninth Conference of the International Association of Practical Theology, Chicago, 2009).

17. The holistic and ecological approach emphasized in the field of social work is taking root within public health through the emphasis on a need for transdisciplinary approaches to major public health concerns. See Debra Haire-Joshu and Timothy D. McBride, editors, *Transdisciplinary Public Health: Research, Education, and Practice* (San Francisco: Jossey-Bass, 2013). Transdisciplinary research also is seen as a means for fostering a deeper level of social justice. See Patricia Leavy, *Essentials of Transdisciplinary Research: Using Problem-Centered Methodologies* (Walnut Creek, CA: Left Coast Press, Inc., 2011).

18. I use the term "para-ecclesial communities" to denote intentional gatherings of groups of people, whether lay or ordained, who are shaped by faith perspectives, but who may not choose to call themselves a "church" and/or who function outside the boundaries of any formal denomination or across denominations or religious faith groups. Ecclesial in this sense also is broadened to any formal religious community beyond the Christian tradition.

19. See the main website of the LDBPI at http://www.ldbpeaceinstitute.org (accessed November 29, 2013) and the main website of the UUTRM at http://www.traumaministry.org (accessed November 29, 2013).

20. For a complete examination of these two case studies, see Michelle A. Walsh, "Prophetic Pastoral Care in the Aftermath of Trauma: Forging a Constructive Practical Theology of Organized Trauma Response Ministries" (PhD diss., Boston University, 2014, ProQuest AAT 3610856).

21. In the particular case of the Louis D. Brown Peace Institute, it continues to be important to note that I approached my relationship with the Peace Institute from the perspective of being a survivor of my goddaughter's nephew's murder and as having utilized their services initially with my goddaughter's family at the time of his murder in September of 2006—as well as having led a youth ministry that suffered from several homicides. I also was involved in an ethnographic immersion as a volunteer prior to the beginning of formal research, providing some assistance with the formation of the Peace Institute's interfaith committee, as well as providing volunteer supervision for two master's level social work interns over a nine-month period in 2009–2010. In the case of the UU Trauma Response Ministry, it should continue to be noted that I am an ordained UU minister and hence have some natural immersion in and knowledge of UU communities, though my prior interactions with each person interviewed had been minimal to nonexistent. As I found during my pilot studies, it also was impossible to completely separate the role of researcher from my role of minister when I engaged participants in questions that at times provoked painful memories and tears or anger. This was a struggle for both case studies, regardless of the level of my involvement. As Mary Clark Moschella has noted, pastoral care and ethnographic research can be intertwined for the minister of a congregation, and I found the same was true for myself as a participant-observer engaging in research on trauma. See her text *Ethnography as a Pastoral Practice: An Introduction* (Cleveland: Pilgrim Press, 2008). See also Sarah Pink, *Doing Sensory Ethnography*, 2nd Edition (Thousand Oaks, CA: Sage Publications, 2015), particularly her discussion of "embodiment" and "emplacement" for ethnographers, 27–28.
22. See http://www.uua.org/giving/awardsscholarships/presidentsannual/31417.shtml (accessed September 13, 2015).
23. Beyond the fact that the original case study did not seek to be a full congregational study of the TVUUC, there also was another congregation impacted by the shooting that morning to which the UUTRM responded, and this posed an additional limitation for the breadth of capacity for this particular study. I was unaware that the Westside UU

church also had one congregant killed and several injured who were in attendance that morning. In some ways, this particular case study replicated the heartfelt neglect experienced by the Westside congregation, by TVUUC leader reports, of attention to their losses as well as their struggles in the aftermath. For this replication, I am particularly regretful that the economic limitations and study restrictions did not permit an expansion to include Westside at the time that this became known to me upon my site visit to Knoxville. It is hoped that future researchers will correct this neglect and also expand congregational studies of these particular congregations.

24. Michael Quinn Patton, *Qualitative Research and Evaluation Methods*, 3rd ed. (Thousand Oaks, CA: Sage Publications, 2002), 247–248.
25. A transitions director assists with ministerial placements and transitions, while a district executive is an employee of the UUA who manages congregational support in one of multiple national district or regional offices.
26. In my use and understanding of "cultural worldview," I am indebted to the grassroots work and training of indigenous activist Robette Dias and the work of Crossroads Antiracism Organizing & Training http://crossroadsantiracism.org (accessed March 2, 2016). In Chap. 4, I begin to suggest and develop alternative language to "worldview," that of "world/sense."
27. Judy H. Watts, "Building a New Paradigm: Transdisciplinary Research Comes to the Forefront." *Social Impact*, Fall 2009, 16 (Brown School of Social Work, Washington University, St. Louis, MO). I thank a social work colleague, Betty J. Ruth, for initially calling my attention to the significance of the transdisciplinary approach in public health through this particular article.
28. Ellen L. Idler, ed., *Religion as a Social Determinant of Public Health* (New York: Oxford University Press, 2014).
29. One of the most painful examples of this I have witnessed is the loss by indigenous cultures of their languages, symbolized most poignantly in a documentary where Windy Boy recounts, with trauma-induced embodied flashbacks visually recorded, how his abuse in Indian boarding schools caused him to lose his native tongue so

that he could no longer talk to his spirits because "Our Spirits Don't Speak English." The documentary is available through http://www.richheape.com/boarding-school.htm (accessed March 12, 2016). For a fascinating example of an indigenous group's reclamation of their language and spiritual experience, see the documentary of the Wampanoag people of Cape Cod, MA, USA here http://www.makepeaceproductions.com/wampfilm.html (accessed March 12, 2016).

30. See Caroline B. Brettell, *Anthropological Conversations: Talking Culture Across Disciplines* (New York: Rowman & Littlefield, 2015), chapter three in particular.

2

Challenges and Possibilities in Interdisciplinary Encounters

Tales from Cross-Cultural Encounters Between Academic Disciplines

In the sense that as we grow older, we may come to see that our lives are like different chapters from a book—once upon a time, I was a US clinical social worker trained in assessment for violent trauma and sexual abuse, and I also went to seminary after ten years in the field of urban social work and lay community ministry. I wanted to be ordained as a Unitarian Universalist (UU) clergyperson and was quite comfortable with my Buddhist mindfulness practices, as many clinical social workers are in their secular trainings. I found my Buddhist practices enormously and personally helpful to me for processing and living compassionately with my ongoing exposure to violent trauma, in both my professional clinical work and my lay ministry with urban youth. Indeed, my first exposure to Buddhist practices came on a spirituality retreat sponsored by my school of social work—the timing of which followed an experience of listening to an urban mother describe the violence that occurred regularly on her street—and the felt experience of breathing pain in and breathing compassion out was powerful for me at the time.

The vast majority of seminaries were Christian in orientation and structure, however, including those nearest to my home. I was rather unfamiliar with the historical Christian tradition, and certainly had never read the bible in any great detail. I discovered that I needed to take at least four classes in the bible while in my Christian seminary, two in the Hebrew Scriptures and two in the New Testament—and I found it helpful to know that scholars at this seminary respected the Hebrew Scriptures on their own cultural terms rather than calling them "the Old Testament," as I understood them to be called in the larger US dominant popular culture.

I was eager to learn historical approaches to understanding the bible and its formation and found it very interesting overall. At orientation, one of the associate deans stressed that seminary could be an anxiety-provoking process of losing one's faith. The associate dean made a light-hearted analogy to temporarily "losing one's mittens," but not to worry, that each of the students would "find your mittens again before you finish." Since my faith tradition was open to many spiritual paths, including the social sciences as tools of revelation, I could not quite relate to this concern and lacked empathic grounding for it. However, I indeed witnessed some students becoming quite distressed in my first semester as they were exposed to this historical approach to the bible, including a young person who ended up dropping out that first semester when she experienced shock that Moses actually did not write Exodus in the bible, among other things.

As a clinician with some background in cognitive developmental psychology, I realized the enormity of what was happening for these students in the cross-cultural encounter between their living religious traditions and an academic discipline's tool for historical analysis of the bible. I began to read these particular students as experiencing a form of psychic trauma to their cultural worldviews under the pressure also of meeting academic standards. Their inner tools for translating their lived experiences within the power structure of the academy could not bridge the gap, and at least some "mittens" were temporarily, if not permanently, lost in the process, unable to be held fully for the finding in compassionate community between students, staff, and faculty.

In my second semester of seminary, I decided to take a course in the anthropology of religion, as well as my second Hebrew Scriptures course in the biblical text Ezekiel. I found myself marveling at how alien this text was to me in the bizarreness of the imagery and story, and I grappled with finding an inner tool to help me understand the text. As I did so, I found myself drawn to thinking about the lived experiences of the people from whom the writer Ezekiel came and their endurance of the destruction of Jerusalem and the Babylonian Exile as a form of cultural trauma. I began reading and relating to essayists who drew from anthropology and psychology to understand the text of Ezekiel. As a therapist, I imagined the horrific lived experiences of a people exposed to violent trauma and how the writer of Ezekiel might be engaging in these extraordinary images to express the aftermath of this living reality and the impact of it on the connection of his people to their God.

As I initially began to explain in a midterm and a book review my reactions to the text drawing me in as a reader through this empathic and embodied form of imaginative meaning-making, my professor in turn struggled to understand what I, as her student, was saying—pointing out that there was no evidence in the textual language itself for some of these reactions. Gradually, both the professor and I came to realize that the cultural worldviews and practices of academic disciplines were being crossed, that together we were no longer in an area solely of textual and literary criticism. For this "social work clinician forming as clergy," reading with the lens of trauma called forth an embodied hermeneutic of the text attached to the lived experiences of a people, and this required a deep and empathic imagination for their particular historical and cultural experiences, including as lived through their bodies.

The Philosophical Significance of Lived Religion for Studies of Violent Trauma

Often I am asked by those in nonacademic contexts, including cross-disciplinary professional contexts, something along the lines of, "What the heck is lived religion and why should I care?" In highly simplified terms that some will contest, I define "lived religion" as a field of study of the beliefs and imaginative, embodied, and material practices of sacred meaning-making, whether these are of formal religion or in popular folk religious or secular spiritual form. On a personal level for some of us academic types, consciously seeking out opportunities for living encounter with these differences in meaning-making can be a form of religious or spiritual practice in and of itself, transformative and contributing to our own constant sense of sacred meaning-making in and of the world.[1] However, when cross-cultural encounters of difference in the context of power relations sometimes lead to violent rather than sacred ends, as the people of Ezekiel's time found, as well as so many people of our time find, an ethical and sociological mandate begins to arise for each of us to pay attention to lived religion studies of violent trauma, culture, and power.

Such seeking out and paying attention goes beyond reading a religious or spiritual text, however, and begins to embrace other tools in lived religion studies, such as phenomenological and ethnographic interviews and direct experiences with what a person/people consider as sacred. What is termed "hermeneutics," or a method of textual interpretation in religion, including of a religion's source documents or traditions, cannot be separated from meaning-making through the culturally embodied and enlanguaged particular person/people that shape that text and the tradition. An early effort to recognize this was made by a pastoral theologian named Anton Boisen, who argued that human beings are "living human documents."[2] It is significant that Boisen had to bridge metaphorically "living human" beings even with the language of "documents," the dominant Protestant academic worldview for understanding religion at the time. It prompts me to ask from where the drive comes to strip the living body on its own terms from our understanding of religion? Hermeneutics as a method cannot be separated from the impact of power relations embedded in that person/people's historical, cultural, embodied, emplaced, and material communal life—including in our use of particular academic disciplinary lens. This especially is true for the study of violent trauma.

Dr. Bessel van der Kolk, a leading international researcher in trauma, studies human beings impacted by different forms of trauma, including war violence. He has discovered that trauma constrains human imagination and results in a worldview shaped by the lingering embodied impact of trauma on the body's capacity to feel fully alive, a core underpinning to meaning-making through imagination and language. Van der Kolk writes, "Imagination is absolutely critical to the quality of our lives ... Without imagination there is no hope, no chance to envision a better future, no place to go, no goal to reach."[3] When the body is impacted, individuals and communities can become caught in cycles of expecting further trauma and seeing the world through a more limited vision and range of possibilities for action. Creative and flexible connections and responses can be muted, dampened, or lost entirely. Yet it also is the case, under certain circumstances, that human creativity in the aftermath of trauma can thrive and grow in unexpected and unique ways. Studies drawing from lived religion interdisciplinary approaches can aid in documenting these circumstances. Given the magnitude of violence through action and speech in our larger world, this uniquely positions lived religion studies of violent trauma to make significant contributions to understanding human resiliency through religious or spiritual meaning-making practices. It can do so by drawing different disciplines into relationship for the ethical purpose of studying embodied and material practices of imagination that address and ameliorate violence at its contextual roots. This book seeks to make one contribution to these efforts by highlighting the strengths, resiliencies, and creativity of practices, including practices of resistance and transformation, in two culturally and socioeconomically diverse communities affected by ongoing and/or sudden violent trauma.

Between Body, Philosophy, Theology, and Experiences of Worlds

Culture and power in the academy have a lot to do with how the academy is structured in relating to and talking about particular bodies that are impacted, or subject to being impacted, by violent trauma. The ongoing and unaddressed historical legacies of colonialism and slavery in our contemporary shared world also shape, through various power structures, who has access even to talk or write about this impact—who has the ability to share their concealed stories to a larger public. Through this book, I have been granted privilege to convey aspects of my own lived experiences and story and the lived experiences and stories of those I interviewed. There is an ethical mandate also to consider the meaning of who has access to tell their story and who does not, as well as the reasons why this is the case.

For example, postmodern philosophy and theology both have made a turn toward highlighting the significance of the body and material life in the past two decades, including the embodiment of the mind and influence of embodied experiences in shaping language and other expressive modalities of meaning-making. Both of these disciplines, philosophy and theology, also provide a larger context for some of the tensions experienced within lived religion studies and between academic disciplines today, tensions that sometimes constrain developing the fullest possibilities for lived religion to contribute to studies of violent trauma. Philosopher Mark Johnson has written, "Without imagination, nothing in the world could be meaningful. Without imagination, we could never make sense of our experience. Without imagination, we could never reason toward knowledge of reality."[4] Imagination itself is *embodied*, Johnson goes on to argue, as imagination comes from the "novel connections that arise out of our experience ... Creativity occurs at all levels of our experiential organization."[5] In partnership with linguist George Lakoff, Johnson has argued that the discovery of metaphoric connections, rooted in bodily experiences, is the source of both ordinary daily creativity and extraordinary creativity—it is the ongoing creative movement of "philosophy in the flesh."[6]

Within postmodern theology, some also have noted the human capacity for language and textuality as a common denominator enabling human community and meaning-making. R. Ruard Ganzevoort, a Protestant practical theologian, finds value in describing practical theology as "hermeneutics of lived religion." In defining hermeneutics, Ganzevoort deemphasizes "the classic focus on the relation between the text and reader," preferring to describe it more broadly as a narrative "approach that stresses the process of human interpretation" with all due respect for the "intrinsic normativity" of each religion studied on its own terms.[7] According to Ganzevoort, lived religion as hermeneutics thus entails "attending to the most fundamental processes of interpreting life through endless conversations in which we construct meaning."[8] Yet as Catholic theologian Michael J. Scanlon[9] ironically noted a few years earlier:

> conversation requires tongues, and tongues come with bodies ... Through the emphasis on the linguisticality of human existence the human body is rediscovered as a basic symbol ... Body is the basic human sacrament through which the human person effects itself in freedom in interdependence with the embodied selves of other human beings in their common commerce with the material world.

Bodies *constrained* in freedom, however, by trauma or structural forces of oppression have tongues that often are sensitive to the creative expressive struggle for language in the aftermath, as literary scholar Elaine Scarry documents in her studies of pain, war, torture, and meaning-making.[10] Perhaps this also is why I find a deeper awareness of the body in the writings, or other corporeal/material performative expressions, of those who are colonized, raced, gendered, disabled, sexual, or religious survivors of violent abuse, as well as those who live with the embodied knowledge of their ever-present capacity to be such survivors. Long before Lakoff and Johnson, two white males in the US context, wrote the words "philosophy in the flesh," a radical collective of women of color organized a section of their writings with the words "theory in the flesh."[11] "Bodies" is the first category listed in the "Lexicon of Debates" for a textbook reader covering centuries of development of feminist theory across disciplines and cultures, and it has remained so through four editions.[12] While not drawn out as a category for special focus except in two essays, "the body" is a substantial category of index across many essays in a recent volume on feminist theology and globalization as well.[13]

While Christian practical pastoral and public theologians continue to elaborate on the metaphor of "living human documents"[14] within a "living human web,"[15] the sensorial and visceral concreteness of "the body" more often goes missing as a specific and separate category of reference or metaphorical exploration, with further implications for assuming white normativity in power and culture in relation to the body.[16] Kelly Brown Douglas, a Protestant womanist black scholar of religion, is among those calling contemporary attention to the body, sexuality, and race. She points particularly to the philosophical legacy of mind/body dualism, with a denigration of the body left by Christianity's exposure to Greek Hellenistic philosophical influences, that was then carried forward as a justification for transnational and US slavery.[17] M. Shawn Copeland, an African American Catholic theologian, argues, "The body provokes theology," recognizing that freedom is always "enfleshed."[18] Thandeka, an African American UU minister and scholar, influenced by the psychoanalytic intersubjectivity tradition, also points to the theological turn to the body as "the magisterium of human knowledge" for common mystical experiences and enlivenment of worship and other practices of ecclesial coherence across diversity, a type of "neurotheology" she terms "affect theology,"[19] drawing on Schleiermacher's work in the creation of this term.

Human beings thus are embodied and enfleshed, enlanguaged and encultured, *emplaced*[20] and embedded in spatial, material, historical, and geographic power relations, and also en-neuroned and enhormoned when we add that the mind is enfleshed physiologically in a *particular* brain impacted by all of these life experiences, including trauma. Yet for all of this turn to the living body in both philosophy and theology, it remains important not to reduce the complexity of human lived experience to the body and its visceral realities alone, sometimes a danger in purely an affect theology or neurological approach and a risk factor in interdisciplinary explorations, on which I will say more in Chap. 4.[21] Likewise, there is a similar danger in attending to textuality, narrative, and story without acknowledging and representing (not necessarily through the spoken word alone) the underpinning of a full range of embodied sources of experience. As meaning-making creatures, our worlds come alive or die to us through our embodied relational connections to other human beings and through our embodied and material expressive practices. Such practices are inclusive of art and of our storytelling bonds of communal heritage over time as well as the lived realities of our experiences under power structures of privilege or oppression.

A recent living and poignant example of this embodied narrative meaning-making in the face of such centuries of violent oppression, and current US police violence against black men, is Ta-Nehisi Coates' expressive letter as an American black male father to his son. In a spiritual practice of resistance worthy of the notice of lived religion studies of violent trauma, and despite Coates' own explicit disavowal of religious belief or practice in the letter, he writes:

> There is nothing uniquely evil in these destroyers or even in this moment. The destroyers are merely men enforcing the whims of our country, correctly interpreting its heritage and legacy. It is hard to face this. But all our phrasing—race relations, racial chasm, racial justice, racial profiling, white privilege, even white supremacy—serves to obscure that racism is a visceral experience, that it dislodges brains, blocks airways, rips muscle, extracts organs, cracks bones, breaks teeth. You must never look away from this. You must always remember that the sociology, the history, the economics, the graphs, the charts, the regressions all land, with great violence, upon the body ....[22]

> This was the week you learned that the killers of Michael Brown would go free ... What I told you is what your grandparents tried to tell me: that this is your country, that this is your world, that this is your body, and you must find some way to live within all of it ... The greatest reward of this constant interrogation, of confrontation with the brutality of my country, is that it has freed me from ghosts and girded me against the sheer terror of disembodiment.[23]

In these two short passages, Coates simultaneously rejects metaphors that mute and disembody the lived reality of racial oppression on the black body, while also imparting his living practice of meaning-making in the aftermath to his teenage son. I consciously call this public performance of a letter in writing to his son both a spiritual practice and a work of art and claim it as a phenomenon worth of study in lived religion interdisciplinary explorations of violent trauma, culture, and power. I also argue that there are a vast range of other stories worthy of lived religion studies that have yet to be told or may never be told simply because these particular storytellers lack power and access to a mediator and an audience—or because their stories and lives are not deemed worthy or are actively repressed as dangerous by those in power or with power to do so.

For example, without explicit textual or ideological references to formal religious practices and doctrines, some might challenge that this act of meaning-making by Coates as an avowed atheist falls under lived religion and thus exclude it from interdisciplinary consideration or focus. Part of this stems from an "unfortunate family quarrel"[24] that has developed and existed for centuries in the dominant Western philosophical and theological tradition, with its consequent legacy of colonialism and slavery, that originates in the very mind/body dualism to which Kelly Brown Douglas points. This has resulted in gaping chasms between the academic guilds and the disciplines of philosophy, theology, religion, science, social sciences, as well as the humanities overall—and more importantly to my ethical sensibilities, between the aforementioned and the "common" people. Finding shared ground for conversation and embodied experiences of encounter in border crossing these chasms is challenging, to say the least, yet ethically necessary in our contemporary shared world at risk and on the brink from the impact of significant trauma, let alone the hovering catastrophe that is climate change.

The Tragic Impact of a Centuries-Long "Unfortunate Family Quarrel"

An example of this tension within lived religion itself is the struggle to defend spiritual practices of popular culture as an object of study, which bears on the case studies of this particular book. Depending on the cultural context, some people might find it odd that a practical theologian would need to construct an argument that gardening is a spiritual practice worthy of study within lived religion. For example, a "spiritual but not religious" (SBNR) person in the US cultural context might take it for granted that gardening can be a spiritual practice—certainly students in my "Spirituality and Social Work" course have never questioned that automatic assumption, though they have certainly experienced visceral discomfort with, and a tendency to reject, other cross-cultural spiritual or religious practices.

2 Challenges and Possibilities in Interdisciplinary Encounters

Yet this is the dilemma R. Ruard Ganzevoort needs to address for a cross-cultural international academic audience.[25] To do so, Ganzevoort must transcend the academic limitations imposed by a definition of religion often restricted in the international context to formal authorized institutional practice and doctrinal Christian narrative. His goal is to broaden an international understanding of religion, rather than abandon it to a dichotomy fostered by the SBNR movement.[26] In doing so, he finds common ground with the work of a US scholar and sociologist of lived religion, Nancy Ammerman, who studies the everyday religious and spiritual practices and finds significance to "sacred stories" held by "spiritual tribes" that go beyond narrower understandings of definitions in religious studies.[27] I share common ground with both Ammerman and Ganzevoort in a larger ethical commitment to lifting up the voice and stories of those some dismiss as bearing normative weight in religious studies. I also share some common ground with the work of Jeff Astley in his empirical lived religion studies as well, though his metaphoric turn to a language of "ordinary theology" is complicated by embracing a philosophical and hierarchical divide I explicitly do not.[28]

In many ways, I see this divide as representative of the classic mind/body dualism in the Western tradition, with mind, reason, cognition/narrative, and science being given more political and institutional status or weight than that which is associated with the body, affect, or nature, which also can include the feminine, as anthropologist Sherry Ortner long ago noted.[29] In truth, as I tell my sometimes secular social work students, the very language of "spirit" and "spirituality" comes from a lengthy heritage in the Jewish and Christian traditions. There is no escape from culturally embodied and enlanguaged communal heritage, even if terms change over time in metaphoric meaning to express shifting cultural worldviews. The definition Ganzevoort constructs *is*, in essence, more spiritual and relational, expanding the realm of meaning-making and sense of the sacred studied to practices that fall outside of those recognized within formal religion: "we propose to define religion as the transcending patterns of action and meaning, emerging from and contributing to the relation with the sacred. This definition accepts that there can be a variety of what counts as sacred in the lives of people, from institutionalized traditions to idiosyncratic experiences."[30]

"This clinician formed as social justice minister" finds the energy expended on such debates a bit distracting, given the ethical weight of societal challenges, yet also strives to enter empathically into the academic culture of intellectual debate. The Hebrew scriptural tale of Ezekiel remains my back pocket biblical story of human wisdom for interdisciplinary reflection. God asks Ezekiel (37:1–14), "O, mortal, can these bones live again?" as they look together over the valley of the dry bones, a visually traumatic scene of great carnage and long dead slain. Reflecting on the analogy to trauma studies, "this clinician formed as minister, shaping as academic" asks if or when the study of lived religion can live in all of its popular and formal embodied fullness without need of ongoing defense, even intellectual war between academic positions? Paralleling the slow and painstaking process of Ezekiel's God making the "vast multitude" of dead come to life, sinew by sinew, can interdisciplinary explorations enflesh and embody the breath of spirit, the breath of life, into the life bones of lived religion studies through the lens of trauma for both their experientially transcendent and immanent dimensions and expressions? Historical culture and power relations between the academic disciplines become an additional sociological factor, if not societal challenge, to address in doing so.

Sociologist Randall Collins writes, "Conflict over attention space is a fundamental social fact about intellectuals. It follows that intellectuals produce multiple competing views of reality. And this disagreement will go on in the future, as long as intellectual networks exist."[31] Having access to "attention space" is a factor of relational access to institutional power, however. Ever broadening access can have the paradoxical impact of democratizing attention space for ideas and practices as well as consolidating fiefdoms or citadels of truth claims that then struggle to be in relationship with one another, let alone cooperate on a substantial societal problem for our time such as violent trauma. This has been the long and glorious path of humanity since we emerged from local agrarian villages and societies into the complex governmental, religious, economic, educational, and media-driven interdependent networks of today.

Like some divided human families, we may protect our fiefdoms, citadels, and academic guild territories with claims to higher status— and have access to power to do so—but it does not mean we are any less dependent on one another for our survival, nor that we are unaffected when we shut ourselves off to the fullest possibilities and dimensions of the human experience. As Archie Smith, Jr., an African American clinical and pastoral psychologist writes, "You cannot lead where you have not been,"[32] and we cannot lead together in addressing shared societal challenges, such as violent trauma or climate change, if we have not been able to enter into each other's disciplinary cultural worldviews, lived experiences, and language for common ethical cause. As any experienced therapist knows, however, sometimes in crisis lies new opportunities and motivation for change. The magnitude of the impact of the societal challenge of violent trauma is one such contemporary crisis—and perhaps the one pressing most deeply in on humanity as a motivator finally to work through our divides and conflicts will be the looming of climate change and its potential for traumatic impact.

In contemplation, this "clinician now formed as social justice minister and forming as academic" also might see human metaphoric wisdom for our interdisciplinary explorations through the Hebrew biblical story and images of the building of the Tower of Babel and the later Christian story of the coming of Pentecost. In the former (Genesis 11:1–9), God sees that the people "had the same language and the same word" as they worked to build a glorious tower together. Concerned that "then nothing that they may propose to do will be out of their reach," God decides to "confound their speech there, so that they shall not understand one another's speech," scattering them then all "over the face of the whole earth" so that they could no longer build their tower to the sky, a vain project indeed. In the latter Christian story (Acts 2:1–4), the Spirit of God descends from heaven on the gathered community. "Divided tongues, as of fire, appeared among them, and a tongue rested on each of them. All of them were filled with the Holy Spirit and began to speak in other languages, as the Spirit gave them ability." In this story, it is interesting to realize that the people are not restored to one language but learn to speak in the language of others as given the ability. Perhaps this is the crux of the matter for interdisciplinary studies as well, pointing also toward the eventual possibility of richer transdisciplinary studies.

A Brief Note on Social Construction, Sociological Realism, Truth Claims, and Power

Interestingly, sociologist Randall Collins also will say, "Truths do not arise in isolated brains or disembodied minds ... Thought is always linked in a flow of verbal gesture from human body to body, among mutually focused nervous systems, reverberating with shared rhythms of attention ... Truth arises in social networks; it could not possibly arise anywhere else."[33] I find usefulness in partnering Collins' work with that of Mark Johnson in pointing to fruitful ways to solve the dichotomies that pit suggested relativism from socially constructed truth claims against what Johnson terms illusory "Objectivism" from "God's Eye" when risking interdisciplinary conversations or encounters. To have *any* type of knowledge requires *form* for that knowledge, which for Johnson means embodied form, or "embodied understanding," through the human body, which *is* "real" knowledge—our realism in this sense is a form of "internal realism."[34] This is the immanent rather than the transcendent dimension of truth claims, which can become transcendent in community. Through structures of imagination and metaphoric play derived from bodily experiences, we come to create *shared understandings of what is real.* Johnson writes:

> Truth-as-correspondence is still a workable notion only if it is not understood in the Objectivist fashion, as requiring a God's-Eye-View of an external relation between words and the world ... we can see the world through shared, public eyes that are given to us by our embodiment, our history, our culture, our language, our institutions, etc. ... Thus we can still preserve a notion of truth-as-correspondence, as long as it is contextually situated.[35]

Yet the key issue here is that *truth as contextually situated* must be considered in relationship to *sociological structures of power*, as Collins would recognize:

> The social constructivist theory of intellectual life, far from being antirealist, gives us an abundance of realities. Social networks exist; so do their material bases, the churches and schools and the audiences and patrons

who have fed and clothed them; so do the economic, political, and geopolitical processes which constituted the outer sphere of causality. These successive layers of contest for the minds of philosophers display no sharp borders. There is no criterion for arbitrarily stopping, for declaring that "I concede that social reality exists; but the world of material nature does not." It is all of a piece, all on the continuum in media res.[36]

And, of course, long before two white males were enabled to make these valuable claims known in print and offer them for the essential philosophical and sociological truths that they are to a larger public, people living under circumstances of significantly less privilege or direct oppression also were living the reality of their truths in embodied and material meaning-making contexts with less institutional access to "attention space," if any at all. They are known by different names in the academy—such as the marginalized, the oppressed, the colonized, or the subaltern—yet less often by the names *they* would claim for themselves. Even less often do they have access in direct cross-cultural personal encounter to an equal playing field of power, with mutuality of influence and transformation in cultural worldviews at stake for possibilities in the aftermath through living encounters with these differences.

The Interdisciplinary Context of Lived Religion Studies of Violent Trauma

Hans-Günter Heimbrock, a process theology-oriented practical theologian, consistently has argued that current practical theology methodologies need to be expanded to capture the full range of possible phenomenology in lived religion, that there is a need to develop additional conceptual tools for the analysis of "lived experience."[37] By implication, this includes the varieties of lived experience of violent trauma and its aftermath. In his essay, "Reconstructing Lived Religion," Heimbrock issues a call "to design concrete methods appropriate to the particular phenomenon"[38] to be studied, including phenomena "which at first glance are not labeled religious in a traditional sense."[39] Heimbrock's intent, similar to Ganzevoort's, is to enlarge empirical research and the ability to reconstruct lived religion in connection to formal religion as well as to popular culture, inclusive of material culture, while also understanding that this is an "approach [to] that which can never be reached completely."[40] It is only "a finger pointing" to that which is larger and beyond complete capture by words alone, the "something more" of lived experience. *"Theology . . . claims truth . . . in metaphoric and poetic description of reality,"* he writes (emphasis added).[41]

In connecting theology—or the religious or spiritual truth claims of different communities—to metaphor and poetry, Heimbrock implicitly is emphasizing the mediating, as well as playful and creative, role of language, narrative, and story in conveying lived experiences of "truth" or "reality" for the reconstruction of lived religious studies. Crossing disciplines into psychology, Ryan Lamothe, a psychoanalytic pastoral counselor writes, "bodily aliveness is visceral validation,"[42] and trauma psychiatrist, Bessel van der Kolk writes, albeit in a noninclusive gendered fashion, on the work of Donald Winnicott and attunement, "The way a mother holds her child underlies 'the ability to feel the body as the place where the psyche lives.' This visceral and kinesthetic sensation of how our bodies are met lays the foundation for what we experience as 'real.'"[43] Between these respective disciplines, a theologian's emphasis on lived experience and metaphor in communally shared stories of transcendence and psychology's emphasis on the visceral of the body in expressing or making stories come alive in their immanence, I see interdisciplinary connections to previous discussions from philosophical and sociological perspectives. What is experienced as "true" or "real" is connected holistically to *both* narrative and the body—to transcendence and to immanence. When trauma severs this connection, including through the interruption of structures of power and oppression, the result can be a "less than real" state of being—the essence of disassociation. Lived religion studies can contribute to understanding practices that bring people and communities back to a state of vitality and sense of "realness" again.

Crossing disciplines once again, a sociologist and anthropologist of religion, Meredith B. McGuire,[44] also argues for the linkages between lived religion, popular practices, and the storytelling nature of human beings across cultures. Embracing openness to the varieties of human meaning-making as a practical theologian or social science researcher entails a need to study practices beyond institutionally authorized forms of religions:

> Lived religion is constituted by the practices by which people remember, share, enact, adapt, and create the "stories out of which they live." And it is constituted through the practices by which people turn these "stories" into everyday action. Ordinary material existence—especially the human body—is the very stuff of these meaningful practices ... Understanding religions-as-lived requires, then, that we take seriously the full range of human religious practice, not only as we find it in religious institutions but equally as we find it in everyday embodied practices.[45]

This type of storied, embodied, and material interdisciplinary "lived religion" approach again is uniquely suited to the study of trauma's disruptive bodily impact and survivor practices of meaning-making in its aftermath.[46] This includes *their* language for and personal narratives of those spiritual practices they find effective for their own healing and empowerment—their *particular* language for their *particular* lived bodily experiences as *truth claims of their experience of reality*. Therefore, if survivors claim that "God's spirit," or the divine or sacred *as named* by different religious, spiritual, social, or cultural communities, is assumed to move through, or be present in, material reality and human embodied existence, then both materiality and human experience are important normative theological *and* social scientific empirical sources of witness to the divine or sacred in human experience. Such sources need to be attended to through practical theological and social scientific research, with the results of such research providing the capacity to "speak back" to existing normative theoretical constructions, including religious or theological ones, as well as to the religious or human service theories and practices of different social and cultural communities, inclusive of academic disciplines. This is the inherent power and significance of lived religion studies, particularly for the study of sociological challenges such as violent trauma.

Lived religion methodologies thus have a capacity to support liberative and decolonizing[47] goals in social science and practical theological research by testing, challenging, expanding, and reconstructing theories and theologies of trauma, as well as religious and human service theories of and practices for trauma. This capacity is fulfilled when normativity is tied to accountable relationship with the actual embodied and material practices, language, and narratives used by survivors—honoring their lived experiences and wisdom as "primary theologians,"[48] beyond "ordinary theology" in theological or religious studies terms, or as "survivor as experts" in sociological terms as well, in the words of interviewees from the Peace Institute case study. This is inclusive of studying survivors from different communal and demographic contexts and their popular religious or spiritual practices. Lived religion can entail a variety of interdisciplinary approaches, including sociology, history, psychology, phenomenology, anthropology, and ethnography, among others. In my lived religion approach to these two case studies, I emphasize oral history, phenomenology, and ethnography and draw in psychology through trauma studies as an additional conceptual tool.[49]

In doing so in this book, I continue to be influenced by a zeitgeist of philosophical and religious interest in the power of metaphor. Within this zeitgeist, I specifically argue for renewed attention to the role of metaphor, alongside the body, in interdisciplinary and correlational approaches for lived religion studies of trauma. Throughout my interdisciplinary exploration of the case studies from which I draw, I give equal mutual critical correlational and ethical weight to the study participants' own stated faith traditions, experiences, and language and to the research and language of the social sciences. As previously discussed, Heimbrock writes: "Theology ... claims truth ... in metaphoric and poetic description of reality."[50] Practical theologians James N. Poling and Donald E. Miller note that all language "is less a mirror of reality than a series of metaphors about reality, and no particular linguistic expression corresponds exactly with any experience."[51] If, as philosopher linguists George Lakoff and Mark Johnson argue, all language is metaphorical and *embodied* in origin, this includes the languages of science as well. If science itself is grounded in linguistic metaphors, it too is subject to an ethical call for granting normative equality, alongside other academic disciplines such as the social sciences and humanities, in the study of lived religion. Each academic discipline stands as its own cultural linguistic embodied metaphoric world, including the sciences, with its own ethical sphere of phenomenological concern.

For example, and dovetailing well with Lakoff and Johnson's work, Daniel Tiffany,[52] a specialist in comparative literature, writes of the reliance of science on poetry, images, and metaphors:

> Certain plausible correspondences between science and poetry can therefore be traced to shared forms of material and imaginative practice, but also the basic inclination of materialism: to make the intangible tangible. Both science and poetry proceed, in part, by making pictures of what we cannot see (or what merely escapes our notice), by attributing corporeal qualities to inscrutable events.[53]

This points to the capacity to mutually correlate religious and scientific metaphors, generally through the realm of bodily or sensory experiences—the corporeal and material realms—in the interdisciplinary study of lived religion.[54]

Theology, religion, and the social sciences thus are seen as separate *metaphorical* spheres of experiential description and truth claims about reality—as cultural worldviews in my argument—but also ones that can be correlated through the multivalent capacity of metaphor to mutually support, critique, or challenge each other. This includes embodied metaphorical correlational approaches to trauma—leveling some of the academic playing field of power when survivor experiences are prioritized in their own language. Granting such normative priority to the lived experiences and language of the oppressed also may address the cautionary note raised by feminists that even scientific metaphors have been used by elites to reinforce power, privilege, and oppression.[55] An *embodied metaphorical and mutual critical correlational approach* will be further illustrated in Chap. 4 while exploring specific interdisciplinary bridge tools for the lived religion study of trauma.

The lens of trauma in lived religion studies helps to keep a holistic perspective on human being. One cannot ignore the visceral and physiological bodily impact of trauma, the limitations or innovations of embodied and material practices of story and imagination in the aftermath, or the larger destructive forces of historical and social oppression in creating *truth contexts*. There is an organicity of relationship between all of these, holistically and ecologically, which is better suited to the metaphor of "kaleidoscope," as one participant in my studies drew upon for description of practices of "healing" in the aftermath of trauma. Interdisciplinary and transdisciplinary explorations likewise call us to appreciate the beauty and complexity of shifting our lens for three-dimensional viewing— perhaps even to four-dimensional viewing (such as a metaphor of a "holographic kaleidoscope")—beyond simple mutual correlational models. This ultimately needs further philosophical, ethical, and practical development—for which my varied readership may be grateful lies beyond the further scope of this particular book and case studies. I merely point to the larger task left for others, while I turn now to an orientation to the two particular case studies on which this book is based.

Notes

1. In this, I agree with practical theologian R. Ruard Ganzevoort that "theology is tracing the sacred" (broadly metaphorically conceived interreligiously) and with his citation of Tom Beaudoin that such tracing can be considered a spiritual practice in and of itself. See Ganzevoort, "Forks in the Road when Tracing the Sacred: Practical Theology as Hermeneutics of Lived Religion," 5–6.
2. Charles V. Gerkin, *The Living Human Document: Re-visioning Pastoral Counseling in a Hermeneutical Mode*. Nashville: Abingdon Press, 1984.
3. Bessel van der Kolk, *The Body Keeps the Score: Brain, Mind, and Body in the Healing of Trauma* (New York: Penguin Books, 2014), 17.
4. Mark Johnson, *The Body in the Mind: The Bodily Basis of Meaning, Imagination, and Reason* (Chicago: The University of Chicago Press, 1987), ix. See also Mark Johnson, *Moral Imagination: Implications of Cognitive Science for Ethics* (Chicago: University of Chicago Press, 1993) for his extension of this into ethical theory.
5. Ibid., pp. 169–170.
6. George Lakoff and Mark Johnson, *Philosophy in the Flesh: The Embodied Mind and Its Challenge to Western Thought* (New York: Basic Books, 1999).

7. R.Ruard Ganzevoort, "Forks in the Road when Tracing the Sacred: Practical Theology as Hermeneutics of Lived Religion," 4–5.
8. Ibid., 5. For a very useful brief summary of the postmodern and postcolonial turn to narrative theory and approaches, including a summary of critiques, see also R.Ruard Ganzevoort, "Narrative Approaches" in *The Wiley-Blackwell Companion to Practical Theology*, edited by Bonnie Miller-McLemore, 214–223 (Malden, MA: Wiley-Blackwell, 2014). The narrative approach is crucial as a theoretical approach to the case studies, and I also seek to expand the narrative approach more deeply in embodied and material ways of poetic or metaphorical and artistic expression.
9. Michael J. Scanlon, O.S.A., "The Postmodern Debate" in *The Twentieth Century: A Theological Overview*, ed. By Gregory Baum (Maryknoll, NY: Orbis Books, 1999), 230. See also Paul F. Knitter, *Introducing Theologies of Religions*. Maryknoll: Orbis Books, 2002. Knitter also points out that the Catholic tradition, through a preeminent theologian Karl Rahner, "has always taken seriously what contemporary anthropology and psychology insist on—that human beings are *embodied* and *social* beings. Everything that we are and know and believe and commit ourselves to has to come to us through our bodies and through other people ... It has to be the way God or the Spirit will deal with us—through our bodies and through other people. Therefore, Rahner's conclusion—*grace must be embodied*. God's presence has to take some kind of material shape (70)." Through such recognition, the Catholic tradition has less discomfort finding correlations to the social sciences.
10. See Elaine Scarry, *The Body in Pain: The Making and Unmaking of the World* (New York: Oxford University Press, 1985).
11. Cherrie Moraga and Gloria Analdúa, eds. *This Bridge Called My Back: Writings by Radical Women of Color*, Fourth Edition (New York: Suny Press, 1981/2015), 19. See also Jerry H. Gill, *The Tacit Mode: Michael Polanyi's Postmodern Philosophy* (New York: State University of New York Press, 2000). Polanyi has influenced many feminists and other writers from the margins to affirm the importance of lifting up the personal as a way of breaking through dominant paradigms. This

includes in science through Thomas S. Kuhn, *The Structure of Scientific Revolutions*, 2nd edition, enlarged (Chicago: The University of Chicago Press, 1962, 1970).
12. Wendy K. Kolmar and Frances Bartkowski, eds., *Feminist Theory: A Reader*, 4th Edition (Boston: McGraw-Hill, 2013).
13. Mary McClintock Fulkerson and Sheila Briggs, eds., *The Oxford Handbook of Feminist Theology* (Oxford: Oxford University Press, 2013).
14. "The living human document" is a term initially used by Anton Boisen and reclaimed by Charles V. Gerkin in *The Living Human Document*.
15. Bonnie J. Miller-McLemore, "Pastoral Theology as Public Theology: Revolutions in the 'Fourth Area.'"
16. Recent encyclopedia style essays on practical theology may focus on religious or spiritual practices that involve the body, such as categories of eating, consuming, suffering, and playing, yet beyond language such as "embodied knowing," or a brief attention to disability theologies, they do not center on the visceral dimensions of the body as a separate category of theological reflection. More often, one finds recognition of visceral dimensions in queer theology. See two different practical theology volumes, one from the Protestant tradition and one from the Catholic tradition, both edited by white female practical theologians: Bonnie J. Miller-McLemore, ed., *The Wiley-Blackwell Companion to Practical Theology* (Malden, MA: Wiley-Blackwell, 2014) and Claire E. Wolfteich, ed., *Invitation to Practical Theology: Catholic Voices and Visions* (New York: Paulist Press, 2014). See then a classic of queer theology as well—Marcella Althaus-Reid, *From Feminist Theology to Indecent Theology: Readings on Poetry, Sexual Identity, and God* (London: SCM Press, 2004). Queer studies and queer theology, as well as a fuller attention to disability theology and challenges to dominant cultural normative conceptions of "the body," await a fuller integration into both practical theology and interdisciplinary or transdisciplinary studies as well.
17. Kelly Brown Douglas, *What's Faith Got To Do With It? Black Bodies/Christian Souls* (Maryknoll: Orbis Books, 2005).

18. M. Shawn Copeland, *Enfleshing Freedom: Body, Race, and Being* (Minneapolis: Fortress Press, 2010), 7.
19. Gary Dorrien, *The Making of American Liberal Theology: Crisis, Irony, & Postmodernity, 1950-2005* (Louisville: Westminster John Knox Press, 2006), 452–455. Also see Thandeka, *The Embodied Self: Friedrich Schleiermacher's Solution to Kant's Problem of the Empirical Self* (New York: State University of New York Press, 1995).
20. In her work, *Doing Sensory Ethnography*, Sarah Pink draws on the work of sociologist Amanda Coffey in her recognition of the importance of spatial emplacement in ethnographic participant fieldwork. I expand the use of the term "emplaced" here in connection with ecological perspectives from the field of social work to recognize that each person and community is emplaced in time, history, culture, power structures, and geography. Another useful work for understanding power, privilege, and geography in this sense is *Geographies of Privilege*, edited by France Winddance Twine and Bradley Gardener (New York: Routledge, 2013).
21. Affect theology continues to be a new and promising field of development for interdisciplinary and transdisciplinary studies. For a recent interesting interdisciplinary theological dissertation in this area that draws on queer and feminist theories and affect, disability, and political theologies, see Karen Bray, "Unredeemed: A Political Theology of Affect, Time, and Worth" (PhD diss., Drew University, 2016).
22. Ta-Nehisi Coates, *Between The World and Me* (New York: Spiegel & Grau, 2015) 10.
23. Ibid., 11–12.
24. Initially, a humorous reference I heard made by the Reverend Ralph Mero, a UU community minister, who was referring to "the unfortunate family quarrel in the 19th century" that led to a split then between Unitarian and Trinitarian Congregationalists in what would today be called the UUA and the United Church of Christ.
25. R.Ruard Ganzevoort and Johan H. Roeland, "Lived Religion: The Practice of Practical Theology," *International Journal of Practical Theology 18(1)*, 2014, 91–101.

26. For three different perspectives on the SBNR movement, see http://www.nytimes.com/2014/07/19/us/examining-the-growth-of-the-spiritual-but-not-religious.html?&_r=1 (accessed September 14, 2015). Polarization at times of spirituality and religion is noted in studies of spirituality and social work as well. See Margaret Holloway and Bernard Moss, *Spirituality and Social Work* (New York: Palgrave Macmillan, 2010), 24.
27. Nancy Tatom Ammerman, *Sacred Stories, Spiritual Tribes: Finding Religion in Everyday Life* (New York: Oxford University Press, 2014).
28. See Jeff Astley, *Ordinary Theology: Looking, Listening and Learning in Theology* (Burlington, VT: Ashgate Publishing Company, 2002). I appreciate Astley's attention to the significance of popular practices, including an appreciation of the affective dimensions, while I grant more normativity to these voices and experiences than I believe at present Astley does.
29. Sherry B. Ortner, "Is Female to Male as Nature Is to Culture?" in *Woman, Culture & Society*, edited by Michelle Zimbalist Rosaldo and Louise Lamphere (Stanford: Stanford University Press, 1974), 67–87.
30. Ibid., 96.
31. Randall Collins, *The Sociology of Philosophies: A Global Theory of Intellectual Change* (Cambridge: The Belknap Press of Harvard University Press, 1998), 876.
32. Archie Smith, Jr., "You Cannot Teach What You Do Not Know: You Cannot Lead Where You Have Not Been," in Eleazar S. Fernandez, ed., *Teaching for a Culturally Diverse and Racially Just World* (Eugene, OR: Cascade Books, 2014), 88–108.
33. Collins, p. 877.
34. Johnson, 205.
35. Ibid., 210–211.
36. Collins, 861.
37. Hans-Günter Heimbrock, "Reconstructing Lived Religion" in *Religion: Immediate Experience and the Mediacy of Research—Interdisciplinary Studies, Concepts and Methodology of Empirical Research in Religion*, ed. Hans-Günter Heimbrock and Christopher P. Scholtz (Germany: Vandenhoeck & Ruprecht, 2007b), 149.

38. Ibid., 152.
39. Ibid., 150.
40. Ibid., 152.
41. Ibid., 154.
42. Ryan Lamothe, *Becoming Alive: Psychoanalysis and Vitality* (New York: Routledge, 2005), 40.
43. Van der Kolk, 115.
44. Meredith B. McGuire, "Embodied Practices: Negotiation and Resistance," in *Everyday Religion: Observing Modern Religious Lives*, ed. Nancy T. Ammerman (New York: Oxford University Press, 2007), 187–200.
45. Ibid., 197–198.
46. Embodied knowing is deeply intertwined with Heimbrock's understanding of theological anthropology. See "Practical Theology as Empirical Theology," *International Journal of Practical Theology* 14 (2011): 153–170 as well as "Reconstructing Lived Religion."
47. See Linda Tuhiwai Smith, *Decolonizing Methodologies: Research and Indigenous Peoples*, 2nd Edition (New York: Zed Books, 2012); Chela Sandoval, *Methodology of the Oppressed* (Minneapolis: University of Minnesota Press, 2000); and Soyini Madison, D. *Critical Ethnography: Method, Ethics, and Performance*, 2nd Edition (New York: Sage Publications, Inc., 2012).
48. Mary Clark Moschella, "Ethnography," in *The Wiley-Blackwell Companion to Practical Theology*, ed. Bonnie J. Miller-McLemore (Malden, MA: Blackwell Publishing Limited, 2012), 224–233, again as distinguished from ordinary theology as discussed in the introduction. For another example of the difference in this type of approach to lived religion ethnographic studies, see a recent dissertation by María Cristina Vlassidis Burgoa, "*Sobre la Marcha:* The Fiesta of Santiago Apóstol in Loíza, Puerto Rico" (PhD diss., Harvard University, 2016) in which she discusses "ethnographies of the particular" and her indigenous methodological approach to studying a Puerto Rican religious festival under threat of tourist oppression.

49. See again Patton, *Qualitative Research and Evaluation Methods*, as well as James P. Spradley, *The Ethnographic Interview* (Belmont, CA: Wadsworth Group, 1979).
50. Heimbrock, "Reconstructing Lived Religion," 154. The power of metaphorical approaches to theology was initially outlined in Sallie McFague's classic work *Metaphorical Theology: Models of God in Religious Language* (Philadelphia: Fortress Press, 1982). McFague writes: "Most simply, a metaphor is seeing one thing *as* something else, pretending 'this' is 'that' because we do not know how to think or talk about 'this,' so we use 'that' as a way of saying something about it . . . metaphorical thinking constitutes the basis of human thought and language" (15). Pastoral psychotherapists who approach their work through narrative therapy also draw heavily on the power of metaphor for spiritual direction, as illustrated by James L. Griffith and Melissa Elliott Griffith, *Encountering the Sacred in Psychotherapy: How to Talk with People about Their Spiritual Lives* (New York: The Guilford Press, 2002). "Metaphor plays a critical role in most forms of spirituality by posing abstract concepts in terms of images and events drawn from daily life. A metaphor is a way of conceiving one thing in terms of another" (64).
51. James N. Poling and Donald E. Miller, *Foundations for a Practical Theology of Ministry* (Nashville: Abingdon Press, 1985), 24. Poling and Miller also reference critical correlational approaches to practical theology drawn from the works of Don Browning and David Tracy (82–86). My approach is more consistent with Tracy's mutual critical correlational approach, particularly as Tracy has more recently highlighted the importance of an aesthetic correlation within practical theology. See Tracy, "A Correlational Model of Practical Theology—Revisited," in *Religion, Diversity and Conflict*, edited by Edward Foley (New Brunswick: Transaction Publishers, 2011), 49–61, reprinted also in *Invitation to Practical Theology: Catholic Voices and Visions*, edited by Claire E. Wolfteich (New York: Paulist Press, 2014), 70–86.
52. Daniel Tiffany, *Toy Medium: Materialism and Modern Lyric* (Berkeley: University of California Press, 2000).

53. Ibid., 5.
54. In *Metaphors We Live By* (Chicago: The University of Chicago Press, 1980/2003), George Lakoff and Mark Johnson also have argued that all language is metaphorical with embodied roots: " . . . we typically conceptualize the nonphysical *in terms* of the physical" (59). As narrative pastoral therapists, Griffith and Griffith, *Encountering the Sacred in Psychotherapy*, draw heavily from Lakoff and Johnson's work.
55. See in particular Sandra Harding, *The Science Question in Feminism* (Ithaca: Cornell University Press, 1984).

3

Two Case Studies by a Researcher Living Between Worlds

Desire, Access, and Projection in Navigating Between Cultural Worlds

As a US clinical social worker "shaping as clergy," I initially shaped as a lay urban minister alongside my social work identity. While my roots were working class, and this gave me a certain comfort level in the urban context, my suburban congregation was predominantly white and middle class and far removed from the challenges facing the children and families to whom I served as a bridge person for the youth ministry in my lay capacity. Over the years, as a clinical social worker/lay community minister, I worked hard at relationship building between these diverse cultural worlds, while holding the tension of the multiple gaps in the bridge between profound desires for connection, abundant moments of real joy and authentic mutuality, and still the monumental realities of different lived experiences in power and privilege, including my own. In my predominantly white suburban lay ministry world, I began to hear, with great discomfort, myself described by my fellow lay people as "our saint," while clergy during my formation as one among them made expectant and, to me mysterious and rather unnerving, comments such as, "It will be very interesting to see what you do." In my predominantly African American urban lay ministry world, I heard, with some humor, myself described as "the little white girl" who didn't seem afraid to be out in their neighborhoods late at night, though they were concerned for me in doing so. Over time, this urban world also claimed me as a lay minister and then clergy through our shared experiences of life and death.

As I arrived on the doorstep of the academy for a doctoral program, I brought all of these lived experiences with me. I discovered myself once again thrust into the role of bridge person between cultural worlds—this time for an academy that longed for access to the urban world of my relationships, as well as for an urban world that often felt disconnected from or used by the predominantly white academy. As a "clinical social worker and clergyperson now shaping as academic researcher," I also heard, again with a bit of detached wonderment and discomfort, some urgency in the tone of questions, desires, and even fierce demands of me, usually by white academic mentors: "I would like to know more about these street memorials—they are not studied so often." "I want to know about the memorial buttons—tell me about the buttons!"

Simultaneously, I heard, with poignant empathy, the suspicion from my urban world: "Researchers come and go. We get requests all the time for access to our work—what's in it for us? We won't do it unless you can guarantee we're going to benefit in some way." To deny the academic research gaze without comparable guarantee of mutual benefit seemed to be the one power left to the communal urban gatekeepers, a demand of equity for their stakeholders—those whom privileged academics might call the marginalized, colonized, or subalterns and without voice of their own in the world of the academy. How to navigate the expectations and desires between these cultural worlds with authenticity and respect became my clinical social work and ministerial call as a researcher. This call stood alongside a need to attend to the human queerness of living between both worlds, one that made me a survivor of violence and of the costs of residing in the borderlands as well.

A Founding Story for an Urban Ministry: Case Study One

One day, Louis was in his bedroom playing with his cousin Antonio and his friend Anthony. They were talking about what they wanted to be when they grew up. Louis said to them: "I am going to be the first black president of the United States when I am thirty-five years old." Antonio was so happy to hear that, he jumped off the bed where he was sitting. "Wow!" he said. "That means you will also be the youngest president ever. Fantastic, then I will be your vice president." "Good," said Louis. "I want you guys and all my friends to be with me in the White House."

One night, Louis was watching the news on television. The news anchor reported that earlier that day two young men had been arguing about drugs, and one had shot the other and killed him. Louis got very sad. He looked at his father with tears in his eyes. "Too many kids are dying on the streets," he said to his father. "Why are there so many guns around? Why do people have to use drugs? That stuff can hurt you, and it can kill you." Louis sat silently for a moment. Then he shook his head and said to his father: "If things don't change by the time I become president, I will be alone in the White House – none of my friends will be around. They will all be in jail, all addicted to drugs, or all dead."[1]

History and Organization of the Louis D. Brown Peace Institute

History of Formation

In the late 1980s and early 1990s, Boston was struggling with a rash of homicides and street violence, reaching a peak of 152 murders in 1990.[2] Amid this context, on December 20, 1993, Louis David Brown, age 15, was on his way to a Christmas party being given by the organization *Teens Against Gang Violence* when he was shot and killed, caught in a cross fire between two rival gangs though he himself had never been involved in a gang. His mother and co-founding ministry leader of the Peace Institute recalls that Louis wanted to be the first African American president, and he is quoted in Peace Institute in-house pamphlet literature as saying: "If true peace is to be achieved it will be up to my generation, regardless of which side of the streets we come from." Current ministry leaders of the Peace Institute, who had never met this young man, cited the legacy of his life and story as foundational to their work and guiding mission. One stated: "[The Peace Institute] became a safe place in the community for people who lost somebody to violence—because of Louis' story."

The initial years of the Louis D. Brown Peace Institute (LDBPI or Peace Institute) took two directions, directions that continue to inform their work and ministry: (1) creating peace curriculums and education based in large part on Louis' life story for use in the Boston public schools and (2) providing outreach and advocacy education to family survivors of homicide. A third direction today is the coordination and training of other providers who serve families of homicide victims. The Peace Institute's peace curriculums are deeply intertwined with their overall mission and became nationally recognized during the Clinton administration in the 1990s for assisting in the reduction of juvenile crime in Boston.[3] However, their survivor outreach services, including their Leadership Academy, and work coordinating Boston area human service providers remain their primary source of recognition locally. These latter services were the main focus of this particular case study, drawing lessons from the Peace Institute's practices for "transforming pain and anger" after homicide, practices that educate and empower families to become peacemakers and advocates for justice in their larger communities.[4]

Mission

As found in its current formal mission statement, the Peace Institute "serves as a center of healing, teaching and learning for families and communities dealing with murder, trauma, grief and loss," with an emphasis on restorative justice theories in their process.[5] They further state on their website that the focal point of their programming includes schools, families, and the broader community. The overarching tagline throughout their literature and website is: "transforming pain and anger into power and action," as well as an emphasis on their seven Principles of Peace: "love, unity, faith, hope, courage, justice, and forgiveness." While some study participants spoke to more or fewer dimensions of this mission, depending on their experiences, none contradicted this perception of the Peace Institute's mission. Sample survivor comments included: "The model is . . . take your pain anger and turn it into power and action . . . [as well as] . . . the mission is to help empower the family to find the strength . . . to cope with . . . this journey, this life change, this life-altering experience . . . to . . . help us create that peace environment . . . to help stop the *cycle* of violence . . . like a wrap-around or comprehensive place for that specific goal . . . ."

For the founding ministry leader, this mission is linked to larger oppressive historical forces and a country founded on violence: "Again this country was founded on violence and . . . in the name of peace, we go to war and we think it's okay, so . . . what's our role in all of this, you know? We're quick to blame people [but] where do we go and how are we accountable? . . . [H]ow are we leading by example?" In the philosophy of the Peace Institute, each person first must learn how to foster peace within, so that one then can foster peace out in the larger community. Several institutional supporters also would use language such as "comprehensive" and "wraparound services" to describe the mission of the Peace Institute. They stated that the Peace Institute's overarching mission is not only to *support* survivors in the aftermath of violence but also to *prevent* violence by "support[ing the survivors] in making this link between personal healing and policy . . . to educate survivors in policy and systems change" and to foster "safer and healthier communities." This intertwining of a micro pastoral and clinical focus on internal peace with the need to engage in the macro prophetic and social justice work of *system change* lends itself to ecological interdisciplinary and transdisciplinary perspectives from fields as diverse as social work, education, public health, and pastoral care.

The motto threaded throughout the Leadership Academy literature remains striking in this regard: "transforming pain and anger into power and action." This philosophy of "healing through action" comes from the Honduran culture and lived experiences of the founding ministry leader, an immigrant to this country as a child with her family. She spoke of her culture teaching her to believe that there is an inner wisdom and capacity for "healing" anger and grief through one's personal capacity for transformative and embodied action. She explicitly attributed her experiences and beliefs to racial, class, and cultural differences:

> I don't know ... as whether it's white people that you have the luxury of going to a counselor and sitting, and in my country as a poor person, that's not a luxury you have, so you find your way of not denying but of dealing with your issues whether it's sewing, cooking, cleaning but different methods of dealing with grief ... [you don't] have this luxury of grievin', of a safe space, you've got to go, go, go because you have other children and that's just the way the world is, you don't have luxury of goin' to a support group because that's not what we believe in . . . ..

Though not an explicit component of their public mission statement, leaders of the Peace Institute also clearly experienced and identified their work as ministry, and some survivors and institutional supporters did as well. Ministry in this sense centered on meeting people where they were at and serving immediate needs, but doing so with a deep and connected sense of compassion and love. This sense of ministry was grounded in each leader's Christian faith tradition or background as lay people and a common belief in "servitude" rather than a specific religious form of Christianity. Ministry leaders interviewed at the time of the initial study most often experienced the work as a calling or mission from God to help with providing love and healing and opportunities for the transformation of pain and anger into power and action. In the grassroots nature of the Peace Institute at the time of the study, formal degrees were not considered necessary for this work so much as a strong base in love and humility as well as personal experience with survivor needs.[6]

As mentioned in their mission statement above, and threaded throughout all of the programs and services of the Peace Institute, are the seven Principles of Peace: Love, Unity, Faith, Hope, Courage, Justice, and Forgiveness. All ministry leaders interviewed agreed that the principles had biblical roots as they understood them. The founding ministry leader specifically described them as coming to her as a message from God in 2002 after she and her husband separated and she became the sole director of the Peace Institute. She explained emphatically (pounding on the desk during the interview) that these principles were divinely revealed to be the core of her peace work. For the founding ministry leader interviewed, a sense of connection to and calling by God also was part of the narrative that turned her outward, pushing her to grow in her own self-confidence and transform her own pain and anger. She experienced her work as a God-given mission to impart the seven Principles of Peace not only to survivors but also to the larger community as well, in her language to work toward "the fullness of God's peace."

While ministry leaders at the time of the interviews identified as coming from lay Christian backgrounds, a newer dimension of the turning outward of their ministry was their engagement in interfaith work through the use of these seven Principles of Peace. They reported discovering that these peace principles could be seen as universal aspects of human experience. This allowed them to operate equally well across cultures in secular public school, health, and clinical settings as in interfaith settings, enhancing the Peace Institute's overall "missionary" capacity and drive to end suffering and create lasting peace in a broader community. The founding ministry leader pulled out and recited a quote to me by the Cambodian Buddhist monk, Maha Ghosananda, in a research interview: "We must find the courage to leave our temples and enter the temples of human experience, temples that are filled with suffering. If we listen to the Buddha, Christ, Mohammad or Gandhi, we can do nothing else. The refugee camps, the prison, the ghettos, and the battlefields will then become our temples. We have so much work to do." Thus she and other ministry leaders learned from different religious traditions, looking for points of connection with their values, language, and practices, while also remaining firmly grounded in their own Christian values and narrative (Fig. 3.1).

Philosophical Influences

Two models and philosophies of anti-violence intervention, a public health model and an anti-oppression analysis, both would help to shape the mission of the Peace Institute in its founding years and also be

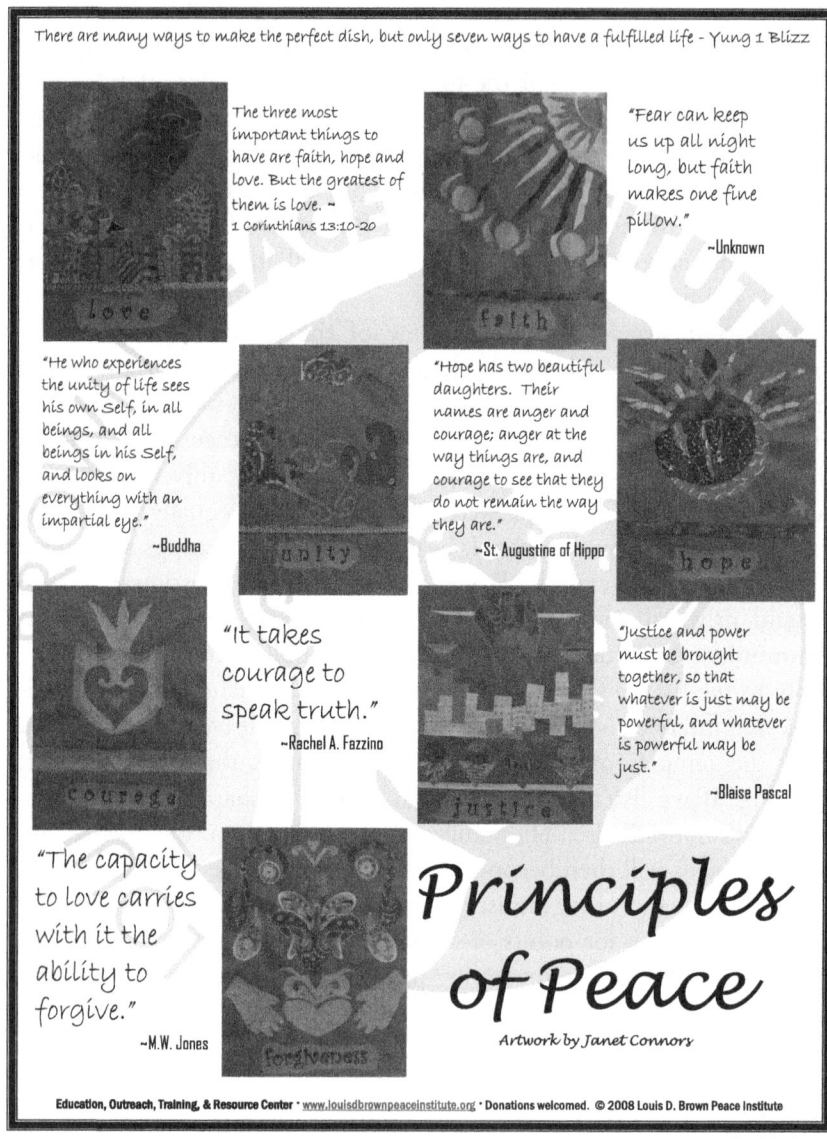

Fig. 3.1 *Peace Institute's Seven Principles of Peace.* The Peace Institute's seven Principles of Peace illustrated with quotes. An example of their efforts to make some interfaith connections can be seen in the quote by Buddha (Artwork by Janet Connors)

recognized in the grassroots work the Peace Institute already was engaging. The respective models were introduced to the founding ministry leader by fellow black female leaders and institutional supporters, both of whom she experienced as important relational mentors in her life. The public health model of violence prevention is most deeply associated with the work of Dr. Deborah Prothrow-Stith, whom the co-founders met in the early 1990s and who assisted in writing the Peace Institute's *Peacezone* curriculum for grades K-5.[7] A ministry leader spoke of the public health model giving "language" to the work in which they were already engaged.

The public health model consists first of recognizing that violence *is* a systemic public health problem, not solely a criminal justice problem, and that as a public health problem it is preventable through a wide range of services, programs, and approaches. Before meeting the founders of the Peace Institute, Prothrow-Stith wrote that, as a public health doctor, she rejected "that the medical community was powerless to prevent young black males or members of any group from hurting one another."[8] In her view, *all* social institutions have a role to play in preventing violence by providing diverse and integrated educational programs to address anger management as a realizable goal:

> My own view is a pragmatic one. To me a problem that destroys health by causing so much injury and death is a health problem . . . I am convinced we can change public attitudes toward violence and that we can change violent behavior. What is required is a broad array of strategies; strategies that teach new ways of coping with anger and aggressive feelings. I believe we can and we must mobilize schools, the media, industry, government, churches, community organizations, and every organized unit within our society to deliver the message that anger can be managed and aggressive impulses controlled.[9]

The second model and philosophy of anti-violence intervention that both helped to shape Peace Institute services and was an intuitive match with work they had already engaged was a model of anti-oppression analysis.[10] This model also gave the staff language and tools for deepening their understanding of their work, language and tools that were seen to match with the public health violence prevention model with which they were already familiar, particularly in gun violence prevention. The anti-oppression institutional supporter interviewed affirmed that it was a natural match with the Peace Institute's focus on internal insight work as the grounding for effectively engaging in peace and social justice work in the community (correlating disciplinary cultural worlds and language, it was a match with both the Peace Institute's Christian prophetic pastoral care approach and their implicit secular ecological systems social work and public health approach). The anti-oppression institutional supporter stated:

> ... our approach to community engagement and to community change is based on the assumption that we have to look personally inside—interpersonally—and then at the systems around, as well as at the culture that we're all swimming in ... survivors need to do personal healing, and they also need to develop advocacy skills ... 'Cause we can heal every individual, and then if we don't do something about the policies and practices that create this condition, then we're still stuck.

As a consultant to the Peace Institute's Survivor Leadership Academy, this institutional supporter developed educational programs to enable survivors to be effective in engaging in social justice and policy advocacy. These programs made explicit the links between the personal and the public at four levels—the personal, interpersonal, institutional, and cultural—and provided language for anti-oppression concepts as well as education in history and policy (e.g. modern racism, classism, sexism, heterosexism, religious oppression). This approach also integrated well with the public health model's focus on primary preventive care through teaching personal and interpersonal skills of conflict, grief, and trauma resolution. A focus on emotional and cognitive literacy was tied to the ability to engage in effective public policy advocacy for both models. The Peace Institute's ministry leaders recognized that personal pastoral and clinical awareness enhanced the skills of systemic prophetic social justice action, and this was foundational to the shape of their ministry.

This institutional supporter also stressed that the theories introduced were a match with what the Peace Institute already was doing on a grassroots level, but that the provision of *theory and language* enabled

3 Two Case Studies by a Researcher Living Between Worlds

the ministry leaders to engage their work more explicitly. It helped them to understand their own need to heal and communicate with each other, as well as to educate the survivors they were serving on this more explicit level:

> [I]t's kind of given them a language ... how do you communicate ... with awareness of power differentials, which be they race or gender or status or age or whatever, and how do those impact how well we do our work? ... It's a language ... and giving them some more tools for how to understand their feelings, how to talk about it with each other, and then also, I don't think that they had explicitly made the link between racism, oppression, and the institutionalization of gun violence ... I mean, it wasn't like it wasn't there, but I don't think they had been focused on how do you *teach* people about that, and I think they're beginning to do more of that.

While both of these particular institutional supporters interviewed stressed that the Peace Institute already was engaged in work reflecting a public health violence prevention model, as well as an anti-oppression stance, ministry leaders affirmed that trainings by these institutional supporters gave them language and theory for sharpening their understanding of the healing and advocacy work in which they were engaged. Language and theory gave them tools of analysis that not only enabled growth in the aftermath of lived experiences of violent trauma but also improved their ability to become more effective *imaginaries and teachers of community peacemaking*.

In bell hooks' essay, "Theory as Liberatory Practice,"[11] she affirms the importance of theory as a liberative means of interpreting and healing personal pain by linking the pain to its source from systemic oppression and beginning to imagine a different world. She writes:

> Living in childhood without a sense of home, I found a place of sanctuary in "theorizing," in making sense out of what was happening. I found a place where I could imagine possible futures, a place where life could be lived differently. This "lived" experience of critical thinking, of reflection and analysis, became a place where I worked at explaining the hurt and making it go away. Fundamentally, I learned from this experience that theory could be a healing place ... When our lived experience of theorizing is

fundamentally linked to processes of self-recovery, of collective liberation, no gap exists between theory and practice.[12]

LDBPI ministry leaders and survivors consistently reported they came to understand the power of theory and language in this way, as both a source of personal "healing" and a source of collective liberation and more effective shared action through deepened understanding.

Programs and Infrastructure

At the time of the interviews, the Peace Institute consisted of four paid staff and a large number of volunteers managing the vast majority of referrals for families whose lives had been impacted by homicide in and around the greater Boston area. There were two main departments which reflected their early origins: (1) Peace Education, under which their ongoing work with their various peace curriculums in Boston public schools fell and (2) Survivor Outreach Services, under which they provided a variety of healing, educational, and empowerment programs for survivor families. While these departments were separated to prioritize staff responsibilities, there often was an intertwining of program influences and developments.

For example, sibling and teen groups offered to survivors through outreach services also were seen as related to peace education work being done in schools. The public health institutional supporter interviewed stated: "[It] became clear that helping children deal with fear and anger and pain and loss was an absent part of the typical violence prevention education activity. That people were going in, teaching character, teaching conflict resolution, teaching skills, but not at all addressing that emotional trauma." One Peace Institute ministry leader spoke of the Survivor Outreach sibling program as arising from the use of their peace curriculums in the public schools and the desire "to literally teach peace to children," particularly since many children already had been exposed to violent traumatic losses in Boston. This was seen to be particularly crucial as the public health doctor interviewed estimated "that something like

10 percent of the children [in Boston] had witnessed a significant episode of violence by the age of 6."

Ministry leaders saw the work of sibling groups as crucial to the prevention of further generational violence. Such groups affirmed that these youth were "peculiar people" who could be stigmatized, isolated, and otherwise at-risk for striking back in pain and anger.[13] Per a ministry leader, such youth needed opportunities to connect with their fellow peers and to learn different vehicles, including artistic ones, for expressing pain and loss:

> [W]e like to use the slogan "hurt people hurt people" ... predisposed possibly, potentially, to violence themselves. They feel the sense or the need to retaliate often, and many times that takes place very subconsciously, if you will ... So recognizing that, [the] Peace Institute sought to develop a siblings program where we could provide ... an atmosphere where these young children could come and could recognize that there are other folks or other children like them. They are not the same people that they were prior to that experience of murder and bereavement and funerals and that whole picture. They are a peculiar people, if you will ... imagine a young kid who is asked about his brother's murder in school or in the playground or wherever. You can only imagine the trauma that he goes through having to try to answer ... "What happened to your brother? Was your brother in a gang? Was your brother a gangbanger? Was he on drugs?" ... So in an effort to address that, the Peace Institute sought to have this group, and it helps these young kids express themselves through arts, express themselves through writing, through poetry, through song ... through different positive avenues of expression, then that sort of takes the place of expressing themselves in negative ways ....

Today, the Peace Institute is best known for its crisis management services under Survivor Outreach, providing support services to families in the immediate aftermath of a homicide. These services include the use of the Peace Institute's *Burial and Resource Guide: What to Do After Leaving the Hospital, A Step-by-Step Workbook*,[14] as well as the creation of specialized orders of funeral services and memorial buttons. From her personal experience of violent loss, the founding ministry leader spoke of the confusion and sense of being overwhelmed with feelings and logistical tasks in the face of a family homicide—from experiencing the emotional trauma itself, to where to start with funeral arrangements, to suddenly having to cope with police and media presence as well as the judicial system in one's life, to needing to find immediate and significant financial resources for the burial and notify as well as coordinate family and friends, to being bombarded with service providers or abandoned by service providers, etc. These experiences motivated her creation of the burial guide over several years. Each of the Peace Institute ministry leaders also was available when a homicide occurred to provide pastoral care, no matter their official paid role. Such care involved immediate, supportive crisis counseling services and walking the family through practical logistical details to find or advocate for the resources they needed.

Once a family moves through the initial crisis management with clinical and pastoral care, other types of programs are available to them through Survivor Outreach Services. At the time of the initial case study, these included the Peace Institute's Holistic Healing Center activities (inclusive of various art activities and body healing practices) and many programs of the Leadership Academy, including educational and empowerment workshops (such as court preparation, understanding police processes, networking with human service providers, public policy advocacy); "By Men for Men" (an individualized program for male survivors led by the male ministry leader); and "Tuesday Talks" (a weekly evening support group for adult survivors, which would come to be named the "Peace Warriors" during the initial case study period and from whom survivors interviewed were drawn).

These "Tuesday Talks" became an early organizing basis for giving public testimony about the needs of survivors and advocacy for public policy changes. Their current and growing outreach to the broader community includes ongoing training for providers; legislative policy advocacy; a peace fellows program with various local universities; an intergenerational justice program with a restorative justice focus; and a wide variety of public events during their Survivors of Homicide Awareness Month (November 20–December 20 annually by proclamation of the Massachusetts governor); as well as their annual Mothers' Day Walk for Peace (their major fundraiser and community event on the streets of Boston, which at the time of writing of this book was entering its 20th year and marching from their local community in Dorchester to Boston City Hall for the first time).

Violent Intrusion, Chaos, and a Call for Help: Case Study Two

A Scene from July 27, 2008 in Knoxville, TN: I was the church administrator and I was going to see the children's play [the musical "Annie"] to show some support for the music director ... I usually go to the left and I decided I would go to the right ... And later I thought boy, that had a lot of impact, that little decision ... So I was on the bad side for the shooting ... And then as it happened it was a very scary moment in the play where little orphan Annie's backing away with her flashlight through the woods thinkin' people were gonna get her. And then all of a sudden, just this enormous loud sound. And my first thought was, as an administrator ... somebody really screwed up because we're gonna get a lot of complaints about this, whatever it was ... And I was jokin'; I was sitting next to a person here. I said, "I bet we look like meerkats if you could see us." Because we both looked up to see [the] cause [of] what happened and you couldn't tell. We thought a sound thing had blown up. And then we both looked around this way and then saw the man. And then hit the ground, but it was just that sort of figuring out moment. So we hit the ground and, um, he was about 15 feet away, and I've just never seen such hostility on a face before ... it felt like, um, sort of a supernatural force of destruction. It really did.

... the other thing that was kind of funny, but not funny was when I was down on the floor I was thinking, did I get the catastrophic violence insurance? As the administrator. And I thought they are going to kill me if I didn't pay that bill or whatever it was, you know? It's funny cause here I am worried about losing my life, but I'm also like I'm in so much trouble if that insurance isn't paid up, you know? And so I had a lot of stress just about my role, you know, afterwards like what's the administrator supposed to do now? ... And I also realized ... later that I'd been trying to cram my head into a space where it wouldn't fit, just very animalistic, you know? And I went like, "What was I doing there? That's not gonna fit. Why didn't I go this way?" Anyway, so—it's just that kind of waiting and just thinking this is so wrong. And then when somebody figured out that we could get out, which was probably like three seconds later, I don't know. Seeing the light from the curtain being open and then going, "Run, run, run, run, run." So we're all like scrambling like Marines on our bellies and stuff and getting' scratched up. Later you're like, "Gee, I really got scratched up." And then later wondering if you hurt somebody or . . . "Did I crush you?". . . And then we went out on the hillside there and—there was a lot of quiet. Seemed very quiet to me at that time. Everyone was just processing . . . . So then . . . I just went to the office and called [the minister] who . . . was on break and left him a scary message. And this was sort of in a daze. And in retrospect I think it's odd that I didn't . . . have the wherewithal to go see what was goin' on. Like my first instinct was to get on my cell phone and call everybody and tell them I'm okay . . . mostly I just was in a daze really and not super functional.

Setting the Context of the Knoxville, TN, Church Shooting and Response

Prior to the shock and tragedy of this day, and prior to the minister's response in calling for help to the UUTRM, the TVUUC had long testified and witnessed to the prophetic social justice power of their faith tradition. This history and context is important for understanding the shape of religious and spiritual practices in the aftermath of the shooting. The UUTRM arrived on site and entered into a cultural world of strength, resiliency, risk-taking, and points of vulnerability already long-standing for this vibrant Southern suburban congregation.

The Tennessee Valley UU Church (TVUUC) proclaims proudly that they have been "a beacon of liberal religious faith in Eastern Tennessee for more than 60 years." This is a prominent statement in their PowerPoint introduction for newcomers, a narrative put together during a time of church growth after the 2008 shooting and from which the below history is drawn. One TVUUC leader, who was the designated initial informant for this study by the minister and the TVUUC board, stated that the church has always had an "evangelical" bent, having spun off three additional UU congregations in the area. He also shared that he was "nominated for church president because I was president of a group I started here called the Society of Unitarian Universalist Evangelists." This particular TVUUC leader also played a significant role in the creation of the PowerPoint narrative, an artifact that both shapes and expresses through images and narrative the religious identity of this particular congregation.

There had been failed attempts to start Unitarian churches in Knoxville, but finally on February 6, 1949, 122 members signed a charter and began renting space at a local school. They would advertise themselves in local newspapers and radio sermons as "The church with the open mind and optimistic program." According to the church narrative, in the segregated US South of 1950 a retired African American railroad worker named Jim Person (pictured in their newcomer PowerPoint) came to the church, pointed to their "Everyone is Welcome" sign, and asked "Does that mean me?" When the usher said yes, the church began a process of embracing integration during the US civil rights era as part of its prophetic social justice mission. The church also suffered the consequence of this when the school system chose not to renew their rental agreement, beginning what the PowerPoint described as their "wandering in the wilderness phase," meeting in different locations until a house eventually was purchased.

The PowerPoint narrative goes on to state that the TVUUC became a "leader in integrating Knoxville," offering housing to traveling integrated groups, participating in lunch counter and other sit-ins, and running integrated summer day camps for children. Again, there were consequences, such as being accused of communism and, according to a former minister who spoke during their sanctuary rededication ceremony, also having to move their integrated summer camps from place to place in an effort to avoid harassment by the local Klu Klux Klan, who had exploded or riddled with shotgun their mailboxes. In the 1970s, when the church hosted the area's first openly gay congregation, the front windows of their home-based church were shot out at the end of that congregation's service.[15]

Eventually the TVUUC was able to purchase land for a formal church building. This new building was not designed for church growth, however, according to the power point narrative, since the architect did not believe there would ever be more than 200 Unitarians in the city of Knoxville. The church did continue to grow, however, and spin off congregations, including the Westside UU Church (members of whom were present in the TVUUC sanctuary and also impacted on the day of the shooting). In the 1980s, the church continued its social justice work and participated in the interfaith sanctuary movement by hosting a refugee family from Guatemala. Then, in 1989, a new church building was completed upon the same property, designed to follow the "natural contours of the land to integrate with the earth" and to emphasize "natural light." Also noteworthy in the architecture of the new building was the prophetic inscription of 18 values associated with UU theology.[16] These included values expressed in the TVUUC affirmation of faith, "Love," "Service," and "Peace." This affirmation originally was written by the Unitarian minister and poet James Vila Blake, and this version (or a different but similar one by a Universalist author) can be found in many UU congregations around the country: "Love is the spirit of this church, and service is its law. To dwell together

Fig. 3.2 *TVUUC Partial Exterior Building View.* The arc of the building as it curves with the landscape can be seen, along with long shots of the exterior panels with UU values inscribed

Fig. 3.3 *TVUUC Sample Exterior Panels.* Two sample panels of 18 from the exterior of the church testifying to UU values

in peace, to seek the truth in love, and to help one another, this is our great covenant (Figs. 3.2 and 3.3)."[17]

In 1993, the TVUUC was recognized formally as a "Welcoming Congregation" within the UUA, a designation meaning that they had completed a formal educational process to welcome gays and lesbians.[18] Though the congregation completed the formal welcoming and educational process at that time, there were ongoing disputes within the congregation about making a *visible* sign of this commitment on the church's main entrance. A former board president would write: " ... there was sentiment that if we put a symbol up for one group, we could be led into a tacky décor characterized by an array of symbols for every disenfranchised group."[19] Finally, early in July 2008 and just prior to the traumatic events of July 27, a task force decided on a temporary solution that would become a form of material testimony to their prophetic social justice history and values (Fig. 3.4):

Fig. 3.4 *Permanent Welcoming Congregation Plaque*. This was installed after the church shooting. Interview participants remarked a permanent plaque had been a particular focus of Greg McKendry to see accomplished

We made up a simple 8-1/2 x 11″ sign that read "Everyone Welcome" and had the rainbow flag underneath it. The text on the back of the sign explained that this sign harkened back to the church's history when a simple "Everyone Welcome" sign in 1950 had welcomed a black man named Jim Person to our doors. The new laminated paper sign was minimalist in design but drew on our church history of welcoming all persons while being able to incorporate the rainbow flag and be specifically welcoming to the GLBT community . . . .[20]

There are multiple news accounts available through the internet, as well as the Unitarian Universalist Association (UUA's) website, as to the traumatic events of July 27, 2008 and into the following year, thus I briefly will outline some of these events only, with no intent of capturing the vividness of emotions and responses conveyed by those interviewed.

3 Two Case Studies by a Researcher Living Between Worlds 71

For their summer service that day, the children of some of the local UU congregations, including Westside, were performing the musical "Annie" at TVUUC. Around 10:15AM, a gunman entered the church carrying a shotgun in a guitar case and opened fire in the crowded sanctuary. He killed an usher in his path, Greg McKendry, age 60, a very active member of TVUUC, as well as Linda Lee Kraeger, age 61, a member of the Westside congregation, and physically injured several others (all were adults, no children were physically injured, all children having successfully fled out a rear door, with some taking shelter at the Presbyterian church further up the hill). Ultimately, the gunman was subdued by members of the congregation. It was learned later, through a letter he wrote as well as through his conversations with police, that the gunman had deliberately targeted the church for its liberal religious teachings and values.[21]

A Bill Moyers Journal episode[22] reported on the police news conference that described the white gunman, age 58, as an "unemployed truck driver" who was motivated by his "lack of employment" and "frustration" and "stated hatred for the liberal movement." The police reported that the gunman said: " ... that all liberals should be killed because they were ... ruining the country, and that he felt that the Democrats had tied his country's hands in the war on terror and ruined every institution in America." He specifically targeted the UU church because of "its liberal teachings" and " ... because he could not get to the leaders of the liberal movement ... he would target those that had voted them into office."

In the direct aftermath of the shooting, the TVUCC minister requested that a colleague contact the UU Trauma Response Ministry (UUTRM), who arrived on site and began to provide assistance immediately and remained connected over the next year(s). Despite this traumatic and violent incident, the church continued to grow in membership throughout the next year and experienced many renewing moments according to TVUUC leader reports, including their annual Christmas pageant and the celebration of their 60th anniversary with the installation of permanent memorial plaques in the church. They also underwent stresses and strains, particularly around governance as well as renewed publicity with the trial of the shooter, hitting a crisis point about nine months after the initial traumatic event. Stresses and strains took the form of multiple congregant health issues emerging, further personal tragedies, exhaustion for staff and church leaders with leadership departures, tense budget negotiations, and an eruption on their email list serve when a transgender woman experienced herself as excluded from a nonofficial church event.[23]

The combination of these events, particularly some occurring on the minister's sabbatical again, required the congregational leadership to request the intervention of the District Executive, who recommended a closer examination of church governance and organizational weak points, as well as some behavioral changes by the membership. These stresses and strains on the church leadership became significant for the recommendations offered by the TVUUC leaders back to the UUTRM leaders in the course of this particular case study. I turn now to examining the larger context of formation of a trauma response team in a denominational setting and the UUTRM's particular involvement in the aftermath of the TVUUC shooting.

History and Organization of the Unitarian Universalist Trauma Response Ministry

History of Formation

Personal experiences with providing chaplaincy services at Ground Zero after 9/11 was the starting place for all UUTRM leader stories of recognizing the need for creating an institutionally based trauma response ministry within the UUA. One UUTRM leader was formally dispatched to Ground Zero as a member and founder of her state's Corps of Fire Chaplains, and another persistently and creatively battled her way into access to Ground Zero when she lacked formal recognition for her chaplaincy role. While working at Ground Zero, these eventual UUTRM leaders came to the conclusion that a UU liberal religious voice and interfaith perspective was needed to bring "a sense of hope" rather than a message of "punishment" or "God's wrath" to survivors of traumatic situations, including large-scale social disasters. As previously discussed, the UU tradition is grounded in a liberal religious tradition of ethical principles and shared practices, drawing from a wide variety of

3 Two Case Studies by a Researcher Living Between Worlds 73

sources for religious wisdom, rather than being based in particular doctrines or creeds. One UUTRM leader argued:

> I think when Unitarian Universalists are there ... we bring a spiritual perspective that's not tied to any particular creed ... we knew that we wanted to be available for all people at all times and we wanted to have that sense of hope that Unitarian Universalism brings, that, in the midst of chaos, hope does arise, and that it's not about punishment or not about God's wrath, it's about walking with people through whatever the circumstances [are] ....

The UUTRM leader who had to find creative linkages to get into and stay at Ground Zero would share, in sharp terms, specific concerns of conversations or behaviors she witnessed by other chaplains at Ground Zero that were antithetical to UU values:

> I encountered all kinds of evangelical people who were talking about how either this was God's will, or they were witnessing to people and basically proselytizing. And I met one guy [and all] I remember is that he said he had really felt like he had had a good day because he witnessed to someone and believed he had relieved them of their lesbianism ... I was just enraged. And I kept thinking to myself, "There's gotta be a liberal religious response to this, other than, 'This was God's will,' or, 'This is God's punishment'"... And so I started thinking about it and looking around online and I realized almost every other denomination had a disaster response team. You know, the Baptist men have just taken over the Earth in terms of cleaning stuff and getting people back into their houses. The Mennonites do kids. The Episcopalians do food. Almost everybody does something, here we sit, you know, twiddling our thumbs. So I started calling all the people that I knew who had been like police chaplains or fire chaplains and just kinda bitchin' and moanin', talking to people about it ....

Within a year, these experiences and conversations would lead to a gathering of various UUs with backgrounds in trauma response and interest in, as well as a passionate commitment to, forming a UUTRM, supported also by an initial grant from a UU congregation of $15,000.

Mission

The UUTRM was founded in 2002, and, according to its current mission statement the UUTRM focuses upon the provision of "culturally sensitive spiritual care to survivors of mass disasters and other significant trauma."[24] This includes a focus on education, provision of resources, deploying response teams, and networking with other trauma organizations. In the establishment of their original mission, however, there were occasional differences among UUTRM leaders as to the hoped for scope of their vision. The clear majority of those interviewed, including their UUA institutional supporters, viewed the UUTRM's role to be intra-associational/intra-denominational in focus, due both to their limited capacity and to a perceived unique value in having such a focus. One UUTRM leader argued: "where we had the most potential to impact . . . was to train and educate, and inform and work with district entities, and work with individual congregational teams and ministers to prepare congregations to respond to these kinds of things effectively." Another UUTRM leader would express strong opinions on the need to limit the prophetic pastoral care scope of the mission and any possibility of "mission creep." "I have no desire to organize . . . for the rest of the world 'cause there are other organizations that are doing it well and better."

However, the African American UUTRM leader interviewed passionately expressed a much more expansive vision of the UUTRM mission, citing her experiences in growing up with a "black church ethos" as a rationale and the value placed on responding to the needs expressed regardless of official certification or perceived limitations:

> [M]y whole thing is that if we're gonna do this work for Unitarian Universalists, then we need to do whatever they need us to do. It's not about whether or not it's in our purview. Disaster's not in anybody's purview, really. And I think a lot of that comes from, even though I didn't grow up in the black church, I kinda grew up with the black church ethos, undergirding cultural life. And ministry in that context is whatever you need to do by whatever means necessary. So if your people can't get loans, you start a bank. If your folks can't read, you start a literacy program.

It's not like, "Okay. Well, I'm not certified as a community minister or I'm not a banker, so I can't do this." So?

Worth noting is the emphasis and debate in much of the above on the need for effectiveness of scope, training, and authority *versus*, at least in small part, a "make do" philosophy and willingness to take some risks in operating beyond perceived boundaries or limitations under certain extreme circumstances. There was a heavy emphasis among all UUTRM leaders interviewed, as well as their UUA institutional supporters, on the need for trauma-specific training and clear lines of authority, with mission focus regarding their limited capacity. There also was a passionate wish expressed by at least one UUTRM leader for a greater vision of their capacity and a willingness to push against aspects of those perceived constraints at times when needs were presented in the provision of care. UUTRM leaders generally expressed empathy for the larger vision but more often felt constrained by resources and capacity. The particular UUTRM leader who expressed these opinions on mission and vision also did agree with the need for hierarchy and authority during crises, however, as well as an overall need for trauma-specific training.

An understanding of the larger overall UUTRM mission was significantly more limited, however, by TVUUC congregational leaders interviewed. In most cases, the UUTRM mission was seen by these leaders as primarily to support and advise the senior minister in his recovery and in his ministry to the congregation (though the minister himself had a deeper awareness of the overall work of the UUTRM from exposure to a UUTRM-led workshop at the UUA national General Assembly). Most TVUUC leaders interviewed had no awareness of the existence of the UUTRM prior to their encounter with their services in the aftermath of the shooting. This lack of perceived clarity as to the UUTRM mission, and its role and authority in relationship to the larger congregational leadership, was seen as a particular challenge by some TVUUC leaders in this case study.

Philosophical Influences

Within the UUTRM mission statement, one can see the emphasis on and philosophical influence of a particular type of training, Critical Incident Stress Management (CISM) modalities,[25] though other training modalities were added as the UUTRM grew with experience over time. These included the National Organization of Victims Assistance (NOVA) training,[26] deemed more suitable for working with crime victims and homicide traumas by UUTRM leaders interviewed. UUTRM leaders frequently stressed that the specific kind of training needed for trauma response was significantly different from the forms of pastoral care training clergy might receive through Clinical Pastoral Education (CPE) and that these particular trainings gave them these added skills. In responding to 9/11, however, some level of *at least* CPE training was a form of legitimizing one's credentials as a chaplain, this according to the UUTRM leader for whom that became a crucial point of credibility in gaining access to Ground Zero (many other denominational chaplains on the ground apparently had not had CPE or any other formal training by her report).

One UUTRM leader spoke in strong terms to the failure of CPE training to prepare ministers fully in the specific skill sets needed as trauma responders:

> I'm doing a CPE residency now, and I'm more and more convinced CPE ... doesn't train you to do crisis and trauma work .... it's a cult ... I mean, CPE can be helpful if you've done your own work on it ... that's certainly gonna be an asset. But the idea that hospital chaplaincy trains you with the skill sets you need to do trauma work is a complete falsehood and just propaganda that they say that they do. So that's my opinion, on the record.

The institutional supporter who was the former UUA president at the time of the UUTRM's formation also believed that the response to trauma requires an additional level of training and skills beyond providing merely a pastoral listening presence:

> Trauma, particularly large-scale societal trauma, in my experience and in my judgment, actually has some dynamics that need to be understood if you're

gonna be helpful and ... the simple act of presence is good but it's not all that's necessary, and that's why I was delighted that [the UUTRM] had searched out some additional education for themselves ... so that they could show up in situations of trauma, not merely with ... a pastoral presence, but with a pastoral presence that understood some of the dynamics of trauma over time and could interact with the people who were going through those various stages of response ... with some information and knowledge about what resources are appropriate at the various stages. So they show up doing a better job of ministry is the short version.

Regarding the need for trauma-specific training combined with clear lines of authority and accountability, all UUTRM leaders agreed that this was a profound human need due to the chaotic nature of traumatic impact. The at times frequent militaristic language and hierarchical protocol in their descriptions (such as "deploy," "chain of command," "command structures," "proper channels") often was striking to me given their UU ministerial and pastoral context. This can be seen when one UUTRM leader stressed the need for accountability to minimize chaos, particularly in the aftermath of traumatic disasters:

> I think the worst possible thing that can happen in disaster scenarios, where chaos reigns supreme and people are trying to put structures in place, is to have groups of people that arrive without any particular authority or direction, and so we're very clear that ... we do not deploy unless we are invited to do so by the proper channels ... And that's really about being accountable and making certain we don't simply add to chaos in an already chaotic situation ... I think people don't understand that it's not just about showing up. It's about being able to show up and *function* to bring the necessary resources to bear in a particular situation ... .

My sense became that this might be the way military chaplains are trained and that there are parallels perhaps between large-scale disaster training responses and military training responses. I found myself struck by the difference in tone, language, and cultural response between the two case studies in this sense, given their different cultural contexts of operation often as well. A question in my mind became: When does a traumatic incident reach a scale requiring a more hierarchical or military-style response? One perhaps might see this need in situations of mass shootings as well as natural disasters, but what about the more gradual, chronic, and accumulated traumas of violent loss for particular communities that reflect multiple rather than single incidents?[27] Another UUTRM leader also spoke to the importance of this hierarchical form of response in the aftermath of violent trauma, but of the challenge this posed to a religiously liberal UU movement culturally wedded to democratic governance:

> Because it's order in the middle of chaos. Everything's nuts. Somebody has to be in charge ... I think one of the biggest problems we have with trauma response in our movement is that it is hierarchical in a way that is not familiar ... to us unless we have people who have served in the Army. You don't get to just do whatever you feel like doing. Somebody has to be in charge ... you still have to follow a chain of command. That's antithetical to the open democratic process.

UUA institutional supporters also agreed that authorization, training, accountability, and legitimacy are acute needs for care in traumatic crises, and that having these enable a deeper layer of trust and effectiveness to be brought to bear, as one would state:

> ... a strong motive for organizing the UUTRM came as a result of the need to kind of legitimate our ministers who would so serve, so that not every cat and dog could come in and make a mess of things, but to make sure that there was membership, that there were qualifications, and so on. That was an administrative but it was also a quality control issue.

In a situation of large-scale group or social trauma, the reestablishment of order amid chaos, and a sense of control and safety, conveyed by UUTRM leaders and UUA institutional supporters, dovetails with much of the existing literature on human needs in trauma recovery. As Judith Herman writes, "Traumatic events call into question basic human relationships ... Traumatic events destroy the victim's fundamental assumptions about the safety of the world, the positive value of the self, and the meaningful order of creation ...."[28] This leads to the question of specific religious and secular care strategies for reestablishing order amid the chaos, particularly in large-scale versus smaller-scale traumatic situations—or as Carolyn Yoder writes, "What *degree* of safety? What *kind* of safety?"[29] Is it also possible that the reestablishment of safety can come at some other emotional or spiritual cost to survivors depending on context?

For example, clearly UUTRM leaders and UUA institutional supporters interviewed placed a heavy emphasis on trauma-specific training and certification of legitimacy, as well as on clear lines of authority and accountability within a clearly defined and limited scope of action. This entailed comfort with structured, hierarchical approaches consistent with those of government and military agencies during large-scale socially traumatic events. What happens when such approaches clash with established cultures or "ways of relational being?" for smaller-scale contexts and events, such as in culturally different communities or religious settings? Can such clashes in and of themselves actually create more anxiety and less safety in certain contexts, or, at a minimum, a failure of expectations that then can deepen a loss of trust on certain levels? How are groups, religious communities, and society educated on or prepared for this potential clash of cultures in large-scale trauma responses as well?

There is a significant difference between cultural expectations of "doing whatever is necessary" to meet emergent needs in care based on whoever might volunteer to step forward in a moment to offer a skill *versus* following very specific "chains of command" to discriminate which needs should be met and which not based on perceived limited capacity and resources in a major social emergency. Such differences in cultural expectations and access to power do have implications for the ecclesial or religious context when congregations or religious communities that are accustomed to more "democratic" and time-consuming ways of functioning encounter a traumatic situation and need to make rapid and multiple decisions. Their normal democratic processes and/or culturally expected roles may not be available or possible. There are even greater implications for impact if an organization external to the normal ecclesial or religious context is added to this mix in the provision of care. If the experience of trauma is *cognitively* as well as emotionally destabilizing, as Ronnie Janoff-Bulman has argued,[30] then such a clash of cultures or worldviews in the clinical or pastoral response, as well as in the guiding relational images or cultural narratives expected or offered, may certainly compound the experience of the trauma and lack of control. Indeed, some of these tension points emerged in this particular case study of the UUTRM and the TVUUC—and beyond this particular case study, there are implications in such culture and power clashes for different types of communities as well.

Outline of Programs and Infrastructure

It is important to know that the UUTRM is not an official institutional arm of the UUA, which is organized as a voluntary association of congregations through a congregational polity form of governance. This lack of a formal institutional affiliation for the UUTRM is inclusive of a lack of formal institutionalized affiliation with the UUA's district or regional offices and the financing of those offices by the UUA and district congregations. Within this governance structure, the UUTRM is a voluntary and separate nonprofit organization that seeks to maintain a Memorandum of Understanding with the UUA for the services that it provides to its member congregations. At the time of the original interviews, this memorandum had no formal automatic mechanism for review or renewal with each new UUA administration. Hence, the UUTRM was heavily reliant on general fundraising and volunteer efforts and coordination for its operations, as well as on internal accountability mechanisms and a high level of trust with UUA staff members.[31] This form of organization posed a certain level of structural challenges and limitations. However, it also offered the possibility of greater operational freedom for the UUTRM, both dimensions of which will be discussed later. UUTRM leaders stated that there was an ongoing discussion as to the best form of infrastructure to support their mission and ultimate vision.

Corresponding to their mission statement, the UUTRM seeks to provide education on trauma and preparedness training and also to provide resources in the event of a traumatic situation impacting on the life of a UU congregation, including the deployment of a UUTRM team as requested. The provision of resources may occur as simply as through a telephone call, including ongoing coaching and consultation by phone, or more fully in the deployment of UUTRM volunteer team members within 24 hours via a response coordinator who assesses and coordinates the meeting of needs. There is an 800 number carried by an on-call Management Team representative that is often the first mechanism of contact with the UUTRM. Additional resources might include assistance with pulpit supply for ministers who need to leave their congregations to help with a trauma event, as well as the provision of assistance in locating respite care for trauma victims.

Developing educational programs and being able to respond with such resources listed above appeared to be the primary capacity of the existing infrastructure of the UUTRM, per its current leadership and institutional supporters at the time of the original interviews. Affiliating with other trauma organizations (apart from participating in trainings), or deploying teams beyond local disaster situations involving UU congregations, were not as frequently mentioned in interviews. It is clear that the UUTRM does coordinate with other organizations, however, such as the Red Cross, when possible and needed, including in this particular case study.

The UUTRM also provides trainings and workshops to UU clergy and laity in the context of the UUA national General Assembly, at minister convocations and district assemblies, in one-on-one settings, and through website information. UUTRM leaders report that they continue to expand their capacity and accomplishments in these areas. Some of the types of workshops they have provided, per one UUTRM leader, include: "introduction to trauma ministry; workshops on the lifecycle of a disaster in faith-based communities; emergency preparedness for congregations, faith-based institutions; the pastoral crisis intervention for professional religious leaders"; etc. Traumatic situations to which they have responded include not only the more well-known ones such as the TVUUC shooting and Hurricane Katrina but also church-related traumas inclusive of fires, floods or tornados, auto accidents, suicide, criminal acts impacting on congregants, sexual misconduct, etc. Each volunteer team member is required to participate in a minimum of 40 hours of crisis response team training, including a variety of other requirements as documented in a formal application, and to comply with a UUTRM Code of Ethics.[32] A quarterly newsletter was reported to be a means of maintaining regular contact with UUTRM volunteer team members across the country.

In working with both of the case studies, I bring the strengths and challenges of being immersed within their respective cultures through lived experiences and being simultaneously outside of their respective cultures through social identity or location. As I move into a more specific exploration of interdisciplinary tools for application in the next chapter, I bring my lived experiences of these cultural border crossings to my selection and suggestion of particular tools that seem to correlate with my observations and interviews. The "truth" of the correlations, as previously suggested in Chap. 2, lies in resonance found in body and narrative by my collective readership, but most particularly, for me also, in and by the communities I studied and to whom I experience myself most accountable as a researcher.

Notes

1. Joseph M. Chery, "The Story of Louis D. Brown," section titled "Dream High" found in *Peacezone: A Program for Teaching Social Literacy, Grades 4-5 Teacher's Guide* by Deborah Prothrow-Stith, et al., 24.
2. For more detailed information on this period of Boston's history and the organizing efforts to reduce homicides, including an unprecedented cooperation between clergy and police represented by the Ten Point Coalition, see "Religion and the Boston Miracle: The Effect of Black Ministry on Youth Violence" by Jenny Berrien, Omar Roberts, and Christopher Winship in *Who Will Provide? The Changing Role of Religion in American Social Welfare*, edited by Mary Jo Bane, Brent Coffin, and Ronald Thiemann (Boulder, CO: Westview Press, 2000). 266–285.
3. See US Attorney General Janet Reno's remarks in "Youth Violence: A Community-Based Response, One City's Success Story," 1996. See https://www.ncjrs.gov/txtfiles/boston.txt (accessed April 20, 2013).
4. It is important to note that the Peace Institute is currently moving in the direction of a greater focus on training providers in the methodology of their work and ministry in the hopes of replicating it and decreasing their focus on direct service outreach. This is due to their

own recognized limited capacity in staffing and funding to enable their vision and mission to have the type of reach they desire.
5. See the Peace Institute's website in particular: http://www.ldbpeaceinstitute.org/mission.html (accessed April 1, 2016) for the mission statement and quotes that follow above.
6. Since the initial study from which the book draws, the Peace Institute has continued to grow and to incorporate more professional staffing, while also seeking to remain true to its overall culture and origins.
7. While the Peace Institute is known best for its *Peacezone* curriculum currently, the founders had also developed other nationally recognized peace curriculums based on literature and community service learning prior to the *Peacezone* curriculum. There are multiple Peacezone curriculums for different grades, but one sample is Deborah Prothrow-Stith, et al., *Peacezone: A Program for Teaching Social Literacy, Grades 4-5, Teacher's Guide*.
8. Prothrow-Stith, *Deadly Consequences*, 132.
9. Ibid., 28.
10. Further information on this form of approach to antiracism/antioppression/multicultural education can be found in Valerie Batts, "Is Reconciliation Possible? Lessons from Combatting 'Modern Racism'," in *Waging Reconciliation: God's Mission in a Time of Globalization and Crisis*, ed., Douglas, I.T. (New York: Church Publishing, Inc., 2002), 35–69.
11. bell hooks, *Teaching to Transgress: Education as the Practice of Freedom* (New York: Routledge, 1994), 59–75.
12. Ibid., 61.
13. I found the spontaneous use of the term "peculiar people" by this ministry leader rather striking as it immediately recalled for me how Southern slaveholders had called slavery "the peculiar institution" out of their own embarrassment and shame, hence associations to stigmatized institutions and people. See Kenneth M. Stampp's classic study, *The Peculiar Institution: Slavery in the Ante-Bellum South* (New York: Vintage Books, 1956/1989). The work of James Gilligan on the role of shame and honor in the creation and perpetuation of violence, particularly for men, is useful in understanding the

importance of peer groups for adults and youth, as well as the importance of providing alternative vehicles for expressing emotions and reducing stigma and shame. See his work *Violence: Reflection on a National Epidemic* (New York: Vintage Books, 1997). Other writers who speak specifically to the African American male experience include Geoffrey Canada, *Fist, Stick, Knife, Gun* (Boston: Beacon Press, 1996) as well as his *Reaching Up For Manhood: Transforming the Lives of Boys in America* (Boston: Beacon Press, 1998), and also John A. Rich, *Wrong Place, Wrong Time: Trauma and Violence in the Lives of Young Black Men* (Baltimore: The Johns Hopkins University Press, 2009). A final interesting historical and cultural perspective on the impact of slavery, violence, honor, and shame that bears on contemporary struggles is a classic work by Bertram Wyatt-Brown, *Honor and Violence in the Old South* (New York: Oxford University Press, 1986).
14. Internal ongoing publication of the LDBPI.
15. The bulk of this extra anecdotal material was shared by a former minister, which I observed when watching the archived videotaped rededication service.
16. The inscribed values included: Diversity, Justice, Freedom, Peace, Experience, Grace, Question, Struggle, Dignity, Hope, Service, Love, Mystery, Sorrow, Humility, Reason, Growth, Joy.
17. See the Commission on Appraisal, *Engaging Our Theological Diversity*, 102–104, for more information on these covenants.
18. Later UUA educational programs would include information on welcoming bisexual and transgender persons as well. More information on the current process for becoming an officially designated "Welcoming Congregation" within the UUA can be found at this link: http://www.uua.org/lgbtq/welcoming/program/57699.shtml (accessed on February 11, 2013).
19. See Ted Jones, *Straightening Up: The Recovery of the Tennessee Valley Unitarian Universalist Church From an Attack* (Unpublished manuscript, 2010), 9. There are parallels in the church's struggle in this area to other challenges articulated in becoming a "Welcoming Congregation," including comments such as "We are already welcoming,

why should we single out a particular group?" as found in another practical theological study I conducted during my master of divinity program. See Michelle Walsh, "Theological Analysis Project: The Welcoming Congregation Program as a Successful Model for Engaging Unitarian Universalists on Behalf of Social Justice" (Unpublished manuscript, 2004).
20. Jones, *Straightening Up*, 9.
21. The shooter's former wife also had been a member of the church several years ago and apparently experienced domestic violence from the shooter, though this was not known during the time of her membership according to the TVUUC minister.
22. See "Shock Jock: Rage on the Radio," *Bill Moyers Journal*, available at http://www.pbs.org/moyers/journal/09122008/watch.html (accessed January 31, 2013).
23. Jones, *Straightening Up*, 54–57.
24. See the UUTRM website at http://www.traumaministry.org (accessed February 11, 2013).
25. More information can be found on CISM trainings, approaches, and definitions through the International Critical Incident Stress Foundation at https://www.icisf.org (accessed April 1, 2016). Also mentioned in the course of this research was that every state participates in the National VOAD—the National Voluntary Organizations Active in Disaster, and more information regarding this organization can be found at http://www.nvoad.org (accessed February 11, 2013).
26. More information regarding NOVA—the National Organization for Victims Assistance—may be found at http://www.trynova.org (accessed on February 11, 2013).
27. In this era of domestic police militarization and BLM in the US context, this is actually not a small question in terms of appropriate levels and cultural forms of response during times of community unrest or protest, particularly for communities long suffering under institutional and cultural forms of oppression. See Radley Balko, *Rise of the Warrior Cop: The Militarization of America's Police Forces* (New York: Public Affairs, 2014).

28. Judith L. Herman, *Trauma and Recovery* (New York: BasicBooks, 1992), 51–51.
29. Carolyn Yoder, Carolyn, *The Little Book of Trauma Healing: When Violence Strikes and Community Security is Threatened* (Intercourse, PA: The Good Books, 2005), 51.
30. Ronnie Janoff-Bulman, *Shattered Assumptions: Towards a New Psychology of Trauma* (New York: The Free Press, 1992).
31. An example of such trust is that one UUA institutional supporter provided a UUTRM member with his personal credit card number late one weekend night so that she could get an immediate flight to "respond quickly and easily without a lot of bureaucracy or silliness." He said this does not happen a lot but has happened more than once when there was a need to respond with informality and speed in certain situations. This required a high level of personal trust and "credibility," as this institutional supporter would say, in their relationship.
32. More information can be found in a UUTRM internal document, their "Standard Operating Procedures" manual, a copy of which was provided to me during the research process.

4

Trauma in a Lived Religion Perspective

The Eyes as Windows to a World of Pain

I will never forget the first time I met a parent who lost her child to homicide. This memory lays tucked into a viscerally experienced wordless area of my brain—a world of fierce pain communicated only through her eyes, eyes that were tearless and awake yet inward and radically broken in human connection, surreal in their disassociation from this particular reality. I realized how powerful the eyes could be in communicating a vastness beyond words, even communicating when one is living in or near the land of death—and I realized also my own powerlessness to connect with, let alone heal, those eyes, leaving guilt and a gaping sorrow in the wake. While serving as a "lay community minister/social work clinician," I'd seen similar yet different eyes in the young men who came to the gang outreach program in my early years with the different urban youth ministries. Their eyes seemed never to have experienced childhood—they too were eyes disassociated from the fullness of life, possibilities, and hope, presenting instead with emptiness and guarded cynicism. By their very choice to come to their youth program, however, the eyes also presented with just a hint of desire for something more, something that would renew and restore their bodies with meaning and joy and safety.

With a certain poignancy, I also remember seeing one such young man transforming overnight into a delighted and free young boy, with laughter in his eyes, when taken on a nature outing to an island in another state for the weekend—only then to stand as helpless witness once again while watching the guard come down slowly over his eyes and body as he shifted back into a state of preparedness for re-entering another world different from that of the outing. A different but equally gaping and sorrow-filled chasm seemed to exist between this yearning and desire witnessed and the reality of felt possibility for safety, renewal, and restoration in these particular boys—and in myself as well. All these images and many more I witnessed with my eyes and with my body in the treacherous borderlands between cultural worlds set apart in life giving and life taking. These images leave their marks, "scratches" on the mind, body, heart, and soul, morally and permanently bonding me in their aftermath to all members.[1]

Interdisciplinary Trauma Studies and Meaning-Making

The disruption of personal meaning-making narrative and connection to community under the impact of severe suffering is well recognized and supported by the social scientific literature on trauma. For example, Judith Herman's text, *Trauma and Recovery*, is an early social science classic in the field of trauma studies, and an implied interdisciplinary relationship between trauma and religion and spirituality can be discerned readily in her formulations, including hints of questions of theodicy and meaning-making and the need for personal healing spiritual practices as well as communal healing rituals[2]:

> Traumatic events call into question basic human relationships ... They undermine the belief systems that give meaning to human experience. They violate the victim's faith in a natural or divine order and cast the victim into a state of existential crisis ... Traumatic events destroy the victim's fundamental assumptions about the safety of the world, the positive value of the

self, and the meaningful order of creation . . . Basic trust is the foundation of belief in the continuity of life, the order of nature, and the transcendent order of the divine . . . .

Ronnie Janoff-Bulman, in her classic text, *Shattered Assumptions: Towards a New Psychology of Trauma*, also would write, "The personal insights that are gained from one's traumatic experience have important parallels in religious teachings. Common religious themes emphasize the redemptive and strengthening role of suffering."[3]

More recent social scientific literature on trauma continues to make reference to "disrupted spirituality"[4] in cases of trauma, even impacting the "helper" of the victim (which could include religious helpers as well as first responders, human service providers, or educators). Other social scientific literature calls attention to the possibility of "posttraumatic growth"[5] for survivors, such as spiritual growth. This includes possible "vicarious growth"[6] for their therapists (and by implication, all other helping professionals as well).[7] For instance, what does it mean as examples of post-traumatic growth and/or vicarious growth that individuals or families impacted by violent trauma, whether through personal loss or providing services to survivors, become motivated to found institutional trauma service ministries, such as the Peace Institute and the UUTRM? Are there linkages between the processing of the trauma and a type of religious or spiritual meaning-making and growth through creation of institutions in the aftermath? Could such community institutions constitute, drawing on Nancy Ammerman's work,[8] a type of "spiritual tribe" centered in the "sacred story" of a murdered loved one? Spiritual tribes can shape around this type of sacred story in the aftermath of trauma.

Some correlation to the psychosocial literature on "post-traumatic growth"[9] is possible here given that each of the Peace Institute ministry leaders were themselves survivors of trauma. As these leaders "struggle[d] with loss" and being a "catalyst for change,"[10] they experienced "posttraumatic growth" as survivors themselves, as well as "vicarious growth"[11] when in the role of caring for other survivors as ministry leaders. They used their personal survivor experiences as a relational basis for empathy in their ongoing learning.[12] These experiences in turn nurtured practices at the Peace institute that were designed, through their Christian narrative, to foster a sense of inward control and peace on the personal level, as well as an outward capacity for public action and impact in challenging the larger society ("transforming pain and anger into power and action")—or "leading by example" as the founding ministry leader stated. In these correlations, the case studies also point to how religious or spiritual communities have the potential to achieve a deeper level of healing by giving attention to survivor social justice practices in light of the various socially induced oppressions that lead to violence and trauma.[13] The Peace Institute case study proves to be particularly useful in highlighting the functioning of a "spiritual tribe" through such religiously and spiritually narrated Christian practices in a community suffering under various historical and contemporary structures of oppression.

Healing from trauma, such as the murder of a loved one or exposure to violence, is a lifelong process of reestablishing and maintaining a new social support system that in effect becomes a new life—a radical break with one's former world of meaning-making into a new world of ongoing meaning-making in the aftermath:

> Trauma survivors do not simply get over their experience. It is permanently encoded in their assumptive world; the legacy of traumatic life events is some degree of disillusionment. From the perspective of their inner worlds, victims recover not when they return to their prior assumptive world but when they reestablish an integrated, comfortable assumptive world that incorporates their traumatic experience.[14]

Such reintegration of assumptions and meaning-making in the aftermath of trauma require supportive communal structures, which again could include a religious or spiritual "tribe" or community—this can be through small-group ministry format as well, such as the Peace Institute's "Tuesday Talks" or "Peace Warriors." Such reintegration also necessitates fostering a culture of safety through political, educational, and health institutions, among other social institutions, in addition to individual clinical therapy—an understanding the Peace Institute specifically cultivates through their Leadership Academy.

Interdisciplinary Trauma Studies: *Body Talk* in Metaphors and Images

The largest body of secondary literature upon which I draw for correlations, based on lived experiences with and observations and interviews in the case studies, is from neuroaffective trauma studies. I also draw upon attachment and bereavement studies and relational-cultural, narrative, and internal family systems (IFS) theories. I argue that these theories *metaphorically* can be integrated with and correlated to a richer understanding of meaning-making and human nature within lived religion studies of trauma ministries—an understanding that is more truly embodied and enfleshed, enlanguaged and encultured, en-neuroned and enhormoned, and emplaced and embedded in sociohistorical and material dimensions of power, as discussed in Chap. 2. Memory, time, and bodily connection are key elements in neuroaffective studies of the impact of trauma on the felt sense of self, understanding of reality, and connection to others.[15] Experiences of powerlessness and being overwhelmed by the threatening experience also can be part of the experience of trauma. Such experiences can be generational in nature due to societal oppressions over time as well and have been labeled "historical trauma" by some, including in the public health context.[16]

Exposure to a traumatic and violent event means one's sense of safety can be disrupted and memories can become inaccessible or repressed because they are encoded differently by the brain, or even damage the brain's functioning, when associated with highly charged affective situations and flooded with chemical brain reactions.[17] Healing components reestablish a sense of safety and control as well as connection to others, foster commonality (a shared understanding of reality), and create possibilities to reintegrate the trauma into one's narrative sense of self and identity so that new meaning-making can occur. Meaning-making and the creation of a new world/view occurs on one level through narrative and story and also on yet another level through the body.

One "sees" or views one's world through oral or textual story but also *experiences* the world through all of one's bodily senses—hence world/view may require an alternative metaphor of "world sense"[18] or *world/sense* as more richly encompassing of this need for meaning-making.[19] In fact, stories are richly experienced in ways beyond the text, oral transmission of story, or sight. They also can be transmitted through additional sounds, touch, smell, and taste, particularly in dramatic or material reenactment or expressions. It is intriguing to me, even in writing this book, how constrained I felt by the general availability of visual metaphors alone—such as vision, lens, or horizon of meaning, etc.—even though the eyes are powerful in garnering and conveying worlds of meaning, as shared in the opening vignette. I noticed my yearning for other metaphors, however, to enliven and deepen more embodied experiences of my world imagination. Religious and spiritual communities often serve this purpose of world imagination through particular forms of embodied spiritual or liturgical practices. Lived religion studies of "spiritual tribes" from different sociocultural backgrounds also may highlight different metaphors and language and help to stretch our existing metaphors and language in practices.

For example, and paralleling Mark Johnson's work on metaphor and embodied imagination, Sandra Schneiders[20] writes,

> ... a metaphor is a proposition that, if taken literally, is absurd ... By the very fact that it obviously intends meaning (because its propositional structure is intact) but is literally absurd, it forces the mind into action to find meaning at another level ... It is a different kind of meaning, an opening on a realm of significance that cannot be expressed literally but engages the imagination in a cognitive and *affective* [emphasis added] exploration of the subject in and through relationships that seem strange but, in fact, are more illuminating than literal predication.

Schneiders argues that a metaphor becomes an instrument of new meaning precisely because the tension created by juxtaposition of the literal and the absurd is inherently unstable—it "struggles to emerge into clarity at another level ... The metaphor only stays alive and healthy, enriching the imagination with meaning by its simultaneous engagement of cognitive and affective energy, if the tension can be maintained between the 'is' and 'is not' [of the propositional structure]."[21] Embrace, rejection, or juxtaposition of different culturally embedded metaphors through correlation at their embodied cognitive and affective roots, from within or across cultures, can be a source of enrichment across academic disciplines through lived religion studies, when open to visceral experiences fostered by these correlations, as these case studies seek to demonstrate. Through this type of cognitive and affective engagement at a different level than purely analogy in correlations, a deeper interdisciplinary or even transdisciplinary approach might be fostered.

In drawing upon this secondary literature of neuroaffective trauma studies, I thus suggest that the turn back to the *physiological* body (in all of its dimensions) as the site of embodied relational knowing and meaning-making and its correlation to the metaphoric and analytic capacities of relational-cultural and narrative theories, in addition to IFS theory, provide strong interdisciplinary tools for the study of trauma and service provision, including pastoral care through ministries. These conceptual tools also assist in the radical reconstruction of an embodied and social understanding of self and human being, including for a theological anthropology[22] compatible with the multivalent uses of metaphorical theologies of trauma and "spirit."

For example, across the Jewish and Christian faith traditions, "Spirit" has been translated from Hebrew to mean "breath" and has been associated in biblical terms with numerous ecological images, including "wind," and with having characteristics of physical movement, vibration, and energy, as well as wisdom, knowledge, and liberation. Such characteristics have an embodied and ecological tone with metaphoric implications and applicability for interfaith dialogues, as well as correlation to the sciences, when allowed to breathe and dance with life and spirit, finding their points of embodied connection within the "interplay" of their respective "emplacements."[23] Thich Nhat Hanh, a Zen Buddhist, upon hearing that the Holy Spirit could be interpreted metaphorically as the energy of God, would say regarding cross-cultural interfaith dialogue: "It confirmed my feeling that the safest way to approach the Trinity is through the door of the Holy Spirit."[24] I point out that Nhat Hanh stated specifically "it confirmed my feeling," which reflects the ethical organicity of a process of individual interfaith encounters in which narrative and body meet on the ground of equal and affirmational felt possibilities in communicating experiential truth or reality to each other, as I suggested in Chap. 2. I will return to the interdisciplinary focus on trauma, religion, and metaphoric approaches to correlating language at the end of this chapter.

To illustrate this further in relationship to the social sciences, however, if all of our knowing is truly *embodied* knowing, both in verbal and nonverbal expression, particularly as trauma survivors experience, then our theories and their metaphorical formulations need to be reexamined at their bodily roots. Jaak Panksepp argues that cognitive psychology has yet "to deal effectively with the proximal neural causes"[25] of behavior patterns:

> In other words, something is lacking. I would suggest that a missing piece that can bring all these disciplines together is a neurological understanding of the basic emotional operating systems of the mammalian brain and the various conscious and unconscious internal states they generate ... I have chosen to call [this new perspective] *affective neuroscience* ... I look forward to the day when *neurophilosophy* ... will become an experimental discipline that may shed new light on the highest capacities of the human brain—yielding new and scientific ways to talk about the human mind.

Designing new "scientific ways to talk about the human mind" to address the "something lacking" actually may mean finding new *metaphoric* ways of talking about human psychology. Such metaphors would be more embodied, relational, and enculturated and would enhance lived religion studies of trauma in correlation to a more embodied social understanding of human nature. This also would entail testing the new metaphors through a lived religion method that allowed for the critique of academic discipline metaphors and dominant cultural worldviews and emergence of new metaphors and language from those studied. This is necessary not only as a matter of ethical respect in leveling the academic/community power field but also for mutual learning and growth as we jointly face societal challenges such as violent trauma.

Trauma Studies: Embodied *Relationship Talk* in Metaphor and Images

As emerged in my work with the case studies, attachment and bereavement literature provided two such avenues into new metaphoric ways of talking about human psychology for lived religion studies, supporting both the traumatic *physiological* impact of the loss of a key attachment figure, such as an immediate family member, and correlating well with the task of developing a more *socially attuned* understanding of human being, including for use with religious studies and theological anthropology. Thomas Lewis, Fari Amini, and Richard Lannon provide a useful summary of some of this literature, inclusive of integrating the history of neuroaffective and attachment studies. They argue that human beings need "limbic regulation to give coherence to neurodevelopment."[26] Pointing to a wide variety of studies on humans and other mammals that demonstrate, through observable physiological data, the negative impact of failure to attach in childhood (whether by neglect or abuse)—impact that ranges from protest to despair to actual death—Lewis, et al.[27] conclude,

> ... even after a peak parenting experience, children never transition to a full self-tuning physiology. Adults remain social animals: they continue to require a source of stabilization outside themselves ... Stability means finding people who regulate you well and staying near them ... This necessary intermingling of physiologies makes relatedness and communal living the center of human life.

Lewis, et al. also have created new metaphorical language based partially in musical language, "limbic resonance," to describe the regulating and contagious role of emotions between mammals, including human beings. We are not bounded, separate, autonomous, and entirely rational individuals, as much of Western philosophy often has viewed human nature as well as "the body." Instead, the past 50–80 years of science has demonstrated our physiological interdependence and permeability of "bodies" through our limbic systems. "Emotionality is the social sense organ of limbic creatures ... A mammal can detect the internal state of another mammal and adjust its own physiology to match the situation . . . a capacity we call *limbic resonance*—a symphony of mutual exchange and internal adaptation whereby two mammals become attuned to each other's inner state."[28]

A researcher trained in public health and social work/welfare policy, Phyllis R. Silverman, studies loss and grief and also supports a more embodied and socially oriented understanding of human being across cultures. Her research with colleagues challenged classic psychoanalytic paradigms and metaphors[29] that tend to regard "continuing bonds" with the dead as pathological. Silverman and Dennis Klass[30] argue instead that these "continuing bonds" can be, or are in fact, living, growing, and shaping bonds in the ongoing life of the grieving person; they are process and action oriented rather than stable or complete:

> "Internalization" as used by the psychoanalytic school of thought does not accurately describe the process occurring in the experiences reported on in this book. What we observe is more colorful, dynamic and interactive than the word "internalization" suggests . . . Memorializing, remembering, knowing the person who has died, and allowing them to influence the present are active processes that seem to continue throughout the survivor's entire life.

Both case studies, in fact, demonstrated that death did not end the relationship with or moral commitment to the dead, particularly in the loss of their life to violence. Peace Institute families and TVUUC congregants remained connected in active and evolving ways with the dead through various practices. Silverman and Klass[31] continue by proposing the need for new rituals as well as new language for these forms of connection, ones that are countercultural to classical Western conceptions:

> The idea of meaning-making as a continuous process requires that we develop a more adequate language for talking about and to the deceased . . . Most other cultures in the history seem to have supported the notion that the deceased continue to live in some form after death, and they provide mourners with rituals to sustain an appropriate relationship . . . In

the model of grief we propose, we would find *a new language* [emphasis added] to talk not only about loss and the person who is gone, but about connections in general.

A neurophysiological *and* narrative link also is made for this phenomenon of "continuing bonds" in bereavement literature by Edward Rynearson and Alison Salloum, drawing upon an analogy to the phenomenon of "phantom limbs" in the case of amputees. "After death, the living representation of an attachment figure (a part of self 'dismembered' rather than a part of body amputated) is predictably 'remembered' and experienced as a 'phantom' presence."[32] Similar to the felt ongoing presence of an amputated limb, the dead can have a continued felt presence neurophysiologically with the living. There is a need to language and ritualize these lived experiences in the Western context or to document the cultural communities that do so—which, again, I see these case studies as making a small contribution toward in the US context.

Additionally, Marci Hertz, Deborah Prothrow-Stith, and Clementina Chery note that there is a particular impact for survivors of homicide that goes beyond both grief and post-traumatic stress disorder (PTSD) and which needs more theoretical attention: "Homicide survivorship is qualitatively different from survivorship of other violent crimes . . . There is no real 'post' in their compilation of symptoms."[33] Thus these studies and Klass and Silverman, et al.'s work, as well as others in the fields of grief, complicated grief, and traumatic grief,[34] support that there is a crucial need for new metaphorical language and studies of cross-cultural communal rituals, including religious or spiritual rituals, which promote healing from traumatic loss and normalize the ongoing power of ritual embodiment and attachment in human life. Again, this is a purpose that religious communities can serve if prepared for and trained in, and further empirical studies in lived religion, such as these case studies, can make contributions toward meeting some of these needs.

Along with a language of "continuing bonds," I also explore relational-cultural theory and IFS theory as other forms of "new language to talk . . . about connections in general," more "colorful, dynamic, and interactive," per Silverman and Klass above. Rather than metaphoric language rooted in psychoanalytic terms such as "objects" or "selfobjects" (terms that metaphorically connote solidity, separation, and stability and can be fruitful for certain contexts of analysis), relational-cultural theorists (formerly known as self-in-relation therapy)[35] speak metaphorically of "relational images,"[36] which are embodied "pictures" that are not necessarily frozen or static but can shift, move, and change over time in the fluid encounter with new relationships. Relational images are defined as,

> [i]nner pictures of what has happened to us in relationships, formed in important early relationships. As we develop these images, we are also creating a set of beliefs about why relationships are the way they are. Relational images thus determine expectations not only about what will occur in relationships but about a person's whole sense of herself or himself. They often become the unconscious frameworks by which we determine who we are, what we can do, and how worthwhile we are.[37]

This language again may have metaphoric usefulness for "connection talk" and trauma studies across disciplines and cultures, including lived religion. World/views and world/sense are shaped by the nature and quality of relationships growing up in communities—world/views and world/sense become grounded in relational images of expectations, including expectations of being exposed to ongoing trauma or not, inclusive of trauma from structural oppression or protection through access to structural power and privilege. This bears on the different socioeconomic and cultural contexts of the two case studies and the different struggles with meaning-making after violent trauma documented in the following chapters.

One final theory I explore, developed by Richard C. Schwartz, is Internal Family System theory,[38] which draws on multiplicity and systems theories in psychology and a metaphorical language of "parts" within a self system, as well as a cultural system, to illustrate connections and movement within self and between self and others. This language was seen later to have resonance with language some interviewed in each of the case studies spontaneously utilized to describe their experiences. Schwartz also has partially developed this theory for larger sociocultural analysis in relationship to historical trauma and oppressions through his use of the term "legacy burden"—the part of the self that carries the intergenerational weight of cultural burdens across time and which is transmitted through families as well as larger social institutions, thus replicating over time. "Some families have passed burdens from generation to generation—burdens that were first instilled hundreds of years earlier."[39] Schwartz goes on to enlarge this application to the transmission of structural institutional oppressions over time:

> To apply the IFS principles to a society, we have to see it as a large human organism composed of smaller groups (parts) that interact ... all the parts of a society (the component cultural groups) carry burdens from the traumas of their histories. For example, the early American settlers (the British and other Europeans), whose values have evolved into those of what I am calling the dominant, managerial coalition, were generally persecuted or troubled in their own countries and faced what they considered a very hostile and dangerous environment in the New World. In addition, they carried a legacy burden of racism. European racism was in existence long before the settlers arrived, as exemplified by the "doctrine of discovery" ... These burdens of fear, anger, and racism account for the generally barbaric and exploitive ways in which European invaders treated Native Americans, and, later, for their embracing the inhuman institution of slavery for 300 years ... Centuries later, mainstream U.S. culture remains burdened by this same aggressive, individualistic, striving, righteous, and racist mentality, which fuels and is fueled by the extreme present-day versions of capitalism and materialism it espouses.[40]

When IFS theory and relational-cultural theory are combined with narrative theory concepts, they prove useful as additional theoretical frames with rich and flexible metaphor systems within interdisciplinary approaches to lived religion studies of trauma. This includes a remarkable level of attention to sociocultural factors and the expansion of such imagery for expressing the ecological relationship of the micro dimensions of human being with the macro dimensions of society. This ecological relationship of micro and macro encompasses spirituality and religion within cultural world/views and world/sense, as will be seen in further in a section below as well as in analysis of the case studies in the next chapters.

Trauma Studies: Poetic Meaning-Making in Material Form

In smaller pilot research prior to the case studies, and also observed in my ongoing ethnographic immersion with the Louis D. Brown Peace Institute, I became aware of the prominence of artistic and embodied ritualized expressions of traumatic grief as a practice by survivors in the aftermath. These included spontaneous street memorials,[41] as well as displays of pictures of, letters to, and poetry about the lost loved one in the Peace Institute's redesign of orders of funeral services. They also included buttons with the picture of the lost loved one and later the Peace Institute's embrace and use of sandplay with miniature objects for spiritual movement and growth. I realized that such ritualized, albeit popular cultural expressions, could be considered examples of "material religion"[42] within a lived religion approach to trauma studies. Yet there was "something more" that captured and stirred my imagination on an affective level. Various offerings to the dead were made that signaled ongoing connection to and communication with the body of the deceased. These included but were not limited to offerings of the childhood comfort of bodily contact with stuffed animals or favorite foods or other special items connected with the body. These material expressions also often were associated with specific religious and/or spiritual written or material content, including biblical quotes and religious imagery such as the cross, prayers, and wishes for victims to rest in peace or hopes for communal peace. There was a sacred quality of "testimony" in these public expressions (Fig. 4.1).

Material religion is an anthropological theoretical frame that, while growing in significance in contemporary religious studies, is less often applied in practical or public theology or thought of specifically in relationship to the psychosocial study of trauma.[43] Yet the case studies illustrate that it is particularly useful for a lived religion approach to study trauma and survivor practices. Material religion encompasses four specific categories of material culture: "artifacts, landscape, architecture, and art."[44] Use of images and material objects reflect our embodied nature, relationships, and extended sense of self in multisensory contact, as

4 Trauma in a Lived Religion Perspective

Fig. 4.1 *Spontaneous Street Memorial #1*: A typical street memorial at the site of the murder with stuffed animals and flowers wrapped around a street lamp pole at the top. Street memorials are known to remain up often for a year or more and rarely are disturbed in any way unless taken down by officials for various reasons

E. Frances King points out (Fig. 4.2). When linked to media, "the power of the image is almost limitless"[45] as a form of poetic and performative testimony to spiritual and religious ways of being:

> Focusing on the material, rather than the aesthetic or symbolic quality of objects, means that we take into account the haptic (touching) interactions that are . . . a significant element in the human response to, and engagement with, material goods. No mater what their aesthetic criteria, images and pictures and statues are there to be touched, smelled, and sometimes tasted

Fig. 4.2 *Spontaneous Street Memorial #2*: This *bottom* view of a portion of a different, more elaborate street memorial depicts food, a hairbrush, liquor bottles, and candles as offerings

as well as looked at: along with other artifacts they are materialized in physical form.[46]

Writing specifically about material Christianity, and dovetailing with Meredith McGuire's understanding of lived religion, Colleen McDannell argues that it is through the "physical dimensions of religion" that human beings both internalize and express their theologies and religious identities (Fig. 4.3)[47]:

> Throughout American history, Christians have explored the meaning of the divine, the nature of death, the power of healing, and the experience of the body by interacting with a created world of images and shapes ... The symbol systems of a particular religious language are not merely handed down, they must be learned through doing, seeing, and touching ... Experiencing the physical dimensions of religion helps bring about religious values, norms, behaviors, and attitudes. Practicing religion sets into play ways of thinking. It is the continual interation with objects and images that makes one religious in a particular manner.

Fig. 4.3 *Spontaneous Street Memorial #3*: This is a closeup of a different street memorial with a basket containing different items, including scriptural quotes

Pastoral and clinical care with victims of trauma requires attention to the somatic rupturing of self and body, and counter-practices of meaning-making may include reconnection to material objects, physical spaces, and one's surroundings. As I became more deeply aware of the various practices of the Peace Institute in both pilot studies, conjoined with the spontaneous street memorials from my first pilot study, I realized that such practices seemed to be empowering when performed publicly as prophetic testimony and/or social justice protest by survivor families and youth—but also that "something more" was happening beyond a political performance. Survivors were speaking of these practices as sacred, as expressing an ongoing sacred connection that also was vibrant and living. I realized that greater exploration of such material and embodied practices could yield explicit or implicit religious content regarding "the meaning of the divine, the nature of death, [and] the power of healing ...."[48]

Specifically, I realized there was potential methodological fruit for lived religion studies in regarding such material practices as a form of *artistic poetic testimony*. In my original research, I combined analytic perspectives from "material religion" with the literature of a "theopoetics" of *testimony* and *reimagining*, as initially developed by Rebecca Chopp, and with a nod also now to broadening Paul Ricoeur's conception of "testimony."[49] Placing the role of testimony in the metaphorical context of a public trial and with the testifier being seen as a "personally devoted" and "faithful witness," Ricoeur writes, " ... the witness seals his bond to the cause he defends by a public profession of his conviction ... The witness is capable of suffering and dying for his belief."[50] Ricouer continues, " ... the theme of confession-profession is ... the major mark of the prophetic concept of testimony," a confession of historical events that becomes tied to a narrative of larger meaning-making, "binding confession-testimony to narration-testimony."[51] Within the Christian tradition, confession-testimony is bound to the narration-testimony of the story of Jesus as Christ. However, just as Sharon Welch metaphorically broadened the concept of "dangerous memories" beyond solely a Christian narrative and context,[52] Paul Ricouer's concept of "testimony" can be broadened to other religious contexts or social circumstances yet retain its prophetic edge and challenge in root metaphoric meaning by linking confession, profession, testimony, and narration.

This combination of literatures seemed uniquely suited to exploring the implicit and explicit religious and spiritual dimensions of embodied and material artistic practices of pastoral and clinical care in the aftermath of trauma. A "material theopoetics" thus became one interdisciplinary bridge tool between a lived religion incorporation of material religion (purely as anthropology) and practical and constructive theologies of prophetic pastoral care in my original research.[53] I find *poetics* to be the broader term overall across disciplines, however, in light of the metaphoric base of language in various academic disciplines. Hence, my preferred writing style would be "material theo/poetics" as my thinking has evolved more deeply in the desire to foster, with ethical respect, interdisciplinary and transdisciplinary studies in the area of trauma, particularly for the very large global and societal challenge of violent trauma.[54] Each academic discipline has its own poetics and metaphors in its particular cultural world/views or world/sense as previously discussed. Thus we could discuss socio/poetics, psych/poetics, anthro/poetics, philo/poetics, religio/poetics, science/poetics, etc., with the metaphors multivalent in possibilities for connection, yet the integrity of the embodied experiences underlying each discipline respected in that connection. The example of this in religio/poetics would be Thich Naht Hanh's desire to find a connective way into the Trinity in his Buddhist practice, as previously discussed, and doing so through the language of "spirit."

Regarding the power of a poetic approach, Rebecca S. Chopp writes, "As compared to rhetoric, poetics seeks not so much to argue as to refigure, to reimagine and refashion the world."[55] Through metaphor, poetics can "reimagine" the world, bringing new images and possibilities to light and/or bringing discrepant images together for prophetic warning and/or transformative insight, thus enlarging narrative vision.[56] As we witness the embodied, material, and performative practices of trauma ministries, we realize they may *testify* prophetically to alternative lived experiences of trauma, to the sanctification of life in new forms, as well as to alternative religious or spiritual world/views or world/sense.[57] My argument is that "poetics" as an expression of beauty, imagination, metaphoric juxtaposition, or moral call[58] need not be restricted to verbal or literary expressions—that a form of poetic testimony, witness, sanctification, and prophetic challenge can occur through material expressions as well—and this is worthy of interdisciplinary and transdisciplinary attention, particularly sociological attention as well as the attention of lived religion studies.[59]

For example, spontaneous street memorials created in the aftermath of homicide are artistic material renderings and mark implicit, at times explicit, public prophetic protest. They testify metaphorically and theologically to the "dangerous memories"[60] of precious lives lost by virtue of being performed in public spaces,[61] with the potential of such testimony being magnified by the additional public witness of the media. Families, youth, and young adults also often resist the removal of such street memorials from the public space, as self-reported in my research.[62] In an essay on theopoetics and liberation, Rubem Alves writes, "Politics begins not with the administration of the dead but with the resurrection of the dead."[63] Various artistic and material practices mark an ongoing bond with the dead that is not only political but also living, moral, and sacred (Figs. 4.4 and 4.5).

Fig. 4.4 *Public Artistic Memorial—Long Shot*: A picture from a public artistic memorial created by a public charter school class using shoes to represent people lost to homicide in the year 2005. It was displayed at a health center for a few years with a lengthy plaque including the words "Our goal is to eliminate violence and bring forth a new community … In order to prevent more deaths we must understand how violence affects everyone in our whole community. Let us come together as a community and make sure there are no more empty shoes. We should use these shoes as the beginning of our journey to PEACE"

One UUTRM leader also shared her experiences with religio/poetic material rituals used in the aftermath of other traumas as well. For example, after a shooting at a Virginia university that impacted in part on a UU congregation in the area, she worked with the minister to develop a ritual where congregants lit candles to express their concerns and then placed stones down and washed them with "healing water" to symbolize metaphorically the laying down of their "burdens." In Florida, after a hurricane, she worked with a different minister to develop a ritual that symbolized the end of the hurricane season and allowed congregants to "ritually dispose," in a metaphorically controlled manner, what they had not been able to control losing during the hurricane, utilizing wood and paper and pictures or pieces of items that had been lost.

4 Trauma in a Lived Religion Perspective 107

Fig. 4.5 *Public Artistic Memorial—Close Up*: Items also were added to this particular public memorial as they are to many public memorials, for example such as Vietnam War Memorial and the 9/11 Memorial in the US context, sometimes poignantly so as suggested artistically here as a form of material poetics with the child-size shoe attached

Finally, this UUTRM leader shared yet another story from her own parish community of the power of a religio/poetic material ritual and the creation of a permanent memorial and site of ongoing ritual during times of loss or trauma. In the aftermath of 9/11, she suggested the use of granite from the church where she ministers to create a permanent handprint on the town's common as a literal "touchstone" of acknowledgment in the aftermath. This was followed by a multigenerational service in which she said

> So this stone that we have here has a handprint in it, and it's the touchstone now and whenever you're feeling like you've lost your bearings or whenever the world feels really scary to you ... or whenever you feel disconnected, whenever you don't feel like you're part of the community, I want you to remember that this stone is here with a handprint in it, and I want you to come and touch that handprint and then you'll know that you're never too far away from anybody else because we have this place and this time to come together and this is your touchstone to be healed and feel part of it

She elaborated that this was a significant communal healing ritual in the aftermath of trauma because "the healing community is being connected back to common roots, common integrity ... coming back to that place where there *is* a common purpose of hope, love, respect, worth and value of being together and that relationship that we all have." She reported that town members, beyond members of her own congregation, would return to this touchstone when there were communal losses after 9/11 as well (Fig. 4.6).

This embodied and material emphasis in rituals developed by a UUTRM ministerial leader reinforce the power of a material religio/poetics in the aftermath of trauma as a prophetic communal practice as well as a personal pastoral care practice. Embodied metaphors conjoined to material artistic expression is at the heart of many of the rituals described—the holding and placing down of stones that carry a physical weight metaphorically testify to the letting go of "burdens." The pouring of water witnesses to and symbolizes the possibility of purification and healing, a symbolic gesture that easily can be associated to various biblical

Fig. 4.6 *Permanent Town Granite Memorial "Touchstone" Handprint.* This stone handprint sits unmarked underneath the town's US flagpole

ritual traditions involving water. The creation of a handprint from the granite of a historic church also becomes a permanent metaphoric and material site of embodied connection through the physical touch of hands across generations during times of disconnection and loss—a place of continuing embodied and moral bonds that is religious and ecclesial in nature, giving sacred material testimony and witness to a larger spiritual hope and bond across time. For these temporary moments, at least, and through the above embodied and material rituals as well as through street memorials, a "spiritual tribe" can come together in ways that also can create "liminality" that breaks through into sacred "communitas," the creation of sacred space where normally hierarchical or socially constructed roles may be leveled, in anthropologist Victor Turner's[64] classic theory and observations:

> Communitas breaks in through the interstices of structure, in liminality; at the edges of structure, in marginality; and from beneath structure, in inferiority. It is almost everywhere held to be sacred or "holy," possibly because it transgresses or dissolves the norms that govern structured and institutionalized relationships and is accompanied by experiences of unprecedented potency.[65]

In addition to the above examples, I was aware through public documents[66] of the UUTRM's work with a congregation in Knoxville, TN, prior to my own research with members of this congregation. As stated in the previous chapter, on July 27, 2008, a gunman specifically targeting UUs killed two adults and injured seven others during a children's performance of a play. At the rededication service for the sanctuary on August 3rd, ritual reinhabitation of the space, elements of material religion, and a metaphoric transformation of a song all were used to reclaim safety and testify to renewal of hope and sanctification of the space, also as witnessed publicly by the media, as discussed in Chap. 6. My growing awareness of the combined practices of the Peace Institute and the UUTRM solidified my interest in the methodological potential of combining these two different literatures initially through the phrase "material theopoetics" as a way of theologically naming such performative practices. In doing so, I came to realize later that I also now am situated in and contributing to a larger stream of growing literature called "the new materialism," one that also is calling for the crossing of disciplines, including scholars and writers in philosophy, ethics, political theory, anthropology, cultural and media studies, corporeality and the arts, etc.[67] I will return to this in the final chapter in recommendations for further research and interdisciplinary explorations, yet this too reinforced my attention to the power of poetics as a means of connecting disciplines—as in material poetics or theo/poetics or religio/poetics or even socio/poetics, among others.

Trauma Studies: Disciplinary Encounters with Culture and Recognition of Power

My training and background necessarily cross disciplines through clinical social work, ministry, and practical and pastoral theology. These disciplines shape my language and cultural lens and approach—yet there also is variability within disciplines in the degree to which culture and power are taken into account. Beginning with my first disciplinary training, social work taught me to examine the intertwining of the psycho-social-biological and ecological aspects of human being—that human beings are born with a particular biological body and are shaped in their psychology by family relationships within a community and culture. Human beings also exist within a larger social and cultural context shaped by experiences of power and privilege or oppression over time. However, even within the discipline of social work, there is variability in the degree to which the profession and its preferred educational theories attend to the ecological lens of culture and power beyond the purely psychodynamic clinical lens. I previously pointed to the way in which IFS theory begins to integrate this larger lens. Here I point to the necessity of bringing a power analysis and an intercultural lens of encounter to research, examining some of the specific contributions of relational-cultural theory (RCT) and liberation health theory as I also draw on them for application to the case studies in the next chapters.

I argue, first, that a power analysis is a necessary tool for an interdisciplinary, or transdisciplinary, lived religion approach to studying violent trauma in communities either privileged or oppressed by race and class. I draw on my own experiences with grassroots activist trainings developed over the years by feminist organizations and writers[68] in my understanding that power encompasses four dimensions: (1) access to resources, (2) access to decision-making capacity, (3) access to norm/standard-making capacity, and finally through the institutional and cultural weight of the combination of these three, (4) access to the capacity to define "reality" and what will or will not be considered a "problem" within an institutional or sociocultural context—with all elements of such power ultimately being backed by the violent or nonviolent capacity of force (nonviolent capacity often being specifically rooted in cross-cultural religious traditions of radical peaceful protest and disruption).

Second, my lived experiences with being a border crosser of cultures in different contexts of historical and institutional power also lead me to advocate for the necessity of opportunities for intercultural encounter in research. This includes openly drawing upon and illustrating the researcher's own experiences of such encounters, as I strive to do with vignettes in my writing style as well as in particular acknowledgments at times, including in endnotes, throughout this book.[69] Given the scope and impact of violent trauma, developing intercultural interdisciplinary research approaches becomes significant as an *ethical* response during an era of increasing pluralism and diversity, including discrepancy of access to power and significant shared global challenges.[70] For example, Maria Pilar Aquino[71] has written,

> ... the meaning of interculturality is linked to the historical context of each people and each culture, so the meaning depends on the realities, the resources, and the challenges of that context ... intercultural praxis requires that we take into account the different constellations of power in order to analyze the implications and the consequences of the intercultural processes ... Through communication and shared dialogue, intercultural approaches offer alternatives for deliberating about our common commitment to forging, out of our diverse cultural contexts, a world free of violence and injustice.

Within psychology, theories such as RCT and the liberation health model, as well as IFS as previously discussed, can be helpful tools for beginning to incorporate a power analysis and recognition of intercultural impact in interdisciplinary lived religion studies of trauma. In contrast to older critiques of relational-cultural therapy,[72] RCT has developed, and continues to develop, in its theoretical work a power analysis of domination and subordination through various categories and experiences of oppression (race, class, gender, and sexual orientation, among others). RCT's particular power analysis emphasizes concepts of domination and subordination, and temporary versus permanent inequality, and initially was developed by the feminist lens and critique Jean Baker Miller brought to psychoanalysis.[73] RCT also now incorporates concepts by other anti-oppression writers, such as Patricia Hill Collins' concept of "controlling images." These are defined by RCT as, "Images constructed by the dominant group that represent distortions of the nondominant cultural group being depicted, with the intent of disempowering them."[74]

Relational-cultural theory would define "power" and empowerment as "most fundamentally the 'capacity to produce a change'" and as "power with" rather than "power over" and as "mutual empowerment."[75] For example, in fostering group work through their Tuesday Talks format for survivors, as well as their sibling and teen groups, the Peace Institute fosters a model of "power with" rather than "power over" others—experiences of collaboration, creativity, and action, and of mutuality support, rather than experiences of professional distance and talking analysis that sometimes was cited by participants as a barrier in more traditional therapeutic relationships. Consideration of such power dynamics may be helpful for examining how certain "spiritual tribes" or approaches to communal trauma treatment are successful in functioning in particular cultural contexts but not others depending on comfort with particular cultural expressions of power.

Contemporary narrative therapy, as developed originally by Michael White and David Epston in the 1980s, was deeply influenced by poststructuralist analysis of power relations, particularly the work of Michel Foucault, that "storytelling rights are negotiated and distributed through the professional institution and its archives."[76] "The issues of power relations, structural inequalities, and ownership of the storytelling rights of personhood are central to the work of narrative therapy."[77] Narrative therapy is not necessarily grounded philosophically in the individual narrative, though larger sociocultural, political, and economic factors indeed may pressure individual pastoral care providers and clinicians to focus primarily on the individual in practice. Instead, narrative therapy theory shares a similar sociological analysis of power as "a relation" and "productive," operating "at the most micro levels of social relations,"[78] including through the establishment and psychological internalization of "cultural hegemony,"[79] and such relational power needs awareness by the caretaker. Bringing a power analysis to religious care, for those survivors ready to receive it, was shown specifically in the Peace Institute case study to add an additional level of insight and effectiveness to their capacity to assume leadership in a public context through their Leadership Academy.

The encounter between cultures, including elements of power illustrated by cross-cultural controlling images and narratives or language, also holds forth the promise of enlarging and expanding our respective academic disciplines, religious traditions, and shared sociological visions—our respective world/views and world/sense. Beyond purely the idea of cognitive dissonance, and drawing instead on more embodied metaphoric RCT language and narrative for world/view and world/sense, "discrepant relational images"[80] formed in the context of different or new relationships can become a means of changing negative relational images that may be internalized as culturally dominant. "Another world is shown to be possible" now, to paraphrase Indian activist Arundhati Roy, in the imagination of possibilities through the encounter with this/these "discrepant" cross-cultural relationship(s). A link thus can be made between relational-cultural (RCT) and narrative theories through the framework of beliefs and experiences that shape into the stories we tell ourselves as well as the expectations and visions that guide our relationships in particular cultural contexts.[81]

As discrepant relational images can become a basis for fluidity and change, narrative therapy practices would look for the "alternative stories" we tell that can become a basis for change as well—paralleling the concealed, resistance, or emerging/transformation stories of critical race theory mentioned in the introduction.[82] The example of the Peace

Institute creating curriculums based on the story of Louis D. Brown's life becomes not only an alternative story but also a discrepant relational image in this sense to the negative controlling images of young black men in the United States. As discussed further in the next chapters as well, the TVUUC minister would use a sermon series to create a discrepant relational image of the liberal religious person as actually powerful and not weak in response to violence. Intercultural research, to which these case studies seek to contribute, can highlight "discrepant images" and alternative stories carried by oppressed groups in counterpoint to a culturally dominant group's distorted and controlling images—and all academic disciplines might learn something new through this process.

RCT founder Jean Baker Miller wrote, "As other perceptions arise ... the total vision of human possibilities enlarges and is transformed"—the capacity and world/sense of human ways of being is expanded.[83] RCT theorist Maureen Walker also emphasizes that "relational-cultural work represents a *worldview* or *philosophical approach* to healing and human development" rather than simply a collection of therapeutic tools or techniques—thus a shift of traditional academic discipline paradigms for psychology in understanding and language.[84] As I have been emphasizing, and discovered through the case studies, there are intercultural research implications for ethical learning to these concepts as well. Exposure to discrepant cross-cultural relationships, or exposure to alternative cultural stories, language, and experiences, also can enlarge and transform visions and experiences of human possibilities and phenomenological understandings, as will be illustrated further in the next two chapters.

RCT is not alone as a clinical model seeking to make this move—the liberation health social work model does as well.[85] This model, developed historically by radical social workers,[86] helps clients to examine their identified "problem" not only through personal factors but also through the lens of institutional and cultural issues. In this sense, application of liberation health theory is compatible with the philosophical influence of the model of anti-oppression analysis in the Peace Institute case study and my prior reference to bell hooks integration of theory and liberative practice, both as discussed in the previous chapter. The liberation health model is influenced by three streams of theory, per Dawn Belkin Martinez and Ann Fleck-Henderson: (1) Paulo Freire and the Latin American popular education movement, (2) liberation psychology as also developed in Latin America by Ignacio Martín-Baró, and (3) radical social work and members of the rank and file movement in the United States, particularly Bertha Capen Reynolds and Mary van Kleeck.[87]

Core concepts in this theory include, (1) its own focus on "worldview" from a more Marxist orientation and as a reflection of the "dominant ideological messages that we receive [as they] reflect the interests of the dominant class in a society"[88] and (2) drawing on narrative therapy, an emphasis that the therapist must help the client to see "a problem in its totality" by developing a "thick description" of all the personal, institutional, and cultural factors that may go into contributing to the problem, thus "triangulating the problem."[89] Through this process, the problem is "de-ideologized" and a dominant worldview is "deconstructed." The client's consciousness of these larger forces is raised, and the client is transformed from a passive sense of self as "object" upon whom others act and others control and is enabled instead to develop an action plan as "subject" in the client's own life.

One additional significant concept of note is the liberation health model's focus on "rescuing the historical memory of change."[90] The shift from "object" to "subject" is not an individualistic phenomenon—it happens in community through shared learning. By collectively recalling communal acts of resistance historically, the capacity to be a "subject" in the face of current present institutional and cultural oppression is expanded. As discussed in the previous chapter, Peace Institute survivors in particular spoke both of the power of language and theory in their learning from the anti-oppression consultant as well as group programs and activities such as the Leadership Academy as sources of personal and communal liberation and deep healing, empowering their shift from victims to survivors and leaders. TVUUC leaders also would engage in acts of rescuing the historical memory of change through the placement of plaques and a power point presentation for newcomers commemorating historical resistance.[91]

Trauma Studies: Bridging to Religious and Spiritual Language, Body, Culture, and Power

Guiding metaphoric and relational images are long familiar to Christian pastoral care practitioners,[92] particularly classic ones such as Seward Hiltner's "the solicitous shepherd" or Henri Nouwen's "the wounded healer," and increasingly newer ones encompassing a broader range of social relationships and responsibilities, such as Margaret Kornfeld's "the gardener" and Bonnie Miller-McLemore's expanded reconception of Anton Boisen's "the living human document" into "the living human web." Practitioners have used such images to identify their primary pastoral style of practice as well as for theological reflection. Within my original research, I drew upon two different pastoral theologians, Charles V. Gerkin and Larry Kent Graham, to illustrate the significance of integrating Gerkin's guiding narrative image and vision of Christian servanthood with Graham's emphasis on the systemic analysis of structural power for Christian prophetic pastoral care as illustrated in the case studies.[93] Through this, I suggested that a social theological anthropology recognizes that pastoral images are always *relational* images with a potential to determine or guide vision and action, including prophetic action.

Within an interdisciplinary lived religion approach that affirms trauma survivors as experts and subjects of their own lives, or as primary theologians, relational-cultural therapy (RCT) concepts also are useful in metaphorically correlating with and understanding survivor reports of the healing and energizing function of reconnection with others in the aftermath of traumatic disconnection and isolation. Such reports reflect an *embodied* social theological anthropology, or understanding of human being, one that takes seriously the neuroscience of our corporeality. "Connection" in RCT is defined as "an interaction between two or more people that is mutually empathic and mutually empowering. It involves emotional accessibility and leads to the 'five good things' (zest, worth, productivity, clarity, and desire for more connection)."[94]

Strategies of connection and disconnection are central tenets of relational-cultural theory. Such "growth-fostering"[95] connection (including, I argue, ecclesial connections brought through religious or spiritual rituals) permits mutual empowerment. Such connections can counteract the disempowerment and isolation of trauma, or "traumatic disconnection"[96] in RCT language, as will continue to be illustrated with the case studies. This includes particularly intense forms of shame, internalized oppression, and "condemned isolation"[97] that results from trauma compounded by historical and cultural oppression, inclusive of all forms of oppression. Such concepts proved fruitful for metaphorical dialogue with the study of prophetic pastoral care and trauma in my original research, including metaphorical correlation and dialogue with constructive Christian theologies of trauma and "spirit."

For example, per Heimbrock's emphasis on the immanence of the divine in lived religion, these energizing and continuing bonds of physiological experiences also may be correlated to and conceptualized through the lens of theological anthropology and Christian pneumatology, rather than psychology, and in terms of the experience of "spirits" or of the "Holy Spirit" or of "God" or the "Divine" in religious studies. The neuroaffective base of human embodiment may account for a commonality across cultures to the experience of phenomena such as ghosts and spirits and ancestor worship in different religions, beyond solely the Christian tradition, and also may account, as previously discussed, for Thich Nhat Hanh's greater comfort with the language of "spirit" poetically and metaphorically in interreligious dialogue. Additionally, George Lakoff and Mark Johnson have argued that all spiritual experience is embodied experience and that "imaginative empathic projection,"[98] which is an embodied neuroaffective function, is the transcendent *and* immanent root of all spiritual experience, a theological form of panentheism.[99] In the field of clinical nursing,[100] the importance of spiritual experiences of both transcendence *and* immanence through such empathic relationality also has been noted

> The interpersonal dynamic of transcendence is concerned with an extension of the self towards another. When concerned with care, this extension of self is focused on a beneficent attending towards another. As we have suggested, this is an unbalanced equation until we consider what comes back towards the nurse ... The therapeutic essence of giving care is not a restricted,

one-way dynamic ... It may be suggested here that in extending the self to attend upon another, the carer is also cared for and sustained through the elements evidenced in mutuality. If nurses did not experience the freely occurring themes of mutuality and reciprocity the experience of care delivery would be static and sterile ... The response of the patient evidences the human themes of mutuality and reciprocation that enrich the state of being for the nurse. This transmission to the nurse of beneficent and sustaining themes is a process that can be called "immanence" and suggests a balancing element to transcendence .....

These perspectives on spirituality also dovetail with the collaborative work of neuroscientist Andrew Newberg and psychiatrist Eugene D'Aquili,[101] who argued that finding a neurobiological basis for our affective spiritual experiences does not invalidate an alternative theological or religious interpretation. In other words, "God" or the "Divine" needs to communicate revelation through some means and that means can be our neurobiological and somatic nature. Within theological or religious anthropology, the body becomes a point of connection for the experience of "God" or the "Divine," as named by different religious traditions, and makes a contribution to a deeper theological or religious understanding of human existence in relationship to "God" or the "Divine," as well as to other human beings.

For further illustration, if we are neuroaffectively related in our attachment, as Lewis, et al. argue, then some desire for, or possible experience of, "being present and alive" may remain after the death of a loved one in the very neurological fibers of our body, as also suggested by Rynearson and Salloum in their analogy to phantom limbs.[102] This desire or experience is part of mutuality and energy in relationships, per the relational-cultural therapy theorists, and also potentially generates "continuing bonds," per Silverman and Klass, that may last a lifetime, experiences which different cultures language, narrate, or story in different ways, per narrative theory, including in Christian traditions through the language of "spirit."

In the pilot studies referenced in my prelude, for example, young adults uniformly said that wearing buttons or t-shirts with a picture of the murdered loved one led to an actual *visceral* experience of the person still being alive, present, and connected to them—including the person being able to continue to participate in and be aware of the activities of the living. In my original research, and as consistent with both the Christian tradition and my own UU tradition, I languaged this phenomenon as a prophetic and performative practice of testimony and witness to ongoing sacred spiritual connections, a phenomenon that led me later to name this practice theologically as a form of *material theopoetics*. In doing so, I was making a contextualized correlation between religious traditions and the social scientific phenomena I was observing, inclusive of respecting the language and experience of the survivors on their own cultural terms and in their own world/view and world/sense.

Finally, Richard C. Schwartz also has sought to make some linkages between IFS theory and spiritual affective and cognitive states a person may report experiencing in correlation with various world religious traditions and their respective languages, ranging through Christian, Buddhist, Hindu, and other traditions. For his practical theoretical purpose in working primarily with therapists, he has simply translated and termed these "the eight C's of Self-Leadership," which include calmness, clarity, curiosity, compassion, confidence, courage, creativity, and connectedness.[103] Beyond the simplicity of these formulations in the context of psychology rather than religion, what is interesting is that Schwartz seeks an embodied and immanent affective and cognitive grounding to spiritual experiences across religious traditions, which may be languaged metaphorically in different ways for different sociocultural purposes. Schwartz does so here in terms that even secular clinicians might grasp as constituting "mentally and emotionally healthy states" for human beings. This includes clinicians more normalized to accept and be viscerally comfortable with Buddhist mindfulness practices, as well as Schwartz' language of "Self energy" rather than specific religious language, in a Western individualized linguistic metaphoric context such as the United States.

I turn now to an examination of the lessons learned from the two case studies, engaging in further interdisciplinary correlations between my phenomenological observations and experiences with the interdisciplinary bridge tools outlined in this chapter. The voices, language, and practices of survivors, and those who serve them, as they experience or seek God/the divine/the sacred and sustenance and "healing" in the aftermath of violent trauma, continue to serve as my normative point of interdisciplinary reflection. Clearly in a world suffering from violent trauma—and barriers to collective action caused by structural divides of race, class, gender, and religion—case studies that apply a wide variety of tools and disciplines to understanding and removing these barriers could not be more necessary than now.

Notes

1. I draw the metaphor of "scratches" in relationship to images from an older work by Harold R. Isaacs, *Scratches on Our Minds: American Images of China and India* (New York: Routledge, 1980).
2. Judith L. Herman, *Trauma and Recovery*, 51–52.
3. Ronnie Janoff-Bulman, *Shattered Assumptions*, 137–138.
4. Christine A. Courtois and Julian D. Ford, ed., *Treating Complex Traumatic Stress Disorders: An Evidence-Based Guide* (New York: The Guilford Press, 2009), 209.
5. Lawrence G. Calhoun and Richard G. Tedeschi, "Posttraumatic growth: The Positive Lessons of Loss," in *Meaning Reconstruction and the Experience of Loss*, 4th edition, edited by Robert A. Neimeyer (Washington, D.C.: American Psychological Association, 2005), 157.
6. Ibid., 168.
7. "Religious, philosophical, and folk traditions have for thousands of years recognized the possibility that the struggle with major losses in life can be the source of enhanced meaning in life and the impetus for positive change ... The phenomenon of posttraumatic growth has been observed at least in a significant minority ... , and sometimes in the vast majority ... , of people who have experienced a variety of different kinds of loss ... The growth experienced tends to fall into three broad domains: changed sense of self, changed relationships, and changed philosophy of life," ibid., 157–158.
8. Ammerman, *Sacred Stories, Spiritual Tribes*. "Sacred stories also imply audiences—what I will call 'spiritual tribes'—who listen and cocreate the tale. Each story is situated in a context, with circles of listeners

who play a role, sacred or otherwise . . . [beyond religious communities] are there other places where spiritual tribes gather, as well? Are there mediated communities on the internet or in circles of readers, viewers, fans (10)?" I want to suggest that a para-ecclesial ministry such as the Peace Institute and a community ministry such as the UUTRM also might constitute what Ammerman calls a "spiritual tribe" guided by a "sacred story" of their founding.
9. Calhoun and Tedeschi, 157–172.
10. Ibid., 167.
11. Ibid., 159 and 168.
12. Calhoun and Tedeschi, 159, cite studies of survivors who reported growth in the aftermath of trauma. While the survivors reported increased awareness of vulnerability, paradoxically they sometimes experienced themselves as "stronger and more capable" too. They also could report "an increased connectedness with others and a deepened sense of empathy and the ability to connect emotionally with other people." It should be noted that not all survivors report experiencing post-traumatic growth and certainly not all go on to found organized ministries.
13. As I discovered in the original research, Walsh, *Prophetic Pastoral Care in the Aftermath of Trauma*, this is not a new historical perspective in the clinical and pastoral care literature, particularly for literature written by oppressed groups. Within the US context and African American communities, practical and pastoral theologians readily document this natural intertwining of healing and liberation. See, for two examples, Dale P. Andrews, *Practical Theology for Black Churches: Bridging Black Theology and African American Folk Religion* (Louisville, KY: Westminster John Knox Press, 2002) and Carroll A. Watkins Ali. *Survival and Liberation: Pastoral Theology in African American Context* (St. Louis, MO: Chalice Press, 1999). See also Sheryl A. Kujawa-Holbrook and Karen B. Montagno, eds. *Injustice and the Care of Souls: Taking Oppression Seriously in Pastoral Care.* (Minneapolis: Fortress Press, 2009).
14. Janoff-Bulman, *Shattered Assumptions*, 171.

15. Some classic resource literature supporting these statements include Herman, *Trauma and Recovery*; Janoff-Bulman, *Shattered Assumptions*; Babette Rothschild, *The Body Remembers: The Psychophysiology of Trauma and Trauma Treatment* (New York: W.W. Norton and Company, 2000); Daniel J. Siegel, *The Developing Mind: Toward a Neurobiology of Interpersonal Experience* (New York: The Guilford Press, 1999); Daniel J. Siegel, *Pocket Guide to Interpersonal Neurobiology: An Integrative Handbook* (New York: W.W. Norton & Company, 2012); and Bessel van der Kolk, Alexander C. McFarlane, and Lars Weisaeth, ed., *Traumatic Stress: The Effects of Overwhelming Experience on Mind, Body, and Society* (New York: The Guilford Press, 1996).
16. The term "historical trauma theory" appears to have entered into the public health context through the work of Michelle M. Sotero, "A Conceptual Model of Historical Trauma: Implications for Public Health Practice and Research" *Journal of Health Disparities Research and Practice*, Vol. 1. No. 1, Fall 2006, pp. 93–108.
17. See van der Kolk, *Traumatic Stress* and *The Body Keeps the Score*. See also Amy Banks with Leigh Ann Hirschman, *Four Ways to Click: Rewire Your Brain for Stronger, More Rewarding Relationships* (New York: Jeremy P. Tarcher/Penguin, 2015) for an integration of the impact of trauma on the brain with practices for healing the brain.
18. I was captivated by the use of this language of "world sense" recorded in an interview with an African American nurse. The term is more embodied on the visceral level, as in "street sense," as well and also can be thought of along the lines of "Does the world make sense to me?" on a visceral level of connection to reality. See Nancy Rule Goldberger, "Cultural Imperatives and Diversity in Ways of Knowing," in *Knowledge, Difference, and Power: Essays Inspired by Women's Ways of Knowing*, edited by Nancy Goldberger, Jill Tarule, Blythe Clinchy, and Mary Belenky (New York: Basic Books, 1996).
19. As I point to a new metaphor of "world/sense," I continue to situate myself among philosophers and feminists in a phenomenological tradition as discussed in prior chapters. Additionally, this includes Eugene Gendlin's use of the term "felt sense" in *Experiencing and the*

Creation of Meaning: A Philosophical and Psychological Approach to the Subjective (Evanston, IL: Northwestern University Press, 1962/1997) as well as Michael Polanyi's concept of "tacit knowing." For example, Gil quotes Polanyi, "To use language in speech, reading and writing, is to extend our bodily equipment and become intelligent human beings. We may say that when we learn to use language, or a probe, or a tool, and thus make ourselves aware of these things as we are our body, we *interiorize* these things and *make ourselves dwell in them*. Such extensions of ourselves develop new faculties in us; our whole education operates in this way; as each of us interiorizes our cultural heritage, he grows into a person seeing the world and experiencing life in terms of this outlook," 39 in Gill, *The Tacit Mode: Michael Polanyi's Postmodern Philosophy*. I point particularly to his use of the term "world" here in relationship to "seeing" as in "worldview." I am suggesting that our metaphoric conception needs to deepen and embrace that we actually are experiencing "world/sense."

20. Sandra Schneiders, *The Revelatory Text: Interpreting The New Testament as Sacred Scripture* (Collegeville: The Liturgical Press, 1999) 30–31.
21. Ibid., 31. See also Paul F. Knitter, *Introducing Theologies of Religions* (Maryknoll: Orbis Books, 2002) for his discussion of language in comparative religions. He particularly notes that while language can constrain experience, language also is capable of being changed by experience. Schneiders' statements in the context of intercultural encounters point to the direction in which this may happen through the multivalent and polyvalent tensions established by metaphors, which is a different approach to correlations than simply making analogies.
22. For example, Barbara J. McClure recently has argued that there is a need to re-envision a "radically socialized self" within pastoral care paradigms of theological anthropology. See *Moving Beyond Individualism in Pastoral Care and Counseling: Reflections on Theory, Theology, and Practice* (Eugene, OR: Cascade Books, 2010), 188. I agree with the need expressed by McClure's aims but also argue that McClure has not attended adequately to the neurophysiological dimensions of

the body as revealed by trauma and attachment studies for support. I also argue that McClure has not fully grasped the contemporary literature and practices of either relational-cultural theory or narrative therapy theories when she critiques these as failing to contribute adequately to her stated aims.

23. Note that beyond the dictionary meaning of "interplay," there also is a global movement of physical play on which I draw for metaphoric image—see http://interplay.org (accessed September 17, 2015). For a larger context to the word "emplacement" in ethnographic research, see again Pink, *Doing Sensory Ethnography*, 27–28. Some examples of how pneumatology has been expanded in the Christian theological tradition include Catherine Keller's works, such as *Face of the Deep: A Theology of Becoming* (New York: Routledge, 2003), and Peter C. Hodgson's works, such as *Winds of the Spirit: A Constructive Christian Theology* (Louisville: Westminster John Knox Press, 1994) and "The Spirit and Religious Pluralism," in *The Myth of Religious Superiority: A Multifaith Exploration*, edited by Paul F. Knitter (Maryknoll: Orbis Books, 2005), 135–150. Mary C. Grey also uses the language of spirit in ecological contexts, see *Sacred Longings: The Ecological Spirit and Global Culture* (Minneapolis: Fortress Press, 2004). In regards to science and metaphors, see again Tiffany, *Toy Medium*, as mentioned in Chap. 2.

24. See Thich Nhat Hanh, *Living Buddha, Living Christ* (New York: Riverhead Books, 1995), 13–14.

25. Jaak Panksepp, *Affective Neuroscience: The Foundations of Human and Animal Emotions* (New York: Oxford University Press, 1998), 5.

26. Thomas Lewis, Fari Amini, and Richard Lannon, *A General Theory of Love* (New York: Vintage Books, 2000/2001), 88.

27. Ibid., 86.

28. Ibid., 62–63.

29. See Dennis Klass, Phyllis R. Silverman, and Steven L. Nickman, ed., *Continuing Bonds: New Understandings of Grief* (New York: Routledge, 1996) and Phyllis Rolfe Silverman, *Never Too Young to Know: Death in Children's Lives* (New York: Oxford University Press, 2000). Note that contemporary psychoanalytic theory has attempted

to move toward a more relational theoretical frame through object relations theory, self-psychology, and intersubjectivity theories, but the foundational core of psychoanalytic theory and metaphoric language remains framed philosophically by and caught in a Western individualistic anthropology and understanding of human nature or being. For more on this, see Renee Spencer, "A Comparison of Relational Psychologies." *Project Report 5* (2002, Wellesley Centers for Women, Wellesley College, Wellesley, MA) and her feminist critique and review of this literature and shifting paradigms in psychology. See also an edited collection by Robert Neimeyer, *Meaning Reconstruction and the Experience of Loss*, 4th ed. (Washington, D.C.: American Psychological Association, 2005) that reviews shifting paradigms in the literature on loss.

For an additional creative effort, however, to push the boundaries of psychoanalytic theories beyond purely intrapsychic or intersubjective formulations and encompass attention to the impact of culture and social oppression on the lives of women of color through the use of Kohut's recognition of the existence of cultural selfobjects, see Phillis Isabella Sheppard's *Self, Culture, and Others in Womanist Practical Theology* (New York: Palgrave Macmillan, 2011). See also a lesser known essay by Thandeka, "The Self Between Feminist Theory and Theology," in *Horizons in Feminist Theology: Identity, Tradition, and Norms*, Rebecca S. Chopp and Sheila Greeve Davaney, ed. (Minneapolis: Fortress Press, 1997), 79–98 in which she also pushes creatively the metaphoric boundaries of psychoanalytic language in reflecting on a social ontology, "self," and the language of spirit by utilizing the work of D.W. Winnicott in particular, as well as Kohut. In addition, see Pamela Cooper-White, *Many Voices: Pastoral Psychotherapy in Relational and Theological Perspective* (Minneapolis: Fortress Press, 2007). Finally, see again LaMothe, *Becoming Alive*, for his attention to the language of "vitality," culture, and trauma within the psychoanalytic tradition.

30. Klass, et al., *Continuing Bonds*, subsequent quote is from 16 to 17.
31. Ibid., 19–20.

32. Edward K. Rynearson and Alison Salloum, "Restorative Retelling: Revising the Narrative of Violent Death," 179, in *Grief and Bereavement in Contemporary Society: Bridging Research and Practice*, edited by Robert A. Neimeyer, Darcy L. Harris, Howard R. Winokuer, and Gordon F. Thornton (New York: Routledge Taylor & Francis Group, 2011), 177–188.
33. Hertz, Marci Feldman, Deborah Prothrow-Stith, and Clementina Chery, "Homicide Survivors: Research and Practice Implications," *American Journal of Preventive Medicine*, 29 (5S2), 2005: 289.
34. For further studies and summary of the history of developments in psychology in the area of grief, see additional works by J. William Worden, *Grief Counseling and Grief Therapy: A Handbook for Mental Health Practitioners*, 4th ed. (New York: Springer Publishing Company, 2009); Therese A. Rando, *Treatment of Complicated Mourning* (Champaign, IL: Research Press, 1993); and Neimeyer, *Meaning Reconstruction*. See also Hertz, et al., "Homicide Survivors," for further recommendations of the special needs of homicide survivors, inclusive not only of immediate family and friends but also the broader communities impacted. Hertz, et al. note in particular a gap in several areas of research and health provider trainings in relationship to these needs.
35. Jean Baker Miller is widely regarded as the founder of what is now known as Relational-Cultural Therapy, particularly beginning with her *Toward a New Psychology of Women* (Boston: Beacon Press, 1976). Judith Jordan's latest book *Relational-Cultural Therapy* (American Psychological Association: Washington, D.C., 2010) is the first collation in one monograph of the theoretical terms and definitions of relational-cultural therapy (RCT) and is drawn upon heavily for primary definitions throughout this book. Most of RCT's theoretical work is spread out through collections of multiple essays, often focused on direct therapeutic care rather than being organized into an overall theoretical frame, which is what has made this recent volume by Jordan helpful for those who might seek to apply their work across disciplines.
36. Jordan, *Relational-Cultural Therapy*, 49, 107.

37. Ibid., 107.
38. See Richard C. Schwartz, *Internal Family Systems Therapy* (New York: The Guilford Press, 1995). See also Regina A. Goulding and Richard C. Schwartz, *The Mosaic Mind: Empowering the Tormented Selves of Child Abuse Survivors* (Oak Park, IL: Trailheads Publications, 2002). Note that a full chapter is devoted to IFS theory in trauma specialist, van der Kolk's, latest book, *The Body Keeps The Score*.
39. Ibid., 138.
40. Ibid., 187–189.
41. Street memorials are a separate spontaneous phenomenon and do not represent a specific practice of the LDBPI; however, many survivors have participated in this spontaneous practice as well.
42. See E. Francis King, *Material Religion and Popular Culture* (New York: Routledge, 2010) and Colleen McDannell, *Material Christianity: Religion and Popular Culture in America* (New Haven: Yale University Press, 1995). Material religion draws on the broader field of material culture studies, and per McDannell, religious material culture is a neglected area of study. For examples of purely material culture studies, see Daniel Miller's works, such as *The Comfort of Things* (Cambridge, UK: Polity Press, 2008). In arguing for greater attention to material Christianity, McDannell states that the line between the profane and the sacred is much more blurred than religious scholars often credit. Items of popular material culture can be given religious or spiritual significance by virtue of human relationships, actions, and interpretations.
43. Special note should be made, however, of the work of at least one other practical theologian: Stephen Pattison, *Seeing Things: Deepening Relations with Visual Artefacts* (London: SCM Press, 2007). Pattison has studied the human tendency to create personal relationships with visual artifacts. I build upon his work but turn particular attention to the relationship between the expression of material religion (including use of visual artifacts) and the psychosocial experience of trauma. I particularly explore the possibilities in material practices beyond the visual dimension for a more fully embodied range of sensual material expression (sight, sound, touch, smell, and taste). I am also interested

in the use of material culture and religion for prophetic and performative testimony and witness, again drawing upon Jack Santino's work in making this particular link as well, though I also argue that "something more" is happening in these performances beyond the political. For another example of the increased interest in material religion in religious studies, see David Morgan, *The Embodied Eye: Religious Visual Culture and the Social Life of Feeling* (Berkeley: University of California Press, 2012).
44. McDannell, *Material Christianity*, 2.
45. King, *Material Religion and Popular Culture*, xv.
46. Ibid., xiv.
47. McDannell, Material Christianity, 1–2.
48. Ibid., 1.
49. On the prophetic dimension of theopoetics, Rebecca S. Chopp writes in "Theology and the Poetics of Testimony," *Criterion* (Winter 1998): "The poetics of testimony is my way of naming the discursive practices and various voices that seek to describe or name that which rational discourse will not or cannot reveal ... The poetics of testimony, expressed in a variety of particular and distinct forms, is fundamentally concerned with human and earthly survival and transformation, and thus renders a moral claim on human existence. This imperative is also theological, or at least for those of us who live Christianity as practices of emancipatory transformation or, in the words of Albert Schweitzer, as a reverence for life" (2–4). Beyond *discursive* practices can be a *material* dimension to testimony and witness in calling a larger community to moral transformation, I argue. See also Paul Ricouer, "The Hermeneutics of Testimony," in *Essays on Biblical Interpretation*, edited by Lewis S. Mudge (Philadelphia: Fortress Press, 1980), 119–154.
50. Ricouer, 129.
51. Ibid., 132–134.
52. See the Christian use of this phrase throughout Johann Baptist Metz, *Faith in History and Society*. I use this phrase in its expanded metaphorical sense as did Welch, *A Feminist Ethic of Risk*.
53. See again Walsh, *Prophetic Pastoral Care in the Aftermath of Trauma*.

54. In this vein, see also Mayra Rivera's recent contribution, *Poetics of the Flesh* (Durham: Duke University, 2015). Rivera's work is very helpful in summarizing historical philosophical and theological debates about the body, but here I point out her influence by Caribbean writer, poet, and philosopher Édouard Glissant in turning to the language of poetics. "For Glissant, poetics refers not only to styles of writing, but also to modes of knowing, being, and acting in the world. The poetic approach is indispensable for addressing histories marked by disruption, displacement, and irrecoverable loss—such as those of Caribbean peoples, whose very existence emerged from the obliteration of African and indigenous cultures, religions, and languages ... For Glissant, poetics is an approach to knowledge that values processes of creation from 'shattered histories' and 'shards of vocabularies' and acknowledges their discontinuities ... In addition to relating poetics to modes of knowing and ways of writing, Glissant links it more broadly to being in the world ... The world's poetic force creates and expresses itself as Relation (2–3)." Poetics thus understood is helpful for communicating the rupturing dimension of trauma and also can be seen to correlate with language survivors' use in the following chapters as well as with relational-cultural and IFS theories lifted up in this book. For the broader philosophical scope of phenomenology and postmodern poetics, see Richard Kearney, *Poetics of Imagining: Modern to Post-modern* (New York: Fordham University, 1998).

55. Chopp, "Theology and the Poetics of Testimony," 6. Note that Chopp is not dismissing the importance of rhetoric and returns to emphasizing a need "to combine poetics, rhetoric, and hermeneutics in theology" (11) at the end of this same essay, as the relationship between the three appears to overlap at times. In her larger work, she recognizes the power of rhetoric in liberation theology, see for example *The Praxis of Suffering: An Interpretation of Liberation and Political Theologies* (Eugene, OR: Wipf and Stock Publishers, 1986), as well as *Saving Work: Feminist Practices of Theological Education* (Louisville: Westminster John Knox Press, 1995). In this particular essay on "Theology and the Poetics of Testimony," Chopp is emphasizing a constructive theological possibility for poetics as testifying to a moral

vision and social imaginary, one that also holds promise for "practices of emancipatory transformation" (11). See also Heather Walton's recent essay calling attention to Chopp's work, "Poetics," in *The Wiley-Blackwell Companion to Practical Theology*, edited by Bonnie Miller-McLemore (Malden, MA: Wiley-Blackwell, 2014), 173–182; as well as L. Callid Keefe-Perry summary work on the history of theopoetics and his attention to Chopp's work, *Way to Water: A Theopoetics Primer* (Eugene, OR: Cascade Books, 2014).

56. In relationship to Chopp's argument on poetics and rhetoric, Robert Frost's poem, "Fire and Ice," is an excellent example of the use of rhetoric within poetry to provoke eschatological imagination and prophetic warning.

57. I draw particular attention to parallel work being done in theopoetics, corporeality, and materiality, albeit in an entirely different arena of religious studies, by Patricia Cox Miller, *The Corporeal Imagination: Signifying the Holy in Late Ancient Christianity* (Philadelphia: University of Pennsylvania Press, 2009). Miller also is interdisciplinary in her approach, drawing from material culture studies of the late ancient Christian period. She engages in a literary analysis of writings about relics, art, and images of the saints to illuminate their theopoetic and material nature when a "corporeal imagination" is engaged through such writing. Miller writes, "From the perspective of the natural attitude, a relic is simply an object, part of a dead person's inanimate body. However, when a martyr's dust, bone, or body becomes the center of cultic activity and reverence, it loses its character as a natural body and begins to function as a site of religious contact. No longer a mere object, it becomes a thing that does indeed signal a new subject-object relation, a relation of the human subject to the sanctifying potential of human physicality as locus and mediator of spiritual presence and power" (2). My focus in material culture studies is shaped less by the theo/poetics of literary analysis than by the theo/poetics of performance using material culture and the works of Jack Santino, such as *Spontaneous Shrines and the Public Memorialization of Death*. Miller also points to inherent "performativity" in "hagiographical writing" that engage the sensory or corporeal imagination. My

study parallels Miller but focuses on the living experience of sanctification through direct engagement of the senses and theo/poetic testimony and witness using material objects, art, rituals, and surroundings.

58. Deepening this connection between poetics and the prophetic, Chopp continues, 6–7, "Poetics is the discourse that reshapes, fashions in new ways, enlarges, and calls into question the order of discourse within ... the 'social imaginary'... By 'testimony' I mean the discourse that refers to a reality outside the ordinary order of things ... Testimonies enact a moral consciousness and communal, even at times, global responsibility ... testimonies ... are collective and social ... testimony is both private and public ... Testimony invokes a moral claim; it is from someone to someone about something. A decision is called for, a change in reality is required." (6–7). She writes further on the connection between a poetics of testimony and theology: "In the theologies formed as a poetics of testimony, transcendence is a matter of the power and spirit of transfiguration ... Transcendence is, quite simply, not a conceptual problem but a moral summons to imagine hope ... Understanding theology as engaged in continually negotiating to sanctify life may enable us to keep theology more fluid and more multi-dimensional—indeed, more Spiritual— and may allow us a way to combine poetics, rhetoric, and hermeneutics in theology. Imagining theology as engaged in negotiating practices to sanctify life by means of tracing Spirit allows us to appreciate theology as a type of cultural intervention" (10–11). Thus poetic testimony through material religion can have powerful prophetic implications for different societies across cultures and can lend itself to metaphoric theologies of spirit and trauma.

59. The language of "theopoetics," as I am using the term, is traced to Amon Niven Wilder, *Theopoetic: Theology and the Religious Imagination* (Lima, OH: Academic Renewal Press, 1976/2001), who also held a broader vision of theopoetics than simply verbal or literary expressions and was inclusive of the cultural arts in many forms, though this was undeveloped in his work. Wilder wrote, 1–5, "Before any new theologies however secular and radical there must be a

contemporary theopoetic ... Religious communication generally must overcome a long addiction to the discursive, the rationalistic, and the prosaic ... I speak of the need for a richer agenda ... this new sensibility is also evident in the arts with their heightened awareness of the elements of perception, the wonder of what is immediately presented to consciousness in touch, sight, and sound ... I speak of the need today for an enrichment of the methods of theology ... wide scrutiny today of the relation of religion and the arts has opened up the deeper dynamics of communication and meaning." It should be noted that Wilder gives credit to Stanley Romaine Hopper for first describing "theopoetics" in its literary sense, though again Wilder's own broader conception needs further recognition and development. This is happening through the work of L. Callid Keefe-Perry, *Way to Water*, as well as The Association for Theopoetics Research and Exploration, see http://theopoetics.net (accessed May 12, 2016).
60. Welch, *A Feminist Ethic of Risk*.
61. I utilized the works of Jack Santino to understand the commemorative and performative dimensions, real and potential, of spontaneous street memorials in my pilot studies, as mentioned in my prelude.
62. The placement and removal of such public street memorials has been such a point of controversy in Boston that the Boston City Councilor interviewed for my research noted her plan to call a public hearing on it.
63. Rubem A. Alves, "Theopoetics: Longing and Liberation," in *Struggles for Solidarity: Liberation Theologies in Tension*, edited by Lorine M. Getz and Ruy O. Costa (Minneapolis: Fortress Press, 1992), 159–171.
64. Victor Turner, *The Ritual Process: Structure and Anti-Structure* (New York: Aldine de Gruyter, 1969/1995).
65. Ibid., 128. These "experiences of potency," of which Turner writes, are what make this phase in the life of a community particularly powerful, with strong potential for political and artistic creativity and expression. This, in turn, can correlate to a religio/poetic or socio/poetic material expression.
66. Public documents were accessed through the UUA and the UUTRM. See www.uua.org (accessed March 9, 2013) and http://www.traumaministry.org/tragedy-in-knoxville (accessed March 9, 2013).

67. Two helpful summary articles of these trends include David Morgan, "Religion and media: A critical review of recent developments," in *Critical Research on Religion*, 1(3), Sage Publications, 2013, 347–356; and Arjun Appadurai, "Mediants, Materiality, Normativity," *Public Culture*, 27:2, Duke University Press, 2015, 221–237.
68. I specifically credit the Women's Theological Center in Boston for the particular shape of power analysis as I draw on it (see http://www.thewtc.org), and also see Suzanne Pharr, "The Common Elements of Oppression." In *Homophobia: A Weapon of Sexism* (Inverness, CA: Chardon Press, 1988), 52–64.
69. See my original research for writers who influenced the evolution of my thought and method in this approach, Walsh, *Prophetic Pastoral Care in the Aftermath of Trauma*. See also cultural anthropologists George E. Marcus and Michael M.J. Fischer, *Anthropology as Cultural Critique: An Experimental Movement in the Human Sciences*, 2nd ed. (Chicago: The University of Chicago Press, 1999).
70. See Melinda McGarrah Sharp, "Globalization, Colonialism, and Postcolonialism," in *The Wiley-Blackwell Companion to Practical Theology*, ed. Bonnie Miller-McLemore (Malden, MA: Wiley-Blackwell, 2014), 422–431, as well as Nancy J. Ramsey, "Redefining a Time of Ferment and Redefinition," In *Dictionary of Pastoral Care and Counseling*, Rodney J. Hunter, ed., 1349–1369 (Nashville, TN: Abingdon Press, 1990/2005). Beyond self-critical intercultural awareness in pastoral care practices, Sharp points to the emerging importance of interculturality in research methods, a contribution toward which this book seeks to make. However, I also recognize that the very approach of my particular research may be re-inscribing a colonizing and imperialist stance, minimally for those who are racially and socioeconomically different from myself, rather than participating in a fully decolonizing methodological approach to interculturality. See also Smith, *Decolonizing Methodologies*. On the dangers of research, writing, and representation, Smith writes as an indigenous person that, "Representation is important as a concept because it gives the impression of 'the truth.' … reading and interpretation present problems when we do not see ourselves in the text. There are

problems, too, when we do see ourselves but can barely recognize ourselves through the representation," 37.
71. Additional work in this area of interculturality is being done by Latin American feminist theologians in particular, such as Maria Pilar Aquino and Maria Jose Rosado-Nunes, ed., *Feminist Intercultural Theology: Latino Explorations for a Just World* (Maryknoll: Orbis Books, 2007), 14–15 from which Aquino's quote is drawn. I am grateful for my colleague, Sofia Betancourt, in calling my attention to Aquino and Rosado-Nunes' text as she also is employing an intercultural approach in her own forthcoming dissertation through Yale, "Our Mothers Made Do: An Ecowomanist Ethic at the Panama Canal." See also S. Wesley Ariarajah, "Intercultural Hermeneutics—A Promise for the Future?" *Exchange* (vol. 34, no. 2, 2005) 89–101 (13). While not specifically utilizing the language of interculturality, see also Kathleen J. Greider's work distinguishing between "religious plurality," "religious pluralism," and "religious alterity" and her desire to reduce "Christian-centrism" on behalf of ethical concerns for peace and justice, "Religious Pluralism and Christian-Centrism," in *The Wiley-Blackwell Companion to Practical Theology*, edited by Bonnie Miller-McLemore (Malden, MA: Wiley-Blackwell, 2014), 452–461.
72. See, for example, how McClure, in her text *Moving Beyond Individualism in Pastoral Care and Counseling*, continues such critiques but does not explore equally RCT theorists' responses and later developments. See also Cooper-White, *Many Voices*, who usefully summarizes this shifting psychoanalytic frame but does not integrate relational-cultural theory nor narrative theory and metaphor into pastoral theology in her summary focus on changing psychoanalytic trends. Of note, however, is Cooper-White's tangential references to sandplay therapy, which will be explored later in the LDBPI case study, and also her recognition of theories of multiplicity of selves/parts within contemporary psychoanalytic literature. She does not, however, cover IFS theory, though it draws on multiplicity theories of mind in combination with family systems theory.
73. Miller, *Toward a New Psychology of Women*, 6–8. "Once a group is defined as inferior, the superiors tend to label it as defective or

substandard in various ways ... In addition, the actions and words of the dominant group tend to be destructive of the subordinates ... Dominant groups usually define one or more acceptable roles for the subordinate ... A dominant group, inevitably, has the greatest influence in determining a culture's overall outlook—its philosophy, morality, social theory, and even its science. The dominant group, thus, legitimizes the unequal relationship and incorporates it into society's guiding concepts ... Inevitably, the dominant group is the model for 'normal human relationships'." Trauma specialist, Judith Herman, was among a group of women deeply influenced by RCT founder Jean Baker Miller's work and also was supervised by the late Miller in the 1970s through the Somerville Women's Mental Health Collective, as reported by Christina Robb, *This Changes Everything: The Relational Revolution in Psychology* (New York: Picador, 2006/ 2007). Herman also was among the first to point out that the relational and analytic lens of trauma provides new insights into various replicating sociopolitical issues over time, including violence and war.

74. Jordan, *Relational-Cultural Therapy*, 102–103. See also Patricia Hill Collins, "Mammies, Matriarchs, and Other Controlling Images," in *Black Feminist Thought: Knowledge, Consciousness, and the Politics of Empowerment*, 2nd edition (New York: Routledge, 2000), 69–96. Phillis Sheppard also works with Collins' concept of "controlling images" or "controlling icons" in her creative work with Kohut's cultural selfobject, see *Self, Culture, and Others in Womanist Practical Theology*, 49–50, 135. RCT was initially criticized in much academic literature for what was perceived as its essentialist feminist stance as well as for being initially developed by white middle class female academics, but it is important to recognize that it has theoretically grown substantially over the years, including in participation by women of color who identify as RCT theorists, and that some critiques also were misunderstandings of their theoretical frame. See Jordan, *Relational-Cultural Therapy*, for further in response to these critiques. See also recent work by clinical psychologists recommending the use of RCT for exploring experiences of class

differences in therapy, Lauren Appio, Debbie-Ann Chambers, and Susan Mao, "Listening to the Voices of the Poor and Disrupting the Silence About Class Issues in Psychotherapy," *Journal of Clinical Psychology: In Session*, Vol. 69(2), 152–161, (2013). In a lesser known essay, Catherine Keller also briefly discusses the context of her shared perspective with myself that these early feminist works were misread in many ways, see "Seeking and Sucking: On Relation and Essence in Feminist Theology," in *Horizons in Feminist Theology: Identity, Tradition and Norms*, ed. Rebecca S. Chopp and S.G. Davaney (Minneapolis, MN: Fortress Press, 1997), 62. RCT remains a relatively young theoretical movement but one that I argue shows unexamined metaphoric promise for integration into lived religion studies of trauma ministries.
75. Ibid., 105.
76. Stephen Madigan, *Narrative Therapy* (American Psychological Association: Washington, D.C., 2011), 7.
77. Ibid., 21. As I discovered in my case study with the LDBPI, the power of storytelling and the giving of survivor testimony illustrated the usefulness of critical race theory as an additional social scientific theoretical tool for correlation to the prophetic empowerment of survivors, particularly in a community oppressed by race and class. See Lee Anne Bell, *Storytelling for Social Justice*.
78. Madigan, *Narrative Therapy*, 169.
79. Ibid., 164, a term derived from Antonio Gramsci and integrated into narrative therapy by Madigan as follows in definition: "Cultural hegemony is the dominance of one social group over another—for example, the ruling class over all other classes. The theory states that the ideas of the ruling class come to be viewed as the norm and are seen as universal ideologies that benefit everyone, though really only benefiting the ruling class."
80. Jordan, *Relational-Cultural Therapy*, 27, 49, 103.
81. See Maureen Walker, "How Relationships Help," in *How Connections Heal: Stories From Relational-Cultural Therapy*, edited by Maureen Walker and Wendy B. Rosen (New York: The Guilford Press, 2004).

82. See Madigan, *Narrative Therapy*, 163. See also Bell, *Storytelling for Social Justice* regarding critical race theory and narrative applications.
83. Miller, *Toward a New Psychology of Women*, 1.
84. Walker, "How Relationships Help," 7. While RCT theorists kept their language simple and accessible, the totality of the worldview shift should not be underestimated through oversimplification of their concepts, and the therapeutic practice requires a high level of relational engagement and mutual vulnerability, recognizing power differentials in the therapeutic relationship rather than distancing and objectification.
85. See an edited volume of essays by liberation health clinical workers, Dawn Belkin Martinez and Ann Fleck-Henderson, eds., *Social Justice in Clinical Practice: A Liberation Health Framework for Social Work* (New York: Routledge, 2014).
86. For more on the history and failure of radical social work in the United States context, see Michael Reisch and Janice Andrews, *The Road Not Taken: A History of Radical Social Work in the United States* (New York: Routledge, 2002).
87. Ibid., see chapter one for historical theoretical formation.
88. Ibid., 20.
89. Ibid, 22–24.
90. Ibid., 24–25.
91. See also Ammerman, *Sacred Stories, Spiritual Tribes*, 56–57, for her review of theories of practices where she adds another level of distinction to such practices as ones of "strategy" versus "resistance," depending on the experience of power and privilege versus powerlessness. For the context of the Peace Institute and the TVUUC as spiritual tribes experiencing violent trauma, practices of "recovery of the historical moment of change" would seem to correspond to practices and rituals of resistance. Yet one also could see powerful sociocultural institutions using ceremony and material art poetic practices as a strategy to reinforce stock stories as well.
92. For more on each of these pastoral care images, see Robert C. Dykstra's *Images of Pastoral Care: Classic Readings* (St. Louis, MO: Chalice Press, 2005).

93. See my tracking of the history of the creation of "prophetic pastoral care language" as this stemmed from a historical period of sociological and political turmoil in the 1960s and Gerkin and Graham's further development of this phrase, Walsh, *Prophetic Pastoral Care in the Aftermath of Trauma*. See also Gerkin, *Prophetic Pastoral Practice* and Larry Kent Graham, *Care of Persons, Care of Worlds: A Psychosystems Approach to Pastoral Care and Counseling* (Nashville, TN: Abingdon Press, 1992).
94. Jordan, *Relational-Cultural Therapy*, 25, 41, 103. The language of "zest" has particular associations with energy by definition.
95. Ibid., 76, 103.
96. Ibid., 5–7, 83–84, 108.
97. Ibid., 28, 102, RCT term created by Jean Baker Miller.
98. Lakoff and Johnson, *Philosophy in the Flesh*, 565.
99. Ibid., 567. In a volume edited by Heimbrock and Scholz, Andrea Bieler cites the work of Johnson and Lakoff in her own argument for embodied knowing: "It is in, with, and through our bodies that we come to know who God is: this is where we receive a felt-sense of the holy ... It is through the emerging felt-sense that embodied knowing finds ways through movement and langue to express what I have called the pragamtic consciousness," see Andrea Bieler, "Embodied Knowing: Understanding Religious Experience in Ritual," in *Religion: Immediate Experience and the Mediacy of Research - Interdisciplinary Studies, Concepts and Methodology of Empirical Research in Religion*, Hans-Günter Heimbrock and Christopher P. Scholtz, ed. (Germany: Vandenhoeck & Ruprecht, 2007), 52–53. See also an essay by Astrid Dinter on the importance of "nonverbal oriented religious forms such as ritual and meditation as helpful for a reconstruction of meaning," "Searching for a Construction of Meaning: Ritual and Meditation as Necessary Part of Pastoral Work," in *Lived Religion: Conceptual, Empirical and Practical-Theological Approaches, Essays in Honor of Hans-Günter Heimbrock*, Heinz Streib, Astrid Dinter, and Kerstin Söderblom, ed. (Boston: Brill, 2008), 223.

100. Kevin David Kendrick and Simon Robinson, "Spirituality: Its Relevance and Purpose for Clinical Nursing in a New Millennium." *Journal of Clinical Nursing* 2000; 9: 704.
101. Andrew Newberg, Eugene D'Aquili, and Vincent Rause, *Why God Won't Go Away: Brain Science and the Biology of Belief* (New York: Ballantine Books, 2001/2002).
102. See also Daniel Goleman, *Social Intelligence: The New Science of Human Relationships* (New York: Bantam Books, 2006) as well as his earlier work *Emotional Intelligence* (New York: Bantam Books, 1997). Other recent works that seek to integrate the fields of neurophysiology and human relationality include Louis Cozolino's *The Neuroscience of Human Relationships: Attachment and the Developing Brain* (New York: W.W. Norton & Company, 2006) as well as Daniel Siegel's *Pocket Guide to Interpersonal Neurobiology*.
103. See Richard C. Schwartz, *Introduction to the Internal Family Systems Model* (Oak Park, IL: Trailheads Publications, 2001).

5
Attending to "Survivors as Experts": Lessons Learned

The Power to Name and Claim One's Own Reality

During my time as a "lay community minister/social work clinician shaping as clergy," I worked for an urban ministry that expanded greatly in youth programs over the decades of my service. While there were significant grassroots components to the youth ministries at the beginning of their outreach to urban youth, including staff who had grown up and lived in the urban community all of their lives, gradually and over time more and more volunteers from outside of the community also began to participate. These particularly included white suburban and economically and educationally privileged volunteers, who also began to become heavily involved in the shape and direction of the youth programs. This had the advantage of bringing tremendous resources to the youth programs in their expansion, and also, at its best, provided opportunities for communities of people who typically were racially and economically segregated to interact and bond with and learn from each other. Yet I began to wonder if something wasn't beginning to be lost at the same time in this trade for resources as well as access to contact, interaction, and mutual support and learning.

I sat with particular discomfort one day in a meeting in which several prominent and well-meaning white volunteers were explaining to an African American staff person that their education equipped them with the knowledge and skills needed to, in essence, whip the afterschool program into shape in a matter of a year or two. When I suggested that people from the cultural background of the youth might indeed know more than those from outside the community and that they might be being overly ambitious, my sense was that this fell on deaf ears and that the group, again as good hearted and well intentioned as they were, carried a normative sense of cultural superiority rather than cultural humility by virtue of their education and class status.

In their fullest normative sense of the world, they truly experienced that they knew best what was needed and comfortably asserted their power, either directly or indirectly, to name and claim this reality. Tensions such as these rode high in the urban ministry as it continued to expand its program capacity across the borders of race, geography, culture, power, and privilege. How could such different worlds meet on common ground with ethical respect and cultural humility such that learning and growth was mutual for all involved, understanding that these different worlds needed each other if they were to become one shared world in both power and reality? Tensions and questions such as these in many different areas linger with me today, and a leveling of power toward those marginalized or oppressed in particular institutional or communal contexts impresses me as significant for moral address and mutual sustenance—perhaps even mutual salvation, in a broad metaphoric and interfaith sense, when spoken from my clergy identity.

Practices of Meaning-Making After Trauma: Normativity and Lived Experiences

One of the most striking lessons during the completion of both of my original case studies[1] was the importance of attending to the voices and lived experiences of survivors. As deeply as I had lived in the urban context for many years, and had become identified with the Unitarian Universalist

(UU) tradition for the equivalent amount of time, I realized in my studies that I continued to bring assumptions with my very questions and approaches at times—many of which I am sure I will continue to be learning even after the publication of this particular book. What assisted me in attending to at least some of these assumptions was that I had lived in and had a commitment to these communities—and I had already learned from and been transformed by them. There is a transformative bond of mutuality in such a commitment—it is a continuing moral bond that may falter at times but cannot be ignored, or it is ignored at one's own emotional moral risk.

When the Peace Institute in particular stressed the phrase "survivors as experts," I realized that this was compatible with a range of disciplinary approaches—from psychology to anthropology to theology and others—for attending to the innate wisdom apparent in the practices of individuals and communities struggling under experiences of marginalization or oppression. Power and privilege tend to blind would-be human service caregivers and researchers with a normative lens of "the taken for granted" language and dominant cultural way of being assumed to be superior—in the United States context, this means dominant cultural ways of being rooted in whiteness and economic privilege.[2] The full richness of the original case studies will remain in their original documentation for reference by those interested. In this chapter, I pull out some of the lessons I found most powerful between the two case studies when I strove to understand their meaning-making processes, language, and cultural worldviews on their own terms. Through honoring normativity and respect of "survivors as experts" in their lived experiences and sources and practices of religious and spiritual meaning-making, interdisciplinary explorers of lived religion may begin to see and attend to the significance of phenomena in new ways.

Meaning-Making Through Story, Poetic Images, and Poetic Material Art

Both case studies demonstrated the power of meaning-making for survivors through practices of telling their stories in narrative form or with poetic images and engaging in poetic material art expressions. These practices shaped differently for the particular context of each case study, yet commonalities in the power of these particular forms of practice were witnessed.

Key Lessons from the Peace Institute Case Study

"Transforming pain and anger into power and action" is the core principle of every aspect of the Peace Institute's spiritual practices, with an end goal of creating communal peacemakers. The initial drive, by the co-founding parents of Louis, to create and sustain an organized peace ministry itself involved a central power-filled act of meaning-making in the aftermath of their violent traumatic loss. Meaning-making through the use of story—the life story of their son Louis—was a core initial practice and has remained so, embodied in poetic material form throughout their various peace curriculums and peace principles, as well as in the very name of their agency and the ministry leaders' connection to their sense of mission. Louis is lifted up as one who dreamed of and worked toward peace and who had aspirations to be the first African American United States president.

The development of the *Peace Zone: A Program for Teaching Social Literacy* K-5[3] curriculums arose as a partnership of Deborah Prothrow-Stith (then at the Harvard School of Public Health) with the Lesson One Company[4] and the Peace Institute founders in response to these needs for trauma resolution and peace practices. Each curriculum in *Peace Zone* opens with the story of Louis D. Brown and his life values and dreams, as well as the trauma of his murder and its impact on his family and friends. The biography of Louis written for 4th and 5th graders in *Peace Zone* includes many anecdotal stories of his desire to become the first black president of the United States and how his parents reinforced this dream.

They would tell Louis that he was a "guiding light for peace" in choosing to work toward "helping teens stop acting violently and stop using guns" when he joined *Teens Against Gang Violence*, and he would say in response: "I want to teach people how to make peace and live peacefully."[5]

Feelings in response to this story, as well as other stories from Louis' life, are threaded throughout the curriculums' focus on the development of emotional literacy and advocacy skills, such as safety and commitments to peace. This focus is developed through various art activities, games, writing assignments, stories/literature, and community service projects.[6] The Peace Institute's holistic methodology for accomplishing inner peace and communal education and advocacy encompasses the arts, bodily awareness, and emotional and cognitive literacy and integration, *as well as* public action in the community on behalf of peace.

In narrative theory, liberation health, and relational-cultural terms, Louis' life story becomes an "alternative story"[7] that helps to break down some of the stereotypes, to "deconstruct the dominant worldview/dominant discourse"[8] as well as the "controlling images"[9] and meanings assigned to murdered young black men in urban America—images that they are always gang-involved and with implicit meanings conveyed that they are generally less than worthy recipients of society's embrace and support. Because Louis is lifted up as a young black man who specifically was working on gang peace issues at the time of his murder, even though he had not been involved in a gang, his life story becomes a potential imaginary and transformative bridge for those who might otherwise dichotomize the black community into good and bad people via the media or in other ways—a "sacred story" guiding hope for a "spiritual tribe."[10] As a "liberatory practice,"[11] as well as a "liberation health practice,"[12] these peace curriculums also provide young people with language and tools for imagining an alternative vision and transformative peacemaking possibilities for their lives and communities.

This use of Louis' life story also can be termed a type of religious social justice or prophetic pastoral care practice and considered as an example of lived religion in popular culture, one in which meaning-making and a vision of communal peace can happen outside formal religious contexts.[13] A "continuing living bond"[14] with their son is both expressed and transmitted to others through prophetic and poetic communal imagination, a material and embodied poetic communal imagination through the use of the arts and specifics of his life story in their various peace curriculums. These practices engaged through Louis' life story also then are exemplified in lifting up and transforming, through material art form and testimony, the life stories of others lost to homicide—a performative example of a type of religio/poetics or socio/poetics of material religion in this public testimony.

The shape of transformative action takes many forms in the Louis D. Brown Peace Institute (LDBPI)'s spiritual care practices, from the personal level to a more public level, and led several survivors to talk of an eventual transformative impact on their lives overall. On the personal level, the Peace Institute has long found value in the use of the arts for expression and transformation of internal pain and anger,[15] particularly now through their Holistic Healing Center. In the aftermath of trauma in an already oppressed community, participant responses support that the use of the arts to convey one's story and experiences has particular power as a spiritual and transformative care practice.

One ministry leader spoke of the need to find alternative ways for survivors to express traumatic experiences, ways that allowed the neurophysiological and embodied dimensions of healing from trauma to be unlocked. An example she gave, among others from their Holistic Healing Center, was sandplay (Fig. 5.1), in which miniature objects are used to create a symbolic and metaphoric yet somehow living world in the sand (including other earth elements such as fire and water when desired):[16]

> I think that it's so hard to talk about [the trauma] that you have to provide different ways to express . . . sand tray gives you alternative ways to kind of spark that, whatever's going on inside of you to bring it out and be processed. And it's like trauma and these things that are happening, like they can't always be explained in words. You have to feel it and one way that you can feel it is through art and music and literature and sand tray . . . when you play in the sand and just touch it, it opens up that part of your brain that the trauma affected. And . . . the process of playing in the sand and . . . creating [with] the figures . . . a world allows for the trauma to . . . kind of come to the front of the brain to be processed.

5 Attending to "Survivors as Experts": Lessons Learned

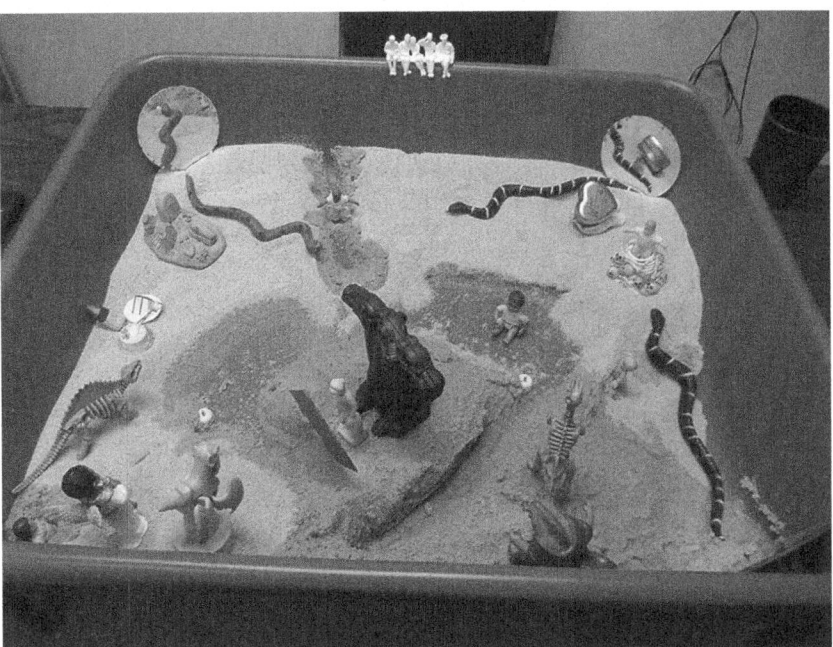

Fig. 5.1 *Peace Institute survivor's sandplay example.* Sandplay in process and performed by a participant following a visit with her son's murderer in jail. In the picture, the participant indicated she was reflecting on self through the figure placed by the mirror. She also indicated she was reflecting on reconciling the perpetrator's innocent child self with the horrific action in which he had later engaged through other figures in the tray. Small white figures perched on the edge of the tray were indicated to be spectators of the sandplay world

By arranging material objects in the sand tray, the survivor can give both theo/or religio/poetic and socio/poetic testimony to their metaphoric world of experiences and be empowered as a witness to the world they have created as well, often a witness in partnership with others. Such religio/poetic and socio/poetic testimony and witness is performative and embodied, functioning on a more *visceral* level of connection to the traumatic loss as material objects become touched by emotional energy—the world is *enlivened* and made sacred in the process. As survivors talk about the world they have created, another type of "sacred story" expressed through material art ensues. One survivor described her sand tray to me as demonstrating her ongoing and transformed connection to her deceased son and to her prophetic, eschatological, and sociological "hope" for "peace in the dark world," revealing also through her words, sighs, tears, tone of voice, and touch the multivalent and metaphoric use of material objects as religio/poetic living and performative symbols in the sand:

> This is my world in here. This is the barrier I want to keep between the outside world and my family. This is the angel watching over my whole world. That's my husband, me, and my younger son. This is the enemy I'm trying to bury. This is my [deceased son—*uses an eagle for the symbol*]. When I see eagles in the sky, I think of him. I keep him near our home. This is the love for my family that is sometimes questioned. The mirror is on hope—I have hope and I want my family to see that too. That was one of my [deceased son's] favorite toys—guarding our family between two worlds. This is the bright world. This is the dark world. I put peace in the dark world hoping for that. [*She rubs the stone lettered "peace."*] If there's peace in the dark world, it can't hurt my world.

Such artistic material expressions through sandplay, quilt, collage, or drawing (Fig. 5.2) often conveyed the survivor's continuing bond to their lost loved one, as well as the ambivalence of unresolved and often unresolvable pain of severed connections, including struggles with forgiveness. Through sandplay and other material artistic renderings, participants gave narrative, metaphoric, and sacred witness to the hidden depths of their personal and communal feelings of loss and separation (e.g. an enemy needing to buried, a love that is sometimes questioned, and a barrier dividing the world into brightness and darkness in the above). Yet they also testified in religio/poetic terms to their prophetic, eschatological, and sociological hopes for transformation, peace, and ongoing embodied and living spiritual connection (e.g. a mirror rests on hope, a peace stone is placed in the dark world, an angel and the son's favorite toy guard the world, and an eagle persists as a symbol of spiritual connection kept near the home).

Fig. 5.2 *Other art by Peace Institute survivors.* Part of a patchwork quilt from the "Express Yourself" project displayed on Peace Institute walls at the time of the original case study. This is one survivor's artistic rendering on forgiveness

The founding ministry leader also spoke of the power of using sandplay to give her control over what she would and would not choose to confront in relationship to her own trauma, a sense of control over her own testimony, witness, and movement through the play, a sense of control that she did not necessarily experience if she chose to engage in talk therapy. Through the play, she maintained control over the pace of her own transformative role in the living world she was creating, whether metaphorically in the moment with one particular sand tray, or also implying real-world prophetic social justice steps she might choose or not choose to take. Here she talks both of her preference for sandplay and her ambivalence as well:

> I don't hafta sit and talk to anybody if I don't want to, you know ... that I have the power ... to choose my course, that I have the power within me to select. Again, the landmines are there, my child was murdered, my husband left me, I can't change that no matter what I do. Do I wanna stay stuck in grief or do I wanna move through the next phase of the journey, and I think

that's what it does for me, it really—and sometimes I wanna stay stuck, I won't even do sandplay because if I do it, I'm gonna reveal somethin' that I know but I don't wanna go there right now, I wanna stay right here, and, again, that's a choice . . . .

Relational-cultural theory (RCT) would identify such ambivalence in moving toward and then away from the power of these forms of artistic embodied and poetic material expressions in the aftermath of trauma as the "central relational paradox," where there is always a desire for growth and connection, for relational life, but various hurts or traumatic violations can build up over time and result in powerful "strategies of survival and disconnection."[17] These serve as a paradoxical form of protection of relational life from further relational hurts, wounds, or traumatic violations. RCT would advise a clinician or prophetic pastoral care provider that such strategies needed to be honored with "radical respect"[18] for their wisdom given a particular context of relational experiences and images available to the survivor, hence also supporting the survivor's strategies of needing control in the aftermath of trauma. In the experience of participants, including the founding ministry leader, sandplay provided this type of needed control as a spiritual care practice, as did many of the artistic material mediums provided, though these types of comments came up most specifically in relation to sandplay.

As previously stressed, the Peace Institute ministry leaders recognized that a multitude of holistic spiritual, social justice, and clinical care practices are necessary in "transforming pain and anger into power and action," but the value of the various artistic peace practices they offered was spontaneously emphasized by several survivors. These included the above practices as well as the sibling group art activities, including the creation of "safe boxes" and "Peaceville" (a three-dimensional ideal city of peace).[19] The Peace Institute's emphasis on family participation and inclusion in these artistic peace practices was particularly valued. One survivor said: "I think it's really important when it's a family affected that you go at the same time. Even though we're not in the same room that we're both reachin' out or getting services around a loss because once again you don't really talk about your feelings." Another would report that her daughter had shut down initially in the aftermath of losing her sibling, but after working with the Peace Institute ministry leaders she gradually began to open up and "express herself." Thus, even for the youth, sacred story-making through spiritual, artistic, and poetic peace practices allowed them to "transform their pain and anger into power and action," as an additional survivor reported:

> ... I have a younger son, so he attends the youth program during the year when there's a particular project, like they did Peaceville ... and they did an appearance at the State House. So he spoke there, him and another youth that are involved at the Peace Institute ... He spoke to different people that were there about his project, and the news reporters that had questions for him ... He's now 13. And he's able to articulate what he feels and expresses himself, whether it's with his hands or verbally.

The Peace Institute's discovery over the years of the spiritual power of art activities and body work, including more recently sandplay and their latest use of yoga, massage, and acupuncture, dovetails with other research that supports the use of embodied modalities in trauma and "healing."[20] This can be witnessed in survivor use of home altars as well (Fig. 5.3). An appropriate cautionary note was raised by ministry leaders and survivors alike that these modalities are so powerful in their embodied experiences that one must in some sense be ready to work with what emotional and visionary energy is revealed in their use—this came out most strongly in relationship to material on sandplay, but the Peace Institute's use of massage, yoga, and acupuncture may prove similar once those modalities are more fully engaged. Above all else, participants stressed that survivors cannot be pushed into post-traumatic growth and the capacity for leadership—the pace of their own "healing process" must be fully in their own control for participation in particular spiritual and social justice practices.

Key Lessons from the UU Trauma Response Ministry Case Study

The need for survivor stories to be heard into being as sacred stories on a personal level, as well as on a religio/social level, in the aftermath of violent

Fig. 5.3 *Home altar example.* Artistic memorial practices continue in the privacy of home as well. A home altar can include pictures of the lost loved one, including t-shirts and memorial buttons, trophies, letters and certificates, etc. (picture used with parent permission)

trauma was stressed again and again as an important religious and spiritual practice for "healing." This also was considered by many to be an example of the type of ministry that Tennessee Valley Unitarian Universalist Church (TVUUC) congregants did for each other and that the Unitarian Universalist Trauma Response Ministry (UUTRM) leaders did for the congregation in the aftermath of the violent intrusion, "*a ministry of presence.*"[21] The former Unitarian Universalist Association (UUA) president interviewed spoke of meeting with the widow of Greg McKendry and her son in the church sanctuary and how she and her son had not yet had an opportunity to tell each other their respective stories of that day. The UUA president said: " ... they needed to tell each other the stories ... ministry can make a space for those stories [to] be told so that they don't go underground in a person and that's a part of healing—of being able to come to terms with your own story and share it so that it's not held in a secret, walled-off place in your spirit." This "ministry of presence," particularly the importance of the UUTRM's presence as fellow UUs, was mentioned by more than one TVUUC leader: "You need someone to receive your pain . . . if there's no one in that role, then it just stays locked up inside you." The TVUUC minister used a bodily metaphor of being a "*pastoral ear*," citing the Sufi mystic Rumi: "You are not God's mouthpiece. Try to be an ear."

For one UUTRM leader, ministry in the aftermath of trauma entailed holding the entire context of their ministry with human beings as connected in and through community, including in how "we understand God": " . . . it's really about grounding us in a *presence* [emphasis placed by UUTRM leader], that we as a team are a manifestation of. We're a manifestation of the history. We're a manifestation of God as we understand God. We're a manifestation of a movement. We're a manifestation of the values that we hold in common. We're a manifestation of beliefs that can make for fuller, healthier, deeper living." For another UUTRM leader, this ministry of presence and meaning-making represented a capacity to hold forth religious *hope* in the aftermath of violent trauma and in the face of evil: " . . . by our very presence . . . we hope our words and actions hold out the hope . . . that the evil thing, the horrible thing, the traumatic thing is not the last word. That's our ministry . . . to make sure goodness has the last word, that hope has the last word, that solidarity and community have the last word."

Threaded throughout the UUTRM and TVUUC leader interviews was a focus on relationships, narrative, and liberation from isolation—both for personal pastoral healing as well as for prophetic social justice witness and challenge. Narratives or stories of pain needing to be shared and received in relation and community, rather than staying "locked up" or "walled off" spiritually and psychologically, were spoken of, with a stress that *all* stories needed to be shared. These included even the "alternative stories"[22] of painful disconnection as these yielded insight into the religious *hope* for a renewal of relationship, of renewal of the sacred continuing bond of their spiritual tribe. Such sharings would be the first step toward relational reconnection. Through such prophetic pastoral care "listening"—the "pastoral ear"—would be found a "ministry of presence" and meaning-making and connection to a larger community of prophetic hope, both as UUs and on an ecumenical and interfaith basis.

Some stated that this ministry of presence also could be found through the humble comradeship of a peer, not necessarily and only through a trained professional.[23] For example, another UUTRM leader focused on the ministerial role being broadly conceived as encompassing both laity and clergy, drawing on a theological frame first offered within her faith tradition by the Unitarian ethicist James Luther Adams.[24] She used his words of "the prophethood and priesthood of all believers" to express her role as a "placeholder" in fostering a larger "connection to hope," one where the work alone "is sacred no matter what the tasks are":

> [T]ruthfully, as UUs with the prophethood and priesthood of all believers, we all have our ministries to do ordained or not . . . personally, it doesn't matter if I'm handing out a bottle of water or cleaning up a bathroom or sitting with someone as they're telling me their story . . . I'm a placeholder at that point. I'm a connection, because I hold my connection to my higher power, to the God of my understanding, and my place as that connection to hope and something bigger than wherever we are. That's what makes it a ministry . . . what we do is sacred, no matter what the tasks are.

This particular UUTRM leader also had been a leader in New York chaplaincy disaster relief and had worked at Ground Zero, though she had joined the UUTRM much later. She spoke to a certain kind of *"credibility"* coming more from life experiences, whether directly as a survivor or from being able to say that one had worked at Ground Zero as a first responder—credibility from some level of shared story in experiences. If the helper was identified as a first responder or survivor, then they embodied credibility and hope and the capacity to *normalize* the trauma survivor's ability to "make it through," as in "We're gonna be OK . . . New York's here." This UUTRM leader also found that the small spontaneously created and peer-led groups in the TVUUC's fellowship hall worked best as debriefings in the aftermath of the shooting. Peers were able to "normalize" their experiences through shared credibility as experts from having lived in through the violent trauma together first

5 Attending to "Survivors as Experts": Lessons Learned

hand, with a UUTRM leader interacting only to highlight and reaffirm their sharings at crucial points.

All UUA institutional supporters saw the fundamental role of trauma ministry to lie in assisting with meaning-making and supporting survivors to find "their own sources of resilience," as well as in helping them to "connect to something larger than themselves, something that can guide their life and provide some solace to them in a different way." At least one UUA institutional supporter also stressed the additional importance of training, however, to provide *credibility* as professional ministers and pastoral care providers. While assisting in the task of meaning-making was one significant component, an equally important component was viewed to be UUTRM leaders' grounding in their religious tradition and UU theology with specific professional ministerial training. This was viewed as important for enabling them to do a different professional care task than social workers, medical professionals, or other professional laity who might work in the aftermath of trauma—one that encompassed an ability to assist with the spiritual aftermath of trauma.

For some TVUUC leaders, however, a sense of disconnection, confusion, disappointment, and disruption of *credibility* also arose when the conception, expectation, and experiences of a "ministry of presence" by the UU Trauma Response team did not conform to needs or preexisting ideas. For example, a TVUUC leader spoke of his disappointment in overhearing a UUTRM representative[25] speak of being "ghostbusters" more than once in a boastful manner. He developed a perception that this representative was arrogant, which tended to generalize to the UUTRM as a whole for him and was at odds with his perception of a ministry of presence that entailed humility with a pastoral image of "servanthood" rather than separateness or presumed professional superiority:

> [T]hey were way too self-aware and not enough of what my old Bible professor would have called the sufferings, or not enough servanthood there, not enough humility there ... I do know that I shied away because that woman said that more than once. And it was sort of said in a joking haha manner, "We're the Ghostbusters." And one doesn't like to think of one's self as the phenomenon even though one is. It's a servant, which I would see them as. Their role is not to lead us through, but to service as we go

through. And a servant doesn't call attention to his separateness from what's going on.

Such sharings demonstrated the potential for different expectations and relational images of religious care roles to exist in the aftermath of trauma. Different expectations and images then can result in "acute disconnection"[26] in that moment with the religious or spiritual provider. However, these painful moments did not necessarily result in chronic or traumatic disconnection since relational resilience and movement also were demonstrated in the very drive to share these alternative stories with the researcher when given the opportunity.[27] Rather than repressing such stories in the interview process, or choosing to separate from the TVUUC in the immediate aftermath of the trauma, these church leaders continued to hope for reconciliation and renewal of their religious connections, their spiritual tribe, through the act of sharing these painful stories and using my identity as a fellow UU and researcher in this case study as a "pastoral ear." Relational "authenticity"[28] in sharing stories and creating religious meaning was valued more highly, and this can be a significant learning and point of awareness for religious care providers, a learning about the power of meaning-making through story that was stressed also by the UUTRM leader and ongoing consultant in the aftermath of the TVUUC shooting.

Troubling the Language of "Healing" and "Wholeness" for Survivors

Key Lessons from the Peace Institute Case Study

As I sought to explore the care practices Peace Institute participants found helpful, I assumed that the word "healing" would be a noncontroversial equivalent to the word "helpful" in my questions.[29] While I also intended to explore what "healing" meant to participants, the use of the word "healing" triggered such a range of reactions from study participants that a pause for more careful thematic attention was signaled. As I listened carefully to survivor responses as expert, their lived experiences of conflicted relationship to this word as a normative reference point for pastoral and clinical care practices began to make more sense. Some participants readily accepted the use of the term without a need to qualify, including most of the Peace Institute ministry leaders and institutional supporters, yet it was viewed as problematic or needing to be rejected as adequate language by some survivors, as well as by the institutional supporter who served as a mental health clinician with survivors. The founding ministry leader herself recognized why the word and concept can be challenging and ambivalent in the aftermath of trauma: "*Yeah* healing means more trauma *[laughter]* because you've got to go through some *crap* to get to that point, so healing is traumatic."

The mental health clinician interviewed as an institutional supporter struggled with words as she expressed the difficulty in finding an alternative language to "healing" for survivors of homicide, recognizing that this word tended to imply a closure not experienced by survivors in practice. She suggested that "movement" might be a better alternative for the care provider to use, a word that doesn't challenge the survivor's right to name, and thereby own, an experience they would rather have never had:

> I think language is complicated and ... you can't assume that you're using them in the same way or that the concept is the same and I think "healing," that word, as with some other words to survivors, suggests ... that there will be an ending to this experience of loss. That there will be a time at which you're over it ... how do you participate in life again once you've gotten through to surviving, how do you participate again in a way that maybe you can imagine, at some point, meaning and purpose ... It suggests movement. We talk a lot about movement, movement, so that things can shift, they can change ... it *[laughter]* takes more—more language, more words than one to sort of get at what the person might be thinking or talking about or contemplating and what we might be doing with them ... and "movement" is a word that comes up a lot because ... that doesn't challenge what belongs to them. As much as they don't want the experience, it's theirs.

For the survivors interviewed, words such as "process," "cope," and "being able to function" and "get up," as well as continued daily movement despite the pain, came up most frequently, including an outright rejection of the possibility of "healing" by some. One survivor called it an "open wound" and that she needed to keep moving or risk being attacked:

> I don't think that you ever heal... Am I healed? No. Just trying to... put one foot in front of the other or just goin' to work... I just feel like it's an open wound... I think that you learn ways of copin'. I think that just tryin' to maintain... it feels like runnin', just stayin' busy... just like the minute you stay still you're attacked by it... Like I just feel like as long as I stand up and can keep my feet movin' I'll be able to function and make it through the day. But I don't feel it as healin', I don't, I just get up.

Another survivor said that she had learned to look at "healing" differently, as an "ongoing journey," or "a big circle," and—in language that resonated with Internal Family Systems (IFS) use of multiplicity and systems theory[30] and "parts"—having enough other "pieces" in place to heal some of the "1,000,001 pieces wounded." She comes to know she will no longer "shatter," though she might "lose pieces" at times and need to "replace them":

> It's huge. I don't know. It's so many different ways you can look at it, but for me I guess one is just to be able to get up and function... I think because healing is so broad, I think you work on little pieces at a time, of yourself. It's not like one straight thing... Something may happen, an experience may happen that may contribute to help heal a certain part of what's wounded inside you, because I feel like I have 1,000,001 pieces wounded inside of me, and today I might feel like I'm okay in this area, and this process has helped me... Something else might come up, and I might forget about that process that I did... because now this over here has... overshadowed what I felt over here, but you don't totally forget about that, and so sometimes you have to reach back into what you've already have to help you work on the next piece, but I think healing is an ongoing journey ... it's just a big circle, and you just continually keep going. It's like endless, but you do get to a *place*... where you're not gonna shatter. You might lose a little piece, but you're not gonna shatter... I just lose pieces and try to replace them.

For the Peace Institute ministry leaders, there was use of a similar metaphor, and again resonance with IFS use of multiplicity and systems theory as applied outward, in the recognition that many different "pieces" are needed for a "kaleidoscope" of practices of "healing" by survivor families, "one size does not fit all," per the founding ministry leader:

> [I]t's not this one-size-fits-all, you know ... healing from trauma is like lookin' in ... kaleidoscopes ... It's not the same thing, you know? Many different people can look inside that kaleidoscope and see something completely different ... bein' able to heal from trauma, there're a lotta different little pieces that we must provide to families and I think that's one of the things that has helped me ....

Participant remarks around the language of "healing," "movement," "wounded pieces," and "kaleidoscope" were particularly striking. Though it became a problematic word in my questions to participants, I did not have a pre-association to the term "healing" that it meant closure rather than an ongoing process, particularly when one has experienced the loss of a child to homicide. However, it was clear that to some survivors, as well as the professional mental health clinician interviewed, the word "healing" can have the metaphoric association of expected closure when used by a care provider in practice—or that it signaled "dominant worldview discourse" from a liberation health perspective.[31] As Hertz, Prothrow-Stith, and Chery indicated, there is no "post" to the homicide of a family member—there is no moving beyond or over.[32]

The language of being in "wounded pieces" and needing a "kaleidoscope" of different "pieces" in the "healing process" also has resonance with the primary cognitive metaphor used by Ronnie Janoff-Bulman in her book on trauma, *Shattered Assumptions*, though the "shattering" expressed by survivors extended along bodily and emotional levels beyond purely the cognitive. This form of "shattering" resulted in an "endless ongoing circle" of losing and replacing wounded pieces. The founding ministry leader reached for the metaphor of a "kaleidoscope" to describe their pastoral, clinical, and spiritual care practices. A kaleidoscope image also is a circular one, constantly shifting and elusive—pieces move and disappear and often reconnect to form in new ways with new images, but still with some familiarity and recognition and still held by one embodied container. Through movement, the lost piece comes to be seen in a new image and form.

The kaleidoscopic and "holistic" nature of "healing" and practices in the aftermath of trauma repeatedly were stressed by the ministry leaders, as one said: "Yeah, healing's just like a lifelong process and it's not any one thing that's gonna help, it's a holistic thing: physically, mentally, spiritually." Connecting and helping survivor families get what they need "in real time" in the immediate crisis period, and on a *practical and logistical* level, can be the first step in providing effective clinical, pastoral, and spiritual care and affirmation, this as well as empathically *normalizing* the full range of their feelings and responses, as another ministry leader stressed:

> ... the more you can contain the immediate crisis and trauma event, the better. And the way that you can do that is like making sure people know step by step what's gonna happen so that there's no like mystery. They know exactly where they can go to get whatever it is that they need. They know who's in place to help them, they know what their rights are, and they know that there's somebody that's gonna be there to help them exercise their rights. Validating them so they don't feel like they're crazy for whatever it is that is on their mind because half the time it's pretty similar for most people and unless you experienced it then you might think it's crazy.

Most specifically, ministry leaders associated "healing" with "*regaining control*" in one's daily life, as another stated: " ... being aware of how the trauma is affecting you on a day to day, physically, mentally, emotionally ... noticing that you don't eat or you eat too much, [then] how are you gonna take steps to kind of control that? So I think healing is really regaining control." This regaining of control requires a holistic range of practices—from assisting with practical logistic details such as raising funds for a burial to providing emotional validation of and normalizing their status as "peculiar people" (adults as well as children) to connecting with others and engaging in healthy body and spiritual self-care practices.

Body practices, such as breathing techniques, emphasized in the LDBPI peace curriculums also now are extended through yoga, massage, and

5 Attending to "Survivors as Experts": Lessons Learned

acupuncture in their survivor outreach Holistic Healing Center as well. The ministry leader who introduced bodywork to the Peace Institute spoke about the importance of having a variety of "holistic health options" because "some individuals did not respond to traditional talk therapy as others may." She particularly stressed that it was important to offer survivors of color in her community alternative forms and paths of "healing," this in light of their spiritual reliance often and solely on God:

> Sometimes with a lot of survivors, in particular survivors of color, it's like we have two options; we go to God or we just deal with it in our way which may be unhealthy or you just, "Okay, that's what we need to do. We're resilient people. We're just gonna bounce back or life goes on." You're dealing with these inner struggles. So this leaves two things that happen. It's not to say oh you don't bring it to God but sometimes we need some additional support. So taking care of yourself in this way as another way to take care of yourself I think is important to have and ... know that it's a healing option ... Then the connection between massage and psychotherapy and that there's been a lot of good research in terms of that connection of bringing those two different modalities together to kind of help people who are suffering from some type of traumatic experience.

Establishing peace in spirit *and* body was seen as key to working toward a fuller embodied communal peace for survivors of color living in an oppressed community.

Finally, for at least one institutional supporter of the Peace Institute, the connection the Peace Institute makes between personal "healing" and the impact of oppression, their stress on the *prophetic social justice change* of larger institutions, was seen as one of the most valuable aspects of the Peace Institute's kaleidoscopic or holistic embodied approach to "healing" in the aftermath of trauma. Through such prophetic pastoral care and social justice practices, and consistent with a liberation health approach as well, "blaming the victim" for what are actually societal problems is avoided:

> [M]ost of the folks that I am aware of that the Peace Institute works with are ... oppressed. Their social conditions make the likelihood of this kinda thing higher than if they were living in a different situation ... I think if

those who are historically excluded understand that that's a *social* issue and not a personal fault or a fluke, then we will be able to better advocate for our own social and physical and mental health ... [because otherwise] they could blame the victim. They could blame themselves and/or their family or community, or ... they could become depressed and hopeless because they could say there's no way out. It helps instill hope and *power* as opposed to just be depressed and giving up.

However, ministry leaders and survivors also were aware that transformation of their pain and anger into power and action on such a societal level was a delicate process that often required pacing and an emphasis on the survivor's own control over the process. Clinical and pastoral care providers, as well as social and public health policy makers, seeking to implement any of these practices would do well to heed those cautions.[33] Survivors need ample time to foster peace within first before they can be expected to foster peace in a larger community. When successfully engaged through such initial pastoral practices for internal transformation of pain and anger, however, survivors were then positioned to enter the public square in testimony with power and action, such as the young people mentioned in the display of their "Peaceville" at the local State House or survivor families participating in the annual Mothers' Day Walk for Peace.

Overall, participant responses led me to ask if the language of "healing" could be reclaimed for survivors of family homicide or if it needed to be abandoned in psychosocial scientific literature, as well as religious care practices, and new metaphors developed and utilized, such as "movement" and a "kaleidoscope" of holistic care practices. As has been recognized, there is a certain "unsayability"[34] to the experience of trauma, one in which "more language," per the mental health clinician, is needed. When validated for the right to name their own experiences as experts by a care provider, embodied metaphors are pushed and reshaped by survivors such that "fracturing" and "movement" appear to be emphasized over stability and solidity, as well as the sheer strength of will to "get up," "cope," and continue to "function" despite the "open wound," despite losing and needing to replace the "pieces." It is clear that there is more theoretical and metaphorical work and research needed to encompass the lived experiences of these particular survivors of family homicide living in already oppressed communities. When one contemplates this challenge across cultures and beyond the United States context, the call to further qualitative research is magnified.

Key Lessons from the UU Trauma Response Ministry Case Study

The impact from this violent trauma also left TVUUC leaders struggling with definitive content for their own ideas of personal and communal healing in the aftermath, though without overt rejection of the language of "healing." Hesitant language of "I guess" or "kinda" often popped up in survivor descriptions of personal healing as their thoughts roamed over different dimensions of experiences and practices the word "healing" might call forth for them. These included getting back to some sense of *normalcy*, such as bodily normalcy or normalcy in the expectation of safety, as a TVUUC leader present that morning would say of the success of various contemplative and body practices in which she had engaged:

> Well, for a long time I, like everyone else, had a lot of jumpiness. And I literally thought I would never be able to sit in that sanctuary again without watching the door constantly. And I find it amazing now that that's totally gone cause it seemed so strong at the time. Like I thought I was gonna jump out of my skin if anybody opened that door. And so there was that kinda healing just in terms of not being so hypervigilant all the time.

Sometimes "normalcy" entailed not only a "getting back to" but also an incorporation of the traumatic event into a new and more positive sense of self, a form of post-traumatic growth. One TVUUC leader spoke of being troubled by the fact that she froze under fire instead of immediately fleeing for her life. She later processed this with a chaplain soldier at a Veterans Affairs (VA) hospital where she also was serving as a chaplain, a career shift after the shooting. She took relief in understanding that soldiers also initially freeze but are trained repeatedly to get up and move despite gunfire. Ultimately, she spoke of the shooting event as "a blessing" that increased her capacities for empathy, relating her posttraumatic growth also to the pastoral care image of the "wounded healer": "I later considered it a great gift ... that I've had this experience ... assimilating that into your reality base of possibilities ... for ministry the more knowledge of things that can happen, the better able you are to help others, the wounded healer thing ... So I felt blessed by the event in an odd way ... Not that I would want it to happen again, could have done without it [*ironic laughter*]." For her, expanded knowledge yielded post-traumatic growth as a pastoral care provider and greater capacity for future control and *efficacy*.

Personal "healing" as associated with practices that allowed for an affirmation of skills or having something to contribute also came from having *a leadership role* to play in the aftermath, which each of the TVUUC leaders interviewed did have. Such a relational role in turn lessened some of the impact of the trauma by allowing control and influence to be exerted through embodied action—again, a form of achieving efficacy in relational connection. For example, though others also spoke to the importance of having a role to play, a TVUUC leader who became heavily involved in media representation as a volunteer felt affirmed in being able to offer his skills in helping in the aftermath: " ... that was such a profound affirmation of who I was that I never expected. I mean the work I did was a profound affirmation for me ... So in that sense of the word, healing wasn't an issue because I had been reached down and touched with the ability to help in ways that I could never have envisioned." However, for some it also was true that laying down the burden of a leadership carried for a long period had a stronger association with the possibility of "healing" and, again, returning to normalcy, as it did for one of the TVUUC board president leaders interviewed: "Getting' back to normal ... like, not being intruded upon ... not being pulled into other responsibilities, and not having that role anymore, basically, would be healing for me."

UUTRM leaders, in contrast to the TVUUC leaders interviewed, often had more elaborated conceptions of the meaning of personal healing in the aftermath of trauma as a guide for their pastoral care practices. One said that personal healing was "the ability to retain or to attain some sense of closure, strength, self-sufficiency, and regaining personal power."

Another would say: "healing is figuring out a way . . . of putting this event in context with your life . . . so that you can go on without being disabled by it . . . ." It also was seen as a return to "functionality," or as one UUA institutional supporter gruffly put it, "[helping people to] kinda regain their sea legs and find their strengths." This focus on effective *pastoral* care as specifically restoring embodied personal *functionality and efficacy* was a common theme among the UUA institutional supporters interviewed in their understanding of "healing" in the aftermath of trauma. UUTRM leaders shared a similar focus on prioritizing *personal* pastoral healing in their practices by providing restoration to a sense of efficacy and control for survivors. However, this pastoral emphasis was *not* disconnected from UUTRM leaders' sense of connection to their larger *prophetic* and communal mission of providing a sense of "hope amidst the chaos" as a liberal religious presence.

This return to strength and functionality, as well as the possibility of post-traumatic growth, also was recognized to be a nuanced and complicated process of *integration* in religious or clinical care, as per a UUTRM leader:

> I am not one who believes that one gets over something. I'm one that believes that we all learn how to integrate difficult experiences into our lives so that over time, they don't require as much energy and attention that we might give to them in their most acute phases. And so healing, for me, is learning how to integrate difficult experiences into one's life in a way that does not impede their health and growth but may, in fact, assist in their health and growth.

Another UUTRM leader reflected that personal functionality could entail a sense of wholeness that was different but still possible in the aftermath of trauma. Here it also is intriguing to see the use of the language of "whole" and "part" in relationship to IFS use of multiplicity and systems theory and "parts." "I don't think people are the same after trauma. But I think that they can be whole. I think that they can incorporate and weave into their lives the loss, that it becomes part of the fabric of who they are. So by then the very nature of that, they're no longer the same. But that doesn't mean that they're so fractured that they can't function." She noted that human nature is fundamentally resilient: "... healing is absolutely possible, because we're resilient. We were created miraculously ... And most people bounce back ... really without much of our help ... and I think that's actually good news ... that most people do not need acute spiritual or mental health care, and they will find whatever healing they get to."[35]

This same UUTRM leader, who was the African American member interviewed and who had worked on many of the UUTRM responses to homicide, spoke more cautiously of "healing" in the aftermath of the murder of a family member, however, paralleling the results from the Peace Institute case study:

> It's harder and harder to make that argument, the closer the circle gets, by the time you're the mother or the daughter or the son of someone who's been murdered, you know that the fabric of their lives is forever changed ... there's always gonna be a hole. But what you try to help people believe is that they'll be able to live, and that their life will mean something, and they'll even be happy again someday. It just won't be the same way.

Nonetheless, turning as did Peace Institute survivors to the language of "pieces," she continued to argue that personal healing was: "Regaining ... after traumatic loss, a new sense of wholeness. And sometimes I think it can be wholeness with pieces missing, that there's still wholeness with pieces missing, and that's what healing has to mean after traumatic loss." Having a hole or pieces missing in the aftermath of trauma was not necessarily a permanent barrier to cultivating a sense of resiliency, hope, and wholeness in her experience of healing and religious or clinical care practices.

Additionally, it was clear that the UUA institutional supporters and UUTRM leaders interviewed were very aware of the potential for burnout by clergy and of the need for clergy to have long-term support and strategies of spiritual self-care for healing.[36] Fewer spontaneous comments arose expressing an understanding of the long-term impact and need for support and healing for church staff and volunteer leaders, except by two UUTRM leaders and the two UU District Executives interviewed, the District Executives more often being involved in the provision of such long-term assistance. The District Executive for the TVUUC, given longer-term familiarity, also was more likely to understand the internal leadership stress dynamics and governance struggles of the TVUUC. Considering the impact of stress and burnout on several of the TVUUC leaders interviewed also yielded insight into this researcher's unexpected experience of having the pastoral and clinical care dimensions of her ethnographic listening presence drawn out at times, her own capacity to provide a "pastoral ear." These particular TVUUC leaders both needed additional pastoral care in the opportunity to share their stories and experiences and also sought to use their access to power through an interview process *prophetically* as a means of *speaking back* their lived experiences in providing recorded and material testimony and learning to others, including the UUTRM. My sense that my research project was providing some added level of "healing" for a few of these participants was confirmed in later emails sent to me. This becomes thematically important phenomenological information for researchers who cross borders and carry different identities into the research—how are the relationships forged in the research shaping what happens as well? Does this make the phenomenon released, so to speak, less valid or objective or is objectivity found in the naming of the character of the relationship?

Claiming Survivor Power Through Communal Unity and Public Testimony

Key Lessons from the Peace Institute Case Study

When the pastoral and the prophetic in religious terms, or the micro and the macro in sociological terms, were successfully linked through a survivor's participation in Peace Institute practices from both their Holistic Healing Center and their Leadership Academy, then a survivor was positioned more effectively to be able to take public leadership, such as has been done by the "Peace Warriors" group. Specifically, when their material poetic-artistic and storied expressions were displayed or performed in a communal context they become prophetic and liberative in their ability to challenge the controlling images of the dominant culture and to educate and call a broader public to personal and political action. Within the broader community, for example, the Peace Institute is most well known for their specialized funeral orders of service (Fig. 5.4) as well as for the memorial buttons they produce. The funeral orders of service, designed by families with the support of Peace Institute ministry leaders, include the standard obituary and order of service, but also give families an opportunity to include multiple pictures of their loved one, as well as letters to or poetry about their loved one. This gives survivor families a larger opportunity to shape and control a unique narrative of their loved one's life, sometimes in counterpoint to stories and stereotypes that are being portrayed in the media—a sense of control important in trauma treatment and also a type of sacred story-making. The funeral orders of service become enlivened by the family's embodied participation in their construction in a process similar to the construction of sandplay worlds—and this enlivened construction then functions as a religio/poetic and socio/poetic testimonial to their lived experiences for a broader community to receive in witness.

A separate unique contribution to these funeral orders of service by the Peace Institute is the inclusion of information about trauma reactions, symptoms, recommendations, and resources. This is both for the sake of the family and also to give prophetic pastoral and psycho-educational guidance to the larger community (sometimes hundreds attend these funerals). Through this information, the gathered community is guided in how to continue to support the family after the funeral, including the importance of remembering special dates and anniversaries and watching for signs of unhealthy grief. Since these specialized funeral orders of service have been permeating these communities for over two decades now, this information and the language of trauma has been widely disseminated. The community also is engaged in learning the seven Principles of Peace[37] and an interfaith Peace Prayer by the Chinese philosopher Lao-Tse, interspersed with the Christian refrain "This I pray,"[38] at the end of the funeral order of service. Various recommended personal and communal spiritual and social justice actions to be taken are included also at the end, such as selecting a principle of peace to focus on as a spiritual practice and/or committing to turning schools and neighborhoods into Peace Zones free from violence.

JUSTICE

When the tragedy and trauma of homicide strikes, countless lives are affected. From siblings to parents, spouses, partners, grandparents, aunts, uncles, cousins, to coworkers, friends and neighbors, we all deal with loss differently. Shock, anger, revenge, self-blaming guilt, and shame; the flood of emotions we go through are seemingly endless. And only through love, support, guidance and compassion can we even begin to make sense of all the grief and pain. Many times when someone we care about is grieving we don't know how to act around them. We may unwittingly end up doing or saying the wrong things.

Here are some suggestions. While it may sound like simple common sense, this advice is coming directly from those of us who have been there, the survivors of homicide victims. It's important that all survivors have a supportive team around them and that they are connected to the proper resources. This is a community in need of specific and targeted intervention that starts with the death notification and goes far beyond the burial, and in some cases the trial.

Keep in touch: Do more than simply visit at the time of the funeral. Call or visit during the weeks and months ahead for these are the loneliest times. As other friends and family begin to go on with their normal routines, your calls and visits will become more valuable than you can possibly imagine.

Learn about loss and grief: This is a natural part of life. The more you know the better you are able to help.

Reading Resources For Adults
Talking With Children About Loss, Maria Trozi with Kathy Massimini
Azim's Bardo: A Father's Journey From Murder to Forgiveness Azim Khamisa
The Bible

Reading Resources For Teens
Fire In My heart, Ice In My Veins A Journal For Teens. By Enid Traisman
Straight Talk About Death for Teenagers: How to Cope with Losing Someone You Love. Grollman, E. A. (1993). Boston, MA: Beacon Press.
The Bible

Reading Resources For Children
After the Funeral;Jane Loretta Winsch, Pamela T. Keating (Illustrator)
Am I Still a Sister? Alicia M. Sims
The Children's Illustrated Bible- The Children's Encyclopedia of Bible Beliefs

9

Fig. 5.4 *Peace Institute funeral order of service, sample resource page.* Resources with recommendations and advice given to community attendees at the funeral so that they may help survivors better in the aftermath of the homicide

At the time of a funeral, the Peace Institute also is known for the creation of buttons with the loved one's picture on it and some wording from the family (sometimes wording related to a peace principle), which are then distributed at the family's discretion to family and friends.[39] One button also is retained for the Peace Institute's Traveling Memorial Button Project (Fig. 5.5), which is prominently displayed at major public events, such as their annual Mothers' Day Walk for Peace. Of the wider purpose of these buttons, the founding ministry leader strikingly drew on an embodied metaphor with the language of "touches" for connection when saying:

> I . . . wanted the larger community to see that violence touches all of us, you know, whether it's inner city, gang violence, domestic, sexual abuse, whatever it is, violence touches everybody, and I wanted the photos to be more than just a number, you know? I wanted people to see the faces are real, the names are real and the impact that it has on the community . . . I mean more

Fig. 5.5 *Traveling memorial button project.* The Traveling Memorial Button Project, seen here displayed at the Peace Institute's twentieth annual Mothers' Day Walk for Peace, is displayed at various events. The bottom reads "When Hands Reach Out in Friendship, Hearts Are Touched With Joy"

than the homicide statistics that they show in the inner city ... take off this myth that it's only gang related in a concentrated area ...

I regard these practices as clearly reflecting poetics in material form—whether termed material theo/poetics, religio/poetics, and/or socio/poetics. They also may be termed "sacred stories" in material form. From the funeral orders of service to the memorial buttons, each of these become powerful and energetically living material and artistic vehicles of prophetic testimony to, and then received in witness by, the larger community. They speak to the need to remember the dead and to construct a sacred poetic and visual narrative through material expression of the lives lived and lost but not gone or forgotten. A continuing bond of living energetic connection is initiated and performed in the testimony of love, conveyed through new material forms with hope for receipt in witness and commitment by a larger community on behalf of peace and justice (a realized eschatology in Christian language or a social justice vision in sociological language), and calling forth a life beyond mere statistics. Through these practices, the dead are marked as and transformed into powerful and still living motivating forces for resistance and prophetic transformative action in the community.

Rebecca S. Chopp writes on the theopoetics of story and testimony: "The telling of these stories is for life, for the mending of life, the healing of life, the ability of life to live and survive and thus conquer ... extremity ... If one is not authorized to live, then surviving is both resistance and hope. These testimonies are discourses of survival for hope and of hope for survival."[40] Lives are indeed lost in one embodied form; yet, they also live on in the public square through a performative testimony that is embodied as much via the material as the oral or literary. They live on in new artistic poetic and material shape through the narratives and pictures of the funeral orders of service, memorial buttons and t-shirts, and banner displays on the streets of Boston during the annual Mothers' Day Walk for Peace. They continue to resist and challenge prophetically the dominant culture's marginalization of lives lost to violence. As lived religion practices, they bear the sacred mark of embodied spiritual energy and an eschatological hope for peace, thus becoming fuel for constructive practical theologies of trauma as well as other religious conceptions of trauma as similar practices are researched and witnessed in other countries and contexts.

Survivor families as experts also took their testimony beyond the streets to the halls and social institutions of power that impacted their lives or purported to serve them. Most institutional supporters directly spoke of the Peace Institute as "unique," as "experts," and as a model of successful and effective collaboration, including in faith-based collaboration as well as in creating secular human service provider networks for serving survivors. The public health doctor interviewed as an institutional supporter said: " . . . there's so much we don't know and . . . survivors really haven't gotten the level of attention that is necessary . . . they still remain the experts at this point, and their stories and their experiences and how they've gotten better represent a starting point for this." She also would go on to say regarding religious institutions:

> I think that the churches and . . . the religious institutions and the funeral homes together should understand the expertise that the Peace Institute has, and together work toward creating protocols that allow for more fluid referrals, but also allow people to do what they do best and not do other things that need to be done but are better done by somebody else. And again, I think until that kind of innovative partnership explores the options, we won't have the best set of strategies for people.

A Peace Institute ministry leader supported that this would require a major cultural shift in awareness, a "mindset shift": " . . . it's really like a whole mindset shift in how to really respond to families impacted by violence. . .in order for institutions really to better serve people impacted by violence, I think that the policies and things in place should be driven *by* the people impacted."

The Leadership Academy is the most explicit example of the Peace Institute's practices in supporting, through training and advocacy, the post-traumatic growth of survivors and their recognition as "experts" and "Peace Warriors,"[41] whether teens or adults, in the larger community. The Leadership Academy educates and empowers survivors and allows the public to witness their often newfound confidence as experts, or as one ministry leader said: " . . . [it] is really good for personal healing because it kind of like flips the script, like survivors are now the experts. And sometimes people who've never felt like an expert in their life but now they are, they are an expert, and you have a program backing you up that you can refer to when you're trying to talk about your own expertise."

For example, one survivor appreciated that, through the Leadership Academy, the Peace Institute encouraged and allowed a fellow survivor, who did not have an advanced degree, to lead the sibling survivors group for a period of time. She argued that more than degrees, "experience was the best education"—that expertise in the ability to connect and help comes first and foremost from being seen to have survivor rather than textbook experience:

> I mean, I'm a firm believer in you can have all education in the world that you need, but sometimes experience is the best education, and dealing with the loss or grief through homicide, you can only educate through experience...if you've never gone through something so traumatic as such, you haven't a clue... one of the surviving mothers...actually had a hand in doing the leadership for the youth sibling survivors. And I thought that was awesome...Because those children know why this one mother is here...It really helped for them...it's better than having a child psychologist come...It's just *not* something that you learn about in a textbook.

This dovetails with the words of some members of the UUTRM's case study as well, though their UUA institutional supporters continued to prefer to see formal education in trauma treatment.

Some of this newfound confidence as experts can be traced to education provided to survivors through the Leadership Academy and the use of theory to understand their pain not as an individual problem of self-blame but as a communal problem demanding communal action. If trauma is pathologized as purely an individual intrapsychic problem, there is a neglect of the social relational context of trauma and the potential for transformative possibilities in the relationship of self to society.[42] The rejection of this individualization of trauma was a strong and consistent thread throughout survivor, ministry leader, and institutional supporter responses, which also is consistent with a liberation health model approach to treatment.

For example, survivors often spontaneously referenced the intersections of race, class, and gender, regardless of the specific question at hand, and these references often revolved around profound questions of "why?" in the aftermath of violent trauma. Their responses alternated between despair and anger—as one survivor painfully demanded: "*Why*, like *why* the African American male? Why did we go through the slavery? Just goin' back to like all of that, and why are these certain areas, like the drug infested and then the projects and why aren't African Americans more motivated ... ?" Survivors repeatedly questioned why their communities were targeted, particularly when such violence should be preventable—where were the sources of resistance? These questions became even sharper in tone when further sociological and institutional education, such as that provided by the Leadership Academy, brought deeper levels of insight and motivated ongoing learning by survivors. One illustration of the transformative impact this social change education brought in empowering and motivating survivors to testify as experts in the public square is found in a survivor's comments:

> I think the Leadership Academy is the most empowering tool that they have ... I've never been to college, didn't know nothing about social change, didn't really care about what was going on in the community as long as like the kids were okay ... and even though this unfortunate tragedy brought me to the Peace Institute, it has brought me to a place in my life where I thought I would never be. Like I said, I'm getting ready to graduate from college. The hunger that I have to wanna just try to make a difference in my community and find out what is needed and where do I fit in and where do I belong and how am I supposed to do this ... .

RCT would identify the practices of the Leadership Academy in empowering survivors as experts in such testimony to be exhibiting some of their core principles in the provision of "growth-fostering relationships" through "mutual empathy" and "mutual empowerment."[43] Such education provides resistance to a pattern of social stigmatization of survivors that can lead to "condemned isolation,"[44] to the pathologizing of the trauma as an intrapsychic problem, resulting in social shame and isolation, rather than as a relational problem attributable to and needing to be engaged by the larger community. Per Judith V. Jordan, "The growth that occurs is both affective and cognitive and leads to an enlarged sense of community . . . a feeling that one's vulnerability will not be taken advantage of or violated . . . people in any growth-fostering relationship are experiencing more aliveness, more clarity, and a greater sense of possibility and potential agency."[45]

IFS theory would note that these practices fostered confidence, courage, creativity, and connectedness for survivors in Self leadership.[46] One survivor spoke of the Peace Institute's spiritual focus as giving survivors the strength to become peacemakers in their communities: " . . . we're taking it back, and we're sharing it with our families, we're sharing it with our coworkers, we're sharing it with our . . . churches . . . we're creating a trail of . . . peacemakers." A ministry leader noted that faith and spirituality became unexpected prophetic components of the public testimonials of survivors, and that this was important to their pastoral healing as well because it was language coming directly from their community. I was struck by the use of the language of "a piece of themselves" to affirm the significance of survivor religious or spiritual parts and the resonance of this with IFS' language of "parts" and use of multiplicity and systems theory. She stated survivors felt confident in witnessing to the power of their relationship with God first and foremost rather than the authority of secular systems or programs:

> . . . the way that we talk about faith and spirituality on a public level in the circles that we talk about it in is sort of unheard of . . . especially when you're like talking to people either in government or like the health world or in academia too . . . I think it's more of a community minded approach. So I think when the community sees us doing it in those settings, it's healing because it's like that's how I feel. They can see themselves in the work. They can see themselves, a piece of themselves in it, and it's in a language that they know and that they drive, you know?

The public nature of the Peace Institute's focus on spirituality even prompted the institutional survivor who is the antiracism consultant to say of their annual Mothers' Day Walk for Peace that "It feels like church": "I think the march is spiritual . . . just that it's a time of the year when hundreds of people come to share that few hours together in a way that's an honoring of the dead and a call for life . . . for the survivors. I find it very moving. It feels like church. It's having a neighborhood witness." If these case studies had not used an interdisciplinary lived religion framework for studying these trauma ministries, some of these metaphors, analogies, and phenomenological data might have been missed in the significance of the Peace Institute's pastoral and public social justice and educational practices with survivors.

In an effort to bring expert survivor witness from the Peace Institute to the halls of government, a listening hearing was organized by the Boston City Council in 2010,[47] and survivors gave testimony on their experiences and needs to begin to use this as a basis for developing protocols among service providers. Reflecting the understanding of survivors as experts, the city councilor interviewed said: "I thought it important that these families be empowered, that government not speak at them, but work with them because as I often sort of define it, they have PhDs in suffering and they are authorities on violence, and we should be engaging them as stakeholders in the solutions to ensure that they're fully informed." Advocacy with police departments, district attorneys, employers, funeral homes, hospitals, and the media[48] were all discussed in this hearing and regarded throughout my interviews as important areas of needed education for social institutions regarding survivor struggles and their painful experiences. The Peace Institute's Leadership Academy often was cited as the means by which survivors gained support in navigating each of these systems and being affirmed in their sense of injustice when a system failed.

Two final areas of themes worth noting in survivor testimonies as experts in the public square were their expectations of the mental health profession as well as the church and other religious institutions. Ministry leaders and survivors both expressed feelings of ambiguity toward the professional mental health field, some having positive experiences but many experiencing the programs and activities of the Peace Institute as providing more "therapy" than traditional forms of "talk" therapy. Feeling "listened to" and having shared experiences of loss and connection were contrasted with experiences of therapists setting an "agenda" for the survivor, therapists who may not have had a baseline for a shared experience. As one survivor pointedly said:

I even said that to my therapist. I said, "I love you, and you're a great support to me, but the Peace Institute is doin' my therapy." ... at the Peace Institute it's about how I'm feeling about my loss, how do I get past this, is this normal, did this happen to you—just we *connect*. We connect because I'm talking to someone who may not know exactly how I'm feeling but have a idea of what I'm going through, not me just talking to you and you're like, "Mm-hm," just lookin' at me, and I'm saying to myself, "You don't even have a clue."

The founding ministry leader's advice to professional mental health clinicians, which has implications for religious care counselors as well, is to place oneself in a more humble, listening, and learning position with survivors—a position of being an ally to the survivor as the expert in their own needs:

> ... just ... stop tryin' to fix somebody. Just really don't if you're gonna work with survivors, don't go in with the notion that you're gonna fix "em that you know, really don't. *Really, really, really* don't ... Go with the attitude of sharing and learning, teaching and learning, hearing and speakin", giving people the opportunity, hear the fullness of what someone is sayin', you know? Don't go in "I'm-gonna-help-you", go in and ask them the question, "I am here, what can I do?" and go in bein' patient. This is not a one-two-three, this is not gonna be as pretty as your textbook.

And most particularly, the founding ministry leader would say, do not make a survivor "dependent" on you as the care provider so that when you are gone, they no longer know what to do. Instead, it remains vitally important to "transform pain and anger into power and action," into the survivor's own ability to work toward communal transformation and peace. There is resonance here with the liberation health model of treatment, as well as with the classic quote often circulated among activists and on social media by an indigenous Australian woman, Lila Watson: "If you have come here to help me, then you are wasting your time ... But if you have come because your liberation is bound up with mine, then let us work together."

Peace Institute ministry leaders also uniformly spoke out on the need for the church and clergy to be a counter role model to the typical conflicts and competition exhibited in the larger society, a need they felt the church often failed to meet. Ministry leaders experienced church leaders as participating in "infighting" and as having "turf issues" in a way that was similar to what caused "gang violence." In their experience, there was little sense of collaboration and more of a sense of competition for grants and money within the faith-based community. "... we're not acting as a peaceful people. To be violent is not just to be physically violent. You can be violent in a very silent way, and by omission we can be violent by not doin' certain things," one ministry leader would say. All providers, from the secular realm to the religious realm, were called upon to exhibit a deep sense of "cultural humility" in respecting survivors as experts in their own needs.[49]

Key Lessons from the UU Trauma Response Ministry Case Study

The immediacy of concrete communal support and denominational presence by the UUTRM and the larger UUA, as well as the Red Cross, were regarded as a key factor in increasing the TVUUC's overall capacity for a public religious response in the aftermath.[50] The overall speed of response and presence of UUTRM and UUA leaders was frequently cited by participants as helpful in organizing the many levels of response—from initial contact with the media to coordinating debriefing groups to developing a service the next night. The ongoing supportive presence of a UUTRM consultant throughout the first year and beyond, and the recognition of the congregation's proud survival on a national UUA level, including its connection to the establishment of a public social justice witness and religious ecumenical and interfaith campaign by UUs, "Standing on the Side of Love," also were cited as helpful, though more long-term and concrete support was viewed as needed in specific crucial areas.[51]

Despite this support in the first year, the need for ongoing support and the importance of ministering to lay leaders, who were overtaxed in the aftermath of the traumatic event, was repeatedly stressed by TVUUC leaders. More often, given their long-range needs, this concrete ministry

5 Attending to "Survivors as Experts": Lessons Learned 179

came through their UUA District Executive than the UUTRM. TVUUC leaders reiterated that it was important not to underestimate the sheer number of logistical issues in need of guidance in the aftermath of such a communal and ecclesial trauma—logistics that ranged from the need to clean the sanctuary professionally; to the hiring of part-time contractors; to the inpouring of cards and money that needed management and response; to the turnover of church leadership from stress, health needs, and physical exhaustion; to the infusion of visitors and prospective new members; etc.

The strain of roles, and expectations attached to those roles, was a poignant point of sharing by TVUUC leaders. Examples included the church administrator, who had been in the direct line of fire that morning, finding herself worrying as to whether or not she had paid the church's catastrophic insurance policy—and the incoming board president, who had shotgun pellets pass within five feet of him that morning, saying his bigger trauma "was the self-perceived responsibility to help people get through it, for the church and the congregation ... worrying about 500 people ... that was a daily impact on me for two years ... I started healing mostly when I quit bein' president."

Impressions varied, however, as to whether the UUTRM was there mainly to support the minister as the primary congregational leader or whether the UUTRM was at the TVUUC with a larger eye on supporting all of the church leadership and congregants in that initial week and beyond, and this role confusion led to mixed expectations and reception at points. Of the TVUUC leaders interviewed, only the minister had any prior awareness of the UUTRM and, of the five TVUUC leaders interviewed, only the TVUUC minister would have the most unqualified enthusiastic response to all of the UUTRM prophetic pastoral care services provided, paralleling the enthusiastic responses of the UUA institutional supporters interviewed as well.

Of the remaining four TVUUC leaders, all would praise many aspects of the UUTRM services, though there also would be specific critiques and recommendations they wanted to offer as well. Two in particular were stressed: (1) while the TVUUC leader who was board president at the time placed great value on the ongoing phone consultation services of the UUTRM, he also expressed frustration that they needed specific and ongoing long-term assistance in particular areas and had lacked guidance and warning about these needs from the UUTRM, requiring them to turn belatedly to their UUA District Executive for the majority of these emerging logistical pastoral care needs;[52] and (2) while all TVUUC leaders interviewed placed great value on the national UU response in supporting the TVUUC, including by the UUTRM, several also argued that there were nuances of culture, governance, relationships, and needs that could not be met by members of a national trauma team flying in and out over the course of a week, that communication breakdowns naturally occurred in the transitions of leadership, and that speed of response at points overwhelmed time and space to build adequate relationships and understand different needs, history, and cultures. These included differing needs for personal recognition as well as for personal spiritual care. In other words, the perceived designation of being considered the UUA's *official* trauma response ministry, even though the UUTRM had no such formal linkage and was volunteer in base, set relational expectations very high and rather naturally led to some level of disappointment or role confusion.

The most definitive statement on practices of communal healing in the aftermath of trauma came from the TVUUC minister, who testified to healing as "*being* a church." Indeed, the clearest emotional expressions, confession, and testimony of inspiration and sustenance among the TVUUC leaders came in describing, often with tears in their testimony, profound moments of connection to a sense of *a larger ecclesial community*, whether this was their church, the Knoxville ecumenical and interfaith community, or the UUA and a larger movement. A UUTRM leader said, using language of connection and energy, which resonates with RCT, though in this case dissipating negative traumatic energy: " . . . I think that one of the best ways to get over a traumatizing event is to start feeling like you're part of the human race again, so . . . any ritual that can get people connected and mitigate, send that energy out, dissipate that energy, is a positive thing and, for me, that's the biggest thing."

UUTRM leaders and UUA institutional supporters alike stressed *the importance of narrative in the communal healing process*—the telling of one's own personal story and the weaving of a story large enough to hold the *multiplicity* of these varying stories and experiences of violent trauma

5 Attending to "Survivors as Experts": Lessons Learned

in an ecclesial context. This case study finding also resonated with possible use of IFS' focus on multiplicity and systems theory for a broader range of congregational studies after trauma. The UUTRM leader who played an ongoing role consulting to TVUUC spoke about his focus on narrative in the healing process as helping survivors of trauma to hold the *"sacred ambiguity"* in these varying experiences—a practice of care that also might be seen to parallel IFS clinical theory stressing that no part in a system should be exiled, all parts need to be welcome. This UUTRM leader regarded this practice as his particular contribution to the overall pastoral care practices of the UUTRM and stated:

> [O]ne of the concepts that is sort of unique to *my* work . . . is a concept that I refer to as the spiritual discipline of sacred ambiguity in relationship to trauma . . . the way in which institutions craft a macro narrative of a traumatic situation can have a huge impact on whether or not people feel included or excluded from the institution and its memory of what happened, and can either aid or inhibit in the healing process of individuals in that institution over time . . . Ministers worth their salt that are in these situations understand that the spiritual discipline is to affirm everyone's experience and to figure out a way to not have to align oneself with a particular aspect of it in order to legitimize that aspect and inadvertently delegitimize every other one.

The TVUUC minister experienced this UUTRM consultant's advice as invaluable in constructing public sermons and rituals that encompassed a broad range of perspectives and possibilities into the ongoing TVUUC ecclesial narrative of the trauma. One other TVUUC leader did as well in understanding the need to bring newcomers relationally into the narrative of what had happened on July 27, 2008. His contribution would be the PowerPoint on the church's history that allowed newcomers to situate this violent event in a larger story of ongoing prophetic resistance by the church, again an example of what liberation health theory might call "recovering the historical memory of change." TVUUC leaders' understanding that there can be different experiences and truth claims in the aftermath of trauma appeared to be the source of grace granted in maintaining their relationships overall, maintaining their spiritual tribe, despite their differences in opinion regarding the media conflict.

"Being church" entailed not only holding stories of difference and supporting one another through stress and burnout. "Being church" also often meant being willing to open the doors to religious strangers, a fully embodied welcome that included those previously stereotyped as potentially hostile to UUs. One UUTRM leader observed a small conservative Christian home church coming in as volunteers to scrub the bathrooms for the TVUUC. She said, using now significant and familiar language of pieces and wholeness again, as well as a reference to the language of "self image" as part of "a bigger community":

> ... *number one*, to see people who probably never heard of the UU before show up for this, unbelievable. *Unbelievable* in terms of making something whole with the pieces missing ... there's always a suspicion of, "Oh, the evangelicals hate us and the Christians think we're this." And ... this little group that nobody knows, well, they know who you are now. And I think by showing up, appreciating, not keeping people out, but finding ways to include, probably helped the healing—some self image healing ... for UUs, as well as getting them into a bigger healing of a bigger community.

Another UUTRM leader said: "I was just floored. I'd never seen that much interfaith amenity. I mean people showed up who couldn't be more antithetical to what UU's believe." The *unexpected* in such experiences was stressed again and again, as well as the connection to a larger relational experience that was countercultural to their existing relational image, hence a discrepant relational experience and image.

The language of "wholeness" and "pieces" also emerged here through the experiences of a different UUTRM leader as an expansion beyond a *personal* pastoral image of healing and into one that was more of an interconnected system, resonating with IFS understandings. This relational image now encompassed a larger *ecclesial* image of ecumenical and interfaith relationships and restoration, at least temporarily, for "wholeness." The unexpectedness of the broken ecclesial faith "pieces" coming forward as a larger experiential and relational "whole" in the aftermath of the trauma surprised and overwhelmed all TVUUC leaders interviewed, and many of the UUTRM leaders on site as well, to the point of tears or awestruck tones of voice in the interviews. This again took on confessional and testimonial tones of "something more" in these moments that are more consistent with findings in lived religion and sacred story and religio/poetic meaning-making experiences and practices. This relational movement toward greater embodied and transformative connection was repeatedly named and experienced as "love" by many TVUUC and UUTRM leaders alike, a love that was to be welcomed, honored, respected, and reaffirmed as the meaning of "being church."

Notes

1. For the most detailed examination of the original case studies, see again Michelle A. Walsh, *Prophetic Pastoral Care in the Aftermath of Trauma*.
2. Critical race theory, inclusive of critical whiteness studies, provides helpful theoretical tools for understanding the dominance of white supremacy culture in the United States context. See Richard Delgado and Jean Stefancic. *Critical Race Theory: An Introduction*, 2nd edition (New York: New York University Press, 2012) as well as Kimberlé Crenshaw, Neil Gotanda, Gary Peller, and Kendall Thomas, eds., *Critical Race Theory: The Key Writings That Formed the Movement* (New York: The New Press, 1995).
3. For the purposes of this book, only the teacher's guide for grades 4 and 5 is referenced in the bibliography, as a sample of one among many LDBPI peace curriculums. See Deborah Prothrow-Stith, et al., *Peace Zone*.
4. More information about Lesson One can be found at their website: http://lessonone.org (accessed August 27, 2013).
5. Prothrow-Stith, et al., *Peace Zone*, 23–26.
6. The Peace Institute also recently completed and published a new workbook for children, *Always in My Heart: A Workbook for Grieving Children* (internal 2011 publication of the Louis D. Brown Peace Institute), which again, similar to their other peace curriculums, is based on an emotional literacy approach with a focus on art and

writing activities, though this workbook is structured particularly around the use of the seven Principles of Peace in addition to the story of Louis D. Brown. It also should be noted that the drawings used throughout the Peace Zone curriculums reflect the ethnic diversity of the Boston student body as the curriculums' primary target audience.
7. Madigan, *Narrative Therapy*, 33–36, 66–70, 163.
8. See concepts discussed in the previous chapter as part of a clinical social work liberation health approach. Martinez and Fleck-Henderson, *Social Justice in Clinical Practice*.
9. Jordan, *Relational-Cultural Therapy*, 28–31, 102–103.
10. See again Ammerman, *Sacred Stories, Spiritual Tribes*.
11. hooks, *Teaching to Transgress*.
12. Martinez and Fleck-Henderson, *Social Justice in Clinical Practice*.
13. Transforming a tragic loss—whether by violence or in other ways—into foundations or institutions named after the person lost can be observed widely in society and also might be understood and labeled as a form of protest, liberation, or prophetic pastoral care practice when the socially transformative intent is made explicit in their mission. I also have suggested that these might be examples of "spiritual tribes" formed around "sacred stories" and exhibiting post-traumatic growth in doing so.
14. Klass, Silverman, and Nickman, *Continuing Bonds*.
15. See for example their use of art and literature activities even in their early years through their various peace education curriculums as previously discussed. They also utilized a well-known local arts therapy university for additional group programs, and ministry leaders frequently incorporate art activities into their work with both the teen and sibling groups and the adult groups, such as the "Tuesday Talks" from which the Peace Warriors emerged.
16. The Peace Institute founding ministry leader specifically was introduced to the technique of sandplay when she spontaneously requested to accompany this researcher to a training during my early period of ethnographic immersion and volunteering. Given the Peace Institute's commitment to the power of the arts in "healing," I thought this particular art form might be of interest to the founding ministry

leader, though her initial request to accompany me was entirely spontaneous. I did not expect how fully and completely the Peace Institute ministry leaders, as well as some survivors, particularly teen survivors, would embrace this particular technique, now regarded as a major component of their Holistic Healing Center with a room fully dedicated to sandplay. Ministry leaders have embarked on further trainings on their own, though it also needs to be noted that I was asked to lead a few early trainings for ministry leaders and some survivors. The particular technique the Peace Institute initially was introduced to and trained in for sandplay (that this researcher is also trained in) is what is known as Sandtray-Worldplay by Dr. Gisela Schubach De Domenico (see http://vision-quest.us/vqisr/about_us.htm, accessed April 20, 2013). They have continued to explore other dimensions of sandplay trainings, and the fullness of their embrace of this constitutes its own phenomenon, including their recent renaming of it as "Peace Play." Sandplay, as a therapeutic technique originally used with children, is traced back to the work of Margaret Lowenfeld in England and later was developed further by Dora Kalff, including uses with adults. See *Sand Tray World Play: A Comprehensive Guide to the Use of the Sand Tray in Psychotherapeutic and Transformational Settings* (Oakland, CA: Vision Quest Images, 1995). For further information and general history, see also Katherine Bradway, Karen A. Signell, Geraldine H. Spare, Charles T. Stewart, Louis H. Stewart, and Clare Thompson. *Sandplay Studies: Origins, Theory, and Practice*, collected by the C.G. Jung Institute of San Francisco. Boston: Sigo Press, 1981, and Kay Bradway and Barbara McCoard, *Sandplay—Silent Workshop of the Psyche* (New York: Routledge, 1997).
17. Jordan, *Relational-Cultural Therapy*, 28, 37, 102, 108.
18. Ibid., 37, 104, 106.
19. "Safe Boxes" was an art project in which the youth decorated boxes and put materials into the boxes that helped them to feel safe. "Peaceville" was another interesting example of a combined religio and socio/poetics of material religion as a spiritual practice. Youth created a their ideal city of peace, a large artistic construction project that amounted to a hoped for fully realized eschatological and

sociological vision—a sacred story. Eventually, it was placed on display at the Massachusetts State House and later within the Peace Institute itself for a period of time.
20. See Peter A Levine, with Ann Frederick. *Waking The Tiger: Healing Trauma* (Berkeley, CA: North Atlantic Books, 1997); Ian Macnaughton, *Body, Breath, and Consciousness: A Somatic Anthology* (Berkely, CA: North Atlantic Books, 2004); Pat Ogden, Kekuni Minton, and Clare Pain, *Trauma and the Body: A Sensorimotor Approach to* Psychotherapy (New York: W.W. Norton and Company, 2006); Babette Rothschild, *The Body Remembers: The Psychophysiology of Trauma and Trauma Treatment* (New York: W.W. Norton and Company, 2000); Robert C. Scaer, *The Trauma Spectrum: Hidden Wounds and Human Resiliency.* New York: W.W. Norton and Company, 2005) and *The Body Bears the Burden: Trauma, Dissociation, and Disease*, 2nd ed. (New York: Routledge, 2007); and van der Kolk, *The Body Keeps the Score.*
21. This specific language was used by UUTRM leaders and institutional supporters separately in the interview process, and Hudson, *Congregational Trauma*, also cites a bomb site volunteer who uses this language in reference to clergy at trauma sites as well (47). In the disciplinary language of pastoral care contexts, this language appears traceable to pastoral care works by Henri Nouwen, who also developed the pastoral care image of "the wounded healer." See Dykstra, *Images of Pastoral Care.*
22. Madigan, *Narrative Therapy*, 163.
23. It is worth noting that relational-cultural theorists also have pointed to the power of self-help peer-led groups, such as Alcoholics Anonymous (AA), on occasion as well. See Christina Robb, *This Changes Everything.*
24. See James Luther Adams' 1947 essay, "The Prophethood of All Believers," in *The Prophethood of All Believers*, edited by George K. Beach (Boston: Beacon Press, 1986), 99–103, as well as in *The Essential James Luther Adams: Selected Essays and Addresses*, edited by George K. Beach (Boston: Beacon Press, 1998), 105–113.
25. I use "representative" here because it was not clear that this particular person was identifiable with any of the known UUTRM leaders on

site who were interviewed for this particular case study. More UUTRM representatives came in and out throughout that week than those interviewed, and UUTRM leaders were among the first to state that there was always a need for ongoing training among those who served on the UUTRM as volunteers, particularly in their early years of formation and operation, such as was the case for this particular case study.

26. Jordan, *Relational-Cultural Therapy*, 5–7, 101.
27. Ibid., 5–7, 36, 107 and Madigan, *Narrative Therapy*, 163. RCT integrates several theoretical frames, including literature on trauma as well as resiliency. Narrative therapy also attends to the possibilities inherent in reframing stories.
28. Jordan, *Relational-Cultural Therapy*, 101–102.
29. My clinical trainings led me to think of the word "healing" in terms of "health," per one root linguistic meaning, and my theological trainings in terms of "wholeness," per another root linguistic meaning.
30. See Schwartz, *Internal Family System Therapy*, as referred to in Chap. 4.
31. See Martinez and Fleck-Henderson, *Social Justice in Clinical Practice*, per discussion in Chap. 4.
32. Hertz, Prothrow-Stith, and Chery, "Homicide Survivors."
33. Indeed not all survivors would utilize these extended offerings of the Peace Institute, either their Holistic Healing Center or their Leadership Academy. Many survivors of family homicide only come to interact with the Peace Institute for its crisis management services, though some may return many years later for their other services. Sustaining the long-term availability of the place and space of the Peace Institute, given the need for survivors to pace and control their "healing" in the aftermath of trauma, is an effective practice noted by institutional supporters.
34. Annie G. Rogers, *The Unsayable: The Hidden Language of Trauma* (New York: Random House, 2006). This may be why symbolic play with material images can be so powerful for survivors of trauma, as seen in the street memorials from my pilot studies as well as in the Peace Institute's use of sandplay and other art forms. The missing metaphorical words for relational images and experiences sometimes

can be more deeply and poetically conveyed through shifting, changing, tactile objects, and images. This bears further investigation, as the embodied role of play is a developing area in practical theological research. There may be usefulness in bringing a material theo/poetics or religio/poetics to this literature. See Jaco Hamman, "Playing," in *The Wiley-Blackwell Companion to Practical Theology*, edited by Bonnie Miller-McLemore (Malden, MA: Wiley-Blackwell, 2014), 42–50. See also Michelle A. Walsh, "Taking Matter *Seriously*: Material Theopoetics in the Aftermath of Communal Violence," in *Post-Traumatic Public Theology*, edited by Shelly Rambo and Stephanie N. Arel (New York: Palgrave MacMillan, 2016).

35. Research into resiliency and trauma supports this statement by the UUTRM leader. See in particular George A. Bonanno, "Loss, Trauma and Human Resilience: Have We Underestimated the Human Capacity to Thrive After Extremely Aversive Events?" *American Psychologist* (January 2004), 20–28.

36. A text recommended by one UUTRM founder for clergy self-care during interviews was Kirk Bryon Jones, *Rest in the Storm: Self-Care Strategies for Clergy and Other Caregivers* (Valley Forge, PA: Judson Press, 2001). The TVUUC minister interviewed clearly did carry an enormous felt weight of responsibility, as initially expressed in his ride home to the church after first hearing the news and his worries that "there are more ways to get this wrong than right." See also again Hudson, *Congregational Trauma*, in support of pastoral care concern for clergy *and* lay leaders. Also see generally for any human service or clinical care provider working in the area of trauma, Laura van Dernoot Lipsky with Connie Burk, *Trauma Stewardship: An Everyday Guide to Caring for Self While Caring for Others* (San Francisco: Berrett-Koehler Publishers, Inc. 2009).

37. One interesting example of the power of such material religio/poetic witness in the space of the Peace Institute itself was the prominent display of seven bricks painted by former social work interns as a gift with the Principles of Peace. These two interns clearly had absorbed the importance of embodied and material practices in their year with the Peace Institute and considered this an appropriate goodbye gift as

a thank you, which it happily was received as, hence the prominent display at the time of the case study.

38. The Peace Prayer recited at the end of the funeral order of service honors the interdependency of peace in the larger world necessitating peace at home and in the heart, as seen in the poem by Lao Tse here http://www.worldprayers.org/archive/prayers/meditations/if_there_is_to_be_peace.html (accessed May 7, 2016).

39. After wearing these memorial buttons had become a prominent practice in the Boston community, young people and families also began to create t-shirts with their loved one's picture displayed as well. These would be worn in different settings, such as the march known as the LDBPI's annual Mother's Day Walk for Peace or for family gatherings. In my pilot studies, the young adults interviewed stated that these memorial buttons and t-shirts gave them a visceral embodied feeling of connection to their lost loved one, a sense that their loved one was physically present when the button was worn—more than simply a memory—and that when more family members wore these buttons or t-shirts at family events, the stronger this energetic sense of connection and presence became for them. This included experiencing the loved one as witnessing events, not being "left out," and feeling the loved one's "vibe."

40. Chopp, "Theology and Poetics of Testimony," 7.

41. The language of "Peace Warriors" came about from one mother attending the "Tuesday Talks" who said she was not a "survivor" so much as a "warrior," and most survivors attending that night embraced this new language. However, one survivor interviewed did express ambivalence for this new language, akin to the ambivalence expressed for the word "healing," stating that she felt more like a "survivor" than a "warrior."

42. Marla J. Arvay, "Shattered Beliefs: Reconstituting the Self of the Trauma Counselor," in *Meaning Reconstruction and the Experience of Loss*, 4th ed., edited by Robert A. Neimeyer (Washington, D.C.: American Psychological Association, 2005), 213–230.

43. Jordan, *Relational-Cultural Therapy*, 3–5, 103–105.

44. Ibid., 28, 102.

45. Ibid., 10–105.
46. Schwartz, *An Introduction to the Internal Family Systems Model.*
47. See the *Report of the Committee on Women & Healthy Communities to Members of the Boston City Council: Family Voices: Strengthening Homicide Response and Family Support in the City of Boston*, by Ayanna Pressley, Chair (Boston, December 15, 2010).
48. The media often is critiqued by the ministry leaders and survivors for setting an immediate narrative as to who is considered an "innocent victim"—hence "good" and worthy of more attention and support—and who is considered "potentially gang involved"—hence "bad" and less worthy. Again, the creation of the specialized funeral orders of service became the Peace Institute's way of giving control of the narrative back to the family, as well as any assistance they provided with drafting statements for the media. One other poignant area that has been a source of personal dismay to me as a minister as I came to know the work of the Peace Institute is the added burden placed on families during the initial period of trauma in the struggle to find money to bury their loved ones in their preferred culturally appropriate way. One survivor shared that she was told by cemetery staff that the gates would be locked upon their arrival if she did not come up with the money in advance for the burial site. The Peace Institute has established a permanent burial fund for survivor families. For me, understanding the importance of and desire to bury their loved one well, often times at quite a bit of expense, was a time of encountering, accepting, and supporting a deep difference in theological beliefs and cultural ways. This was due to my own background as a UU and my comfort with the lesser expense as well as the theological meaning of cremation.
49. Tervalon, Melanie and Jann Murray-Garcia, "Cultural Humility Versus Cultural Competence: A Critical Distinction in Defining Physician Training Outcomes in Multicultural Education," *Journal of Health Care for the Poor and Underserved* (May 1998: 9, 2) 117–125. Tervalon and Murray-Garcia write of the need for a greater level of "cultural humility" rather than continued "cultural competency" trainings by human service providers. Though they focus

particularly on medical doctors in their study, their recommendations could apply equally to mental health professionals, law enforcement officials, politicians, the media, and religious institutions. They write that practitioners and institutions alike need "to identify and examine their own patterns of unintentional and intentional racism, classism, and homophobia," 120, committing themselves to "continually engage in self-reflection and self-critique as lifelong learners and reflective practitioners," 118. The concept of "cultural humility" supplements previously discussed concepts of "power" within relational-cultural theory and "cultural hegemony" within narrative therapy.

50. Hudson, *Congregational Trauma*, notes that the American Red Cross is often the first line of defense in situations of trauma, whether congregational or disaster based, and many denominations join with the Red Cross either through a partnership with the Church World Service (see http://www.cwsglobal.org/what-we-do/emergencies/us-emergency-response/, accessed October 29, 2013) or through some other designated agency (57). However, it should be noted that the American Red Cross is geared toward large-scale disasters and only works in partnership with the US Department of Justice Office for Victims of Crime when acts of terrorism or mass murder occur. The TVUUC shooting constituted an attempt of mass murder in a religious context, hence the immediate response of the Red Cross, whereas other types of traumatic incidents in a congregational or communal setting would not call forth such a response. See US Department of Justice, Office of Justice Programs, *Responding to Victims of Terrorism and Mass Violence Crimes: Coordination and Collaboration Between American Red Cross Workers and Crime Victim Service Providers* (see http://www.ojp.usdoj.gov/ovc/publications/infores/redcross/ncj209681.pdf, (accessed October 29, 2013).
51. Many of these findings on the importance of immediate and logistical response support the case study anecdotal general findings in Hudson, *Congregational Trauma*. For more information on the UUA Standing on the Side of Love campaign, see http://www.standingonthesideoflove.org (accessed October 29, 2013).

52. This particular TVUUC leader said that sheer physical exhaustion proved to be more of point of contention months later than any differing versions of the actual narrative of the shooting (which the UUTRM consultant had advised might be a stressor). He also stated that their long-term support needs were great and varied and completely underestimated by both UUTRM representatives and TVUUC leaders.

6

Cross-Cultural Encounters in the Research: Lessons Learned

Forging Trust, Hearing Stories, and Risking Questions in Cross-Cultural Encounters

One night in the early years of my role as a "lay urban community minister/social worker," I was driving some of the teenage girls home. From the back of the youth ministry van, I heard a sharp comment from one girl to another: "You fight like a white girl!" "Hey," I called out, "What's going on back there?" Laughter broke out in the van, and one of the girls yelled back, "You heard that?" A comical and embarrassed yet earnest conversation ensued with the African American youth explaining the racialized meaning-making stereotypes among them that "white girls" lack the power to be direct or to engage in a physical fight and that this was regarded as a great insult to deliver between African American girls. I listened without challenge and accepted this with a sense of humor, putting it in my memory bank of the stories to which I was privy while living between and having relationships in different cultural worlds of experiences. Clearly there was spiritual meaning for these young people in exercising a sense of superiority and toughness of capacity compared to privileged but soft white girls.

Some stories were more poignant or painful than humorous, however. Of the more painful or challenging sort were questions posed to me such as: "Do you think racist thoughts?" "Is it my fault because I'm black that this is happening to me at work?" "Why do all the white people live out in the suburbs with fancy houses and we live here in the ghetto?" In the conversations accompanying these questions, tremendous suffering was laid bare that yielded an existential crisis of meaning-making for each of us—how to make meaning and sustain relationship in the face of socially constructed and real experiences beyond any of our control. Through the discomfort of living in authentic relationship by sitting with and engaging together honestly such questions, even admitting to ignorance or helplessness with only the capacity to listen empathically and with compassion, still a sense of gratitude remained that the relationship itself was trusted to bear these questions and conversations with mutuality. I needed to embrace that all of these experiences and sources of meaning-making were valid and true in their own right, for they came from vastly different lived experiences than my own in the borderlands of race and class in US cities. I only could share from my reality and learn to listen to different realities and find the possibilities somewhere in the between spaces.

Culture and Power in the Case Studies

Socioeconomic and racial demographics of participants in the two case studies differed enormously, thus exposing different cultural world/view and world/sense and spiritual practices as shaped by historical circumstances and present lived realities.[1] Core cultural values are revealed often through examination of differences in ways of being[2] and communal practices. The cultural world/views and world/sense of most of the Louis D. Brown Peace Institute (LDBPI) case study participants were shaped by their experiences of racialization by a dominant US culture that institutionalizes that black lives do not matter as much as all other lives,[3] particularly through media images and by living in an impoverished urban environment with greater exposure to daily violence and fewer opportunities for higher education and class mobility. Given that single violent events in a survivor's life occurred in the midst of multiple experiences of ongoing oppression, the Peace Institute chose to focus their practices on resistance by transforming survivor pain and anger directly into power and action.

The cultural world/view and world/sense of the majority of Unitarian Universalist Trauma Response Ministry (UUTRM) case study participants, by contrast, were shaped by racialization in a dominant US culture that privileges whiteness, education, and class mobility and expects safety from violence as the norm. Practices focused heavily on narrative and material meaning-making in the aftermath of the Tennessee Valley Unitarian Universalist Church's (TVUUC) experience with a violent event that was seen as alien in the realm of imaginative possibilities. Priority often was given to congregational pastoral care over congregational prophetic social justice action in this meaning-making process, as per the report of those interviewed. Participants carried religious differences as well between the two case studies, one focused on the centrality of the Christian story, especially its call to be peacemakers, and the other on a public ethical and ecclesial tradition shaped by worshiping and acting together within a commitment to welcoming diverse beliefs and spiritual practices.

What is revealed by lived religious examination of these two case studies, and how do their contrasting cultures result in contrasting practices of meaning-making? In asking these questions and stressing the importance of intercultural encounters in interdisciplinary research, I affirm the magnitude and challenge of violent trauma in the US context and globally as a contemporary societal challenge that needs cross-cultural attention, particularly for preventive practices of meaning-making as well as meaning-making practices in the aftermath to ameliorate the impact. I am not "objective" in any classic Western scientific sense of this word when I pose this question either. I view myself as deeply implicated in and by the violence of my world and relationships within it. I affirm my own religious tradition's public ethical commitment to the worth and dignity of every person and to the tradition's recognition that we live in an interdependent web of existence where that which affects the web affects us all.[4] I turn now to intercultural lessons from these two case studies.

Spiritual Experiences and Meaning-Making Through Sacralization of Place and Space

Key Lessons from the Peace Institute Case Study

One of the strongest common themes related to questions of "healing" or "helping" that emerged in the language of nearly all study participants was the spiritual power of an embodied and material culture of peace and safety in the physical space and place of the LDBPI at the time of the interviews. Words such as "comfortable," "safe," "touchstone," "spiritual," "aura," "like family," "supportive," and "culture of peace" repeatedly came up in interviews. It was clear that to the ministry leaders themselves, as well as to survivors and institutional supporters, Peace Institute leaders strove to model what they preached to others and to create an environment in their physical space that gave witness to this culture as well. This was so much the case that several people spoke of being drawn to connect and visit with the Peace Institute if they were merely in the area. A survivor said, "I just felt like it was a place that I could just go talk, but I didn't know what I was gonna talk about 'cause I really didn't realize what I was feeling or whatever. I just felt comfortable being there, and so I would go by and sit and talk ...." Even an institutional supporter said,

> I think again ... it is sort of a touchstone ... that provides some thread of continuity ... there is certainly something that takes action on their part to sustain it, to create that kind of space and culture over time ... I think it's also a place where sometimes people just want to stop by. It represents something. It's solid, it's in the community, it's there. They have associations with it. There's a welcoming sort of aura there *and I* often use it as a place where I'll stop by ... I think it's relationships ... shared experiences ... over time ....

Survivors stressed that the survivor-led nature of the Peace Institute gave them a feeling that they did not need special permission to call or a particular appointment to come over to the Peace Institute or that they needed to explain their presence—they were simply accepted and understood: "You have that outlet like no matter what time ... [the ministry leader] stayed with me on the phone for like an hour ... I could call and cry or don't say anything and they know. They give you that ...." Survivors were provided with a "safe space" to share whatever needed to be shared, and they did not need to share the specific details of their stories: "When you're a survivor, it just seems like we don't ask each other those questions. We *know* why we're there. The story is someone shot and killed your child. That's the story ... they don't need the details ... They know why we're there, and it just seems like we all have that one particular connection. So it's very helpful at times for me to be there."

Both the physical setting and survivor-led culture enhanced the spiritual "aura" of peacefulness and safety experienced by survivors to connect and express the full range of their feelings, even if they were more often distrustful of people, as one survivor reported: "I'm like a hard nut to crack ... [and I think] like there's just an aura around that place, and it's just peaceful. And you know that they have spirituality in their lives and you know that they're good people. So you connect. There's no question about what they're tryin' to do. They're not taking advantage of you. They're experiencing the same thing you have." A Peace Institute ministry leader also stressed that "this *space* is healing in itself" and that "it's a very spiritual space." From the perspective of also being a survivor who has now come to work at the Peace Institute, this ministry leader continued: " ... for me knowing that ... an organization like the Peace Institute existed was healing in itself because at least we can say that we have an organization that does this work in our community and in our state." This ministry leader also would call their work a "survivor-based methodology" that is "real" and "unique" because so many of the ministry leaders have had their own lives touched by homicide; thus there is no "stigma" or "shame" in their connection with the families, "it brings down any walls."

The primacy in value given to *consistency of culture and stability of material place* by nearly all participants also was striking. For an interdisciplinary lived religion approach attending to sacred stories and meaning-making practices in the aftermath of trauma, these experiences have correlational capacity with relational-cultural theories of the power of empathy, mutuality, and connection, and the metaphoric capacity of these theories to suggest embodied energetic connection that could be termed spiritual. As previously discussed, ethnographer Sarah Pink draws on sociologist Amanda Coffey's concept to point to the significance of spatial emplacement.[5] However, an additional correlational tool also might be postmodern place theory, as utilized by Mary McClintock Fulkerson in her ethnographic study of a multicultural church. Drawing on the authors of postmodern place theory, Fulkerson writes, "Place is a structure of lived, corporate, bodied experience . . . a category that characterizes *all* knowledge . . . ."[6] It is through place that unity of experience creates a sense of reality that is fully embodied in our senses and feelings, in our world/sense, and one that also can hold "conflict and contradiction."[7] The people and the place of the Peace Institute came to represent in world/sense both a place that could retrigger ambivalence and painful memories of loss and a place of "spiritual healing," peace, and restoration. All of these lived experiences—the multiplicity of experiential parts of the Self when correlated with IFS theory—were contained and held via place through a spiritual "aura" similar to church, where the material architecture of the place became a form of religio/poetic testimony and witness itself, calling forth poetic religious language such as "aura" for description.

Correlating again with Ammerman's research[8] in the sacred stories of spiritual tribes as enacted also in space, place, and a sense of home, uniformly ministry leaders also spoke of creating *an embodied culture* of peace, love, and support for each other, threaded with their spiritual sense of Christian "calling" as a lay ministry and practicing what they "preach." This meant they strove to be "like family" and to "check each other with love," supporting each other in pastoral practices of self-care while role modeling this pastoral care practice as a prophetic practice to the broader community as well:

> We are very much a family unit, if you will. And that's appropriate because much of what we try to teach or preach or train is that peace starts at home. It starts within. So if we're in turmoil all the time, in chaos all the time and can't see eye to eye with one another most of the time, then what are *we*? And who are we to preach or teach peace? ... [W]e eat together, we talk together, we share together, we cry together, we give ourselves to one another . . . we lift one another up rather than tear one another down. If someone makes a mistake, we don't tear 'em down. We lift them up. We

help them with that mistake, help 'em figure it out and get it right. All those things that we would like for the community to do and to be, we try to be, you know.

The central pastoral care ritual for supporting each other as ministry leaders revolved around their use of the Peace Institute's seven Principles of Peace and striving to internalize them for the culture of staff meetings, as well as board meetings, through check-in's and close-outs: "[W]hat principle are we lifting up today or struggling with today and what do we need to help that struggle? . . . So we just stay engaged with one another so that we're assured that one another is safe." But equally important was shutting down entirely for lunch together, where business was not allowed for discussion, as well as allowing the space for the ministry leaders to partake in the same healing activities available for families, such as art activities, massage, and bible study. Ministry leaders realized that their own pastoral care of self practices were profoundly important for sustaining the prophetic missionary dimension of their Christian lay ministry, and they were self-conscious in implementing this role modeling to others.

Their embodied spiritual culture of peace and safety, of role modeling being a "healthy family" as fellow survivors, also fostered a sense of mutuality, empathy, energy, and empowerment in this "place" that was experienced as immanent. This expanded their capacity for connection to their broader community as well, a connectional expansion consistent with Lakoff and Johnson's understanding of embodied empathy as the root of all experiences of spiritual transcendence and also correlating with the writings of relational-cultural theory (RCT):

> When empathy and concern flow both ways, there is an intense affirmation of the self and paradoxically, a transcendence of the self, a sense of the self as part of a larger relational unit . . . The primary channel for this kind of mutuality is empathic attunement, the capacity to share in and comprehend the momentary psychological state of another person. It is a process during which one's self-boundaries undergo momentary alteration, which in itself allows the possibility for change in the self. Empathy in this sense, then, always contains the opportunity for mutual growth and impact.[9]

For such interactions to grow to their fullest fruit obviously requires a sturdy foundation in pastoral and clinical care practices of trust, safety, and stability over time, particularly in light of trauma theory emphasizing that disruption of control and reestablishment of control are key to creating a sense of safety and connection again. Continuity of ministry leaders and their embodied spiritual culture of peace and safety *holding*[10] these shifting "kaleidoscopes" of feelings, "pieces," and practices *in a particular place* became a repeated value reflected across participant interviews. This stability allowed survivors interviewed to pace their interactions and created a context for a slow post-traumatic growth in feelings of empowerment and confidence as they took the opportunity to experiment with a particular connection or practice. Providing such continuity also required a certain level of vulnerability on the part of ministry leaders as pastoral care providers. This vulnerability was reflected both in their ongoing commitment to these relationships in a particular place and also in their commitment to authenticity in disclosures and sensitivity to impact in relationships, core values expressed also in relational-cultural theory and practices.

An unexpected theme that emerged in response to my questions relating to institutional religious communities as a potential "place" of support was a heavy sense of disappointment with and frequent anger toward the institutional church and clergy by several survivors.[11] Passionate survivor critiques centered on the failure of senior ministers to visit the survivors; a perception that the churches often were more eager to help families survivors of "high-profile" murders of "innocent youth" than others deemed "gang-involved"; and anger that the church's status with wealthier congregants who commuted from the suburbs was perceived as of greater concern than the welfare of the urban communities in which the church was located. When the lived experience of the institutional church failed to embody the power of a spiritual culture of peace and safety, the contrast of survivors' embodied para-ecclesial experiences with the Peace Institute became even more significant. A survivor who experienced discrimination by clergy due to the circumstances of her son's murder would say, " ... I'm so in tuned with the Peace Institute because to *them*, everyone is equal. Even the perpetrator has an equal right of some sort. And that holds a lotta weight with me. A whole lotta weight with me."

While not every survivor had a disappointing experience with a church or clergyperson, it was clear that the quality of pastoral care experience a survivor had in the aftermath of a family homicide could have a lifelong spiritual impact on the survivor. This included their capacity for prophetic social justice engagement of society if support was not given for their experience of righteous anger—unless they found support elsewhere, as many did through the Peace Institute. The founding ministry leader provides one example of a successful pastoral encounter, though she also did speak initially of a family priest failing to reach out personally after her son's murder. Instead, a different priest came to visit on the recommendation of a friend, and this person became an ongoing supportive presence in her life for several years.

In his first impression, he quietly visited their household "like everybody else" and spoke to people and then simply asked to pray with them before he left, continuing this pattern for the next few days. While she continued at a different church in the meantime, this particular priest became important in simply being with her through her process of anger with God, struggles with forgiveness, and ultimately transformation into her present journey and ministry. She specifically experienced him as "humbling" himself and really listening to and learning from her, and she in turn began to respect and engage with him as a result:

> ... I had stopped going to confession because all he wanted me to do was forgive and I'm like, "No, that's too big for me. I've done everything God wanted me to do, I've donated to the needy, I attended mass, I read the bible, I help my children understand, I believe I've done good and then you're tellin' me that this is God's will? You got to do better than that, you've got to help me to understand." And I think him really humbling himself and realizing that, "You can't just tell me forgive, you really can't just tell me to come to confession and ask God to forgive if you haven't taken me through and helping me to understand why would this happen to me ... when I was doin' everything I believed God wanted me to do?" And I think he understood that and didn't take it personally when I told him I couldn't do that, when I told him it wasn't fair that he is not even helpin' me to understand this journey, he didn't take it personally, he would give me books, he would call me after mass and he really, without even ministering to me, he was ministering to me in a way that I respect ....

In the cultural world of the Peace Institute survivors, visitation by clergy, when experienced as a more gentle unassuming "presence" and as a recognition of the extent of the survivor's pain and anger rather than a push toward a particular religious experience or action, often was valued or desired by survivors interviewed. Ideally and preferably, this was from the clergyperson who was the leader of the church where the survivor actually attended. Support of this nature also can take the form of "survivor ministries" that embody a spiritual culture of peace and safety within congregations, as survivors interviewed suggested and agreed based on their experiences with the Peace Institute. Participants suggested that checking in on families during holidays or anniversaries or providing care baskets and support groups also can be experienced as very helpful for surviving families, again particularly when the senior clergyperson embodies such support.

Key Lessons from the UU Trauma Response Ministry Case Study

Providing immediate assistance in reclaiming the sacredness of the TVUUC building and the sanctuary were significant practices in the aftermath of their violent trauma. These practices also illustrated the importance of embodied relationships and material religio/poetic meaning-making in the aftermath. For example, the rededication service one week after the shooting included many elements: a ministry of presence by several former ministers as well as the UUA District Executive; the inclusion of a favored UU hymn that took on new embodied meaning that morning by participant reports, "May Nothing Evil Cross This Door";[12] the giving of artistic material courage awards to the children; the recognition of the courage of many members in helping to keep the church safe that day, followed by a promise from all gathered to continue to help to do so in the future, with all being called to stand physically as able; and a benediction that entailed the minister standing on the spot where Greg McKendry had been shot and died to reclaim and resanctify that space as well.

The words of benediction the minister had always used, and continued to use, also took on new embodied meaning that morning by participant reports: "Prophetic church, the world awaits your liberating ministry. Go forward in the power of love. Proclaim the truth that makes us free."[13] At the end, the children reprised the song "Tomorrow" from the musical "Annie," as they had the night after the shooting at the "interfaith" community service at the Presbyterian church that had sheltered them on the day of the shooting—but this time, they did so while standing at the front of the sanctuary during the rededication service and on the very stage that had been targeted during the shooting. Such ritual and liturgical reinhabiting of the physical space imparted some control to all involved against the experience of ongoing traumatic fear after the shooting and reclaimed the material space as once again sacred for their spiritual tribe.

UUTRM leaders, particularly the long-term consultant, were viewed as providing a significant role in feedback and consultation regarding the sermon, rituals, and creating a sense of physical safety and renewal in the church space—in fact, security was a role that the ministerial consultant played in this initial rededication service, including assisting with evaluating security at the church's one year anniversary as well. To create a sense of safety in the sanctuary itself required some reorientation of and physical changes to the space. To resacralize the space, as the UUTRM leader consultant explained, not only did the damaged and blood-soaked pews need to be removed, but also certain pews were shifted by 15 degrees in their material orientation, as well as the pulpit. These recommendations were made based on the UUTRM leader's understanding of the neurobiology of trauma triggers and the further disruption of spiritual experience these could provoke:

> [W]e didn't want anyone to go back into that space and sit down and be oriented exactly the way it happened. That by simply shifting what a focal point would be would diminish the potential for intrusive memory in that environment, if they happen to be sitting down here ... you can also shift the pulpit from the middle over a little bit, so that when you're sitting here, you're also oriented differently up here. And the notion is that part of what we understand about the neurology of trauma is that environment has a lot to do with the way in which that particular neural map gets triggered, and if

we can alter the environment just a smidgen, we don't tend to continue to re-traumatize over time.

The UUTRM leader and consultant also suggested that the TVUUC might want to save some of its damaged materials and artifacts to create memorials, and this material memorialization also was important for religio/poetic meaning-making in the aftermath—demonstrating continuing bonds. The congregation did in fact choose to rededicate two areas of the building as the Greg McKendry Fellowship Hall and the Linda Lee Kraeger Library (Fig. 6.1).

The current pastoral care office also was designated for a space near the sanctuary stage, next to the still pellet-ridden door that had been the pathway to escape and safety for many children and adults, now preserved carefully and marked with a plaque (Fig. 6.2). This placement of her office in this particular space struck the TVUUC leader interviewed, who also was the former church administrator and now pastoral care minister, as "funny," as in ironic. Yet there was a sense of religio/poetic testimony to life and prophetic hope in such an architectural and material placement of the heart of the TVUUC pastoral care ministry in this location as well.

This same former church administrator also intuitively understood the importance of saving damaged materials and artifacts from that day for their artistic potential, despite those who challenged her in doing so. This TVUUC leader reported that some people thought she was "retraumatizing" herself by wanting to keep the pellet-torn curtain that had covered the entryway to what would become the pellet-ridden door, yet there clearly was great spiritual comfort, significance, and sacred meaning-making for her in keeping this curtain as a potential symbol of the hoped for eventual transformation of this violent event.[14] This same church administrator who had "see[n] the light from the curtain being open" and ran toward it for safety lifted the original pellet-torn curtain up to the light to show me, stressing its religio/poetic symbolic transformative potential as a material artifact:

> For instance, I protected this curtain. No one else seemed to care about the curtain. I thought ... we should keep [it] 'cause I thought somebody could make a piece of artwork out of it at some point and that they would want to,

Fig. 6.1 *TVUUC Linda Lee Kraeger Library Memorial.* Painting by Emily Taylor, a TVUUC congregant, as a tribute to the Westside Unitarian Universalist congregant who lost her life that morning. It celebrates her love for learning and scholarly writing in religious history and witnesses to the power and "lasting reminder" of a life lived in the "pursuit of academic excellence." I note that, as an ethnographer, the selection of this image to include in the book also is my own tribute to the losses experienced by the Westside Unitarian Universalist congregation that day, often overshadowed by the focus on the TVUCC, which my case study unintentionally replicated

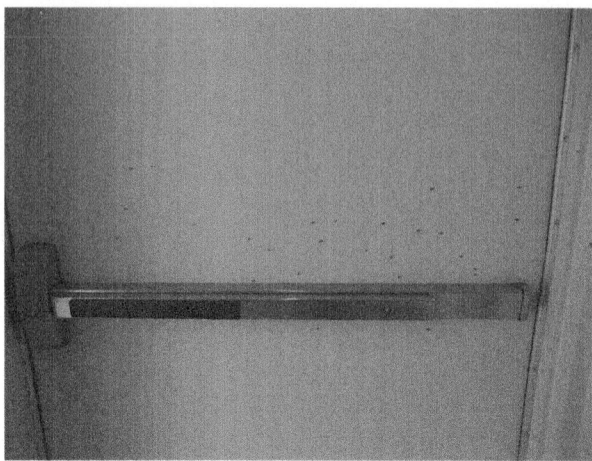

Fig. 6.2 *TVUUC Pellet-Marked and Memorialized Door*. In the aftermath of the shooting, the congregation chose to memorialize the door that both had been riddled with pellets and also had been the door to freedom and safety for many, including the children on the stage. In so marking with a plaque, they also expressed gratitude to the embrace of a larger community of care in the aftermath—specifically "the faith and community organizations that responded to the tragedy, and people throughout the world who expressed their support"

> so I've had it in the top drawer in the office ever since . . . See how the light comes through though? . . . See, that to me seems very symbolic of the transformation from—I mean I just thought there was a lot of good symbolism in this . . . It's like star shine.

Material memorialization was deemed important by UUTRM and TVUUC leaders alike, and memorialization in a way that would not retraumatize but rather would give religio/poetic testimony to the "something more" of the embodied power of the lives lived and lost or injured, even though there might be disagreements on how best to witness to those religio/poetic values. The reported deepest sense of resacralization of space, however, came from the fact that the majority of people did not abandon the church after the shooting—they kept returning and they kept bringing their children, including the immediately following Sunday, and the church did indeed grow in membership in the aftermath. The

TVUUC minister said, "... one of the most *healing* things to happen was tackling that guy as quick as they could," which in turn created a sense of efficacy and capacity for the congregation to keep their church safe. The rededication service affirmed this shared commitment to continuing the spiritual and material form of the church as sacred space, both through the formal call to stand as physically able in affirmation and through the many spontaneous standing ovations that happened throughout that morning. The material pews, floors, walls, and space were resanctified through very bodies of congregants enlivened by energetic connection in joy and hope that day.

A poignant story of this "continuity" of the church in sacred space also was shared by the TVUUC minister regarding the rededication service and involved the head usher who had directed Greg McKendry to stand on the spot where he had ushered and was later killed:

> [T]his is part of what makes that a sacred space almost as much as anything really. [The head usher] had terrible survivor's guilt that first week. And he came in and talked to me. English isn't his first language ... he's a refugee from a war country. So he's got layers of violence. But ... really the moment that makes that space sacred is when I came in ... and there was [the head usher] with the bulletin. He was the usher and he's standing where Greg stood, and ... to me that just was a powerful, powerful moment of continuity.

For the benediction that rededication Sunday, the TVUUC minister went to stand on that spot *with* the head usher, surrounded also by the UUTRM leader and consultant as well as the UUA District Executive. This was an embodied standing of ground that had marked death and now marked renewal of life again. As a ritual action, it gave religio/poetic testimony and witness to resacralization of the material space as well as their continuing *moral* bond to the deceased congregant. The TVUUC minister continued to go to that spot for many future Sundays as well to give his traditional benediction: "Prophetic church, the world awaits your liberating ministry. Go forward in the power of love; proclaim the truth that makes us free."

Such material memorialization processes thus continue to be strong examples of the moral need for "continuing bonds" with the dead and, in the case of the TVUUC, the powerful role a religio/poetics of material religion plays in constructing or reinforcing a religious narrative and sacred story in the aftermath of violent trauma through rituals of resacralization of building and space. The church building itself already materially embodied a historical and religious message and sacred story through the various values inscribed on its exterior walls, as well as through its ecological architectural design, giving testimony to a larger UU religious narrative designed for public witness by others. The newcomer PowerPoint also became a material artifact and gave religio/poetic testimony through its use of the story and image of Jim Person being welcomed into church membership as the first African American, witnessed now across the generations by those who viewed the PowerPoint and, as previously suggested in correlation to liberation health theory, "rescuing the historical memory of change" to reinforce prophetic social justice witness, through material form in this case. The same is true of the inclusion of Jim Person's story and name in the welcoming congregation plaque eventually placed on the building itself.

The decision to leave pellet holes in some walls and also to mark these with a material plaque expressed yet another sacred continuing moral bond to the larger religious story of risk and "*being* a prophetic church," again examples in material form of "recovering the historical memory of change" for resistance and transformation. These all were choices to turn *toward* the trauma, rather than away, as a sign of post-traumatic growth, prophetic hope, resilience, resistance, and overcoming in religio/poetic material testimony and witness through the resacralization of the building. The material building thus is marked in ways large and small with the religio/poetic living relational images and energy of a religious tradition and community in place and history—the embodied and material sacred story as a particular spiritual tribe.

It also was true that the most painful moments, and for some TVUUC leaders a feeling of being wounded again, came during a conflict over use of the space of the sanctuary in the week after the shooting. This central story was touched upon by four of the TVUUC leaders interviewed and entailed different perspectives on, experiences with, and narratives in relation to a local TV station being allowed to film in the church sanctuary. This was a few days after the church shooting but before the planned rededication ceremony. It was clear that the opportunity to tell this story was significant[15] for those who fell on the "losing side" of this conflict. At the time, this conflict revolved around the request and initial authorization by some TVUUC leaders of a camera crew to film a more "neutral," in their perception, part of the sanctuary, such as the empty pulpit, for a backdrop to a news story to be shown later that night. The TVUUC minister was not involved in this initial decision, but a member of the UUTRM became aware and objected in very strong terms, had the camera crew leave, and informed the minister who also then strongly objected to the presence of the camera crew.

Relational, cultural, *and* narrative differences seemed to be at the root in this conflict, as well as sources of power and authority in governance. For the UUTRM leader and the TVUUC minister, the camera crew was viewed as treating the sanctuary as a "crime scene," and their perception was that this relational image and narrative would be retraumatizing for congregants if shown on the news that night, particularly without warning or planning and before the sanctuary had had a chance to be resanctified through a rededication service. The TVUUC minister said, "I really thought it would be important for the first image to be sanctuary rededication and healing and recovery." For the other TVUUC leaders involved in the initial authorization, however, there were personal relationships at stake, they were demonstrating appropriate sensitivity, and they observed cultural differences in attitudes toward the media being expressed.[16] One TVUUC leader explained that the cameraperson

> ... was the son of our longtime congregants ... He's very sensitive to the whole thing. The press people are all our friends ... We know 'em ... We can talk to them and say, 'Hey, this is what we wanna do. We don't wanna do this or that ... So that whole dynamic of fighting with the press and ... being suspicious of the press didn't fit, which I think is part of a north/south, big city/small city kind of issue.

The perception by one TVUUC leader also was that the particular UUTRM representative involved "had a lot of affect" and "basically screamed at me a few times." This was experienced as particularly painful for the TVUUC leader, who said he had to step away from his birthday celebration with his family that night to intervene with the TV station and convince them at the last minute not to show the film they had taken. He reported, "I ended up shakin' like a tuning fork for, you know, months after that ...." Another TVUUC leader who was heavily involved with media relations throughout that week also concurred that a different experience with and attitude toward the press was brought with the UUTRM and that, for at least a short period, this posed significant barriers to a cultural style in which he was more accustomed to operating. The TVUUC minister, in contrast, experienced the "image of chasing the camera people out" as a positive prophetic pastoral image akin to "Jesus chasing the money changers out of the Temple," though this was dissonant to and disconnecting for the experience of other TVUUC leaders whose pastoral relational image and expectation of UUTRM representatives was that they minimally be dispassionate or be a humble servant at all times. Additionally, this conflict over sacred space highlighted points of tension that can occur in a congregational setting when the lines of authority and communication are dispersed or not clear in the aftermath of a trauma.[17]

Cultural Meaning-Making in Narratives of Encountering God and Encountering Evil

Key Lessons from the Peace Institute Case Study

All Peace Institute ministry leaders and survivors interviewed stressed the significance of one's personal relationship with God more than formal religious traditions or church communities, and "God" was the spontaneous language used rather than "Jesus" or "Christ" for most ministry leaders and survivors.[18] Survivors spoke to their sense of God being a primary sustaining force in the aftermath of the murder of their child, helping them to "move" and "function." They experienced this sustaining force through various signs, practices, or the beauty of God's creation, with one survivor explicitly calling it "God's spirit." A survivor spoke of the coffee she needed as mysteriously appearing in the hands of a neighbor, while another survivor spoke of the movement of her son in the moment before he died as a sign from God. Still another said there was a "healing force" in nature, and a survivor and a ministry leader both made spontaneous references to the process of sandplay as an almost physical spiritual guiding of their process by God, a "taking over" of their body.

While most survivors interviewed spoke of their sense of faith being questioned or even shattered in the aftermath of trauma, there still was a sense of God being available as a loving and reassuring presence in their journey, even if in mysterious ways, to the degree that they were able to see the signs. For most of these particular survivors, there was no spontaneous direct association of God's action with the cause of their suffering as a form of punishment, primarily they questioned "why" in the aftermath.[19] This result dovetails with other lived religion research by R. Ruard Ganzevoort and Nette Falkenburg, who also drew on continuing bonds literature in studying parents who lost children to severe illness rather than homicide. They discovered that the parents they studied preferred to focus on the significance of the life of their child in their meaning-making rather than on their death and that this took the shape of a wide variety of spiritual experiences and practices illustrating their ongoing connection to their deceased child and experience of receiving religious support.[20] The Peace Institute founding ministry leader, in particular, spoke of God placing an allotted time frame for one's presence on earth, drawing on Ecclesiastes for her understanding, though not prescribing the form of the end of that time frame. Peace Institute funeral orders of service explicitly suggested that people refrain from telling survivors that the murder of their loved one "was God's will."

Uniformly, all Peace Institute ministry leaders spoke of their personal connection to God as the source of a "calling" or "mission" to engage in the work and ministry of the Peace Institute, and all survivors, as well as most institutional supporters interviewed, minimally viewed the Peace Institute's work as "spiritual." Thus for the Peace Institute ministry leaders, the shape of God's communication was missional and ecclesial in a lay Christian narrative to create a community of peacemakers and transform their larger world toward a vision of God's peace. First and foremost, however, the ministry leaders experienced themselves as called to reflect God's culture of peace in the space and place of the Peace Institute itself—a peace within self first practiced by following the seven principles of Love, Unity, Faith, Hope, Courage, Justice, and Forgiveness—principles considered biblically based and widely applicable from both an interfaith as well as a secular perspective. The interiority and immanence of these peace principles reflecting peace within self first before turning outward to the community also can correlate to Schwartz' efforts within IFS theory to connect embodied affective and cognitive experiences to spirituality across religious traditions as well through the 8 C's of Self Energy, as suggested in chapter four.

When asked direct questions about "healing" and their spirituality or faith, embodiment in their experience of spirituality and faith—a *physicality* to the experience of spirituality and God—was another significant theme to emerge in relation to Peace Institute participant interviews. For example, one survivor spontaneously spoke of sandplay as spiritual and that "something just took over my body," something she could not explain, though it did not frighten her. This survivor was so powerfully affected that she brought in sample trays and objects to lead a mini-training in testimonial for her human service college class:

> And I was tryin' to explain it to my professor. I said, "It just took me somewhere spiritually. I just went somewhere, and I began to just put things in the sand tray . . . I would pick up the pieces and say, 'This is my family,' and then I put my family, I put the house in, and I could remember I felt like I needed to protect my family. I can remember, like, 'Okay, if I put up this wall, I could protect my family.' Then I would move stuff because it didn't represent this, and whatever," but I'm tellin' you like, I can't even really explain that feeling to anybody. I was like, "You have to experience it personally to even understand it 'cause, I'm tellin' you, I felt like something else took over me." But it was a feeling that I wouldn't mind feeling again over and over again. When I left there, I kept thinking about, "Wow, how did that happen? Okay, God, what's really going on?" I wasn't scared, but it was *different*.

6 Cross-Cultural Encounters in the Research: Lessons Learned 213

A ministry leader also spoke spontaneously of sandplay as a spiritual experience of God, as "God working through me" and that it required "a leap of faith" in what God was trying "to show" her:

> I think just the whole process of building the world and then not really knowing where it's going ... it's like taking a leap of faith because I don't know, you're going somewhere. You're going somewhere that you might not necessarily want to go and then once the world comes to you, then you can either shut down or you can explain where you fit in there ... it's just a real deep spiritual moment that happens in sandplay ... I mean that God's working through me and working through me building the world and really trying to show me something.

A different ministry leader spoke about one of the principles of peace, "faith," as representing an embodied movement of spirit. She reported that faith could mean a particular religion, but it also might mean just being spiritual, with spirituality for her meaning a force of energy and connection, a higher power guiding her or placing particular people in her life:

> I think spirituality is hard to explain. It's more of like a feeling, something that you just know, energy, people being connected, and I think that's through spirit ... Like I feel a higher power or something like speak to me or put me in different situations. Like I think that just me being at the Peace Institute is like an example of me following something spiritual. I didn't ever think that I would end up here.

If in the academic discipline of theology, material theo/poetics reflects the movement of God or Spirit in material form, then these artistic and peace practices can be correlated metaphorically to the academic discipline of psychology's neuroaffective studies of an embodied—or perhaps better said en-neuroned—experience of "God,"[21] as referenced in Chap. 2, though without reduction of one academic cultural world/view and language to the other. Such practices also may be correlated to relational-cultural theory when it speaks to "energy, power or 'zest'" in human relationships,[22] if this language is metaphorically reconceptualized in part as one's relationship to God or Spirit as well and how that relationship might be experienced in and through the body:

> The movement of relationship creates an energy, momentum, or power that is experienced as beyond the individual, yet available to the individual ... Empowerment is based on the capacity to turn toward and trust in the relationship to provide the ongoing context for such interaction. This action or movement of relationship, then, transfers to action in other realms as the person has become increasingly response/able and empowered to act.[23]

If survivors are regarded as experts or as primary theologians and granted normativity of phenomenological experience for their own language and narrative, then such metaphorical correlations to the embodied movement of spirit or God in the relationship also has possible implications for speaking back to academic theologians regarding the experience of power and control in one's relationship with God, as well as the location of God and God's embodiment in the human and in the material. Again, I will stress that I am not reducing one academic discipline's cultural world/view and world/sense and language to the other; I am simply seeking to mutually and critically correlate them through the multivalent excess of embodied metaphors and poetics while respecting the inherent normativity of these different phenomenological worlds. Not to engage in such respect would risk the unethical and the imposition of power that historically has been experienced as a colonizing cultural approach to religion and religious studies.[24]

For example, some of these reported experiences by Peace Institute participants included that spirituality was associated with "energy" and "people being connected"—through which a ministry leader spoke of "feeling" her spirituality. The founding ministry leader spoke of a "sense of a warm blanket inside of me, on me" when she attends church and says something similar happens to fellow survivors when they enter the Peace Institute. In regards to sandplay in particular, one survivor reported, "I felt like something just took over my body," while another ministry leader similarly said sandplay was "like taking a leap of faith ... God's working through me ... building the world and really trying to show me something." "God exists here," another ministry leader said of the Peace

Institute itself. God was regarded as an embodied and material *presence* in the space and was tangibly expressed through the quotes and other decorations on the walls. This spirit lingered and created an "aura" for the place of the Peace Institute as a whole, an experience of immanence as discussed in the prior section.

Each of the above statements by participants, as well as others by survivors who spoke of their personal experiences of God outside the context of the Peace Institute, reflected not an abstract distant experience of God or spirit but a relational image that was fully and physiologically embodied, at times material, and deeply personal and directly connected. This included the experience of God being the immanent sustaining force helping a survivor to get up in the morning or being the mysterious presence creating the appearance of a cup of coffee through a friend just when needed. God's movement was experienced spiritually through human-embodied connection to each other, as well as through human-embodied connection to material objects in sandplay and through other artistic expressions created. As explicit language of hope and peace, or a "leap of faith," was used in confession and testimony, *a religio/poetic interpretation* also began to enter for these material expressions, one with ecclesial and eschatological suggestions in a lay Christian theological context, as well as at times socio/poetic political suggestions, interpretations, and protest in other contexts, including in public testimony with memorial buttons, banners, and t-shirts.

Finally, it is important to recognize the role that the evolving theology and spirituality of the Peace Institute's founding ministry leader has played in shaping practices in light of her personal survivor relationship with God, one that complicates the idea that God controls each event of the world. Based on her own as well as survivor experiences, she has made a policy recommendation of what to say and not to say to survivors regarding this personal experience of God. This includes never to say "It was God's will" in reference to a survivor's family member's homicide. Pastoral care recommendations such as these are given religio/poetic material testimony in the Peace Institute's specialized funeral orders of service (Fig. 6.3). A more nuanced theological perspective and experience arose in the founding ministry leader's own personal connection to and discernment of God's will and her missionary calling in the aftermath of

FORGIVENESS

"Forgiveness does not equal forgetting. It is about healing the memory of the harm, not erasing it." Ken Hart

Comfort the surviving children. They are grieving the loss too and they are often forgotten. They need to express strong emotions that may seem awkward to others. Holding their hand, placing an arm around them or giving them a hug are simple ways of showing your emotional support. Be prepared for your gentle touch to set off a flood of tears that they may have been holding back. As difficult or uncomfortable as it may be for you, the greatest gift you can give the children is to give them the freedom and permission to cry openly. Being able to release their pent-up emotions will help them to feel better and to cope with the difficult days that still lie ahead.

Statements to avoid making to, or in the presence of, the family:
"It was God's will" - "He was with the wrong kind of people"
"You shouldn't cry so much." - "I understand how you feel."
"You must be over it by now." - "He lived the wrong kind of life."
"You have to be strong." - "You should let him rest in peace." "Wrong place at the wrong time" - "At least you don't have to worry about him anymore."
While you may be trying to help, these type of declarations usually do more harm than good.

Be on the look out: Sometimes survivors of homicide victims run into a complicated grieving pattern. Watch out for signs that may indicate their grief is becoming unhealthy, such as an appetite change resulting in dramatic weight gain or loss, or alcohol and drug abuse. You may need to be especially vigilant when survivors are going through unusually difficult times, e.g., birthdays, the anniversary of the murder, holidays, etc.

Remember them on special days: The first year after the murder is especially difficult. Anniversaries, birthdays, Father's Day, Mother's Day, Thanksgiving, and religious holidays can send survivors reeling. What were once festive occasions may now be times of sadness and despair. Call, visit, or send a brief note to the survivors letting them know that they are in your thoughts and/or prayers.

10

Fig. 6.3 *Peace Institute Funeral Order of Service, Sample Pastoral Care Advice Page.* Pastoral care recommendations the Peace Institute makes to those who attend the funerals, including religious or theological statements to avoid saying and awareness of days or situations when a survivor may be in need of particular pastoral care and attention. The extent of communal religious or spiritual education accomplished through these services should not be underestimated given the institutional power of the Peace Institute's involvement in pastoral care after the majority of homicides in the greater Boston area

her son's murder. Theologically, as she struggled to come to terms with the murder of her son, she arrived at the belief that human beings experience free will, but God can set an ultimate timetable for individuals, an understanding derived in part from Ecclesiastes 3:1–8: " ... I don't think it was ever God's will for Louis to die the way he did ... He could've been hit by a car ... anything could've happened but that was his time ... There's a given time when we are born, there's a given time when our life is no longer here on this earth ... I think it says somewhere, 'A time to live and a time to die, a time to mourn ... '."

Not every survivor was successful in "moving" through the structured spiritual healing processes created by the Peace Institute. Many never claimed a "Peace Warrior" identity and continued to exhibit broken and tenuous connections. Ministry leaders respected that each person might have an unknown timetable and personal responsibility for recognizing and choosing the path of peace God is "preparing." Formally and explicitly, the Peace Institute embraced the overall "brokenness" or limitations of humanity with compassion. Programmatically, ministry leaders also rejected any intent by God as having a purpose in *causing* suffering in survivors or as designating some of those murdered as "good" and some as "bad." All are loved and worthy of being saved, and there is accountability for choices but not "punishment" in most of these ministry leader and survivor images of God.

For the founding ministry leader in particular, as well as other ministry leaders who spoke in terms contrasting "spirit" and "flesh," suffering was seen as an inevitable aspect of the finitude of the human condition ("there is a season") as well as the God-given capacity of human free will. For this reason, *community* was needed to help each other achieve God's intended peace. Ministry leaders and survivors often strongly conveyed expectations that the church and its ministers should participate prophetically in creating God's peace as role models. They should seek humbly to learn from survivors as experts and prioritize supporting them both pastorally and prophetically. Unfortunately, this expectation often was disappointed, frequently bitterly so in survivor experiences reported. Those interviewed witnessed instead the church and many of its ministers emulating the competitive and status-seeking behaviors of the larger culture. If the church itself could not be an emblem of peace, then alternative communal space, and in many ways an alternative spiritual tribe, was needed and found through the place and practices of the Peace Institute.

Given their experiences with the institutional church and larger society, personal wholeness was seen as complicated by an inevitable "brokenness" and limitation that is part of the human condition, only compounded in the face of violence and trauma. For the founding ministry leader, God also can express a *desire* for how individuals choose to deal with the timetable God has set, though God will not mandate the outcome. Instead, God works actively to prepare individuals for God's calling and desire, though it remains up to the free will of the individual to recognize and receive that preparation:

> [B]ut I also believe ... that we were bein' prepared for Louis not bein' here, and I can only say that now. I can only say that, really now, and now, understanding, why we say, "God won't give you more than you can handle" but in that beginning that's not whatchoo wanna hear ... the choices I could've made was to stay home, to deal with my anger in a different way and that would've been justified because something bad did happen to me but that just wouldn't seem right with ... what I believe I'm being called to do, with what I believe the purpose on earth, my purpose, or we each have a purpose on earth, or with what I believe, again, "Thy will be done on earth as it is in heaven."

This calling and preparation then has implications not only for a particular individual but also for the larger community, church, and society and is an understanding that may come again only with time. For the founding ministry leader, her experience of her call from God became an embodied call to make God's message of peace a Christian eschatological reality in her community and beyond. This mission of peace could take both human and material shape, and the Peace Institute's prophetic pastoral care practices were deeply shaped by her embodied experience and vision of this call.

Key Lessons from the UU Trauma Response Ministry Case Study

Trauma disrupts all sense of normalcy, and for victims of violence, it does so in a way that can be experienced as morally intrusive and deliberate when at the hands of another human being. One TVUUC leader, present in the sanctuary that morning, said when asked about the process, practices, and meaning of "healing" for her:

> I guess healing means coming to a place where I can accept what happened in the sense that this person willfully chose our congregation because of who we are and what we strive to do ... it's hard to *accept* that there are evil people in the world ... I didn't wanna accept that, because I wanted to accept that, you know, life is good. It's what you make of it, you know, dah, dah, dah, dah. And it's hard to accept that somebody has so much hate in them that they want to harm you.

Reconciling prior more optimistic or liberal conceptions of human nature with the experience of being attacked and then failing to see remorse in the perpetrator, seeing that he experienced himself as a "proud offender" instead, left some TVUUC leaders struggling with accepting concepts of "*evil*" in their new frames of reference for their experience of the world. As previously indicated by participant reports, a favorite hymn "May Nothing Evil Cross This Door" took on new religio/poetic meaning in the aftermath of this violent intrusion.

Another TVUUC leader and direct survivor from that morning said, "... I've just never seen such hostility on a face before ... it felt like, um, sort of a supernatural force of destruction. It really did." Jones also would write that congregants had their first direct exposure to the assailant's lack of remorse at his preliminary hearing: "For many this situation challenged their long-held UU beliefs of dignity and worth for every human being. Thoughts about what to do with a murderer who showed no remorse, as well as occasional desires for revenge or atonement, gave rise to complicated emotions and some community debate."[25] Though the UUA historically has taken a public social justice stand against the death penalty, both the consulting UUTRM leader and the UUA president recommended, and the TVUUC ultimately decided, not to take a public stand as a church. To take a stand as either for or against the death penalty was regarded as placing an additional strain on individual congregants and the congregation as a whole in the midst of already turbulent emotions. A UUTRM leader said of their emphasis on the pastoral over the prophetic at that time: "The issue is to get everyone to come together, feel safe, support one another and be together, not polarizing over something like [the] death penalty, which can be so divisive," particularly since this act of violence impacted on an entire "social milieu."

Relational-cultural theory (RCT) emphasizes the role of connection and mutual empathy in human life as the basis of growth and authenticity and that disconnection creates feelings of hopelessness and isolation instead. UUTRM leaders sought to avoid further feelings of disconnection within the congregation amidst their encounter with violent trauma. For survivors of the TVUUC shooting interviewed, the attacker's hatred and failure to exhibit any capacity for remorse, as an expected basis for their own connection to and empathy with his humanity, already left them with a severe sense of visceral disconnection and no language other than "evil" or "supernatural force of destruction," in the sense of experiencing the attacker as alien or "other." This was a cognitively and emotionally disruptive experience for those interviewed, given their historical and sociocultural commitment to a religious tradition that often affirmed the innate goodness and capacity of human beings to love and care for one another and progressively improve over time. This then contributed to ethical and spiritual struggles regarding their proper response to the attacker as UUs committed to the worth and dignity of each person, which in turn overwhelmed their capacity at that time to affirm as a congregation the larger association's social justice commitment against the death penalty.

As pointed out in Chap. 2 and elsewhere, George Lakoff and Mark Johnson view "imaginative empathic projection"[26]—or what might be called imaginative empathic imaging in RCT language—as the basis of all embodied spiritual experiences. A failure to experience such empathy with or from an attacker can disrupt personal and group spiritual experiences for survivors in the aftermath of violent trauma *if* expectations of such experiences of empathy with all human beings have been *normalized* within a group's culture, world/view, or world/sense of spirituality or religion. A clinical or pastoral care provider might readily see how such a disruption of an *expected* embodied felt connection to a fellow human being then could feel alien or abnormal, to the point of being categorized as "evil" or a "supernatural force of destruction," and result in "othering" and a confused, paralyzed, or divisive and polarizing response depending on the religious and sociocultural historical context of those impacted. This also includes how such an encounter might stir uncomfortable feelings of hatred, fear, repulsion, and the desire for revenge—despite explicit spiritual beliefs opposing action on such feelings. The pastoral focus chosen by the UUTRM leaders at the time directed attention to reestablishing communal connections and empathy on this feeling level for TVUUC congregants rather than debate about beliefs and course of action, a longer-range project.

Drawing on IFS theory to broaden and examine this at the cultural level beyond conflicts within the self, parts of a larger social or religious system also can become polarized when the dominant culture's normalized expectations of empathy, diplomacy, or democratic or even "civilized" ways of being are disrupted from and by subdominant cultures. Such polarization can create tremendous situations of polarization in the culture of a religious institution or in a society itself, with human tendencies to "other" and denigrate more pronounced.[27] One UUTRM leader affirmed that UUs struggle with "human evil"[28] and have a need for a richer range of spiritual rituals or practices to help them "mend the potential of one's understanding of the universe":

> I think that UUs don't have a particularly good handle on ... human evil; on the capacity for human beings to do destructive things ... although I think this is less the case now than it was 30 years ago—the dearth of religious language or religious understanding for some people does not give them tools with which to do this work from a spiritual standpoint. It is psychologized but there's very little meaning making that occurs, you know? So I find the people who are most adept at doing this work are able to express themselves in a way that mends their relationship to the ultimate, when that relationship has been severed, by whatever name they call the ultimate ... the trust in the universe—the universe is a good place

... or the church itself is a safe place—and then having to grapple with the fact that it's also a human place and it's susceptible to things that human beings are susceptible to.

Yet another UUTRM leader expressed a passionate yearning for a richer capacity to theologize about and create rituals for recognizing trauma and evil within the UU tradition, a way to "embody" the inherent "brokenness" in our humanity more deeply and create accountability rather than elide the starkness of the encounter with an event that challenges an otherwise positive or optimistic view of human being:

> [S]ome of my strong criticisms of Unitarian Universalism, as a birthright UU, is that we do not have a theodicy. We don't talk about evil. We don't talk about that. We have had this trajectory, since at least the '30s, of onward and upward forever. We will become human perfection. We can do that. And so, that sense does not allow for a way to talk about our brokenness ... We have no understanding of what does it mean to screw up and no rite of reconciliation, as in the Catholic Church where we can say, "I've screwed up. Here's how I want to come back ... "—the fallibility of humankind ... has never been seriously dealt with since we turned away from the Calvinists. And we need to develop a more robust theodicy ... I'd long for something like the Rite of Reconciliation of the Catholic Church where we can say, "You know, I really screwed up." And rather than saying, "Oh no, no, no," someone will take me seriously and say, "Yeah, you did. And how are you gonna change your life now?" That kind of deep accounting, we too often don't do. We have not done very much collectively ... So although we've thrown out original sin, we've thrown out, also, the possibility for people to be human ... And so, collectively, we need more theology that deals with what does it mean to be human? How do we deal with evil? What is evil, how does it exist? How do *we* embody that, in order to be able to even begin to delve into then what is grief, death, loss about because ... especially with traumatic death, if we don't have an understanding of how we get there, we have no way to know how to come back.

The development of vibrant spiritual practices also may hinge on the UU tradition of being able to reconsider aspects of its tendency to normalize a positive theological anthropology or belief in innate human goodness, including the power and significance of reason (as well as formal education for salvation and protection).[29] Correlations to neuroaffective and attachment studies may help with such a project and "speak back" to UU theologians regarding their assumptive worlds and emphasis on cognition and reason, in essence continuing a long Western Christian tradition of mind and spirit over body. As discussed in Chap. 4, Thomas Lewis, Fari Amini, and Richard Lannon argue that we are physiologically interdependent and permeable through our limbic systems as mammals and that through "limbic resonance," emotions are actually contagious and can become communal:

> Because limbic states can leap between minds, feelings are contagious, while notions are not. If one person germinates an ingenious idea, it's no surprise that those in the vicinity fail to develop the same concept. But the limbic activity of those around us draws our emotions into almost immediate congruence … The same limbic evocation sends waves of emotion rolling through a throng, making scattered individuals into a unitary, panic-stricken herd or hate-filled lynch mob.[30]

Emotions can be contagious—whether these are emotions of hate or fear, such as might be "caught" from an experience with a mass shooter, or, on a more positive note, whether these are emotions experienced through shared wonder, awe, laughter, tears, reassurance, or beauty, such as might be felt during congregational worship, including the experiences shared by TVUUC leaders in reference to their "interfaith" and rededication services.

In other words, a correlation with phenomenology observed by the social science of neurophysiology teaches that there is no inherent *enduring* biological disposition toward love and empathy or reason other than a minimal baseline as infants we share with other mammals. Instead, human beings are vulnerable and share emotional and physiological capacities and needs, which include attachment and fear, and these are socialized, nurtured or repressed, and responded to in interaction with family and a larger ecological and institutional environment over time, including through the impact of trauma. As Lewis et al. also write, "Because mammals need relatedness for their neurophysiology to coalesce correctly, most of what makes us a socially functional human comes from connection ... Children who get minimal care can grow up to menace a negligent society ... America produces remorseless killers in bulk."[31] Human beings are capable both of great acts of love and great acts of "evil" or harm, and of an entire range in between.[32] Religious rituals and practices are needed across all traditions to ground us spiritually in the painful complexity of this potential reality—while continuing to foster the social conditions for empathy, compassion, and love. In this, there is a shared ethical responsibility, and in this, also we can learn from intercultural lived religion studies.

As illustrated in Chap. 4, UUTRM leaders did give additional examples of religio/poetic material rituals designed to meet such needs in the aftermath of trauma, including those drawn from other traumatic events to which they had ministered. One example cited by a UUTRM leader was that of the use of "holy humor"[33] to assist holding survivors and their first responders or helpers with compassion through the complex range of human feelings possible in the aftermath of trauma. In particular, she shared a story from serving at Ground Zero as an illustration of how extraordinary and complex emotional tensions may be held and released with humor, affirming how an action that might be experienced as offensive to some actually becomes a release of righteous anger and religio/poetic witness to a different vision of God through the recognition and practice of such empathic "holy humor":

> I'm thinking of a story of Ground Zero and I'm thinking of these born-again Christian missionaries who showed up when it was a little more open and ... one of my jobs was to ... be at the morgue and bless body parts and the bodies as they came in—and these born-again Christians were bound and determined that anyone who died was gonna have the blessings, so that they could go straight to heaven. And two firefighters that I know of went and got socks that had been donated, and after sitting outside for a few days the socks were kinda grungy, and they put 'em in a black plastic bag, and they brought 'em up to these two that had been blessing everybody, you know, "Go straight to heaven" ... and they said to those two guys, "You gotta come because we think we've found a body part," and it was really that the firefighters had taken a black plastic bag, gotten dirty socks, put that

in there and done it. So you might think that's that a really bizarre situation, and it is, but it is a way of dealing with, kind of, that bizarre humor, that holy humor that helps . . . because . . . these firefighters were overwhelmed with having been given the responsibility for the safety of, what they said to me quote unquote, "these two idiots" who were bound and determined that they were gonna get a body part and that they were gonna make sure that this body went straight to heaven. And I said to the firefighters, "Whadda you think about that?" and they said, "We are so busy taking care of everyone and ourselves and we know and trust that ultimately, as horrible as this thing is, God is a God of Love and nobody needs to be blessed. No one would ever not have eternal rest after this experience but we're charged with taking care of these two idiots, so we just conjured up this scheme.". . . Not a lot of people would appreciate that story . . . .

Human service providers might recognize this practice in a secular context as what we have termed "graveyard humor" as a way of releasing extraordinary physiological tension in intense situations—in IFS language, the multiplicity that arises in the self and in the larger community, all vying for attention space in their respective needs. When the language of "holy" is added to this, however, it becomes lifted metaphorically to a new level of the "something more" of meaning-making in significance, lending perhaps a quality of human forgiveness and compassionate and connected poignancy beyond what might otherwise seem cynical or acutely disconnected. The connection in this moment to a ministerial presence through a "listening ear" also serves to bring out the larger sacred story and narrative behind the practice, illuminating religio/poetic dimension as an expression and release of pain for this particular spiritual tribe tasked with holding so much affect—anger, exhaustion, heartbreak, compassion, and hope.

For TVUUC participants interviewed, the memorialization of the TVUUC's minister's 10-part series of sermons on a CD for all congregants proved to be a powerful religio/poetic material artifact testifying to their spiritual continuity and resiliency as a congregation in the aftermath of violent trauma and their experience with "evil." The TVUUC minister self-described his homiletic style as a "journey from irreverence to reverence," and indeed, his sermons were peppered with much responsive laughter, as observed within the first minute of the rededication sermon only one week after the traumatic event. In his tenth and final sermon on the CD, the TVUUC minister used All Soul's Day to highlight the intent to create memorials to the slain *within* the church and also linked this intent to stories of the long line of UU martyrs in history, particularly to the first formally recognized Unitarian martyr Michael Servetus.[34] This narrative act placed the two slain persons as souls in a larger community of guiding UU saints in sacred story making, materially marked in memory now on the church's interior. Such saints then could be pointed to and drawn from in an ongoing communal narration that was both religious and material in nature, as, for example, written in the last line in the dedication plaque for Greg McKendry: "Greg McKendry's love of life and impulse for service inspire everyone who enters this place of fellowship."

All ten sermons, including the rededication sermon, were collected on this CD as a permanent material artifact for members of the congregation and were made available to me as a researcher. Throughout the sermon series, there is a striking narrative use of self by the minister, particularly through the pastoral care image of "the wounded healer"[35] to create a "relational pulpit"[36] and to "story a religious vision" in the aftermath of this traumatic event. He links pastoral care of self and communal prophetic challenge, as well as unity through the public disclosure of his own emotional processes of grief, rage, and anxiety. Two examples are seen in his third sermon, "Healing Waters," and in his fifth sermon, "A New Beginning in the New Normal," in which he openly shares about his own emotional and bodily struggles in the aftermath of trauma, including the "molting of his hands" and role modeling the need to seek out all forms of healing and therapy while also drawing upon communal support to find spiritual healing. The permanent recording of these sermon stories then became a material artifact of religio/poetic testimony to and sacred story of the resilience and resistance of this particular spiritual tribe in the aftermath of violent trauma, witnessed by ongoing and new members to the tribe who received copies of the CD, again what might also be termed an ongoing practice of "recovery of the historical memory of change," per liberation health theory.

The power of a religious narrative to create vision and an "alternative story" in the aftermath of trauma, as well as the recognition of the systemic dimensions of social power, come together in the arc and material preservation of these ten sermons. These sermons intertwine pastoral care and prophetic care by reinforcing a Universalist theological narrative of "God is Love," a mystical unifying love repeatedly seen to undergird all major religions.[37] This experience of God, as preached by the TVUUC minister, calls each to care for self and neighbor but also to honor human limitations and vulnerability in providing such care—including the experience of anger and limitations on forgiveness. This was seen as particularly important by the minister when challenging a dominant cultural discourse of powerful social forces acting to dehumanize entire groups of people, including liberals, through "hate speech."

Sermon themes also preached to the "vulnerable, peace-loving, nonviolent liberal," whom "it does not take much courage to attack and wound." Paradoxically, in the TVUUC minister's experience, this religious liberal finds power in responding to the call of love through prophetic self-defense, as well as public resistance through "self definition" rather than "other definition." This overall combination of homiletic relational images and narrative with a religio/poetic material remembrance amounts to what Edward Rynearson and Alison Salloum also identify as a "restorative retelling"[38] in the aftermath of violent traumatic death—a restorative retelling process in which intrusive violent imagery and narratives are gradually moderated by more "hopeful and purposive"[39] imagery and narratives in the context of historical relationships. A "liberal" is not weak and vulnerable to attack; a liberal is prophetic and powerful in capacity to stand on the side of love in this reframed sacred story, per the TVUUC minister's sermons.

Referring often to their experiences of receiving "love" and affirmation and to the TVUUC covenant "love is the spirit of this church, service is its law," TVUUC leaders placed relationships and a sense of a larger unity at the center of their experience of the sacred or divine in the immediate aftermath of the trauma. This centering in spiritual love explicitly was connected to a common mystical thread in all world religions by the TVUUC minister throughout his sermons, frequently drawing from the Sufi mystic Rumi for quotes as well as the minister's oft-repeated definition of God: "Whenever two or more people gather together to love and support and encourage each other, there is a power greater than ourselves that can renew, restore and sustain us."[40]

Love is thus experienced as the source of renewal and hope, of sustenance, restoration, and service *in* community.[41] UUTRM and TVUUC participant responses were consistent with understanding Unitarian Universalism as being and possessing a *public* theology in ethical and ecclesial practice rather than being a religion of specific doctrines of the divine or sacred.[42] However, despite this heritage of a common public theology focused on ethical relationships, many interview participants often shared deep frustrations with their faith tradition and its perceived limitations for religious practices in the face of trauma. These frustrations and limitations centered on a sense of inadequacy in preparation for understanding and reconciling *in practice* the negative capacities and limits of human nature with the faith tradition's emphasis on more optimistic human possibilities for love, compassion, and progressive rational growth through justice and equality in "beloved community."[43] This inadequacy was experienced as particularly stark when confronted with the reality of violent traumatic intrusion, loss, and human evil.

Through the development of rituals and practices of sacred ambiguity or holy humor, UUTRM leaders also sought to be nuanced and sensitive in holding pastorally the paradoxes and contradictions of human experiences and emotions in the aftermath of trauma, the multiplicity and ambiguity in these experiences, creating healing space for the development of a sense of normality, functionality, efficacy, integration, and transformation over time. For TVUUC leaders, having a leadership role to play at times assisted their healing process by giving them focus and a greater sense of control in the aftermath of trauma. However, both the provision of care and the receipt of care could be marked by confusion, disorientation, fear, anger, frustration, hurt, disappointment, despair, burnout, etc. In my site visit, a TVUUC leader was observed to say in her Sunday morning pastoral prayer that the human heart during normal times "is a mess in there." Trauma compounds this "mess." Rituals are needed to hold and transform the "sacred ambiguity" of this process as well as affirm its "holy humor" when possible, releasing tension through laughter and a loving, compassionate community.

A Few Overall Key Lessons in My Intercultural Encounters

Maintaining an ethical focus of respect in dialogue across difference is consistent with my UU religious tradition's embrace of ethical principles in covenant, including their affirmation of the worth and dignity of each person and promotion of justice. However, I discovered in the course of listening to participants in the case studies that an additional layer of ethical tension exists in any dialogue, particularly intercultural ones, which is the right of naming—the right of claiming the language that expresses one's experiences, worth, and dignity. Valuing such a right also is not inconsistent with my own UU tradition in their practice of right relationship through awareness of power relations and promotion of justice nor with my profession of clinical social work practice. Nonetheless, the extent of the contemporary problem of violence, particularly in the US context, emits its own ethical call for action, interdisciplinary work, and the capacity to forge new links between different communities of language and experiences. Thus I engage the risk entailed in laying out a few more overlapping lessons and wonderings not already explicitly drawn out.

Sources and Language of Sustenance and Connection

While an explicit theism was central to the experience of God for LDBPI ministry leaders and survivors, and love was central to the experience of the divine or sacred for TVUUC leaders, as well as many other UUTRM participant interviews, the need for *relational sustenance* was an important common thread in both studies. Culturally, this took the form of turning to a theistic God for support in getting out of the bed each morning, as well as to fellow survivors for solidarity and support in the Peace Institute study. In the UUTRM study, this took the form of being inspired by the spontaneous human outpouring of communal, denominational, ecumenical, and interfaith support. For both case studies, violent traumatic loss highlighted human vulnerability and the social need for others, whether experienced and named in Christian terms as a sustaining relationship with God and Spirit or with the divine as mediated through human grace and love.

Additionally, the quality of this relational sustenance often was couched in immanent physical terms and embodied rituals, including ones expressing a material religio/poetic. From my initial pilot studies with young adult family members in Boston, I learned that loved ones lost through violent trauma also were felt as an ongoing *visceral* presence, most often when they wore memorial buttons or t-shirts with pictures of their loved one, and particularly when several of them wore them *together* for the same event. Buttons were enlivened with the presence of their murdered loved one in a similar way that sandplay worlds were enlivened. This enlivening in turn is amplified in performative testimony with other survivors as well as with witnesses, buttons worn together with family or on the Mothers' Day Walk for Peace brought forth even more powerfully the still living presence of their murdered loved one. The focus on *relational energy and connection* conveyed through material objects, as well as the place and space of the Peace Institute, gave religio/poetic witness both to God's presence for survivors and to an implicit metaphoric pneumatology of living and embodied spiritual energy.

These testimonies also gave witness to the usefulness of continuing bonds and relational-cultural theory in highlighting this lived religion phenomenon as expressed by survivors through their sacred stories and testimonies in the Peace Institute case study. For UUTRM and TVUUC leaders, a variety of religious practices expressed an expanded and embodied sense of spiritual connection and growth, physical testimonial, and material witness to the divine or sacred, named by these case study participants as love and grace. Thus the experience of God or the divine often would take embodied and material form for participants in both studies, though their particular cultural religious language for that experience might differ significantly by virtue of being a Christian narrative or a UU narrative in religious interpretation of their respective phenomenological experiences and truth claims.

Struggles with Meaning-Making and Forgiveness

It was interesting that both the LDBPI founding ministry leader and the TVUUC minister drew upon the parable of "The Good Samaritan," though in different ways and from different cultural needs—one to propel outward prophetically and the other to justify an inward pastoral focus. The LDBPI founding ministry leader specifically conceptualized her sense of God's call to "Christian neighbor-love" through the Good Samaritan narrative and challenged herself with the question, "Who *is* my neighbor?" This motivated her movement outward from purely a focus on her community of origin to work instead across lines of race and class as well as religion. The TVUUC minister drew differently upon the Good Samaritan narrative to legitimize and normalize the congregation's need to care for its own brokenness first. While he recognized that the one who had inflicted harm also was sick and in need of grace and care, he resisted various pressures "to forgive" and focus on the person who had engaged in harm, as much as this tested a faith claim to care for the worth and dignity of each person. The TVUUC minister distinguished between holding a perpetrator to "accountability" versus the granting of "cheap grace," role modeling instead that "forgiveness has its own timetable" and the "best we can do is be open to forgiveness" while also giving priority to establishing safety and boundaries. These latter points align with the Peace Institute ministry leaders' formal stance that while all are worthy in God's eyes, there is accountability in personal choices.

Both the Peace Institute founding ministry leader and the TVUUC minister found areas of practical agreement that "forgiveness has its own timetable." They agreed that adequate pastoral care first involves the rejection of forced forgiveness on a survivor. Instead, human finitude needed to be honored while also holding tenderly the hope and possibility for a more embracing, inclusive love and letting go that accompanies a deeper internal peace. This included holding such hope at times through the complexity of "holy humor," UUTRM language that also fits the experience of the Peace Institute founding ministry leader calling "forgiveness," one of their seven Principles of Peace, "the 'F' word." She often would laugh as she said this in various contexts, holding the fiercely defiant rage, "I am a very angry woman," together with what she saw as the possibility of a larger letting go in peace, "the fullness of God's peace."

The Language of "Evil" in Cultural Context

Ministry leaders in both case studies were particularly sensitive to the creation of pastoral care practices to hold this complex range of emotional experiences in the aftermath of violent trauma, to hold the tension between the reality of devastation, loss, and anger and the desire for hope and renewal, through a "kaleidoscope" of practices addressing the multiplicity of the many "pieces." However, for TVUUC leaders, the uniqueness of violent trauma occurring in a cultural context that typically experienced itself as sheltered and privileged led to a sense of confusion, as well as a sense of loss, for practices to grapple with human "evil." Escalating anxiety and confusion in the aftermath meant the larger denomination's social justice commitment against the death penalty, based on an ethical commitment to promoting the worth and dignity of each person, had to be deferred for fundamental pastoral care needs first. Such a violent traumatic event was foreign and thoroughly disruptive to the normal lived reality and expectations of UUs, as experienced by TVUUC leaders, adding another layer of traumatic disruption to their world/view and world/sense.[44]

In contrast, a concern for "evil" did not tend to emerge spontaneously in LDBPI survivor and ministry leader interviews, where there more often was an explicit rejection of binaries of salvation, binaries reflecting an understanding that some were innately bad and deserving of punishment while others were more worthy of life. Instead, Peace Institute ministry leaders' interpretations of their lay Christian narrative and culture, and survivors' daily encounters with oppression by race, class, and/or violence, led to more explicit and extensive connection of personal and social salvation, particularly for survivors when educated to see these links through the Leadership Academy. For LDBPI ministry leaders, all were potentially vulnerable, though accountable to a loving God who prepared a path of grace for each. There could be no fullness of personal salvation until all were saved in the realized eschatology of God's peace.

6 Cross-Cultural Encounters in the Research: Lessons Learned   233

While TVUUC leaders professed a UU theological heritage of Universalism and universal salvation and love, *in practice*, the need to engage others who might test such beliefs was not part of their cultural lived religious reality in quite the same way as it was for LDBPI survivors and ministry leaders. Peace Institute participants interviewed sometimes faced having a victim and perpetrator in the same family or needed to reconcile parents or siblings of both victims and survivors being in the same survivor group with each other. A striking example is the founding ministry leader's relationship with the mother of her son's murderer, who volunteers regularly at the Peace Institute and, since the time of the original research, now speaks regularly in partnership with her son and the founding ministry leader on restorative justice practices. There were greater opportunities and need for communal reckoning, restoration, and renewal on a more personal, embodied, and social level in the cultural context of the Peace Institute case study than the cultural context of the TVUUC case study.

"Healing" in the Cultural Context of Power and Privilege Versus Oppression

Both case studies reflected some cultural level of clinical or soteriological belief in the resiliency of human nature and its capacity to "heal" itself, including in the aftermath of trauma, but this belief was sharpest in the LDBPI study as a form of prophetic pastoral care protest that "survivors are experts" with "PhD's in suffering" whose voices and experiences need to be heard at the highest levels of society in order to better shape policies and programs. Seeds of this belief also were present explicitly in the UUTRM study, including in relational images of the "wounded healer" and recognition of the added credibility such experiences might bring. These were heavily tempered, however, by cultural beliefs also in the value of ongoing specific professional training in trauma treatment and ministry, particularly by UUA external supporters of the UUTRM, who sought assurances of authority and ethical competence in UUTRM ministry leaders through such training. Again, this was consistent with a historical tendency for UUs to place a high value on education as enhancing a path to salvation and enlightenment and protection against potential harm to self or others.

This suggests that the needs of participants for "healing" in each case study might have been different by virtue of differing social experiences with oppression or privilege. For LDBPI survivors and ministry leaders, asserting as a social equity and justice practice the public identity of "survivors as experts," including the capacity of survivors to educate themselves and others, provided a counter story to the controlling images of low-income people of color as "less than capable." In contrast, the demand for competency and training in UUTRM leaders both reinforced the need for cultural humility in those deemed more socially privileged while also paradoxically reinforcing that same privilege through social certification, certification that often required time and money to achieve and maintain. Paradoxically also, the hoped for result of humility in "servanthood" by UUTRM leaders did not always play out in the pastoral experiences of some TVUUC leaders for this particular case study, though this certainly was not true of every interaction with UUTRM leaders for all TVUUC leaders, others of whom expressed very positive and overall appreciative interactions.

LDBPI survivors and ministry leaders spoke of finding more "therapy" in the para-ecclesial space and place of the Peace Institute than in a traditional therapist's office—they found more "healing" (or "movement") and empowerment through companionship with fellow survivors who shared their journey and struggles and with whom they did not have to repeat or even speak their stories. TVUUC leaders often found great solace in "being church," in taking leadership roles connecting their story of survival to a much larger story of religious persecution and resistance for both their denomination and their specific church. Even when a greater experience of healing was found in eventually laying the burdens of leadership down, the powerful connection to a larger religious narrative and felt sense of a transcendent "we" in their shared sacred story as a spiritual tribe remained for TVUUC leaders.

Of course, the probability of exposure to violence resulting in homicide was clearly a greater shared and ongoing lived reality for the racial and socioeconomic community served by the LDBPI than for the communities generally served by the UUTRM, or for the TVUUC in particular.

6 Cross-Cultural Encounters in the Research: Lessons Learned 235

Cultural expectations and world/sense by LDBPI ministry leaders and survivors were created against a backdrop of living within a larger reality that constantly presented controlling media images of their oppressed status as racialized survivors. They reported frequently being served by white middle-class educated providers and subjected to a range of microaggressions[45] from the very people tasked with their care, from police to therapists. Hence, a felt need for a permanent para-ecclesial institution to provide structural analysis of the root causes of such violence also was greater in the Peace Institute's lived cultural context.

Consistently, yet only in responses by Peace Institute participants, there was an emphasis on the need for theoretical education regarding issues of systemic oppression and violence, particularly the intertwining of race, class, and gender and a public health approach to violence prevention. Only in Peace Institute participant responses was such education experienced as liberating and motivating toward dismantling structures of oppression and implementing instead a sociological or religious vision of a more peaceful and just community. In contrast to the UUTRM case study, literature that spoke to resisting "cultural hegemony" and "controlling images" from the dominant social culture correlated more frequently with the needs and practices expressed by Peace Institute participants. There were hints of this in the UUTRM case study, primarily in the TVUUC minister's resisting perceptions of the larger society's controlling images of "liberals." Nonetheless, participant responses in the TVUUC context did not draw out the fullest range of correlative possibilities to a specific anti-oppression social analysis or metaphors reflecting a living consciousness of their existence within a dominant culture of power and privilege.[46] However, their explicit cultural struggles with understanding a religious response to "evil," even the labeling such as alien and "other," supported an implicit social analysis appropriate to those living with more power and privilege and normally a wider variety of choices in protection from or response to violent traumatic intrusion.

There also was a shared cultural understanding by the TVUUC minister and LDBPI ministry leaders and survivors that personal peace and social peace are tied together. Both stressed the cultural value of teaching the young the skills of peace, but the two communities proceeded to do this task differently. Only with the LDBPI ministry did this emerge as a specific program of commitment, including their development of a peace curriculum for use in the Boston Public Schools. The UUTRM leaders did embrace a specific anti-oppression commitment to justice in their mission and spoke of various contexts where that commitment came more explicitly to the fore.[47] However, religious trauma experienced by the TVUUC did not bring this intertwining of pastoral and prophetic care practices out in as dramatic a fashion as in the LDBPI study. TVUUC and UUTRM leaders interviewed primarily shared a concern for the pastoral care gap in their capacity to respond effectively to evil and suffering due to the paucity of UU theological resources and rituals for engagement of trauma.

Finally, in examining the cultural power of an *explicit* religious narrative, it is interesting also to note that the public embrace of a specific religious narrative in the context of the UUTRM's work with the TVUUC allowed the minister to consciously and deliberately place the two murdered victims into a larger UU narrative of religious persecution and resistance over centuries. For the LDBPI, which seeks to operate in secular and interfaith contexts, ministry leaders often were less public about their lay Christian cultural orientation. There similar theology of resistance and hope[48] is more frequently muted and only implicit in their various prophetic pastoral care and social justice practices, such as the creation of their traveling wall of memorial buttons displayed at public events, including their annual Mothers' Day Walk for Peace.

The LDBPI thus is limited in some ways in expressing the fullest Christian cultural meanings that might be attached to their particular performative and commemorative practices, ones that also seek to create dangerous memories of testimony and witness to the Christian eschatological vision of "the fullness of God's peace," in the words of the Peace Institute's ministry founder. However, the sacred story they create through the life of Louis as well as the seven Principles of Peace do draw out interfaith and interdisciplinary secular transcendent power in ways that a commitment solely to the Christian tradition might not.

Notes

1. Derald Wing Sue and David Sue define worldview as "how a person perceives his or her relationship to the world (nature, institutions, other people, etc.) ... [N]ot only are worldviews composed of our attitudes, values, opinions, and concepts ... [they also] affect how we think, define events, make decisions, and behave ... [race and ethnicity], economic and social class, religion, sexual orientation, and gender are also interactional components of a worldview." See *Counseling the Culturally Diverse: Theory and Practice*, 4th edition (New York: John Wiley & Sons, 2003) 267–268.
2. "Ways of being" is a language that I have observed used in various activist communities, such as the recent Boston Occupy Movement, to express differences in cultural styles and forms of expression that can sometimes cause conflict between groups seeking to do collaborative organizing. These require explicit uncovering, discussion, and practice to create shared guidelines and agreements.
3. See Michael Omi and Howard Winant, *Racial Formation in the United States*. Also see Dwight N. Hopkins, *Being Human: Race, Culture, and Religion* (Minneapolis: Fortress Press, 2005), 128–160, for an excellent historical summary of the history of the idea of race through a theological lens. A briefer practical theological focus on race in the twenty-first century can be found in Dale P. Andrews, "Race and Racism," in *The Wiley-Blackwell Companion to Practical Theology*, edited by Bonnie Miller-McLemore (Malden, MA: Wiley-Blackwell, 2014), 401–411.
4. It is likely that the language of "the interdependent web" as found in the 7th UU principle draws from a zeitgeist of feminist and process of theological thinking in the 1980s, but there is no formal tracing of the roots of this language. See Commission on Appraisal, *Engaging Our Theological Diversity*, 72–74. I have argued often in other contexts that the language of "the interdependent web" is UU contemporary metaphorical God-talk.
5. Pink, *Doing Sensory Ethnography*.

6. Mary McClintock Fulkerson, *Places of Redemption: Theology for a Worldly Church* (Oxford: Oxford University Press, 2007), 26. I appreciate Fulkerson's use of ethnographic and auto-ethnographic descriptive terms such as "visceral" in this study. I found correlative use for this type language with RCT's use of "zest" and "power" for describing energetic connections as well as in relationship to young adult descriptions in my pilot studies for their experience of their connection to their lost loved one while wearing memorial buttons and t-shirts.
7. Ibid., 29.
8. Ammerman, *Sacred Stories, Spiritual Tribes*.
9. Judith V. Jordan, "The Meaning of Mutuality," 82, in *Women's Growth in Connection: Writings from the Stone Center*, edited by Jordan, Judith V., Alexandra G. Kaplan, Jean Baker Miller, Irene P. Stiver, Janet L. Surrey (The Guilford Press: New York, 1991), 81–96.
10. It is the case that certain psychoanalytic frames of analysis also could be fruitfully applied to this same data, such as D.W. Winnicott's "holding environment"; however, this book seeks to highlight the metaphoric and conceptual possibilities in other social scientific theories, for example, relational-cultural theory (RCT), not typically used for correlation with theological language, in order to explore their metaphoric fit (e.g. RCT's embodied sense of energy and connection and the language of Spirit). For another effort to push the boundaries of the psychoanalytic conception of self and a creative use of Winnicott's concepts in application to theology, including an affirmation of the embodied self and an examination of the relational space between selves via air and water metaphors, see Thandeka, "The Self Between Feminist Theory and Theology." The difficulty with Thandeka's efforts in her essay, as at times with other psychoanalytic correlations to religion, can be the perceived reduction of religion to psychology, e.g. the reduction of the "Holy Spirit" to Winnicott's concept of the "transitional object," rather than holding theology and psychology as separate metaphorical fields to be mutually and critically correlated through the multivalent excess and creative tension of

embodied metaphor rather than reduced one to the other or even stated as purely analogous.

11. My assumption was that the church would be experienced minimally as a helpful resource for the families in the aftermath of homicide through pastoral care and visitation. Hence, I was surprised that this was not the experience of most of the survivors I happened to interview, and this admittedly was disturbing to my own value system as a minister.
12. Unitarian Universalist Association, *Singing the Living Tradition* (Boston: Unitarian Universalist Association, 1993/2000), 1.
13. The TVUUC minister reported that these words are drawn from another classic UU hymn, "As Tranquil Streams," ibid., 145. Though the text of this particular hymn was written in 1933, it also was used for the service honoring the consolidation of the Universalist and Unitarian denominations into their current association in 1961. Complete text for hymns referenced may be found in the current edition of *Singing the Living Tradition*, and more historical information about the hymns may be found in Jacqui James, editor, *Between the Lines: Source for Singing the Living Tradition*, second edition (Boston: Skinner House Books, 1995/1998).
14. This also reminded me of reports by some young adult survivors of family homicide in my pilot studies of the importance to them of keeping the bullet-torn clothing, or even samples of blood, of their murdered loved one from the crime scene. There was a deeper embodied connection through such preservation that also represented hope and a sacred longing for or experience of continued bonds, albeit with a different religio/poetic significance than that given by the former TVUUC church administrator to the curtain.
15. One TVUUC leader wrote an appreciative email later to the researcher that the telling of this story allowed the TVUUC leader to "debrief" in a way that had not happened at that time.
16. Hudson, *Congregational Trauma*, found that working with the media in a situation of congregational trauma was highly sensitive and warranted the devotion of a substantial part of one chapter in terms of pastoral care tips, see Chap. 7, "Surviving in the Public Eye."

17. In Jones, *Straightening Up*, 22, the UUTRM representative involved in the media conflict was reported as angrily saying at one point, "Who's in charge here?!" and this interaction would prompt a lot of reflection afterwards on the complicated realities of church governance for TVUUC leaders in Jones' analysis.
18. "God" also was clearly a classically theistic God (as distinguished from panentheistic or pantheist) as well as a gendered God in the use of male pronouns by all survivors and ministry leaders. This study did not seek to explore personal Christologies, though all ministry leaders and survivors interviewed referenced being raised in Christian traditions. One ministry leader did use explicit Christological language, while another ministry leader stressed that she experienced herself as more "spiritual," and another ministry leader said she historically had experienced a deeper relationship to "Mary" than to "Jesus" in her own faith journey.
19. Two (a survivor and a ministry leader who also was a survivor), however, did raise beliefs that there was a "purpose" or a "test" in their suffering, a larger perhaps mysterious reason that was associated for both participants with their scriptural learning.
20. R. Ruard Ganzevoort and Nette Falkenburg, "Stories Beyond Life and Death: Spiritual Experiences of Continuity and Discontinuity among Parents Who Lose a Child," *Journal of Empirical Theology* 25/2 (2012), 189–204.
21. Newberg, et al., *Why God Won't Go Away*.
22. Janet L. Surrey, "Relationship and Empowerment," in *Women's Growth in Connection: Writings from the Stone Center*, 162–180, edited by Jordan, Judith V., Alexandra G. Kaplan, Jean Baker Miller, Irene P. Stiver, Janet L. Surrey (New York: The Guilford Press, 1991), 172.
23. Ibid., 168.
24. It was beyond the scope of these particular case studies to implement a full decolonizing approach in methodology, and likewise, it is beyond the scope of this particular book to integrate all the work being done in postcolonial studies. Primarily, I seek to lift up the voices, language, and experiences of survivors as experts on their own terms and seek

points of metaphorical contact in correlations with social science theories that reflect their lived experiences and offer liberative frames of analysis. For theologians in particular, however, I do recommend a further and deeper embrace of this material.
25. Jones, *Straightening Up*, 46–47.
26. Lakoff and Johnson, *Philosophy in the Flesh*, 565.
27. I have observed Richard Schwartz in recent annual IFS conferences to be expanding upon his respective IFS concepts of "cultural legacy burdens" and "polarized parts" to apply to larger sociological cultural systems, particularly the current US context.
28. For example, the Universalist belief that "God is love" and the Unitarian belief in optimistic ethical progress for humankind has meant, at times, the place or role of sin, suffering, and evil in UU theology and practices is less than clear. In a 2002 *UU World* edition (the denominational magazine) dedicated to the problem of evil in the aftermath of 9/11, Warren Ross wrote, "Lois Fahs Timmins—the daughter of the great Unitarian religious educator Sophia Lyon Fahs—once criticized her own liberal religious education for failing to address the reality of evil. 'We spent 95 percent of our time studying good people doing good things, and skipped very lightly over the bad parts of humanity,' she said in 1996. 'I was taught not to be judgmental, not to observe or report on the bad behavior of others. Consequently, because of my education, I grew up ignorant about bad human behavior, incompetent to observe it accurately, unskilled in how to respond to it, and ashamed of talking about evil.'" See Warren Ross, "Confronting Evil: Has Terrorism Shaken Our Religious Principles?" *UU World* http://www.uuworld.org/2002/01/feature1.html (accessed July 19, 2013).
29. Twentieth century Unitarian ethicist and minister James Luther Adams also has written on the struggle liberal religious faiths, including Christianity, have had with conceptions of human nature throughout time. See "The Changing Reputation of Human Nature," in *The Essential James Luther Adams: Selected Essays and Addresses*, 51–78 (1941), edited by George K. Beach (Boston: Beacon Press, 1998). On the issue of education as a path of salvation, I note

here very interesting doctoral work being done in this area by Hannah Adams Ingram, a religious studies student at the University of Denver, who presented at the 2016 Bienniel Association of Practical Theology conference on "The Myth of the Saving Power of Education".
30. Lewis, et al., *A General Theory of Love*, 64.
31. Ibid., 218.
32. This is not to dismiss or minimize the spiritual potential and capacity of human beings nor the human capacity for strength and resiliency but merely to temper more understanding of that potential as highly vulnerable when isolated or damaged, particularly by trauma, and in need of communal and institutional protection and sustenance to access that potential, unless the damage is irretrievable through the neurophysiological vulnerability of the body. The social scientific theories utilized in correlation for these studies would be supportive of both strength and vulnerability along a number of levels. I will return to theological correlations on this point in the final chapter.
33. Another UUTRM leader said that one of the ways UUTRM leaders provide pastoral care support to each other is by recognizing that "we have a tremendously morbid sense of humor" in sharing and discharging the buildup of the complex range of emotional tensions they hold.
34. Michael Servetus was an anti-trinitarian, claimed in the heritage of European Unitarianism, who lived in the sixteenth century and wrote several texts opposing the doctrine of the Trinity. Ultimately, he was burned at the stake by the decree of John Calvin for refusing to recant his views. In critiquing this decision by Calvin, Sebastian Castellio would famously write, "To kill a man is not to defend a doctrine. It is simply to kill a man." See Charles A. Howe, *For Faith and Freedom: A Short History of Unitarianism in Europe* (Boston: Skinner House Books, 1997), 41.
35. See Dykstra, *Images of Pastoral Care*, for an outline of the various images of pastoral care that often have been drawn upon as guiding relational imagery by pastoral care providers. The image of "the wounded healer" is particularly associated with theologian Henri

Nouwen and his pastoral theology that the minister is not apart from the shared conditions of humanity, that the minister also is capable of being wounded, but the minister then uses these wounds to relate to humanity more empathically and compassionately in the healing process.

36. See Scott W. Alexander, *The Relational Pulpit: Closing the Gap Between Preacher and Pew* (Boston: Skinner House, 1993), as well as John S. McClure, *The Roundtable Pulpit: Where Leadership and Preaching Meet* (Nashville: Abingdon Press, 1995), on relational and collaborative preaching styles, and also see Jacqueline J. Lewis, *The Power of Stories: A Guide for Leading Multi-Racial and Multi-Cultural Congregations* (Nashville: Abingdon Press, 2008) on the power of prophetic preaching to "story a vision."

37. See also Unitarian ethicist James Luther Adams sounding more like a Universalist in his essay, "God is Love," in *An Examined Faith: Social Context and Religious Commitment*, 213–219 (1947), edited by George K. Beach (Boston: Beacon Press, 1991). However, given that the consolidated UU tradition is covenanted around ethical practices and is social justice oriented, they also fit well with Nancy Ammerman's research in *Sacred Stories, Spiritual Tribes* and what she terms the "Golden Rule Christians," though UUs extend the Golden Rule to embrace wisdom from all the world religions.

38. Rynearson and Salloum, "Restorative Retelling," 177.

39. Ibid., 187.

40. There was a recognized mystical thread in the responses of some other TVUUC leaders as well as UUTRM leaders. This is not surprising and corresponds to the findings of the Commission on Appraisal report *Engaging Our Theological Diversity*, which found that " ... 58 percent of lay respondents said that they have had mystical experiences, compared to 81 percent of clergy. Most such experiences fall under the heading of natural mysticism" (79). Of the many different studies cited in this 2005 report, interview participant responses in the UUTRM case study are highly consistent in values and theological orientations with the 2005 report.

41. This also is consistent with twentieth century Unitarian ethicist and minister James Luther Adams' connection of the language of love with the communal power of "God" metaphorically as "the community-forming Power that we confront in the Gospels and in the Free Churches. This community-forming Power calls us to the affirmation of that abundant love which is not ultimately in our possession but is a holy gift. It is the ground and goal of our vocation." See James Luther Adams, "Our Responsibility in Society," in *The Essential James Luther Adams: Selected Essays and Addresses*, 171 (1953), edited by George Kimmich Beach (Boston: Skinner House, 1998).
42. UU theology is essentially a shared anthropological and ecclesial theology, with a pneumatological underpinning in its emphasis on spiritual experiences. In other words, as *a public theological practice*, UUs recognize the limits of universal claims to know the divine and instead promise through a public affirmation of covenant to a set of ethical principles that they will journey in right relationship with each other in the search for *experiences* and *knowledge* of the divine, experiences most often *publically* named as a "Spirit of Life and Love." Practical evidence of this is the popularity of the hymn "Spirit of Life" in *Singing the Living Tradition*,123, as cited within the Commission on Appraisal's *Engaging Our Theological Diversity* but also as cited by a UUTRM participant in recalling that this song was spontaneously sung as a source of comfort at a General Assembly when a man collapsed just prior to the opening ceremony.
43. Drawing most likely on the Rev. Dr. Martin Luther King, Jr.'s development of this term, "beloved community" has become an often-used phrase to describe a community striving toward justice and right relationship within Unitarian Universalism. See the Commission on Appraisal, *Engaging Our Theological Diversity*.
44. An interesting text to read on the changing conceptions of "evil" in human history in juxtaposition with changing cultural worldviews, particularly in response to traumatic events ranging from natural disasters to the Holocaust, is Susan Neiman's *Evil in Modern*

Thought: An Alternative History of Philosophy (Princeton: Princeton University Press, 2002).

45. See Derald Wing Sue, *Microaggressions in Everyday Life: Race, Gender, and Sexual Orientation* (New York: John Wiley & Sons, 2010). Sue defines microaggressions as "brief, everyday exchanges that send denigrating messages to certain individuals because of their group membership" (xvi).
46. An exception being one TVUUC leader who did notice a gap between responses they received as a congregation in the aftermath of the homicides in comparison to impoverished areas of Knoxville that experienced such violence on a more ongoing basis. This observation was not more broadly engaged in analysis or action.
47. This included trainings in which they sought to teach congregations to know the socioeconomic demographics of their communities and which populations might be most severely impacted by a natural disaster or other communal trauma. This also included references made to anti-oppression work engaged by a UUTRM leader at national conferences of trauma responders on their need for greater interfaith awareness and representation.
48. The language of "theologies of resistance and hope" is drawn from the work of Sharon Welch, *A Feminist Ethic of Risk*.

7

Poetics and Ethics of World/Sense: Cultivating the Lessons

Tales of Normativity, Worldview, Difference, and Ethical Respect

One day, when I was a clinical social worker shaping as clergy and academic, I sat in on a world religions class in a large undergraduate lecture hall. I listened as the professor recounted his encounter with a fellow religious scholar in India to the class. He shared that in a lighthearted moment of conversation, he said to his Hindu colleague with a knowing chuckle, "Listen, you guys don't really believe in reincarnation, do you?" His Hindu colleague with all seriousness replied, "You mean you don't? I thought you believed that you are reborn in heaven." This moment struck me as a powerful example of different experiential worldviews as transmitted through language and narrative stories as well as how easily human beings dismiss what others experience as and believe to be real, while elevating their own experience of reality to a superior level of cultural truth. Internalized superiority in one's sense of reality led so quickly to enforcement of one's superiority when acquiring the power to do so, in ways of being subtle and not so subtle.

I appreciated this particular professor's vulnerability in sharing his cross-cultural encounter with the class, and the ethical respect it transmitted of his own willingness to be called out on his attitude and assumptions. It reminded me of my own decades of being challenged as a young white female lay urban minister and social worker by the young people I served. I remembered how hard it was to be challenged in one's narrative stories and language when one's visceral lived experiences were so radically different. I thought particularly of a time when I witnessed members of an African American urban community speaking back to a predominantly white audience at a church and using the language of "genocide" and "white supremacy" for their lived experiences—how easy it was for some in the audience present to minimize their language, story, and lived experiences, calling it "exaggeration" and thus somehow less than real.

I carried these many experiential and pedagogical moments into my own preferred experiential style of teaching later, most often with secular United States social work students. As I taught my spirituality and social work class, I would begin by saying that I gave them a "money back guarantee" that each them would experience at least one moment of deep discomfort by the end of the course as they encountered a broad range of what human beings might experience as spiritual—and indeed, I have not failed a student in this yet, nor experienced that they did not see the wisdom of such discomfort. The same pedagogy was crucial in teaching my racial justice and my ethics courses in social work as well—students needed living encounters with differences in how reality was conveyed on both verbal and nonverbal levels. They needed to sit compassionately and without judgment of themselves and others in the discomfort stirred and with openness to possible transformation in their own sense of reality. From my heart and my own lived experiences, I believed deeply as an ethical principle that opportunities to cross boundaries and borders of culture and power, and to live with and learn from each other without hierarchy of power in the vulnerable and liminal borderlands of human experience, was a key—a key to begin to unlock the doors for entry into a larger peace and shared understanding and capacity for vision and actions together. A commitment to this pedagogy became my covenant and fulfilled my call to ministry.

Poetic Visions of Peace and Beloved Community from Two Different Worlds

Developing Peace Zones in the Borderlands

Peace Institute ministry leaders poetically imagined, confessed from their world/sense, and testified to a vision of communal transformation that would result in the creation of "peace zones" in every major city, including having their own building and base of operation to train providers in their many decades of grassroots peace-building wisdom. The founding ministry leader viewed such centers as places where "all stakeholders" could come together—"victims, perpetrators, stakeholders within the community"—to "invest" in a model of nonviolence and peace education. This vision was familiar to all participants interviewed in the Peace Institute case study, and uniformly, and sometimes with frustrated laughter, they stated that the primary challenge for the Peace Institute was financial support.

At the time, this frustration seemed to stem from the fact that while the Peace Institute appeared to be recognized and appreciated with ample public praise and many referrals, this was not accompanied always with the necessary funds to support their infrastructure—a dilemma the UUTRM also faced. One institutional supporter observed:

> ... I think that the kind of political capital that the Peace Institute has with the families has elevated its standing in the professional community more. I also think that the Peace Institute has a lot of political support ... I'm not always sure with the political support whether it's political support because, for example, the Peace Institute is really valued or its political support because, "Oh, thank God. Somebody's doing that and now I don't have to worry about it so much." You know? ... So I'm not always sure how genuine it is, but there is a lot of political support in the community for the Peace Institute ... And support ... among academic institutions that have honored [the founder] and the work of the Peace Institute ... there's lots of support in a number of different areas that don't always translate to the kind of on-the-street support that the Peace Institute might need in order to most effectively carry out its mission.

This need for ongoing stable funding was related not only to the challenge of sustaining the Peace Institute's present work, it also was related to their larger hope and vision, shared repeatedly by several survivors, to own a Peace Institute building—a home and a place where they could even more fully express their culture of peace. For another ministry leader, this would entail "tak[ing] our rightful place and really be[ing] seen as the experts that we are and validated as the experts through ways that other experts are validated: through money, through publication, through *money*, [*smiling*] through resources . . . ."

The desire for resources to implement this larger vision, including through increased participation in the Peace Institute's annual Mothers' Day Walk for Peace, led to the creation of an Interfaith Committee at the Peace Institute, but with some unexpected results according to the founding ministry leader: " . . . we got more support from our *white* suburban faith community and our *white* urban faith community than the black faith community. We got a lotta support from the survivors in the African-American faith community that would come, and we've got [only] some support from the African-American faith [community leaders] . . . ." A similar frustration was expressed by a different ministry leader:

> You know, we think that churches sort of get caught up a little bit in their own protocol, in their own programs and kind of forget . . . the larger purpose . . . They may support it in spirit, if you will, but not every church comes out to physically support let's say the Mother's Day Walk for Peace. We think that it would be a powerful, powerful message if the churches in the city could ever set aside that day . . . adjust their service time, so that they could come out and make it to their Mother's Day Walk for Peace . . . it's a citywide event for all people who are concerned about the violence that's taking place in this city [*pounds desk*]. If the church doesn't publicly indicate that concern, it's a problem. And folks see it as a problem.

All institutional supporters also were agreed on the need for better funding and infrastructure support for the Peace Institute, and one specifically wanted to see the Peace Institute receive a grant for a staff position solely related to public policy advocacy, while another wanted to see the Peacezone curriculum expanded in its use in schools. The

7 Poetics and Ethics of World/Sense: Cultivating the Lessons 251

institutional supporter who served as an antiracism/anti-oppression consultant specifically wanted to see survivors continue to be educated in and empowered to lead on the public health model established by Deborah Prothrow-Stith, "helping survivors to make the link to how this is oppressive, and oppression at this level has to do with certain communities get the right to safety and certain don't. That's a policy issue to me ... it's a justice issue ... It's a spiritual issue." Several institutional supporters also expressed concern that the very "variables" that make the Peace Institute successful also make it hard to replicate, including a worry that the founding ministry leader herself was irreplaceable, but also expressing confidence that if the founding ministry leader needed to step down, she and the Peace Institute would work toward a new leader who could "take it to the next level."

While experiences of racism and classism posed both very real systemic and emotional barriers, the enormity of the challenges faced in eliminating violence and in implementing their vision of peace pushed ministry leaders to confront their own world/sense stereotypes or prejudices. The founding ministry leader, for example, spoke to carrying internalized stereotypes prior to the murder of her son and of being a "wannabe suburban mom." She drew upon her Christian faith, including the Good Samaritan parable and question of "Who is my neighbor?," to help her in her own internal transformation of motivation on behalf of the "fullness of God's peace." This included working with her more economically privileged "white neighbor[s]" and learning not to judge them or to divide people into good and bad, despite her anger, and instead to see their common humanity:

> So again ... it was only until Louis was killed that I took off these blinders because I was also in my own world, the violence only happens to certain people, I went to church, I gave to the needy, I hadda husband, I had my home but I still live in the community, I haven't changed my community but ... I had my tunnel vision on. If you're in this perfect world, then nothing bad happens to you, you're protected ... and then *we* allow society to tell us who the good people are and who the bad people are ... and in doin' that we're molding into this world that pits us against each other, the haves and the haves-not, so it's ... goin' back and understanding the

scriptures and understanding the power of God and understanding and what's God's peace and what's this fullness of God ... it's really putting yourself in somebody else's shoe and it's really you experiencin' ... what's the awkwardness of them [her white neighbors] comin' into this community and how do I acknowledge them and not force them to do more but how do *I* do more and hopefully they see the humanity, and not get upset with them when they have more and they can give more but they're not doin' more? How do I not be angry and hold that against them for what they have? But ... how do I speak to what it is God is callin' them to do or what they're studying or what their beliefs say they are and how do I have them to look within that and examine that and then really ask themself that question? You know again who is my neighbor? ... somewhere in the scripture it gives you this parable of the Good Samaritan, you know, that who we expected to help this man didn't help. Anyway, so makin' those type of comparison and really havin' peace, have us take off our blinders and have us see our humanity and have us see also how many of us in wantin' to help sometimes we also have some blinders because we are judging someone else who we believe should be doing more.

The Peace Institute's drive toward inclusiveness in their larger vision of peace extended to an interfaith community across borders of culture, religion, class, and race—and also to perpetrators of violence as well as victims. The founder experienced this interfaith opening, through the world/sense of her Christian tradition, as a new "calling" of and vision for the Peace Institute. She believed the Peace Institute had professional clinical and pastoral training and expertise to offer, not only to secular providers but also to interfaith clergy.[1] Once again, the founding ministry leader also used her personal lived experiences to extend a vision of peace in working with perpetrators of violence, while also holding them accountable through a restorative justice approach. In subsequent years after completion of the original research, she and the mother of the son accused of murdering her own son, as well as this man now released from prison, began to speak together in public contexts about the power of forgiveness and restorative justice practices. This included speaking together at the Peace Institute's historic 20th annual Mothers' Day Walk for Peace, for the first time marching from the streets of Dorchester to Boston City Hall with thousands of marchers from diverse communities.[2]

7 Poetics and Ethics of World/Sense: Cultivating the Lessons   253

The Sacred Ambiguity of Being a Liberal Church for the World

Within the foundational experiences and mission of the UUTRM was the confession of a liberal religious world/sense and testimony to the need for culturally sensitive practices in pastoral care after trauma—a vision which reimagined the possibility of religio/poetic hope and human resilience in the midst of chaos, as well as social justice for a beloved community. For the participants in this case study, the experience of being attacked for their religion left all with a deeper sense of bonding to each other and an embodied connection to the theological narrative and meaning of their UU faith tradition, despite earlier internalized doubt that had been fostered by critique.[3] Some also gained a sense of confidence in claiming and confessing their religious identity and speaking out and testifying on behalf of their religion more publicly and coherently:

> ... it certainly made everybody in the congregation think, "Do I wanna be here or not? Is this worth it?" ... You know, love is the spirit of this church. It has become a much deeper thing that we say every week, and very true. And it's a legitimate way to go about things. It's not kind of a half-sell kind of thing ... love and service become the twin pillars, and that makes a good faith.

For the TVUUC leaders in particular, there was a larger relational context experienced within this theological narrative—one that was historical, value-driven, and deeply intertwined with their sense of their identity, sacred story, and world/sense as a unique UU congregation surviving and thriving in a more conservative Southern context—"a respected oddity" in the words of the TVUUC minister. Feelings of self-worth and being newly affirmed, energized, and empowered in their group identity, that of a UU spiritual tribe, were broadly reported.[4]

However, it was the TVUUC minister, as well as the UUTRM leaders and some UUA institutional supporters, who held the clearest sense of connection between their pastoral care and prophetic social justice practices and the experience of healing in the aftermath of trauma, including in their understanding of their call to give testimony to their faith tradition in the public square. Beyond the minister, TVUUC leaders interviewed waivered in their sense that the church had embraced a clear and consistent social justice call to the public square linked specifically to the violent traumatic event. One TVUUC leader said:

> Well, here's one thing that's bothered me. What I became aware of was that this thing is going on all the time and that poor communities and such are not getting the kind of support we did. You know, like when these random shootings occur in East Knoxville, some black section in town and such—they're not gettin' the kind of support. And so we kind of got flooded with it . . . it just makes you aware that traumatic things happen every day and have probably happened every day up until our shooting where people are not supported at all . . . I mean it's almost embarrassing that we got so much attention . . . Yeah, it's like when a white girl gets kidnapped in Aruba and it's all over the news forever . . . but if it wasn't the blond white girl from a wealthy family in Connecticut or whatever it was, there just wouldn't be that much attention. So the invisible violence that goes on without any acknowledgement.

For UUTRM leaders, in contrast, the connection of their mission to challenging social oppression was woven into the very content of their mission statement, or as one UUTRM leader stated, their mission was "to work within the paradigms of social justice and action that we live as Unitarian Universalists as anti-oppression [and] antiracist" to prepare people in coping with traumatic events.[5] UUTRM leaders gave various examples of how they fulfilled this mission, from the awareness they raised through various national and district trainings to their interfaith commitments.

When interview participants reflected generally on UU struggles with responding to violent trauma with public vision, profession, and action, beyond this particular event, their thoughts turned in one of at least two directions. *First*, the practical and logistical barriers posed by congregational polity, and the operation of the UUTRM as a volunteer-based community ministry; and *second*, a perception of a lack of adequate UU cultural, religious, and theological preparedness for coping with trauma, particularly coping with "evil" when the trauma was violent and human made and put them experientially in conflict with their belief in the inherent worth and dignity of each person. In regards to the former, the informal relationship of the UUTRM to structures available within the UUA, including the UUA's congregational governance polity, often was viewed as a major challenge for the development of adequate financial support for the UUTRM, as well as for its ability to conduct the level of preparedness education and operational connection on a regional national level for congregations that they might otherwise desire.[6]

These structural challenges were viewed as reinforced by a particular UUA institutional culture that sought to respect the rights of each congregation to manage their own concerns. One UUA institutional supporter said: "I think it's part of the culture . . . of UUA staff to . . . not presume to dictate what ought to occur either in congregations or in districts." The exceptions, he would go on to say, were "youth safety issues" due to legal liability as well as ethical concerns. Mandating the need for congregations to receive training related to emergency preparedness and trauma was viewed as potentially subject to "pushback" that would be "counterproductive." An overall UU culture of autonomy and independence also was seen as reinforced at times by the UUTRM leadership itself, creating an ambiguous dynamic of desiring greater institutionalization but also resisting perceived potential losses of creative flexibility, freedom, or control and authority through such institutionalization.

Several UUTRM leaders and UUA institutional supporters confirmed an overarching need for the UUTRM to regionalize its capacity and institutionalize its connection to the UUA more formally. UUTRM leaders also saw a need to expand their membership so that greater diversity was reflected by race, gender, skill sets, and lay positions within a congregation, with more peers working with peers rather than primarily being led by clergy. As one UUTRM leader, who had a dual role as a UUA District Executive, put it, paralleling similar concerns to institutionalizing the Peace Institute's larger vision: "'Cause the only way it's gonna work is if regional teams are created and sustained, that there is a clear sense of structure, and modality, and a clear understanding of it surviving beyond the lives and interests of this *wonderful* group of dedicated people who have done *marvelous* work in our congregations." One UUA institutional supporter also saw the UUTRM's struggles in this area as reflecting a broader problem of the relationship of congregational polity to what are termed "community ministries" within the UUA. Community ministries are ministries that are focused outside the walls of the parish, many of which are not even connected to parish ministries. He saw accountability issues in this as well as a potential to strengthen the promise of community ministries through the positive example of the UUTRM and greater institutionalization throughout the UUA districts.

Beyond the practical and logistical challenges of congregational polity, the socioeconomic status and privileges of UUs often were cited as an experiential barrier—a world/sense barrier—to engaging issues of violence and trauma with sustained spiritual and religious focal attention. Such concerns were raised especially by UUTRM leaders and UUA institutional supporters, often in strong and sometimes sharp terms. One UUA institutional supporter, the former UUA president, spoke to the spiritual paradox of privilege being "both a blessing and a curse," one that gave more resources for effective action, but one which also created a danger of insularity from rather than connection to a larger shared human experience—an insularity of world/sense in this respect. In words that also echoed a Peace Institute ministry leader's concern for the Peace Institute being tasked with the burden a larger society rejects in fully sharing, the former UUA president said of the UUTRM, lived experiences of trauma and suffering, and UU congregations:

> The privilege of most of our members and most of our communities is both a blessing and a curse. And the blessing is that we are persons who, A, have resources both personal, financial, educational ... so that we are able to actually be more effective than many. The curse is that ... most of us personally, we're insulated from much of what is normal life for many people ... a good colleague of mine describes it as ministry to the shallow affluent—and I say that not to denigrate that ministry, because ... all people are important to receive ministry. But it means that there's a whole range of human experience that we don't often directly engage ... it's no small thing to be able to understand that we are a part of one human family, and it's *easy* to say, "I'm glad we've got a Trauma Response Ministry," you know, "They're taking care of that piece of my response to being human for me. I don't have to do that" and there's a spiritual danger in that.

7 Poetics and Ethics of World/Sense: Cultivating the Lessons

Repeatedly, both UUTRM leaders and UUA institutional supporters experienced UUs as struggling spiritually and religiously with the reality and world/sense of traumatic suffering and evil in light of both their privilege as well as their resistance to authority, optimistic view of human nature, and denial that anything truly hurtful might occur to them. For example, using physiological metaphoric language for depth, a UUA institutional supporter said: "I think it's core in our DNA. I think it's part of what has led many of us to leave our traditional religious background, if we had a traditional religious background ... a deep down engrained resistance to authority, a deep down engrained belief that we know what's best for us and you can't tell us what to do." One UUTRM leader also spoke to a cultural rationalistic tendency of UUs to seek to control chaos and the possibilities of anything bad ever happening to them, so much so that UU's forget the "awe, mystery and wonder": "I think there's an arrogance *[laughter]* about us that we think we've got the universe all figured out ... our tendency to be rational ... and that once we've figured it out then nothing bad can happen ... We forget awe. We forget awe, yeah, awe, mystery and wonder and that we're not in control."

There were significant lived truths of ironic holy humor, sacred ambiguity, and passionate frustration expressed in these participant experiences and analyses of world/sense limitations to a UU capacity to fulfill a religio/poetic vision of the liberal church in responding to trauma, particularly human-made violent trauma.[7] Yet there also was truth witnessed and hope experienced that something *in* the UU tradition *did* exhibit relational resilience—as perhaps might be the case for any sustained religious tradition. Something in the tradition itself did yield the capacity to bring forth an alternative narrative and ecclesial world/sense experience in the very birthing and sustenance of the UUTRM, even as the UUTRM, like the Peace Institute, struggled with institutionalizing its own support within the larger denomination.

Through each of these small trauma response community ministries studied, one lay and urban and one denominational, particular practices and rituals are seen to continually evolve in response to violent trauma, beginning also to encompass larger religio/poetic narrative visions and world/sense through opportunities and power taken for public testimony. For the Peace Institute participants, this entailed a vision of a home of their own with interdisciplinary and interfaith Peace Zones across the state in which peace within individuals and peace in the larger community might be actively fostered and practiced, while also bringing the voices, body, and material witness of this vision through survivors as experts to Boston City Hall and beyond. For the UU participants, this entailed connection to the denomination's larger Standing on the Side of Love national campaign, sparked in its public format by the Knoxville tragedy and furthered in public recognition through marriage equality and immigration rights. This later situated the campaign to launch another level of public activism with Black Lives Matter banners in support of the original Black Lives Matter movement.[8] These two culturally diverse case studies illustrate that the embodied interplay of lived religious experiences with narrative and material practices enables religio/poetic vision and world/sense to continue to reimagine and metaphorically expand in capacity, including for public confession and testimonial.

Speaking as Experts from the Bottom to the Top of the Power Hierarchy

Shifting the Paradigms in Clinical, Pastoral, Health and Human Service Care

Embracing a poetics of world/sense and a power analysis for interdisciplinary and transdisciplinary clinical, pastoral, and health and human service care means taking survivors seriously when they ask to be seen as the experts in their experiences, needs, and particular expressive forms of world/sense. This often is a paradigm shift for professional training in clinical, pastoral, health and human service (including medical) care—one that requires trust in inner client and communal wisdom and a focus on partnership and mutuality as stressed in the five primary clinical theories that correlated with survivor descriptions in the case studies: narrative theory, RCT, IFS theory, liberation health theory, and continuing bonds. This paradigm shift requires an even deeper level of trust and cultural and intercultural humility in approach to clients and an ethical respect for choice of language and cultural methods of communication, including nonverbal and material expressive forms. This paradigm shift also entails an appreciation for the embodied affective and cognitive dimensions of *immanence* rather than solely transcendence in religious spiritual experiences.[9] Finally, this paradigm shift also requires attention beyond talk and narrative therapy to holistic engagement of the body and structures of power, particularly when considering the long-term impact of violent trauma on the neuroaffective and interdependent physiological dimensions of the body and community. Again, through world/view reconsidered metaphorically as our world/sense, we are seen to be embodied and enfleshed, enlanguaged and encultured, en-neuroned and enhormoned, and emplaced and embedded in sociohistorical and material structures of power.

For example, the studies illustrated that comfort with the language of "healing" was refracted through the lens of both *the nature* of the violent trauma—loss of a child to murder distinct from violent intrusion and murder in a church context—as well as through class, race, and comfort with a discipline's professional cultural language. Perceptions and experiences of survivors themselves could differ, as seen in the case of the origin of the language of "Peace Warriors" versus the language of "survivors" in the Peace Institute case study. One mother stated that in their "Tuesday Talks": "...honestly I got tired of being called a survivor. And I had said to them, 'I'm not a survivor, I'm a warrior,' 'cause I have to get up every day and fight this . . . And so from that day, everybody kept sayin' they were warriors." While another mother said: "I don't like to take away from the fact that I *am* a survivor. I commend my fellow Warrior moms who are able to step up and [say], 'I am a warrior.' . . . Me, personally, I'm still a survivor . . . This drains me. This takes a whole lot out of me . . . on a regular basis, it consumes a lot of my life." Language is complex with significant metaphoric implications. Language needs to be contextualized fully to the lived experiences of the particular client and community. Even what might be termed the same event, such as the violent church intrusion and its aftermath, could be experienced in different ways by different people, including different aspects of an event heightened, emphasized, or recalled in stories shared. All stories needed to be shared, heard, and affirmed for their lived experience—if not adequately so, the story returned in some sense when given the opportunity, as experienced with the TVUUC through my interviewer presence.

In reconsidering attention to metaphor and survivor chosen language and narratives, the Peace Institute case study illustrated that many survivors experienced themselves as being physically weighted down by and bonded to their lost loved one, such that it was a challenge to get up and function, let alone put one foot in front of the other. The desire expressed was not to sever the bond despite this weight but to learn to carry and move with it in a different way so that the loss did not "attack" and paralyze them completely. Clinical, pastoral, health and human care providers might need "to play" or experiment with relational and metaphorical images for such bonds, including through use of expressive material arts and in consultation with survivors—this includes *communal* moral bonds that continue in the aftermath of other forms of violent trauma, as highlighted in both case studies. Clinical, pastoral, health and human service care providers may be positioned to help clients to reshape these connections as ongoing physiological bonds that are recognized to be experienced naturally as embodied connections when languaged with a poetics of science if this resonates with the clients. But they also could help clients to attend to their religious traditions and spiritual tribes for embodied or material poetic metaphors as a source of strength and resilience—as happened with the Universalist language of "all souls" in the TVUUC minister's sermon. The task would be to emphasize survivor control in reimagining the weight of carrying this bond more lightly, rather than severed, with possibilities through their own sacred communal story, and also perhaps with an elasticity that prevents shattering as well as an adhesion that allows for the reassembly of lost pieces—including pieces that take new religio/poetic but physically lighter material and embodied form in their expressions, such as through art and body practices or material memorialization.[10]

Seeking alternative embodied metaphors and narratives, including sacred stories, for healing that are more consistent with the lived experiences of family survivors of homicide dovetails with existing narrative theory and practice.[11] This also is consistent with clinical, pastoral, health and human service care practices of empowerment, such as liberation health and IFS, that prioritize a survivor's ability to claim their particular

7 Poetics and Ethics of World/Sense: Cultivating the Lessons 261

language for their lived experiences and burdens under larger sociohistorical systems of cultural and structural oppression. Consistent with RCT, I suggest that clinical, pastoral, health and human service care providers also may learn new relational images, metaphors, and language from lived religion studies of intercultural and interreligious encounters, particularly in the aftermath of trauma. Such attention by care providers and lived religion scholars also may prove useful both in expanding the world/sense of clients and freeing them to find and claim their own personal and communal language as well.

For example, intercultural exposure to the concept of "han" from Korean culture can illustrate that not all cultures exhibit a world/sense of individualism or disconnection from the larger forces of history and collective struggle. "Han" specifically expresses suffering as a world/sense of interdependency in the collective experience of a people under colonial oppression. Choi Hee An describes "han" as "a fundamental feeling of defeat, resignation, the tenacity of life, unresolved resentments, or grudges" but also as situated in the "interconnections of classism, racism, sexism, colonialism, neocolonialism, and cultural imperialism ... It is the suppressed, accumulated, and condensed experience of oppression caused by the carrier of a message from the collective unconscious in Korean historical and social structures ... *Han*, as a symbol for the cry of oppressed people, has become a political metaphor."[12] Used in the Korean context, "han" is a felt experience of world/sense and not easily translatable because it is connected to the specific historical experiences of a particular people with repeated invasions by colonial powers. Drawn from the Korean context and expanded metaphorically, however, it also can become a word to express the contextualized world/sense of others living collectively under oppression. Lifted up in a clinical, pastoral, health or human service care context as an example, such a practice also can free others to find or develop their own cultural metaphors and language to express the felt experience of collective systemic oppression as a people.

Finally, the embodied neurophysiological nature of human interdependency and its potential for fostering vicarious trauma or vicarious growth in impact on clinical, pastoral, health and human service care providers *as well as* survivors came up as a lesson stressed in both case studies. At the Peace Institute, internalizing self-care practices through communal support and role modeling their culture of peace was recognized by institutional supporters as crucial for the long-term sustenance and effectiveness of the ministry leaders. The mental health clinician interviewed discussed the importance of self-care in light of her professional experiences and the impact of vicarious trauma, with implications for the Peace Institute's ministry leaders when they were in the care taking role as well:

> ... there can be a cumulative impact and effects of working with people who are *suffering* so much ... and also a cumulative effect in seeing such bravery, so ... It's part of the professional responsibility, keep *track* of where you are because it affects how you work with survivors ... [you can get] vicarious trauma ... you can distance yourself, you can remote, you can get overwhelmed, you can absorb more than is good for you or for the work that you're doing ... I had a supervisor who ... said to me, "You hafta learn how to walk up to the abyss, so that you can get close enough but you can't go into that abyss. Survivors don't need you there, they've got people there. You hafta use whatever you might offer." So staying, finding that place where you can stand, where you're very present and connected but you're not falling into that place ....

UUTRM leaders also stressed awareness and self-care practices for providers when working in the aftermath of trauma, and the TVUUC minister demonstrated vulnerability in the pulpit in role modeling this for his spiritual tribe as a leader as well.

Brief Implications for Secular and Religious Educators

Lessons learned of the value of a holistic approach to clinical, pastoral, health and human service care through the case studies point to a need for broader consideration of the value of such approaches for secular and religious educators as well across a broad range of age groups and contexts, particularly in light of the impact of trauma within educational settings. Through their Peacezone curriculums and active involvement with the Boston Public School system, as well as the emphasis placed on anti-oppression education and analysis through their Leadership Academy, this was most evident in the Peace Institute case study. A commitment to the value of expressive art and embodied practices in all forms for this education, including bringing this forth in public testimony to their larger communities through projects such as Peaceville, were threaded throughout their curriculums and activities. Attention to the impact of trauma on children and youth was very much part of the religious education practices in the UUTRM work with the TVUUC as well, including artistic material practices during the rededication service and ongoing attention and care in their religious education program. These lessons serve as a general and significant reminder for educators that embodied practices of learning, including use of the arts and with contextualized attention to larger social systems of oppression with opportunities to put learning into action, are significant across the age span and worthy of respect and further research development in holistic, integrative learning, including through lived religion studies.[13]

To Social and Religious Institutions: "Nothing About Us Without Us"[14]

What struck me as a researcher was how often survivors interviewed in both case studies saw my research presence as an opportunity to publicly document and testify to the ways in which they experienced larger institutions they expected to serve them—whether social or religious—as having missed the mark in many ways. The public health institutional supporter interviewed in the Peace Institute case study again would affirm the importance of the need for further research attending to survivor voices and experiences as the "experts":

> ... I think the medical, social service, public health and criminal justice organizations need to pay more attention to this. I mean, this ... should be the subject of some very intentional evaluation. I mean, there's some things that are very similar to what other parents who experienced the death of a child would need. But I think there's some very different aspects that deserve additional attention. And I think depending on where they are in their healing process, there's the capacity to heal through helping. But ... that's not everybody, and ... I don't know well enough *when* in the process ... I just think there's so much we don't know and that survivors really

haven't gotten the level of attention that is necessary to really answer that question. I think they still remain the experts at this point, and their stories and their experiences and how they've gotten better represent a starting point for this.

Survivors interviewed in the Peace Institute case study in particular more often did not experience themselves being regarded as the expert in their own needs by larger social institutions. Instead they reported being confronted with a bewildering array of bureaucracy to navigate or treated with indifference if not callousness by the very institutions meant to serve them, often law enforcement and judicial institutions were singled out in particular.

> It was really, really difficult. No support. The mayor didn't knock on my door. The chief of police didn't knock on my door. The cop who actually was dealing with the incident with my son, knocked on my door, handed me an envelope. "Here's your son's belongings," and walked away, *literally*. Literally, *never* stepped foot inside my door. "Oh, I just want to drop this off. These are your son's belongings." Like *really*? [*harsh ironic laugh*] But it's the assumptions that . . . I had to deal with.

The founding ministry leader had sharp words at the time regarding professional therapists, some of which were based in repeated experiences of being dismissed or minimized as a survivor when she first turned toward professionals, including being asked if she wanted medication for depression when she did not. She repeatedly felt that survivors were placed in a particular "role" by a larger system, a role which circumscribed their ability to make a contribution to necessary knowledge, a role she also experienced as a racialized rather than empowering and authentic and in counter-distinction to a liberation health model:

> Why are ya gonna give me medication if you're tellin' me this is something normal? Then why are ya gonna give me somethin' to suppress what's normal and . . . Professional white women, yeah. That's a funny one . . . this is coming from my own perspective that I believe people saw me a survivor and [for] clinicians, survivors have a role, survivors have their place, you know? Survivors can advocate. Survivors are called to gun control, death

penalty, you know, survivors are called to tell their story, and I think, with me, I can do all that but I also need to know who you are, I also need to understand whadda you know about me and I think that's the difference between me and other survivors. I wanted to understand all this grief and trauma. I wanted to understand all of that, I wanted to be educated. I also wanted to know what your role was ... I wanted to know what everybody role was, so that I can understand who are the people in place to help and that I can also again share [with] other survivors ... the providers have gotten to trust us but providers are also stubborn ... I still believe, as a black woman doin' this work and as a survivor, I still believe I'm not bein' heard the way I should be heard and that our expertise and wisdom as survivors is still not bein' valued because ... [they] have no issue in calling me and havin' me come to the table and still don't get compensated.

One survivor expressed a cautionary note, however, that there are times when professional help *is* necessary, that there are risks that "signs and symptoms" of suicidal ideation and severe depression, for example, might otherwise be missed by the lay ministry leaders at the Peace Institute— though she also noted that even the professionals can get it wrong when she spoke of a therapist misdiagnosing her child with anxiety attacks when the child actually was experiencing medical seizures. The Peace Institute ministry leaders also admitted to struggling at times with the policing role of professionals in filing child abuse and neglect reports rather than working foremost with confidentiality and trust building for families. Since the original case study, however, I have observed that the Peace Institute is working cooperatively with hospitals and agencies for grants to maintain therapists on site, hence a mutual and trusting relationship has deepened overall, though they continue to shift toward institutional trainings for human service and clergy providers and further away from direct care. Overall, the "provocateur" role of the Peace Institute was deemed valuable by institutional providers in the larger social arena in that they could agitate at times in ways licensed service agencies might be restricted politically in doing so, per the mental health provider interviewed: "I think that, you know, *[laughter]* ... they certainly have played the role, intentionally or not ... to some extent as a *provocateur*, as, ya know, just a *voice* for, and sometimes a pretty rowdy voice for, people who struggle and suffer...."

The case studies also highlighted the importance of localization of religious trauma response to assist in the development of time, energy, and resources for greater creative capacity and cultural sensitivity in diverse spiritual care practices, as well as for consistency in meeting practical logistical needs and preventing leadership burnout for the long run. This recommendation was highlighted as much by the success of the Peace Institute's para-ecclesial grounding through place and space in community as by the frustrations signaled by TVUUC leaders with the limitations of continuity of care by a national trauma response team. Both case studies demonstrated that organized local and secular trauma responses do exist through local mental health agencies and local deployment by the Red Cross. The Peace Institute case study highlighted the cultural preference of several survivors in their particular community for more peer led interventions than solely professional mental health interventions, and the TVUUC leaders also demonstrated that relationality through shared cultural context was significant for them as well.

Responses needed to violent trauma, however, often exceed the capacity of religious institutions solely, and this may be significant for all to understand in the disappointment and frustration expressed by survivors in both case studies to relational responses by clergy at times. Religious institutions and clergy can be subject to higher expectations than other secular social institutions due to the added weight of sacred meaning-making and relational images of care held by all involved—in essence projections based in desires for the "God-like" perfect caretaker, with gender and race adding additional intercultural variables to those expectations. The pain of disappointment in this area carries enormous implications, as one Peace Institute survivor indicated by generalizing her personal disappointment to her experience with church overall:

> I personally feel like that the churches can be doin' more ... I want to hear from the pastor from the church and I had been goin' and goin' and goin' and he was too busy to come out. He kept sending other people. When he did connect—and I feel like I hurt—I go to listen to your voice every Sunday and I needed you to be here and he wasn't ... he did *not* come. He

did *not* call and I kept calling church and begging. And he called me probably like three or four weeks later ... I said, "I need you to come." And no he did not come. So since that day I have not been back to church.

For a different Peace Institute survivor, there was a felt discrimination between who is regarded as an "innocent" victim and hence worthy, and who is considered part of the street life and hence less worthy by clergy and religious institutions. Her critique of the church differed from her feelings about her experiences with the Peace Institute and their restorative justice practices. She spoke of this discrimination occurring before her son's murder, when clergy would visit her son regularly in prison but not upon his release, and then also did not come to see her after his murder:

> You can't pick and choose. You can't pick and choose those you wanna help or those you wanna reach out to. *Everybody* should be treated as an equal ... My son was 20, *was* into the street life, but *still* shouldn't a never happened to him. So they just can't pick and choose. And I always keep in the back of my head that you're human ... And I don't make my son's story a secret. When people ask me, and I say to them, "This is *not* your fairytale killing here. He was the intended target. It was the life that he lived." But no one still had the right to do that. And it doesn't make his life any less valuable, which is another reason why I'm so in tuned with the Peace Institute because to *them*, everyone is equal. Even the perpetrator has an equal right of some sort. And that holds a lotta weight with me. A whole lotta weight with me.

Religious institutions, including in the UUTRM and TVUUC case study, may need to consider the weight of these relational expectations and the significance of pain created that can carry implications for the life of the survivor family in relationship to institutions and their practices, while also recognizing that trauma is often societal in nature and religious institutions cannot bear the burden alone. There may need to be additional practices developed that assist survivors and their caretakers to be more aware of both the naturalness and the inherent limitations of these expectations, including practices of reconciliation and repair when needed.

The scope of this needed social response was witnessed in the Boston City Council hearing with Peace Institute survivors, with implications again for the UUTRM and TVUUC case study as well. The range of providers impacting the lives of homicide survivors included the police department, district attorney offices, hospitals, emergency medical services, public schools, government, grief and trauma services, and the media. A small sample of many concrete recommendations at this particular hearing included: increase funding for grief counselors and defray the burial costs for those who cannot pay; allow families to ride in the ambulance or get police escort if they cannot; improve hospital response and sensitivity to family members as well as follow-up with services; have trauma response teams available in all schools; require trauma training for all school staff; increase the number of bereavement days after the loss of an immediate family member; improve gun-control laws; ensure the media notifies families before publishing information and that the media is accountable for the accuracy of information published; and develop a prerelease victim/offender dialogue program with also increased support for young men with criminal records.[15]

Practical recommendations from the UUTRM case study included stressing the need for better overall emergency preparedness training, beyond the creation of a "Go-Bag" with important documents and supplies, as well as the need for ongoing emotional and financial support to survivors in the aftermath. One UUA institutional supporter wished for a "centralized, organized, transparent, and comprehensive plan" in the event of social traumas, having experienced that "we don't have one as a country." A UUTRM leader hoped for a greater understanding of survivor resiliency in the aftermath of trauma, as well as for the reduction of stigma and self-consciousness in interacting with survivors. Other specific suggestions included seeing "churches continue to sponsor communitywide groups for people who have been survivors of violence," as well as creating local partnership programs with public service agencies such as the police or their local Red Cross. One UUTRM leader also strove to use UUTRM educational workshops as opportunities to develop consciousness in religious institutions about their larger community and the needs of the most marginalized in emergency preparedness:

7 Poetics and Ethics of World/Sense: Cultivating the Lessons 269

... one of the things that I talk about is a congregation wide advocacy so that it touches on not just things like groups for victims of violence and trauma but also things like do you know what you're zoning regulations are for flood plains? Do you know how vulnerable your poorest populations are in the community to particular disaster scenarios, whether it be chemical or explosions? So that communities recognize that they have the potential to be an advocate for the most marginalized in the community as part of their own emergency preparedness programs ... to make certain that they understand that, you know, they have a larger role to play in being present with the community to get word out, like pandemic flu response materials, you know, you name it. I think there's a lot that we can do as churches ....

Other UUTRM leaders echoed that it would be useful if more congregations, rather than individuals, specialized in trauma responsiveness and took up opportunities for education in this area. Currently, the UUTRM is the primary vehicle within the UUA for engaging in this continuing education—and one UUTRM leader pointed out that in her national trauma training experience, the UUTRM is unique for its internal denominational focus rather that purely engaging in externally focused disaster relief efforts with specialized practical ministries. Overall, the intercultural lessons of the case studies demonstrated that social and religious institutions must work in partnership with secular agencies at local levels. Such partnerships must be in depth, fostered from mutual education and practical encounters in developing a shared power analysis, as well as a shared narrative vision that taps the veins of enduring embodied metaphoric truth and world/sense correlated between sociocultural academic language and religious traditions.

Implications for Theological and Religious Scholarship

Implications for theologians and scholars of religion do not stand alone without some interdisciplinary support. The public health doctor interviewed in the Peace Institute case study spontaneously introduced the term "theological" when referencing the Peace Institute's inclusion of a process of forgiveness in their work, stating that it was hard for her to imagine being able to do this particular work in this community without a ministerial focus and that there was a need to develop research techniques, per the lived religion focus of this book:

> I know [the founder looks at it as ministry], and I think that's a pretty healthy way to look at it ... I think there's a certain part of the work that's definitely spiritual or even theological in that it holds especially true when you're dealing with issues like forgiveness and the rationale for forgiveness or the basis for forgiveness or even the process for forgiveness ... I suspect, depending on the community, you're going to get the cultural and spiritual influences of that community. So it's hard for me to imagine that it could be done without it being a ministry of sort ... I actually think that forgiveness, even as a healing strategy, is an interesting and evaluatable concept. But it's really hard. It's easier to recommend helping as a way of healing. I think it's much more difficult and probably inappropriate to recommend forgiveness as a way of healing. But I think to understand that process and to be able to talk to others about it would be a helpful addition to those service providers' repertoire of what happens.

Indeed, the idea and language of forgiveness did come up in the two case studies, with differences dependent on their respective cultural contexts. For example, one Peace Institute survivor spoke at length of her spiritual struggles with their peace principle of forgiveness. She spoke of finally of being able to "let this go" and come to a greater sense of "ease" and "control" in her life: "You know when you don't forgive people, they really do have power over you? It's like they control how you think, how you feel, and how you act. I don't want the enemy havin' control over me like that." This survivor spoke of needing "to let go" of "bad thoughts or animosity" to be fully connected to God—that the desire for revenge was acting as a physical barrier to her natural connection with God and making her feel so controlled that she could contemplate using her body in a vengeful way. Only when she "let go" did she feel a sense of regaining personal control and power over her body and a sense of peace and "ease" becoming available again, a sense she associated with her natural embodied connection to God being reestablished. For her, this initial disconnection also was associated with her struggle with anger and the meaning of "forgiveness." As God forgives her, she also sought to be a Christian role model in being able to forgive others, and even if she could never completely

7 Poetics and Ethics of World/Sense: Cultivating the Lessons 271

forgive, a physical easing occurred as she practiced "letting go" and forgiving. An embodied language of connection was threaded throughout her responses.

Within the UUTRM case study, the capacity for forgiveness was complicated by a theological frame that affirmed the worth and dignity of each person without a thickness to practices that also incorporated a place for the human capacity for harm or "evil" and acts of reconciliation or restorative justice approaches. In a 1998 talk at a UU General Assembly that I heard in person and lingered with me, sociologist Robert Bellah, after reviewing UU Commission on Appraisal reports and demographics, argued that the overt UU commitment to an "ontological individualism" and right to dissent placed UU's "religiously and therefore culturally, [at the] mainstream, right at the American center." Such demographics, beliefs, and practices diluted transformative UU social witness in the world. Bellah challenged UUs to reexamine their theological anthropology and "recover your fundamentally social nature " and, even more radically perhaps, to place "the interdependent web of existence" as the first UU principle.[16] Only by doing so, in Bellah's implied soteriological critique, would UU's achieve a depth to their missiological visions.

As per the former UUA president, there was a "spiritual danger" in the experience of privilege that could insulate people from a shared humanity and necessity to forgive in this context, whereas in the Peace Institute study, harm often was being done by community members against each other, sometimes with victims and perpetrators in the same family. When experienced as living in the same world, the moral bonds could not be disassociated and survivor vengefulness or guilt needed to be addressed for life to feel free to move again. When the shared impact of trauma was not owned or addressed, then there were different cultural legacies for those who lived with privilege and those who lived with oppression. In IFS language, these cultural legacies and burdens included emotional, moral, and practical legacies for religious traditions and communities, all of which could bear further tools of analysis within religious, as well as theological, studies. Essayist, literary scholar, and activist Elaine Scarry[17] places the language of "world making and unmaking" at the center of her study of human creativity and the constricting and unmaking effect on the world of a person whose body is in pain. There is theological fruit in her innovative language for this process, including "dissolving world-extension" or "lack of world-extension" to describe the privileged who keep themselves from the moral bonds of suffering and pain—in essence, disassociating from the connectedness of survivor's guilt. Are there theological and religious implications to beginning to view living in worlds of privilege as disassociated states from possibilities of moral injury[18] or survivor's guilt?

For theologians, there is a need to reconsider theologizing from this place of world/sense—particularly how different world religious traditions beyond solely Christianity find resources within their respective narratives and practices to theologize from human being as embodied and enfleshed, enlanguaged and encultured, en-neuroned and enhormoned, and emplaced and embedded in sociohistorical and material structures of power. The lived experience of trauma challenges us particularly to theologize from the *physiological, interdependent body in community*—and to attend to survivors as primary theologians who give expert testimony through their voices, language, and embodied and material practices as guides. As pointed to in my original research, some theologians of trauma have begun to do so—yet they vary in the normativity they grant to the lived experiences of survivors, including to fellow theologians who openly write as survivors and who lay claim to a fierceness of testimony in their survival, such as Rebecca Parker and Rita Nakashima Brock in particular.[19] Theologians of trauma also vary in the levels of their attention to physiological dimensions beyond the flesh, including physiological interdependence.

Here I only will point out the usefulness I discovered in conjoining trauma theology with disability theology for constructive and practical purposes within Christian theologies. In particular, I highlight the work of Thomas Reynolds and his development in a Christian context of the language of "vulnerable communion."[20] Metaphorically expanding the concept of 'vulnerable communion' beyond solely a Christian context was helpful for reconsidering normative theological associations of the language of perfection with wholeness. As survivors in both case studies indicated, there is a need to theologize from the place of vulnerability and wholeness even with pieces missing and needing to be replaced. I also lift up from my original research the less referenced works of Jennifer Beste and Nancy Pineda-Madrid for the significance of their theological attention to the centrality of communal bonds as sources of resiliency under the impact of suffering and trauma.[21]

Beste is interesting as a Catholic theologian for her effort to seek to shift the locus of human freedom and mediated grace from the individualized wounded victim to the caretakers—"grace as mediated through supportive relationships," because she recognizes the depth of physiological woundedness may require dependency on others.[22] Pineda-Madrid proposes a "social-suffering hermeneutic" in theological studies that also should be of interest to religious studies scholars, a hermeneutic which recognizes the importance of "naming the experience of suffering"; "the presence of interests in naming our suffering"; "the interplay between societal problems and personal suffering"; and the ways in which "cultural representations and symbols mediate the construction of social and self-identity" and hence expressions of suffering.[23] Each of these had correlative possibilities with the case studies in my original research.

For scholars of religion, there also is a need for further congregational and community case studies, inclusive of community-based, para-ecclesial ministries across cultures and religions, to study the intercultural range of possible trauma responses, not only to violent trauma but also to other forms of trauma.[24] This book has suggested the usefulness of a variety of social science, theological, spiritual, and linguistic conceptual tools for correlation to the lived experiences of trauma survivors, including prophetic pastoral care, neuroaffective trauma studies, continuing bonds literature, narrative theory, RCT, liberation health theory, IFS theory, and an embodied metaphorical and mutual critical correlational interdisciplinary approach, inclusive of attention to material poetics. Further tools and methods may be needed to attend more adequately to phenomena that arise in the face of cultural oppressions, inclusive of the need for intercultural dialogue and encounters across lines of difference by race, class, gender, ability, sexual and affectional orientation, and religion among others, with a larger openness by all academic scholars to disclosing their own social identities and locations in the research as well. This study drew from relational-cultural, narrative, liberation health, IFS, and critical race theories to highlight some of these intercultural factors and dynamics of power between the two case studies.[25]

Interdisciplinary Encounters with Intersectional Signs of Hope

If our emplacement and embeddedness as embodied and enfleshed, enlanguaged and encultured, en-neuroned and enhormoned beings also is contextualized by sociohistorical and material dimensions of structural power, then the call for intercultural research that is more forthcoming in documenting our own contextualized emplacement and experiences as researchers is an ethical mandate. Hints of this are sometimes seen across disciplines, including trauma researcher Bessel van der Kolk openly discussing his own experiences with trauma and therapy as a source of motivation and insight for his research.[26] An excellent example also of this type of more forthcoming intercultural encounter with radical difference in written research is that of Mattjis van de Port, a cultural anthropologist and white European gay male.[27] In his description of his first encounter with a Candomblé spirit possession ceremony in Bahia, Brazil, he shares the mutuality of impact on himself when one by one those around him fall into a trance. For van de Port as an anthropologist of religion, withholding himself from the research, withholding the data of his own lived experiences of these encounters, would mean that he was withholding important phenomenological data about the living power of these religious experiences, experiences which in turn challenge his own normativity of world/view beliefs and world/sense ways of being. He writes:[28]

> The drums were beaten evermore frantically. Each time someone would fall into a trance there was a lot of cheering and applause. I felt nervous. I was overwhelmed by the sight of behavior I could only interpret as a complete lack of self-control. And I was scared that I too would fall to the floor, with but with no narrative other than "hysteria" to make sense of it. I panicked; it was only a sense of professionalism that kept me for wrestling my way back to the exit. I recall that I crossed my arms over my chest. I tried to disassociate myself from the scene by rummaging in my rucksack to look for nothing in particular. I urged myself to breathe deeply and calmly. I told myself that I do not believe in spirits. I forced myself to think of what anthropologist have been saying about possession trance, invoking the

7 Poetics and Ethics of World/Sense: Cultivating the Lessons 275

spirits of science to protect me from whatever it was that was creeping toward me that rowdy night. What calmed me down, in the end, was the sight of a dog. Not a Saint Bernard dog, to be sure, but a breed akin to a German Shepherd. The animal had been walking around freely over the dance floor, pursuing its own canine pursuits. Undisturbed by the interactions of people and spirits, the dog offered a reassuring image of normalcy to hold onto.

This is a different style of research writing, one that incorporates reflexivity at a vulnerable level, an experience more common within ethnographic writing. I note particularly his reach for cultural academic language to help him make "world/sense" of the situation, that is, "hysteria," and also that his bodily comfort and "image of normalcy" is reestablished by connecting in that moment to the commonness in his "world/sense" of seeing a German Shepherd calming walking around. I use this striking example to suggest that just as the use of the third party voice normatively in our research writing styles[29] actually may be hampering our ability to attend to our ethical call to see and hear in new ways for the societal challenges of our times, the white male normative ideological ideal of "objectivity" also may be limiting our ability to be faithful to all phenomena we are experiencing in our interdisciplinary research, particularly in our qualitative research. Paradoxically, by bringing more of our self—our intersectional "I" of lived experiences and identities—openly into our writing and our research, we may begin to develop a more faithful practice to the complexity of living world/views and world/senses and ultimately to the diversity of forms of human sacred meaning-making, including in relationship to formal religion.[30] In making this statement, I situate myself in larger reflexive dialogues common to ethnographers within anthropology, dialogues that could be fruitfully brought into broader interdisciplinary discussion as well as into lived religion studies of trauma.[31]

As I begin to close where I began, I note that there are interdisciplinary parallels occuring between these case studies focused on peace in the aftermath of violence, with their various religio/poetic material practices, and the work of what are termed "the New Materialists" emerging in this era of climate change, with climate change's potential for traumatic impact as well. Circling back to my references to the power of embodied metaphor as a correlational tool between religious and spiritual communities and the sciences, inclusive of the language of 'spirit,' I point particularly to new materialists Clayton Crockett, religious studies, and Jeffrey W. Robbins, philosopher,[32] who state:

> ... we suggest that this crisis [of ecology, energy, and finance] could provide an opening for a new kind of orientation to thinking and acting, a new way of being in and of the earth. This opening is an opening onto a new materialism that is neither a crude consumerist materialism nor a reductive atomic materialism, but a materialism that takes seriously the physical and material world in which we live. The New Materialism is a materialism based on energy transformation. Energy itself is not reductive matter but resonates with "spirit" and "life" . . . .

The looming of climate change adds its own ethical challenge to find the points of connection across disciplines and across the fields of human embodied and material existence—a going back to ancient wisdom indigenous peoples have long known in their own world/sense, which others of us now are attempting to recapture with new language for Western and planetary salvation. For example, referencing Bruno Latours' concept of "actant," and forging a paradigm shift in the face of destructive ecological forces, Jane Bennett, a political theorist,[33] is drawn ethically to argue that matter is *vibrant* and *vital*, and that these are characteristics constitutive of matter itself rather than added by traditional dichotomous ideas of matter and spirit, as passed down through a dominant Western cultural heritage and world/sense.

In this, I draw particular attention to the works of anthropologist Birgit Meyer[34] as well, who is keenly aware that the "mentalistic approach" of the Western Protestant Enlightenment world/sense defines and constrains "religion" through its history of colonialism, creating a need for a major integration of cross-disciplinary studies to defamiliarize the "academic canon":

> The point is to grasp the specific dynamics of power that constitute and "normalize" the academic study of religon within historically and socially

7 Poetics and Ethics of World/Sense: Cultivating the Lessons   277

specific formations, showing how ways of studying religion reflect ways of perceiving the world at large. We need to spotlight biases, blind spots and inadequacies in these established and perhaps all-too-familiar ways, enabling us to imagine new, alternative directions for our work.[35]

In point of fact, according to Meyer's studies, and as I have suggested above, indigenous cultures understood that "religious" experiences, the sense of "something more," *always* were mediated through human action and material means—and this is a significant and promising area of interdisciplinary research, as lived religion studies often demonstrate:

> I propose to place at the centre of scholarly inquiries the very concrete ways through which humans "fabricate"—by mobilizing texts, sounds, pictures, or objects, and by engaging in practices of speaking, singing, being possessed and so on—a sense of presence of something beyond. Foregrounding "fabrication" prompts very concrete empirical questions about the specific practices, materials and forms employed in *generating* a sense of something divine, ghostly, sublime or transcendent ... the *genesis* of a sense of extraordinary presence ... as practices and materials are indispesable for religion's existence in the world as a social, cultural, and political phenomenon, they need our utmost theoretical and empirical attention ... Intended as a provocative shout to signal the need for a new approach, "material religion" is in fact a pleonasm that will become obsolete once the study of religon has been materialized.[36]

Meyer's particular contribution of a methodological tool is the term "sensational form" in "religious mediation," mediation that also takes seriously embodied and material dimensions of power: "This notion refers to a configuration of religious media, acts, imaginations and bodily sensations in the context of a religious tradition or group" that are "authorized and authenticated" mediators of the religious experience.[37] Fostering the "shared partaking in religious mediation sustains collective identities ... within a particular material environment ... ," one in which "the sensation-power nexus needs to be taken seriously."[38] I embrace much in the approach of these New Materialists, particularly in the work of Birgit Meyer. I raise additional issues related to normativity and power—who authorizes and who authenticates?—and maintain an

Fig. 7.1 *Intersecting issues at the Mothers' Day Walk for Peace.* Young people clearly understanding the intertwining relationship between violence, justice, outreach and the need for jobs as they illustrate their banner with the 7 Principles of Peace and names, pictures, and buttons of the dead

appreciation for an embodied metaphorical correlational approach that honors the linguistic systems, verbal and nonverbal, that express different cultural world/sense across academic disciplines.

Finally, beyond all the academic disciplinary struggles, there also is what is happening on the ground among the people outside the walls of academia, walls that often are labled ivory towers in their disconnectedness. How connected those towers seek to be to the struggles in the streets, including the seriousness with which the streets are taken in the academy and research, is both an individual and collective act of ethical accountability

7 Poetics and Ethics of World/Sense: Cultivating the Lessons

Fig. 7.2 *Intersecting issues at a climate change protest.* Activists from West Roxbury and the surrounding Boston area communities protesting the installation in process of a natural gas lateral pipeline carrying fracked gas, understanding the implications for issues of race and class as well as the environment

and a matter of world/sense in the attribution of sacred meaning to the living, pulsing, power, and reality of those streets.[39] So here I choose to leave my readers with signs of such intersectional hope on the streets of Dorchester, in a climate change protest, and in a youth movement embracing the living power of a new sacred story through a spiritual tribe of activism. If a larger peace is to be achieved, it may come more through those who demand it with their bodies and work to build embodied connections than through those who only write about it (Figs. 7.1, 7.2 and 7.3).

280 Violent Trauma, Culture, and Power

Fig. 7.3 *Intersecting issues through youth activism and new stories.* There is an international grassroots network of young activists training under the narrative vision of the Harry Potter stories and called the Harry Potter Alliance. This picture was taken at a related organization's conference, The Granger Leadership Academy, where teens and young adult activists took part in a wide variety of social justice workshops, ranging from "Planning to Change the World A Lot" to "Showing Up for Racial Justice" to "Wake Up and Smell the Environmental Racism" to "Transgender Advocacy 101." Embodying young adult literature becomes a new story and path to peace and justice

Notes

1. The primary advice of ministry leaders to clergy in the immediate aftermath of violence was not to focus on theology but to focus on *practical logistical care*. Time and again, survivors would say that this

7 Poetics and Ethics of World/Sense: Cultivating the Lessons   281

type of compassionate and practical case management was an aspect of the Peace Institute's crisis services that they most valued. If they did not have the money to bury their loved one or if they had a housing crisis, the Peace Institute's focus was first and foremost on these logistical practical details of care to reestablish survivor safety and control. UUTRM leaders would concur in this as well.
2. For media coverage, see https://www.bostonglobe.com/metro/2016/05/08/thousands-gather-for-mother-day-peace-walk/nxxmwkwmZQBUqIdgZoe6pJ/story.html (accessed May 9, 2016).
3. A TVUUC leader specifically referenced a book some had studied together that had critiqued the UU faith tradition, see Michael Durall, *The Almost Church: Redefining Unitarian Universalism for a New Era* (Tulsa, OK: Jenkin Lloyd Jones Press, 2004).
4. For further conceptual work within RCT on the energizing power of group identity and a sense of "we," see Stephen J. Bergman and Janet L. Surrey, "Couple Therapy: A Relational Approach," 167–193, and Nikki M. Fedele, "Relationships in Groups: Connection, Resonance, and Paradox," 194–219, in *The Complexity of Connection: Writings from the Stone Center's Jean Baker Miller Training Institute*, edited by Jordan, Judith V., Maureen Walker, and Linda M. Hartling (New York: The Guilford Press, 2004), as well as Karen Skerrett, "Moving toward 'We': Promise and Peril," 128–150, in *How Connections Heal: Stories From Relational-Cultural* Therapy, edited by Walker, Maureen and Wendy B. Rosen (New York: The Guilford Press, 2004); and most recently Judith V. Jordan and Jon Carlson, editors, *Creating Connection: A Relational-Cultural Approach with Couples* (New York: Routledge, 2013).
5. This sense of the founding mission of the UUTRM was consistent with the UUTRM leader's angry reaction to the possibility of conservative faith traditions oppressing gay, bisexual, lesbian, or transgender (GBLT) persons in the 9/11 disaster.
6. See again Hudson, *Congregational Trauma*, where she lays out a range of practical tips from the need for specific information, agencies that help in particular contexts, Christian worship suggestions, and tips for working with the media among others. Many of these tips and

strategies were employed in the provision of basic pastoral care in the aftermath of trauma for both case studies.

7. A recent contribution to the dilemma that UUs experience in living into their profession of the worth and dignity of each human being is Nathan C. Walker's book illustrating the engagement of moral imagination to cultivate empathy, *Cultivating Empathy: The Worth and Dignity of Every Person—Without Exception* (Boston: Skinner House, 2016). See also Kathleen D. Billman and Daniel L. Migliore, *Rachel's Cry: Prayer of Lament and Rebirth of Hope* (Cleveland: United Church Press, 1999) for possible useful material in this area, including for Unitarian Universalists.
8. See http://www.standingonthesideoflove.org/the-power-of-the-black-lives-matter-banner (accessed May 20, 2016).
9. In addition to clinical theories and approaches lifted up in this book already, see also the intercultural approach to pastoral care developed by Carrie Doehring, *The Practice of Pastoral Care: A Postmodern Approach*, revised and expanded edition (Louisville, KY: Westminster John Knox Press, 2015), and also an essay on immanence in pastoral psychotherapy by Daniel Shaw, "Immanence and Intersubjectivity," in *The Skillful Soul of the Psychotherapist: The Link Between Spirituality and Clinical Excellence*, edited by George S. Stavros and Steven J. Sandage (New York: Rowman & Littlefield, 2014). The collection of essays in this latter volume as a whole are useful examples of clinical self-reflection in the practice of therapy and spirituality. The embodied affective and cognitive experience of immanence is an under-conceptualized and under-studied interdisciplinary area in most definitions of spirituality, including for lived religion studies as well as in spirituality and social work in my experience where the language of transcendence tends to be more prominent. See Holloway and Moss, *Spirituality and Social Work*, as well as Edward R. Canda and Leola Dyrud Furman, *Spiritual Diversity in Social Work Practice: The Heart of Helping*, 2nd edition (New York: Oxford University Press, 2010). See also the efforts of Srdjan Sremac to research such an immanent experience as conversion within substance abuse populations,

"Conversion and the Real: The (Im)Possibility of Testimonial Representation," *Pastoral Psychology*, Springer, published online April 28, 2016.
10. Some art therapy texts have previously been recommended. Here I call particular attention to Helen Land, *Spirituality, Religion, and Faith in Psychotherapy: Evidence-Based Expressive Methods for Mind, Brain, and Body* (Chicago: Lyceum Books, 2015).
11. See Griffith and Griffith, *Encountering the Sacred in Psychotherapy*. Griffith and Griffith are pastoral psychotherapists who speak to the importance of "multichannel listening," 61, and "eliciting multiple metaphors," 67, when working with clients. No single metaphor is usually sufficient in facilitating a client's capacity to reframe their life story for healing or movement and empowerment. See also Herbert Anderson and Edward Foley, *Mighty Stories, Dangerous Rituals: Weaving Together the Human and the Divine* (San Francisco: Jossey-Bass, 1998) for additional examples of meaning-making through story and ritual, albeit through the Christian tradition.
12. Choi Hee An, *Korean Women and God: Experiencing God in a Multireligious Colonial Context* (Maryknoll: Orbis Books, 2005). Also see Andrew Sung Park, *From Hurt to Healing: A Theology of the Wounded* (Nashville: Abingdon Press, 2004).
13. For a few different recent examples of this across different contexts see Loretta Pyles and Gwendolyn J. Adam, eds., *Holistic Engagement: Transforming Social Work Education in the 21st Century* (New York: Oxford University Press, 2016); Christopher Emdin, *For White Folks Who Teach in the Hood...and the Rest of Y'all Too: Reality Pedagogy and Urban Education* (Boston: Beacon Press, 2016); and Courtney T. Goto, *The Grace of Playing: Pedagogies for Leaning Into God's New Creation* (Eugene, OR: Pickwick Publications, 2016). See also classics such as Paulo Freire, *Pedagogy of the Oppressed*, 30th edition (New York: Continuum, 1970/2003) and Henry A. Giroux and Peter McLaren, eds., *Between Borders: Pedagogy and the Politics of Cultural Studies* (New York: Routledge, 1994). Also see another classic Barbara G. Wheeler and Edward Farley, eds., *Shifting Boundaries: Contextual Approaches to the Structure of Theological Education*

(Louisville, KY: Westminster/John Knox Press, 1991)—and I call particular attention to two essays in this volume: Paul F. Knitter, "Beyond a Mono-Religious Theological Education" 151–180; and Mark K. Taylor, "Celebrating Difference, Resisting Domination: The Need for Synchronic Strategies in Theological Education" 259–293.

14. Paralleling the political advocacy of the disability rights community, I can see how survivors are often not treated as the experts in their own experiences and needs by larger institutional and professional communities. Hence, I have drawn on the title of this classic book for this subheading, which in turn draws on a phrase from the disability rights movement: James I. Charlton, *Nothing About Us Without Us: Disability Oppression and Empowerment* (Berkeley: University of California Press, 2000).

15. See *Report of the Committee on Women & Healthy Communities to Members of the Boston City Council,* entire.

16. Robert N. Bellah, "Unitarian Universalism in Societal Perspective," Unitarian Universalist Association, General Assembly, Rochester, NY, June 27, 1998. Bellah also did point out that James Luther Adams did not share an ontological individualism view of human nature. See also Robert Bellah, Richard Madsen, William M. Sullivan, Ann Swidler, and Steven M. Tipton, *Habits of the Heart: Individualism and Commitment in American Life* (New York: Harper & Row Publishers, 1985).

17. Scarry, *The Body in Pain.*

18. The literature on moral injury is growing and originates in the context of war, though it also has applicability to other contexts. Here I wish to suggest the usefulness of integrating continuing bonds theory into this literature along with revisiting the older concept of survivor's guilt. See Rita Nakashima Brock and Gabriella Lettini, *Soul Repair: Recovering from Moral Injury After War* (Boston: Beacon Press, 2013) for an accessible text in this area.

19. See Rita Nakashima Brock and Rebbeca Ann Parker, *Proverbs of Ashes: Violence, Redemptive Suffering, and The Search For What Saves Us* (Boston: Beacon Press, 2001). See also Walsh, *Prophetic Pastoral Care in the Aftermath of Trauma* for my engagement with a wide

variety of constructive theologians of trauma based on the results of the case studies and the ways in which their works reflect or do not reflect survivor experiences. Of particular concern was a tendency for theologians to disregard contextuality of sociocultural location in constructing theological claims.

20. See Thomas E. Reynolds, *Vulnerable Communion: A Theology of Disability and Hospitality* (Grand Rapids, MI: Brazos Press, 2008). See also Walsh, *Prophetic Pastoral Care in the Aftermath of Trauma* for my development of the usefulness of disability theology when linked to trauma theologies.

21. Jennifer E Beste, *God and the Victim: Traumatic Intrusions on Grace and Freedom* (Oxford: Oxford University Press, 2007); Cynthia Hess, *Sites of Violence, Sites of Grace: Christian Nonviolence and the Traumatized Self* (New York: Lexington Books, 2009); and Nancy Pineda-Madrid, *Suffering and Salvation in Ciudad Juarez* (Minneapolis: Fortress Press, 2011). Two additional classics in the field of trauma and theology include Serene Jones, *Trauma and Grace: Theology in a Ruptured World* (Louisville, KY: Westminister John Knox Press, 2009); and Shelly Rambo, *Spirit and Trauma: A Theology of Remaining* (Louisville, KY: Westminster John Knox Press, 2010). Rambo's work is particularly helpful for theologians wishing to theologize from the place of immanence rather than always transcendence. Jones' work is noteworthy for her attention to "liturgies of the flesh," 156.

22. Beste, *God and the Victim*, 101.

23. Pineda-Madrid, *Suffering and Salvation in Ciudad Juarez*, 21–24.

24. Studies such as this have been mentioned in prior chapters. One additional recent ethnographic study that examined economically privileged urban congregations in their responses to poverty in their midst is a dissertation by Andrew Stephen Tripp, "Poverty and Urban Ecclesial Discipleship: A Practical Theological Investigation Of Congregations Caring For The Poor" (PhD Dissertation, Boston University, 2015).

25. Again, further attention is needed to decolonizing approaches in research and writing that take seriously mutuality of learning power relations. The ongoing work of Kwok Pui-lan is significant for

religious and theological studies, for example her classic *Postcolonial Imagination & Feminist Theology* (Louisville, KY: Westminster John Knox Press, 2005). In broader scope for intersectional issues of power, see the works of Andrea Smith, beginning with her essay "Heteropatriarchy and the Three Pillars of White Supremacy: Rethinking Women of Color Organizing," in *Color of Violence: The Incite! Anthology*, edited by Incite! Women of Color Against Violence (Cambridge, MA: South End Press, 2006). Also see the classic work of Chandra Talpade Mohanty, *Feminism Without Borders: Decolonizing Theory, Practicing Solidarity*, 3rd Edition (Durham, NC: Duke University Press, 2004). Finally also see David Chidester, *Empire of Religion: Imperialism and Comparative Religion* (Chicago: University of Chicago Press, 2014).

26. van der Kolk, *The Body Keeps the Score*.
27. This is excerpted and edited from my paper presentation given at the Association for Practical Theology 2016 Biennial Conference, "Examining Whiteness: Recovering the Intersectional 'I' and Experiences of 'Peoplehood' in Writing and Research" (New York: Fordham University, April 9, 2016). See also the historical role of feminists in bringing attention to intersectionality and contextual knowledge as well, such as through standpoint theory. Sandra Harding, ed., *The Feminist Standpoint Theory Reader: Intellectual and Political Controversies* (New York: Routledge, 2004). See also Goldberger, Nancy, Jill Tarule, Blythe Clinchy, and Mary Belenky, eds., *Knowledge, Difference, and Power: Essays Inspired by Women's Ways of Knowing* (New York: Basic Books, 1996).
28. Mattjis Van der Port, *Ecstatic Encounters: Bahian Candomblé and the Quest for the Really Real* (Amsterdam: Amsterdam University Press, 2011) 65.
29. For example, while using a first person rather than third person voice to my opening chapter vignettes, I am inviting the reader to enter into the particularity of my experiences with their own experiences, thus grounding any effort at generalizing or universalizing.
30. I lift up here the work of James W. Perkinson in theology. Perkinson broke some initial barriers in academic writing as a white male by

integrating his lived experiences into his now classic text, *White Theology: Outing Supremacy in Modernity* (New York: Palgrave Macmillan, 2004). See also another early work not as often referenced in the area anti-racism work in the academy and ministry: Jennifer Harvey, Karin A. Case, and Robin Hawley Gorsline, eds., *Disrupting White Supremacy From Within: White People On What We Need To Do* (Cleveland: Pilgrim Press, 2004).

31. See again Brettell, *Anthropological Conversations*. Brettell sees anthropology as an academic discipline naturally situated for these types of interdisciplinary efforts. I agree, though I also see other disciplines naturally suited for such efforts as well, such as social work and public health. Brettell's text does provide an excellent summary of these efforts within anthropology, including intersections with psychology and trauma though primarily through psychoanalytic theories.

32. Clayton Crockett and Jeffrey W. Robbins, *Religion, Politics, and the Earth: The New Materialism* (New York: Palgrave Macmillan, 2012) xv–xvi.

33. Jane Bennett, *Vibrant Matter: A Political Ecology of Things* (Durham, NC: Duke University Press, 2010) viii–ix.

34. Birgit Meyer, "Mediation and the Genesis of Presence: Toward a Material Approach to Religion," Inaugural Lecture, Universiteit Utrecht, October 19, 2012. Meyer's interest in decolonizing and defamiliarizing methodologies follows my own, as illustrated in my introduction. Her focus solely on a Protestant legacy may be questioned by those who argue the mind/body/spirit split is deeply rooted overall in the encounter of Christianity with Hellenistic culture and Plato. See again for example, Douglas, *What's Faith Got To Do With It?*. See also W.J.T. Mitchell, *What Do Pictures Want?: The Lives and Loves of Images* (Chicago: The University of Chicago Press, 2005) as part of this emerging zeitgeist of the New Materialists.

35. Ibid., 8–10.

36. Ibid., 22–23.

37. Ibid., 26. See also *Aesthetic Formations: Media, Religion, and the Senses*, ed. by Birgit Meyer (New York: Palgrave Macmillan, 2009).

38. Meyer, "Mediation and the Genesis of Presence," 30.

39. In addition to Black Lives Matter and beyond the former Occupy movement, two other grassroots movement in the United States are worthy of attention. First is the Moral Monday Movement, with its focus on intersectional fusion politics, led by Rev. Dr. William J. Barber II. See his two recent books documenting the rise of this movement that began in North Carolina: *Forward Together: A Moral Message for the Nation* (St. Louis, MO: Chalice Press, 2014) and *The Third Reconstruction: Moral Mondays, Fusion Politics, and the Rise of a New Justice Movement* (Boston: Beacon Press, 2016). Also of note for immediate attention is the secular and interfaith Showing Up for Racial Justice Movement led by white allies in support of Black Lives Matter. See Chris Crass' books in partial documentation of the growth of white anti-racist education and movement building: *Towards Collective Liberation: Anti-Racist Organizing, Feminist Praxis, and Movement Building Strategy* (Oakland, CA: PM Press, 2013) and *Towards the "Other America": Anti-Racist Resources for White People Taking Action For Black Lives Matter* (St. Louis, MO: 2015). Finally, see also a recent work examining nonviolent grassroots social movements on an international scale during this century: Mark Engler an Paul Engler, *This Is An Uprising: How Nonviolent Revolt Is Shaping the Twenty-first Century* (New York: Nation Books, 2016).

A Queer Postlude of Intersections in the Aftermath

This manuscript was finalized on the day after my fifth wedding anniversary, a special date known as Loving Day[1] that we consciously chose to be married on as an interracial couple. Loving Day occurs during the Pride celebration month of June and is a day honoring the United States Supreme Court's 1967 decision to overturn state legal bans on interracial marriages. Ironically, the couple's last name in the legal challenge was Loving. As I finished posting a few picture reminders of the wedding for my husband and friends on Facebook in celebration of this particular Loving Day, June 12, 2016, I began to hear with growing horror and anger reports coming from the television of a mass shooting at a lesbian, gay, bisexual, transgender, and queer (LGBTQ) nightclub in Orlando, FL—the news only worsened throughout that day as the number of the dead rose to at least 50, inclusive of the shooter himself who was being termed a self-radicalized Islamic terrorist.[2]

When the number so quickly reached 50, the mass media began to term this the deadliest mass shooting in the US history—yet those of us who know that the history of the United States is founded in violence also know that that is not true, that there have been other mass shootings known and unknown, inclusive of Wounded Knee among others.[3] The

© The Author(s) 2017
M. Walsh, *Violent Trauma, Culture, and Power*,
DOI 10.1007/978-3-319-41772-1

289

violence that erupted in the Orlando nightclub carried a relationship to all the mass shootings and historical US violence that went before it, the violence known and the violence unknown. We record, remember, and memorialize our history selectively by whose bodies are marked as significant at any particular time—and by who have the power to record, remember, and memorialize particular stories of particular lives. Social media became a powerful tool once again in the aftermath of this particular June 12th. Material poetic and artistically designed images of mourning and protest rapidly began to appear—Facebook profile images shaded with rainbows, a wolf howling in a Facebook profile juxtaposed against rainbow lines of candles, hearts with rainbow colors affirming love, and many, many more, alongside the posting of articles and memes calling for further gun control laws.

This particular social media explosion also came on the heels of yet another turbulent week of social media activity spotlighting gender violence and rape culture, focused particularly on higher education campuses in the United States.[4] The publication of the victim witness letter of a campus rape survivor prompted remarkable outpourings from many corners, including further sharing of gender-based violence in both small and large public and private groups. Members of Congress also made plans to read her letter into the US congressional record, a CNN reporter read parts of it out loud on television, and the sitting US Vice President wrote a public heartfelt response, calling her a "warrior."[5]

Ironically, the ready-made intersectional link available between these two violent events, separated in time by barely a week, was still too distant for some media analysts, even one who spoke clearly to patterns of dominance and control being examples of "toxic masculinity"[6] in US history and its aversion to gun control. Power, domination, and control can lead to violence across a spectrum of cultural identities when given the opportunity—we've seen this in the militarization of police culture and its impact particularly in poor communities of color, as stated in my introduction. To understand intersectionality on an embodied level is to understand that there is a queerness inclusive of, as well as beyond, experiences of sexual or affectional orientation and gender status.

This is the queerness that occurs when one crosses also between borders and into the borderlands of race, class, religion, ability, and the academic disciplines—into the borders between worlds or world/sense—through the markings of social constructions and lived experiences and through the push and play of language and expanded metaphors. This is the queer sense of being in an unfamiliar, peculiar, or strange land where one's visceral sense of the world is challenged and where one's grasp on felt reality seems to shift, with anxiety and desire for control often resulting. As a final though different example as I complete the writing of this book manuscript, the candidate also mentioned in my introduction who shamelessly called for a ban on Muslims entering the United States and for building a wall along the Mexican border appears to have garnered the nomination of a major political party. There can be a felt experience of queerness in this as well for those whose sociohistorical world/sense has not included an intellectual and visceral understanding of the rootedness of violence, patriarchy, and white supremacy in the United States—that the emergence of this candidate represents, drawing on Malcolm X's controversial phrase, "the chickens coming home to roost."

As our paradigms shift in understanding human being, intersectionality, and our essential embodied relatedness to and dependency on one another, as well as on our shared though endangered planet, then the call to enter into these borderlands of queerness becomes louder and more imperative—and to enter while we have an opportunity to do so freely without being forced to do so from the lived experience of trauma queering us into a new world. For the lived experience of trauma, particularly violent trauma, marks many of us as liminal people and members of a shared tribe across all of these borders, as well as within the borderlands, of a multitude of social and professional identities. We are the embodied "spiritual tribe" of the "scar clan," as Catholic Jungian analyst, poet, post-trauma recovery specialist, and multiracial daughter of indigenous immigrant and refugee families, Clarissa Pinkola Estés, might call us[7]—and in sharing tribal status as scar clan members, perhaps there also is power in sharing our "sacred stories" of survival as scar clan. Through our creative practices in embodied narrative and material poetic or artistic form, we may find metaphorical bridges and the intersectional liminal common ground of communitas for constructing peace in our larger shared and troubled world.

Are we able to heed this call to enter into the borderlands of queerness with an open and compassionate heart, as well as with ethical respect and an intent to level social, cultural, and institutional power? Do we share in witness to the ethical urgency to do so in light of global violence as well as the looming threat of climate change? Heeding such a call means leaving our respective academic or professional disciplinary, religious, or secular comfort zones or ivory towers in more ways than we might possibly imagine at present. It means engaging the visceral realities of different world/sense encounters and risking the potential for transformation involved in such engagement. The reward may yet be a more peaceful, sustainable, and equitable shared world. As my self that always will remain a community minister at heart would say, even in and to an academy that may find a minister queer in its midst, "May it be so. Amen, Amen, Ashe, and Blessed Be."

Notes

1. See http://lovingday.org/learn (accessed June 13, 2016).
2. See http://www.cnn.com/2016/06/12/us/orlando-nightclub-shooting/index.html (accessed June 13, 2016).
3. See http://indiancountrytodaymedianetwork.com/2016/01/01/truth-about-wounded-knee-massacre-162923 (accessed June 13, 2016).
4. See http://www.csmonitor.com/USA/Justice/2016/0609/Outcry-over-Stanford-case-hints-at-shift-in-rape-culture (accessed June 13, 2016).
5. See http://www.huffingtonpost.com/entry/stanford-sexual-assault-victim-letter-congress_us_5758d597e4b00f97fba74969 (accessed June 13, 2016) and https://www.buzzfeed.com/tomnamako/joe-biden-writes-an-open-letter-to-stanford-survivor?utm_term=.klx5Z1G2Y#.vhMKY2x5D (accessed June 13, 2016) and http://www.cnn.com/videos/justice/2016/06/06/stanford-rape-survivor-letter-brock-allen-turner-ashleigh-banfield-orig.cnn/video/playlists/stanford-rape-case/ (accessed June 13, 2006).
6. See http://www.salon.com/2016/06/13/overcompensation_nation_its_time_to_admit_that_toxic_masculinity_drives_gun_violence/?source=newsletter (accessed June 13, 2016).

7. Clarissa Pinkola Estés, *Women Who Run With Wolves* (New York: Ballentine Books, 1996). See also her website for a complete list of her works going back decades. Trauma theologian Shelly Rambo, influenced also by philosopher Richard Kearney's works, has postulated the significance of theorizing about the scar as well as the wound. "While trauma is figured as wound, its afterlife might be figured as scar, as a textured surface that serves as a critical crossing between death and life, interior and exterior, hidden and revealed. Moving between wounds and scars requires theorizing the textured surface of the skin. (p. 266)" See Shelly Rambo, "Refiguring Wounds in the Afterlife (of Trauma)," in *Carnal Hermeneutics*, 263–278, edited by Richard Kearney and Brian Treanor (New York: Fordham University Press, 2015). Per my writings, there also are the wounds and scars that are not relegated to the surface of the skin alone but are internal and neurophysiological, which also need theorizing and metaphorical exploration across academic disciplines, including theology. There also are interesting pastoral care considerations to make as to the value of adding to the "wounded healer" pastoral care image that of the "scarred healer."

Bibliography

Adams, James Luther. 1986. *The prophethood of all believers*. (ed. George K. Beach). Boston: Beacon Press.
Adams, James Luther. 1991a. *An examined faith: Social context and religious commitment*. (ed. George K. Beach). Boston: Beacon Press.
Adams, James Luther. 1991b. God is love. In *An examined faith: Social context and religious commitment*, ed. George K. Beach, 213–219 (1947). Boston: Beacon Press.
Adams, James Luther. 1991c. Root metaphors of religious social thought. In *An examined faith: Social context and religious commitment*, ed. George K. Beach, 243–255 (1973/1988). Boston: Beacon Press.
Adams, James Luther. 1998a. The changing reputation of human nature. In *The essential James Luther Adams: Selected essays and addresses*, ed. George K. Beach, 51–78 (1941). Boston: Beacon Press.
Adams, James Luther. 1998b. Our responsibility in society. In *The essential James Luther Adams: Selected essays and addresses*, ed. George Kimmich Beach, 153–177, 171(1953). Boston: Skinner House.
Adams, James Luther. 1998c. The prophethood of all believers. In *The essential James Luther Adams: Selected essays and addresses*, ed. George K. Beach, 105–113 (1947). Boston: Beacon Press.
Alexander, Scott W. 1993. *The relational pulpit: Closing the gap between preacher and pew*. Boston: Skinner House.

Alexander, Michelle. 2012. *The new Jim Crow: Mass incarceration in the age of colorblindness*, rev. ed. New York: The New Press.
Althaus-Reid, Marcella. 2004. *From feminist theology to indecent theology: Readings on poetry, sexual identity, and God*. London: SCM Press.
Alves, Rubem A. 1992. Theopoetics: Longing and liberation. In *Struggles for solidarity: Liberation theologies in tension*, ed. Lorine M. Getz and Ruy O. Costa, 159–171. Minneapolis: Fortress Press.
Ammerman, Nancy T. (ed.). 2007. *Everyday religion: Observing modern religious lives*. Oxford: Oxford University Press.
Ammerman, Nancy T. (ed.). 2014. *Sacred stories, spiritual tribes: Finding religion in everyday life*. New York: Oxford University Press.
An, Choi Hee. 2005. *Korean women and God: Experiencing God in a multi-religious colonial context*. Maryknoll: Orbis Books.
Anderson, Herbert, and Edward Foley. 1998. *Mighty stories, dangerous rituals: Weaving together the human and the divine*. San Francisco: Jossey-Bass.
Andrews, Dale P. 2002. *Practical theology for black churches: Bridging black theology and African American folk religion*. Louisville: Westminster John Knox Press.
Andrews, Dale P. 2014. Race and racism. In *The Wiley-Blackwell companion to practical theology*, ed. Bonnie Miller-McLemore, 401–411. Malden: Wiley-Blackwell.
Appadurai, Arjun. 2015. Mediants, materiality, normativity. *Public Culture* 27 (2): 221–237, Duke University Press.
Appio, Lauren, Debbie-Ann Chambers, and Susan Mao. 2013. Listening to the voices of the poor and disrupting the silence about class issues in psychotherapy. *Journal of Clinical Psychology: In Session* 69(2): 152–161.
Aquino, Maria Pilar. 2007. Feminist intercultural theology: Toward a shared future of justice. In *Feminist intercultural theology: Latino explorations for a just world*, ed. Maria Pilar Aquino and Maria Jose Rosado-Nunes, 9–28. Maryknoll: Orbis Books.
Aquino, Maria Pilar, and Maria Jose Rosado-Nunes (eds.). 2007. *Feminist intercultural theology: Latino explorations for a just world*. Maryknoll: Orbis Books.
Ariarahah, S. 2005. Intercultural Hermeneutics—A promise for the future? *Exchange* 34(2): 89–101 (13).
Arvay, Marla J. 2005. Shattered beliefs: Reconstituting the self of the trauma counselor. In *Meaning reconstruction and the experience of loss*, 4th ed,

ed. Robert A. Neimeyer, 213–230. Washington, DC: American Psychological Association.
Astley, Jeff. 2002. *Ordinary theology: Looking, listening and learning in theology*. Burlington: Ashgate Publishing Company.
Balko, Radley. 2014. *Rise of the warrior cop: The militarization of America's police forces*. New York: Public Affairs.
Banks, Amy, and Leigh Ann Hirschman. 2015. *Four ways to click: Rewire your brain for stronger, more rewarding relationships*. New York: Jeremy P. Tarcher/Penguin.
Barnard, Ian. 20014/2008. *Queer race: Cultural interventions in the racial polities of queer theory*. New York: Peter Lang.
Barber, Rev. Dr. William J. 2014. *Forward together: A moral message for the nation*. St. Louis: Chalice Press.
———. 2016. *The third reconstruction: Moral Mondays, fusion politics, and the rise of a new justice movement*. Boston: Beacon Press.
Batts, Valerie. 2002. Is reconciliation possible? Lessons from combatting 'Modern Racism'. In *Waging reconciliation: God's mission in a time of globalization and crisis*, ed. Ian T. Douglas. New York: Church Publishing Incorporated.
Beach, George K. (ed.). 1998. *The essential James Luther Adams: Selected essays and addresses*. Boston: Skinner House Books.
Beach, George K. (ed.). 2005. *Transforming liberalism: The theology of James Luther Adams*. Boston: Skinner House Books.
Bell, Lee Anne. 2010. *Storytelling for social justice: Connecting narrative and the arts in antiracist teaching*. New York: Routledge.
Bellah, Robert, Richard Madsen, William M. Sullivan, Ann Swidler, and Steven M. Tipton. 1985. *Habits of the heart: Individualism and commitment in American life*. New York: Harper & Row Publishers.
Bellah, Robert, Richard Madsen, William M. Sullivan, Ann Swidler, and Steven M. Tipton. 1998. *Unitarian Universalism in societal perspective*. Rochester: Unitarian Universalist Association, General Assembly.
Bennett, Jane. 2010. *Vibrant matter: A political ecology of things*. Durham: Duke University Press.
Bergman, Stephen J., and Janet L. Surrey. 2004. Couple therapy: A relational approach. In *The complexity of connection: Writings from the Stone Center's Jean Baker Miller Training Institute*, ed. Judith V. Jordan, Maureen Walker, and Linda M. Hartling, 167–193. New York: The Guilford Press.
Berrien, Jenny, Omar McRoberts, and Christopher Winship. 2000. Religion and the Boston miracle: The effect of black ministry on youth violence. In *Who will

provide? The changing role of religion in American social welfare, ed. Mary Jo Bane, Brent Coffin, and Ronald Thiemann, 266–285. Boulder: Westview Press.

Beste, Jennifer E. 2007. *God and the victim: Traumatic intrusions on grace and freedom.* Oxford: Oxford University Press.

Betcher, Sharon V. 2007. *Spirit and the politics of disablement.* Minneapolis: Fortress Press.

Bieler, Andrea. 2007. Embodied knowing: Understanding religious experience in ritual. In *Religion: Immediate experience and the mediacy of research – Interdisciplinary studies, concepts and methodology of empirical research in religion*, ed. Hans-Günter Heimbrock and Christopher P. Scholtz, 39–59. Göttingen: Vandenhoeck & Ruprecht.

Billman, Kathleen D., and Daniel L. Migliore. 1999. *Rachel's cry: Prayer of lament and rebirth of hope.* Cleveland: United Church Press.

Bonanno, George A. 2004. Loss, trauma, and human resilience: Have we underestimated the human capacity to thrive after extremely aversive events? *American Psychologist* 59: 20–28.

Bradway, Kay, and Barbara McCoard. 1997. *Sandplay—Silent workshop of the psyche.* New York: Routledge.

Bradway, Katherine, Karen A. Signell, Geraldine H. Spare, Charles T. Stewart, Louis H. Stewart, and Clare Thompson. 1981. *Sandplay studies: Origins, theory, and practice*, Collected by the C.G. Jung Institute of San Francisco. Boston: Sigo Press.

Bray, Karen. 2016. *Unredeemed: A political theology of affect, time, and worth.* PhD dissertation, Drew University.

Brettell, Caroline B. 2015. *Anthropological conversations: Talking culture across disciplines.* New York: Rowman & Littlefield.

Brock, Rita Nakashima Brock, and Gabriella Lettini. 2013. *Soul repair: Recovering from moral injury after war.* Boston: Beacon Press.

Brock, Rita Nakashima, and Rebbeca Ann Parker. 2001. *Proverbs of ashes: Violence, redemptive suffering, and the search for what saves us.* Boston: Beacon Press.

Bronfenbrenner, Urie (ed.). 2005. *Making human beings human: Bioecological perspectives on human development.* Thousand Oaks: Sage.

Calhoun, Lawrence G., and Richard G. Tedeschi. 2005. Posttraumatic growth: The positive lessons of loss. In *Meaning reconstruction and the experience of loss*, 4th ed, ed. Robert A. Neimeyer, 157–172. Washington, DC: American Psychological Association.

Canada, Geoffrey. 1996. *Fist, stick, knife, gun.* Boston: Beacon Press.

Canada, Geoffrey. 1998. *Reaching up for manhood: Transforming the lives of boys in America*. Boston: Beacon Press.
Canda, Edward R., and Leola Dyrud Furman. 2010. *Spiritual diversity in social work practice: The heart of helping*, 2nd ed. New York: Oxford University Press.
Centers for Disease Control and Prevention. 2011. Homicides—United States, 1999–2007. *Morbidity and Mortality Weekly Report*, Supplements, 60(01): 67–70 (January 14, 2011).
Charlton, James I. 2000. *Nothing about us without us: Disability oppression and empowerment*. Berkeley: University of California Press.
Chery, Joseph M. 2005. The story of Louis D. Brown, section titled "Dream High." In *Peacezone: A program for teaching social literacy, grades 4–5 teacher's guide* by Deborah Prothrow-Stith, Joseph M. Chery, Jon Oliver with Clementina Chery, Marci Feldman, and Fern Shamis. Champaign: Research Press.
Chidester, David. 2014. *Empire of religion: Imperialism and comparative religion*. Chicago: University of Chicago Press.
Chopp, Rebecca S. 1986. *The praxis of suffering: An interpretation of liberation and political theologies*. Eugene: Wipf and Stock Publishers.
Chopp, Rebecca S. 1995. *Saving work: Feminist practices of theological education*. Louisville: Westminister John Knox Press.
Chopp, Rebecca S. 1998. Theology and the poetics of testimony. *Criterion* (Winter 1998): 2–12.
Coates, Ta-Nehisi. 2015. *Between the world and me*. New York: Spiegel & Grau.
Collins, Randall. 1998. *The sociology of philosophies: A global theory of intellectual change*. Cambridge: The Belknap Press of Harvard University Press.
Collins, Patricia Hill. 2000. *Black feminist thought: Knowledge, consciousness, and the politics of empowerment*, 2nd ed. New York: Routledge.
Commission on Appraisal. 1983. *Empowerment: One denomination's quest for racial justice 1967–1982*. Boston: Unitarian Universalist Association.
Commission on Appraisal. 1997. *Interdependence: Renewing congregational polity*. Boston: Unitarian Universalist Association.
Commission on Appraisal. 2005. *Engaging our theological diversity*. Boston: Unitarian Universalist Association.
Cone, James H. 2007. Strange fruit: The cross and the lynching tree. *Harvard Divinity Bulletin* (Winter 2007): 47–56.
Cooper-White, Pamela. 2007. *Many voices: Pastoral psychotherapy in relational and theological perspective*. Minneapolis: Fortress Press.

Copeland, M. Shawn. 2010. *Enfleshing freedom: Body, race, and being*. Minneapolis: Fortress Press.
Courtois, Christine A., and Julian D. Ford (eds.). 2009. *Treating complex traumatic stress disorders: An evidence-based guide*. New York: The Guilford Press.
Cozolino, Louis. 2006. *The neuroscience of human relationships: Attachment and the developing social brain*. New York: W.W. Norton & Company.
Crass, Chris. 2013. *Towards collective liberation: Anti-racist organizing, Feminist Praxis, and movement building strategy*. Oakland: PM Press.
———. 2015. *Towards the "Other America": Anti-racist resources for White people taking action for Black Lives Matter*. St. Louis: Chalice Press.
Creamer, Deborah Beth. 2009. *Disability and Christian theology: Embodied limits and constructive possibilities*. New York: Oxford University Press.
Crenshaw, Kimberlé, Neil Gotanda, Gary Peller, and Kendall Thomas (eds.). 1995. *Critical race theory: The key writings that formed the movement*. New York: The New Press.
Crockett, Clayton, and Jeffrey W. Robbins. 2012. *Religion, politics, and the earth: The new materialism*. New York: Palgrave Macmillan.
Damasio, Antonio. 1999. *The feeling of what happens: Body and emotion in the making of consciousness*. New York: Harcourt, Inc.
De Domenico, Gisela Schubach. 1995. *Sand tray world play: A comprehensive guide to the use of the sand tray in psychotherapeutic and transformational settings*. Oakland: Vision Quest Images.
Delgado, Richard, and Jean Stefancic. 2012. *Critical race theory: An introduction*, 2nd ed. New York: New York University Press.
Dinter, Astrid. 2008. Searching for a construction of meaning: Ritual and meditation as necessary part of pastoral work. In *Lived religion: Conceptual, empirical and practical-theological approaches, essays in honor of Hans-Günter Heimbrock*, ed. Heinz Streib, Astrid Dinter, and Kerstin Söderblom. Boston: Brill.
Doehring, Carrie. 2015. *The practice of pastoral care: A postmodern approach*, rev. and exp. ed. Louisville: Westminster John Knox Press.
Dorrien, Gary. 2006. *The making of American liberal theology: Crisis, irony, & postmodernity, 1950–2005*. Louisville: Westminster John Knox Press.
Douglas, Kelly Brown. 2005. *What's faith got to do with it? Black bodies/Christian souls*. Maryknoll: Orbis Books.
Dunbar-Ortiz, Roxanne. 2014. *An indigenous peoples' history of the United States*. Boston: Beacon Press.

Durall, Michael. 2004. *The almost church: Redefining Unitarian Universalism for a new era*. Tulsa: Jenkin Lloyd Jones Press.
Dykstra, Robert C. 2005. *Images of pastoral care: Classic readings*. St. Louis: Chalice Press.
Edman, Rev. Elizabeth M. 2016. *Queer virtue: What LGBTQ people know about life and love and how it can revitalize Christianity*. Boston: Beacon Press.
Eiesland, Nancy L. 1994. *The disabled God: Toward a liberatory theology of disability*. Nashville: Abingdon Press.
Emdin, Christopher. 2016. *For white folks who teach in the hood…and the rest of y'all too: Reality pedagogy and urban education*. Boston: Beacon Press.
Engler, Mark an Paul Engler. 2016. *This is an uprising: How nonviolent revolt is shaping the twenty-first century*. New York: Nation Books.
Estés, Clarissa Pinkola. 1996. *Women who run with wolves*. New York: Ballentine Books.
Fedele, Nikki M. 2004. Relationships in groups: Connection, resonance, and paradox. In *The complexity of connection: Writings from the stone center's Jean Baker Miller Training Institute*, ed. Judith V. Jordan, Maureen Walker, and Linda M. Hartling, 194–219. New York: The Guilford Press.
Freire, Paulo. 1970/2003. *Pedagogy of the oppressed*, 30th ed. New York: Continuum.
Fulkerson, Mary McClintock. 2007. *Places of redemption: Theology for a worldly church*. Oxford: Oxford University Press.
Fulkerson, Mary McClintock, and Sheila Briggs (eds.). 2013. *The Oxford handbook of feminist theology*. Oxford: Oxford University Press.
Gaede, Beth Ann (ed.). 2006. *When a congregation is betrayed: Responding to clergy misconduct*. Herndon: The Alban Institute.
Ganzevoort, R. Ruard. 2009. Forks in the road when tracing the sacred: Practical theology as Hermeneutics of lived religion. Presidential Address to the Ninth Conference of the International Academy of Practical Theology, Chicago.
Ganzevoort, R. Ruard. 2014. Narrative approaches. In *The Wiley-Blackwell companion to practical theology*, ed. Bonnie Miller-McLemore, 214–223. Malden: Wiley-Blackwell.
Ganzevoort, R. Ruard, and Nette Falkenburg. 2012. Stories beyond life and death: Spiritual experiences of continuity and discontinuity among parents who lose a child. *Journal of Empirical Theology* 25(2): 189–204.
Ganzevoort, R. Ruard, and Johan H. Roeland. 2014. Lived religion: The practice of practical theology. *International Journal of Practical Theology* 18(1): 91–101.

Gendlin, Eugene. 1962/1997. *Experiencing and the creation of meaning: A philosophical and psychological approach to the subjective.* Evanston: Northwestern University Press.
Gerkin, Charles V. 1984. *The living human document: Re-visioning pastoral counseling in a hermeneutical mode.* Nashville: Abingdon Press.
Gerkin, Charles V. 1991. *Prophetic pastoral practice: A Christian vision of life together.* Nashville: Abingdon Press.
Gill, Jerry H. 2000. *The tacit mode: Michael Polanyi's postmodern philosophy.* New York: State University of New York Press.
Gilligan, James. 1997. *Violence: Reflections on a national epidemic.* New York: Vintage Books.
Giroux, Henry A., and Peter McLaren (eds.). 1994. *Between borders: Pedagogy and the politics of cultural studies.* New York: Routledge.
Goldberger, Nancy Rule. 1996. Cultural imperatives and diversity in ways of knowing. In *Knowledge, difference, and power: Essays inspired by women's ways of knowing,* ed. Nancy Goldberger, Jill Tarule, Blythe Clinchy, and Mary Belenky. New York: Basic Books.
Goldberger, Nancy, Jill Tarule, Blythe Clinchy, and Mary Belenky (eds.). 1996. *Knowledge, difference, and power: Essays inspired by women's ways of knowing.* New York: Basic Books.
Goleman, Daniel. 1997. *Emotional intelligence.* New York: Bantam Books.
Goleman, Daniel. 2006. *Social intelligence: The new science of human relationships.* New York: Bantam Books.
Goto, Courtney T. 2016. *The grace of playing: Pedagogies for leaning into God's new creation.* Eugene: Pickwick Publications.
Goulding, Regina A., and Richard C. Schwartz. 2002. *The mosaic mind: Empowering the tormented selves of child abuse survivors.* Oak Park: Trailheads Publications.
Graham, Larry Kent. 1992. *Care of persons, care of worlds: A psychosystems approach to pastoral care and counseling.* Nashville: Abingdon Press.
Greider, Kathleen J. 2014. Religious pluralism and Christian-centrism. In *The Wiley-Blackwell companion to practical theology,* ed. Bonnie Miller-McLemore, 452–461. Malden: Wiley-Blackwell.
Grey, Mary C. 2004. *Sacred longings: The ecological spirit and global culture.* Minneapolis: Fortress Press.
Griffith, James L., and Melissa Elliott Griffith. 1994. *The body speaks: Therapeutic dialogues for mind-body problems.* New York: BasicBooks.

Griffith, James L., and Melissa Elliott Griffith. 2002/2003. *Encountering the sacred in psychotherapy: How to talk with people about their spiritual lives*. New York: The Guilford Press.

Grodzins, Dean (ed.). 2004. *A language of reverence*. Chicago: Meadville Lombard Press.

Haire-Joshu, Debra, and Timothy D. McBride (eds.). 2013. *Transdiciplinary public health: Research, education, and practice*. San Francisco: Jossey-Bass.

Hall, David D. (ed.). 1997. *Lived religion in America: Toward a history of practice*. Princeton: Princeton University Press.

Hamman, Jaco. 2014. Playing. In *The Wiley-Blackwell companion to practical theology*, ed. Bonnie Miller-McLemore, 42–50. Malden: Wiley-Blackwell.

Harding, Sandra (ed.). 1984. *The science question in feminism*. Ithaca: Cornell University Press.

Harding, Sandra (ed.). 2004. *The feminist standpoint theory reader: Intellectual and political controversies*. New York: Routledge.

Harris, Mark W. 2004. *Historical dictionary of Unitarian Universalism*. Lanham: Scarecrow Press.

Harvey, Jennifer, Karin A. Case, and Robin Hawley Gorsline (eds.). 2004. *Disrupting white supremacy from within: White people on what we need to do*. Cleveland: Pilgrim Press.

Heimbrock, Hans-Günter. 2007. Reconstructing lived religion. In *Religion: Immediate experience and the mediacy of research – Interdisciplinary studies, concepts and methodology of empirical research in religion*, ed. Hans-Günter Heimbrock and Christopher P. Scholtz, 133–157. Göttingen: Vandenhoeck & Ruprecht.

Heimbrock, Hans-Günter. 2011. Practical theology as empirical theology. *International Journal of Practical Theology* 14: 153–170.

Heimbrock, Hans-Günter, and Christopher P. Scholtz (eds.). 2007. *Religion: Immediate experience and the mediacy of research – Interdisciplinary studies, concepts and methodology of empirical research in religion*. Göttingen: Vandenhoeck & Ruprecht.

Herman, Judith L. 1992. *Trauma and recovery*. New York: BasicBooks.

Hertz, Marci Feldman, Deborah Prothrow-Stith, and Clementina Chery. 2005. Homicide survivors: Research and practice implications. *American Journal of Preventive Medicine* 29(5S2): 288–295.

Hodgson, Peter C. 1994. *Winds of the spirit: A constructive Christian theology*. Louisville: Westminster John Knox Press.

Hodgson, Peter C. 2005. The spirit and religious pluralism. In *The myth of religious superiority: A multifaith exploration*, ed. Paul F. Knitter, 135–150. Maryknoll: Orbis Books.
Holloway, Margaret, and Bernard Moss. 2010. *Spirituality and social work*. New York: Palgrave Macmillan.
Hooks, Bell. 1994. Theory as liberatory practice. In *Teaching to transgress: Education as the practice of freedom*, 59–75. New York: Routledge.
Hopkins, Dwight N. 2005. *Being human: Race, culture, and religion*. Minneapolis: Fortress Press.
Howe, Charles A. 1993. *The larger faith: A short history of American Universalism*. Boston: Skinner House Books.
Howe, Charles A. 2007. *For faith and freedom: A short history of Unitarianism in Europe*. Boston: Skinner House Books.
Hudson, Jill M. 1998. *Congregational trauma: Caring, coping & learning*. Bethesda: The Alban Institute.
Idler, Ellen L. (ed.). 2014. *Religion as a social determinant of public health*. New York: Oxford University Press.
Isaacs, Harold R. 1980. *Scratches on our minds: American images of China and India*. New York: Routledge.
Jakobsen, Janet R. 1997. The body politic vs. lesbian bodies: Publics, counterpublics, and the use of norms. In *Horizons in feminist theology: Identity, tradition and norms*, ed. Rebecca S. Chopp and S.G. Davaney, 116–136. Minneapolis: Fortress Press.
James, Jacqui (ed.). 1995/1998. *Between the lines: Source for singing the living tradition*, 2nd ed. Boston: Skinner House Books.
Janoff-Bulman, Ronnie. 1992. *Shattered assumptions: Towards a new psychology of trauma*. New York: The Free Press.
Johnson, Mark. 1987. *The body in the mind: The bodily basis of meaning, imagination, and reason*. Chicago: The University of Chicago Press.
Johnson, Mark. 1993. *Moral imagination: Implications of cognitive science for ethics*. Chicago: University of Chicago Press.
Jones, Kirk Byron. 2001. *Rest in the storm: Self-care strategies for clergy and other caregivers*. Valley Forge: Judson Press.
Jones, Serene. 2009. *Trauma and grace: Theology in a ruptured world*. Louisville: Westminister John Knox Press.
Jones, Ted. 2010. *Straightening up: The recovery of the Tennessee Valley Unitarian Universalist Church From an Attack*. Unpublished Manuscript.

Jordan, Judith V. 1991. The meaning of mutuality. In *Women's growth in connection: Writings from the stone center*, ed. Judith V. Jordan, Alexandra G. Kaplan, Jean Baker Miller, Irene P. Stiver, and Janet L. Surrey, 81–96. New York: The Guilford Press.
Jordan, Judith V. (ed.). 1997. *Women's growth in diversity: More writings from the stone center*. New York: The Guilford Press.
Jordan, Judith V. 2010. *Relational-cultural therapy*. Washington, DC: American Psychological Association.
Jordan, Judith V., and Jon Carlson (eds.). 2013. *Creating connection: A relational-cultural approach with couples*. New York: Routledge.
Jordan, Judith V., Alexandra G. Kaplan, Jean Baker Miller, Irene P. Stiver, and Janet L. Surrey (eds.). 1991. *Women's growth in connection: Writings from the stone center*. New York: The Guilford Press.
Jordan, Judith V., Maureen Walker, and Linda M. Hartling (eds.). 2004. *The complexity of connection: Writings from the stone center's Jean Baker Miller Training Institute*. New York: The Guilford Press.
Kearney, Richard. 1998. *Poetics of imagining: Modern to post-modern*. New York: Fordham University.
Keefe-Perry, L. Callid. 2014. *Way to water: A theopoetics primer*. Eugene: Cascade Books.
Keller, Catherine. 1997. Seeking and sucking: On relation and essence in feminist theology. In *Horizons in feminist theology: Identity, tradition and norms*, ed. Rebecca S. Chopp and S.G. Davaney, 54–78. Minneapolis: Fortress Press.
Keller, Catherine. 2003. *Face of the deep: A theology of becoming*. New York: Routledge.
Keller, Catherine. 2006. The flesh of God: A metaphor in the wild. In *Theology that matters: Ecology, economy, and God*, ed. D.K. Ray. Minneapolis: Fortress Press.
Keller, Catherine. 2008. *On the mystery: Discerning divinity in process*. Minneapolis: Fortress Press.
Kendrick, Kevin David, and Simon Robinson. 2000. Spirituality: Its relevance and purpose for clinical nursing in a new millennium. *Journal of Clinical Nursing* 9: 701–705.
Keshgegian, Flora A. 2000. *Redeeming memories: A theology of healing and transformation*. Nashville: Abingdon Press.
Keshgegian, Flora A. 2008. *God reflected: Metaphors for life, time for hope*. Minneapolis: Fortress Press.

King, E. Frances. 2010. *Material religion and popular culture*. New York: Routledge.
Klass, Dennis, Phyllis R. Silverman, and Steven L. Nickman (eds.). 1996. *Continuing bonds: New understandings of grief*. New York: Routledge.
Knitter, Paul F. 1991. Beyond a mono-religious theological education. In *Shifting boundaries: Contextual approaches to the structure of theological education*, ed. Barbara G. Wheeler and Edward Farley, 151–180. Louisville: Westminster/John Knox Press.
Knitter, Paul F. 2002. *Introducing theologies of religions*. Maryknoll: Orbis Books.
Knitter, Paul F. (ed.). 2005. *The myth of religious superiority: A multifaith exploration*. Maryknoll: Orbis Books.
Koepping, Elizabeth. 2008. *Food, friends and funerals: On lived religion*. Berlin: LIT VERLAG.
Kolmar, Wendy K., and Frances Bartkowski (eds.). 2013. *Feminist theory: A reader*, 4th ed. Boston: McGraw-Hill.
Kuhn, Thomas S. 1962/1970. *The structure of scientific revolutions*, 2nd ed, enlarged. Chicago: The University of Chicago Press.
Kujawa-Holbrook, Sheryl A., and Karen B. Montagno (eds.). 2009. *Injustice and the care of souls: Taking oppression seriously in pastoral care*. Minneapolis: Fortress Press.
Lakoff, George, and Mark Johnson. 1980/2003. *Metaphors we live by*. Chicago: The University of Chicago Press.
Lakoff, George, and Mark Johnson. 1999. *Philosophy in the flesh: The embodied mind and its challenge to Western thought*. New York: Basic Books.
Lamothe, Ryan. 2005. *Becoming alive: Psychoanalysis and vitality*. New York: Routledge.
Land, Helen. 2015. *Spirituality, religion, and faith in psychotherapy: Evidence-based expressive methods for mind, brain, and body*. Chicago: Lyceum Books.
Leavy, Patricia. 2011. *Essentials of transdisciplinary research: Using problem-centered methodologies*. Walnut Creek: Left Coast Press, Inc.
Levine, Peter A., and Ann Frederick. 1997. *Waking the tiger: Healing trauma*. Berkeley: North Atlantic Books.
Lewis, Jacqueline J. 2008. *The power of stories: A guide for leading multi-racial and multi- cultural congregations*. Nashville: Abingdon Press.
Lewis, Thomas, Fari Amini, and Richard Lannon. 2000/2001. *A general theory of love*. New York: Vintage Books.
Lightsey, Pamela. 2015. *Our lives matter: A womanist queer theology*. Eugene: Pickwick Publications.

Lipsky, Laura van Dernoot, and Connie Burk. 2009. *Trauma Stewardship: An everyday guide to caring for self while caring for others*. San Francisco: Berrett-Koehler Publishers, Inc.

Lofton, Kathryn. 2015. *Queer Christianities: Lived religion in transgressive forms*. New York: New York University Press.

Macnaughton, Ian. 2004. *Body, breath, and consciousness: A somatic anthology*. Berkely: North Atlantic Books.

Madigan, Stephen. 2011. *Narrative therapy*. Washington, DC: American Psychological Association.

Madison, D. Soyini. 2012. *Critical ethnography: Method, ethics, and performance*, 2nd ed. New York: Sage.

Marcus, George E., and Michael M.J. Fischer. 1999. *Anthropology as cultural critique: An experimental movement in the human sciences*, 2nd ed. Chicago: The University of Chicago Press.

Martinez, Dawn Belkin, and Ann Fleck-Henderson (eds.). 2014. *Social justice in clinical practice: A liberation health framework for social work*. New York: Routledge.

McClure, John S. 1995. *The roundtable pulpit: Where leadership and preaching meet*. Nashville: Abingdon Press.

McClure, Barbara J. 2010. *Moving beyond individualism in pastoral care and counseling: Reflections on theory, theology, and practice*. Eugene: Cascade Books.

McColgan, Daniel T. 1940. *Joseph Tuckerman: Pioneer in American social work*. PhD dissertation, The Catholic University of America.

McDannell, Colleen. 1995. *Material Christianity: Religion and popular culture in America*. New Haven: Yale University Press.

McFague, Sallie. 1982. *Metaphorical theology: Models of God in religious language*. Philadelphia: Fortress Press.

McGuire, Meredith B. 2002. New-old directions in the social scientific study of religion: Ethnography, phenomenology, and the human body. In *Personal knowledge and beyond: Reshaping the ethnography of religion*, ed. James V. Spickard, J. Shawn Landres, and Meredith B. McGuire, 195–211. New York: New York University Press.

McGuire, Meredith B. 2007. Embodied practices: Negotiation and resistance. In *Everyday religion: Observing modern religious lives*, ed. Nancy T. Ammerman, 187–200. New York: Oxford University Press.

McGuire, Meredith B. 2008. *Lived religion: Faith and practice in everyday life*. New York: Oxford University Press.

Metz, Johann Baptist. 1977/2007. *Faith in history and society: Toward a practical fundamental theology*. Trans. J. Matthew Ashley. New York: The Crossroad Publishing Company.
Meyer, Birgit (ed.). 2009. *Aesthetic formations: Media, religion, and the senses*. New York: Palgrave Macmillan.
Meyer, Birgit (ed.). 2012. Mediation and the genesis of presence: Toward a material approach to religion. Inaugural Lecture, Universiteit Utrecht, October 19, 2012.
Miller, Jean Baker. 1976. *Toward a new psychology of women*. Boston: Beacon Press.
Miller, Daniel. 2008. *The comfort of things*. Cambridge: Polity Press.
Miller, Patricia Cox. 2009. *The corporeal imagination: Signifying the holy in late ancient Christianity*. Philadelphia: University of Pennsylvania Press.
Miller, Jean Baker, and Irene Pierce Stiver. 1997. *The healing connection: How women form relationships in therapy and in life*. Boston: Beacon Press.
Miller-McLemore, Bonnie J. 1990/2005. Pastoral theology as public theology: Revolutions in the 'Fourth Area'. In *Dictionary of pastoral care and counseling*, ed. Rodney J. Hunter, 1370–1380. Nashville: Abingdon Press.
Miller-McLemore, Bonnie (ed.). 2014. *The Wiley-Blackwell companion to practical theology*. Malden: Wiley-Blackwell.
Mills, C. Wright. 1959. *The sociological imagination*. New York: Oxford University Press.
Mitchell, W.J.T. 2005. *What do pictures want?: The lives and loves of images*. Chicago: The University of Chicago Press.
Mohanty, Chandra Talpade. 2004. *Feminism without borders: Decolonizing theory, practicing solidarity*, 3rd ed. Durham: Duke University Press.
Moraga, Cherrie, and Gloria Analdúa (eds.). 1981/2015. *This bridge called my back: Writings by radical women of color*, 4th ed. New York: Suny Press.
Morgan, Edmund S. 1975. *American slavery American freedom: The ordeal of Colonial Virginia*. New York: W.W. Norton & Company.
Morgan, David. 2012. *The embodied eye: Religious visual culture and the social life of feeling*. Berkeley: University of California Press.
Morgan, David. 2013. Religion and media: A critical review of recent developments. *Critical Research on Religion* 1(3): 347–356, Sage.
Morley, Jefferson. 2013. *Snow-storm in August: The struggle for American freedom and Washington's Race Riot of 1835*. New York: First Anchor Books.

Morris, Leslie Takahashi, Chip Roush, and Leon Spencer. 2009. *The arc of the universe is long: Unitarian Universalists, anti-racism and the journey from Calgary*. Boston: Skinner House Books.

Moschella, Mary Clark. 2008. *Ethnography as a pastoral practice: An introduction*. Cleveland: Pilgrim Press.

Moschella, Mary Clark. 2014. Ethnography. In *The Wiley-Blackwell companion to practical theology*, ed. Bonnie J. Miller-McLemore, 224–233. Malden: Blackwell Publishing Limited.

Muir, Fredric John. 2001. *Heretics' faith: Vocabulary for religious liberals*. Annapolis: Unitarian Universalist Church of Annapolis.

Neiman, Susan. 2002. *Evil in modern thought: An alternative history of philosophy*. Princeton: Princeton University Press.

Neimeyer, Robert A. (ed.). 2005. *Meaning reconstruction and the experience of loss*, 4th ed. Washington, DC: American Psychological Association.

Newberg, Andrew, Eugene D'Aquili, and Vincent Rause. 2001/2002. *Why God won't go away: Brain science and the biology of belief*. New York: Ballantine Books.

Newcomb, Steven T. 2008. *Pagans in the promised land: Decoding the doctrine of Christian discovery*. Golden: Fulcrum.

Nhat Hanh, Thich. 1995. *Living Buddha, living Christ*. New York: Riverhead Books.

Ogden, Pat, Kekuni Minton, and Clare Pain. 2006. *Trauma and the body: A sensorimotor approach to psychotherapy*. New York: W.W. Norton and Company.

Omi, Michael, and Howard Winant. 2014. *Racial formation in the United States: From the 1960's to the 1990's*, 3rd ed. New York: Routledge.

Orsi, Robert A. 2005. *Between heaven and earth: The religious worlds people make and the scholars who study them*. Princeton: Princeton University Press.

Ortner, Sherry B. 1974. Is female to male as nature is to culture? In *Woman, culture & society*, ed. Michelle Zimbalist Rosaldo and Louise Lamphere, 67–87. Stanford: Stanford University Press.

Owen-Towle, Tom. 1998. *Freethinking mystics with hands: Exploring the heart of Unitarian Universalism*. Boston: Skinner House Books.

Panksepp, Jaak. 1998. *Affective neuroscience: The foundations of human and animal emotions*. New York: Oxford University Press.

Park, Andrew Sung. 2004. *From hurt to healing: A theology of the wounded*. Nashville: Abingdon Press.

Pattison, Stephen. 2007. *Seeing things: Deepening relations with visual artefacts.* London: SCM Press.
Patton, Michael Quinn. 2002. *Qualitative research and evaluation methods*, 3rd ed. Thousand Oaks: Sage.
Perkinson, James W. 2004. *White theology: Outing supremacy in modernity.* New York: Palgrave Macmillan.
Pharr, Suzanne. 1988. The common elements of oppression. In *Homophobia: A weapon of sexism*, 52–64. Inverness: Chardon Press.
Pineda-Madrid, Nancy. 2011. *Suffering and salvation in Ciudad Juarez.* Minneapolis: Fortress Press.
Pink, Sarah. 2015. *Doing sensory ethnography*, 2nd ed. Thousand Oaks: Sage.
Poling, James N. 1991. *The abuse of power: A theological problem.* Nashville: Abingdon Press.
Poling, James N. 1996. *Deliver us from evil: Resisting racial and gender oppression.* Minneapolis: Fortress Press.
Poling, James N. 2002. *Render unto God: Economic vulnerability, family violence, and pastoral theology.* St. Louis: Chalice Press.
Poling, James N. 2011. *Rethinking faith: A constructive practical theology.* Minneapolis: Fortress Press.
Poling, James N., and Donald E. Miller. 1985. *Foundations for a practical theology of ministry.* Nashville: Abingdon Press.
Prothrow-Stith, Deborah, and Howard R. Spivak. 2004. *Murder is no accident: Understanding and preventing youth violence in America.* San Francisco: Jossey-Bass.
Prothrow-Stith, Deborah, and Michaele Weissman. 1991. *Deadly consequences: How violence is destroying our teenage population and a plan to begin solving the problem.* New York: HarperCollins Publishers.
Prothrow-Stith, Deborah, Joseph M. Chery, Jon Oliver, Clementina Chery, Marci Feldman, and Fern Shamis. 2005. *Peacezone: A program for teaching social literacy, Grades 4–5, Teacher's guide.* Champaign: Research Press.
Prud'homme, Sheri M. 2015. *Gleam of the infinite majesty: The interplay of manifest destiny and ecotheology in Thomas Starr King's Construction of Yosemite as sacred text.* PhD dissertation, Graduate Theological Union.
Pui-lan, Kwok. 2005. *Postcolonial imagination & feminist theology.* Louisville: Westminster John Knox Press.
Pyles, Loretta, and Gwendolyn J. Adam (eds.). 2016. *Holistic engagement: Transforming social work education in the 21st century.* New York: Oxford University Press.

Rambo, Shelly. 2010. *Spirit and trauma: A theology of remaining*. Louisville: Westminster John Knox Press.

Rambo, Shelly. 2015. Refiguring wounds in the afterlife (of Trauma). In *Carnal hermeneutics*, ed. Richard Kearney and Brian Treanor, 263–278. New York: Fordham University Press.

Ramsey, Nancy J. 1990/2005. A time of ferment and redefinition. In *Dictionary of pastoral care and counseling*, ed. Rodney J. Hunter, 1349–1369. Nashville: Abingdon Press.

Rando, Therese A. 1993. *Treatment of complicated mourning*. Champaign: Research Press.

Reisch, Michael, and Janice Andrews. 2002. *The road not taken: A history of radical social work in the United States*. New York: Routledge.

Report of the Committee on Women & Healthy Communities to Members of the Boston City Council: Family Voices: Strengthening Homicide Response and Family Support in the City of Boston. By Ayanna Pressley, Chair. Boston, December 15, 2010.

Reynolds, Thomas E. 2008. *Vulnerable communion: A theology of disability and hospitality*. Grand Rapids: Brazos Press.

Rich, John A. 2009. *Wrong place, wrong time: Trauma and violence in the lives of young black men*. Baltimore: The Johns Hopkins University Press.

Ricouer, Paul. 1980. The hermeneutics of testimony. In *Essays on biblical interpretation*, ed. Lewis S. Mudge, 119–154. Philadelphia: Fortress Press.

Rivera, Mayra. 2015. *Poetics of the flesh*. Durham: Duke University.

Robb, Christina. 2006/2007. *This changes everything: The relational revolution in psychology*. New York: Picador.

Rogers, Annie G. 2006. *The unsayable: The hidden language of trauma*. New York: Random House.

Ross, Warren R. 2001. *The premise and the promise: The story of the Unitarian Universalist Association*. Boston: Skinner House Books.

Ross, Warren R. 2002. Confronting evil: Has terrorism shaken our religious principles? *UU World*, XVI 1 (January/February 2002): 18–25.

Rothschild, Babette. 2000. *The body remembers: The psychophysiology of trauma and trauma treatment*. New York: W.W. Norton and Company.

Rynearson, Edward K., and Alison Salloum. 2011. Restorative retelling: Revising the narrative of violent death. In *Grief and bereavement in contemporary society: Bridging research and practice*, ed. Robert A. Neimeyer, Darcy L. Harris, Howard R. Winokuer, and Gordon F. Thornton, 177–188. New York: Routledge Taylor & Francis Group.

Saleeby, Dennis. 2000. Power in the people: Strengths and hope. *Advances in Social Work* 1(2 Fall): 127–136.
Sandoval, Chela. 2000. *Methodology of the oppressed*. Minneapolis: University of Minnesota Press.
Santino, Jack. 2001. *Signs of war and peace: Social conflict and the uses of symbols in public in Northern Ireland*. New York: Palgrave MacMillan.
Santino, Jack (ed.). 2006. *Spontaneous shrines and the public memorialization of death*. New York: Palgrave MacMillan.
Scaer, Robert C. 2005. *The trauma spectrum: Hidden wounds and human resiliency*. New York: W.W. Norton and Company.
Scaer, Robert C. 2007. *The body bears the burden: Trauma, dissociation, and disease*, 2nd ed. New York: Routledge.
Scanlon, Michael J., O.S.A. 1999. The postmodern debate. In *The twentieth century: A theological overview*, ed. Gregory Baum. Maryknoll: Orbis Books.
Scarry, Elaine. 1985. *The body in pain: The making and unmaking of the world*. New York: Oxford University Press.
Schneiders, Sandra. 1999. *The revelatory text: Interpreting the New Testament as sacred scripture*. Collegeville: The Liturgical Press.
Schulz, William F. 1993/1997/2004. Our faith. In *The Unitarian Universalist pocket guide*, ed. William G. Sinkford, 4th ed, 1–6. Boston: Skinner House Books.
Schwartz, Richard C. 1995. *Internal family systems therapy*. New York: The Guilford Press.
Schwartz, Richard C. 2001. *Introduction to the internal family systems model*. Oak Park: Trailheads Publications.
Sharp, Melinda McGarrah. 2014. Globalization, colonialism, and postcolonialism. In *The Wiley- Blackwell companion to practical theology*, ed. Bonnie Miller-McLemore, 422–431. Malden: Wiley-Blackwell.
Shaw, Daniel. 2014. Immanence and intersubjectivity. In *The skillful soul of the psychotherapist: The link between spirituality and clinical excellence*, ed. George S. Stavros and Steven J. Sandage. New York: Rowman & Littlefield.
Sheppard, Phillis I. 2011. *Self, culture, and others in womanist practical theology*. New York: Palgrave Macmillan.
Siegel, Daniel J. 1999. *The developing mind: Toward a neurobiology of interpersonal experience*. New York: The Guilford Press.
Siegel, Daniel J. 2012. *Pocket guide to interpersonal neurobiology: An integrative handbook*. New York: W.W. Norton & Company.

Silverman, Phyllis Rolfe. 2000. *Never too young to know: Death in children's lives.* New York: Oxford University Press.
Skerrett, Karen. 2004. Moving toward 'We': Promise and peril. In *How connections heal: Stories from relational-cultural therapy*, ed. Maureen Walker and Wendy B. Rosen, 128–150. New York: The Guilford Press.
Smith Jr., Archie. 1982. *The relational self: Ethics & therapy from a black church perspective.* Nashville: Abingdon.
Smith, Andrea. 2006. Heteropatriarchy and the three pillars of white supremacy: Rethinking women of color organizing. In *Color of violence: The Incite! Anthology*, ed. Incite! Women of Color Against Violence. Cambridge: South End Press.
Smith, Linda Tuhiwai. 2012. *Decolonizing methodologies: Research and indigenous peoples*, 2nd ed. New York: Zed Books.
Smith Jr., Archie. 2014. You cannot teach what you do not know: You cannot lead where you have not been. In *Teaching for a culturally diverse and racially just world*, ed. Eleazar S. Fernandez, 88–108. Eugene: Cascade Books.
Sotero, Michelle M. 2006. A conceptual model of historical trauma: Implications for public health practice and research. *Journal of Health Disparities Research and Practice*, 1(1, Fall): 93–108.
Spencer, Renee. 2002. A comparison of relational psychologies. *Project Report 5* (2002) Wellesley Centers for Women, Wellesley College, Wellesley, MA.
Spradley, James P. 1979. *The ethnographic interview.* Belmont: Wadsworth Group.
Sremac, Srdjan. 2016. Conversion and the real: The (im)possibility of testimonial representation. *Pastoral Psychology*, Springer, published online April 28, 2016.
St. Clair, Michael. 1994. *Human relationships and the experience of God: Object relations and religion.* Eugene: Wipf & Stock Publishers.
St. Clair, Michael. 2004. *Object relations and self psychology: An introduction.* Belmont: Thomson-Brooks/Cole.
Stampp, Kenneth M. 1956/1989. *The Peculiar Institution: Slavery in the Ante-Bellum South.* New York: Vintage Books.
Stavros, George S., and Steven J. Sandage (eds.). 2014. *The skillful soul of the psychotherapist: The link between spirituality and clinical excellence.* New York: Rowman & Littlefield.
Streib, Heinz, Astrid Dinter, and Kerstin Söderblom (eds.). 2008. *Lived religion: Conceptual, empirical and practical-theological approaches, essays in honor of Hans-Günter Heimbrock.* Boston: Brill.

Sue, Derald Wing. 2010. *Microaggressions in everyday life: Race, gender, and sexual orientation.* New York: Wiley.
Sue, Derald, and David Sue. 2003. *Counseling the culturally diverse: Theory and practice*, 4th ed. New York: Wiley.
Surrey, Janet L. 1991. Relationship and empowerment. In *Women's growth in connection: Writings from the stone center*, ed. Judith V. Jordan, Alexandra G. Kaplan, Jean Baker Miller, Irene P. Stiver, and Janet L. Surrey, 162–180. New York: The Guilford Press.
Taylor, Mark K. 1991. Celebrating difference, resisting domination: The need for synchronic strategies in theological education. In *Chifting boundaries: Contextual approaches to the structure of theological education*, ed. Barbara G. Wheeler and Edward Farley, 259–293. Louisville: Westminster/John Knox Press.
Tervalon, Melanie, and Jann Murray-Garcia. 1998. Cultural humility versus cultural competence: A critical distinction in defining physician training outcomes in multicultural education. *Journal of Health Care for the Poor and Underserved* 9(2): 117–125.
Thandeka. 1995. *The embodied self: Friedrich Schleiermacher's solution to Kant's problem of the empirical self.* New York: State University of New York Press.
Thandeka. 1997. The self between feminist theory and theology. In *Horizons in feminist theology: Identity, tradition, and norms*, ed. Rebecca S. Chopp, and Sheila Greeve Davaney, 79–98. Minneapolis: Fortress Press.
Thandeka. 2000. *Learning to be white: Money, race, and God in America.* New York: The Continuum Publishing Company.
Tiffany, Daniel. 2000. *Toy medium: Materialism and modern lyric.* Berkeley: University of California Press.
Tinker, George E. 1993. *Missionary conquest: The Gospel and Native American cultural genocide.* Minneapolis: Fortress Press.
Townes, Emilie M. (ed.). 1993. *A troubling in my soul: Womanist perspectives on evil and suffering.* Maryknoll: Orbis Books.
Tracy, David. 1981. *The analogical imagination: Christian theology and the culture of pluralism.* New York: The Crossroad Publishing Company.
Tracy, David. 2011. A correlational model of practical theology—Revisited. In *Religion, diversity and conflict*, ed. Edward Foley, 49–61. New Brunswick: Transaction Publishers.
Tracy, David. 2014. A correlational model of practical theology revisited. In *Invitation to practical theology: Catholic voices and visions*, ed. Claire E. Wolfteich, 70–86. New York: Paulist Press.

Tripp, Andrew Stephen, 2015. *Poverty and Urban Ecclesial Discipleship: A Practical Theological Investigation of Congregations Caring for the Poor*. PhD Dissertation, Boston University.
Turner, Victor. 1969/1995. *The ritual process: Structure and anti-structure*. New York: Aldine de Gruyter.
Twine, France Winddance, and Bradley Gardener (eds.). 2013. *Geographies of privilege*. New York: Routledge.
Unitarian Universalist Association. 1993/2000. *Singing the living tradition*. Boston: Unitarian Universalist Association.
van der Kolk, Bessel. 2014. *The body keeps the score: Brain, mind, and body in the healing of trauma*. New York: Penguin Books.
van der Kolk, Bessel A., Alexander C. McFarlane, and Lars Weisaeth (eds.). 1996. *Traumatic stress: The effects of overwhelming experience on mind, body, and society*. New York: The Guilford Press.
Van der Port, Mattijs. 2011. *Ecstatic encounters: Bahian Candomblé and the quest for the really real*. Amsterdam: Amsterdam University Press.
Velez Caro, Olga Consuelo. 2007. Toward a feminist intercultural theology. In *Feminist intercultural theology: Latino explorations for a just world*, ed. Maria Pilar Aquino and Maria Jose Rosado-Nunes, 248–264. Maryknoll: Orbis Books.
Vlassidis Burgoa, Maria Cristina. 2016. *Sobre la Marcha: The Fiesta of Santiago Apóstol in Loíza, Puerto Rico*. PhD dissertation, Harvard University.
Walker, Maureen. 2004. How relationships help. In *How connections heal: Stories from relational-cultural therapy*, ed. Maureen Walker and Wendy B. Rosen, 3–21. New York: The Guilford Press.
Walker, Nathan C. 2016. *Cultivating empathy: The worth and dignity of every person—Without exception*. Boston: Skinner House.
Walker, Maureen, and Wendy B. Rosen (eds.). 2004. *How connections heal: Stores from relational- cultural therapy*. New York: The Guilford Press.
Walsh, Michelle A. 2004. Theological analysis project: The welcoming congregation program as a successful model for engaging Unitarian Universalists on behalf of social justice. Unpublished manuscript.
Walsh, Michelle A. 2014. *Prophetic pastoral care in the aftermath of trauma: Forging a constructive practical theology of organized trauma response ministries*. PhD dissertation, Boston University. ProQuest (AAT 3610856).
Walsh, Michelle A. 2016. *Examining whiteness: Recovering the intersectional 'I' and experiences of 'Peoplehood' in writing and research*. Paper presented at the

Association for Practical Theology 2016 Biennial Conference. New York: Fordham University, April 9, 2016.

Walsh, Michelle A. 2016. Taking matter *seriously*: Material theopoetics in the aftermath of communal violence. In *Post-traumatic public theology*, ed. Shelly Rambo, and Stephanie N. Arel. New York: Palgrave Macmillan.

Walton, Heather. 2014. Poetics. In *The Wiley-Blackwell companion to practical theology*, ed. Bonnie Miller-McLemore, 173–182. Malden: Wiley-Blackwell.

Watkins Ali, Carroll A. 1999. *Survival and liberation: Pastoral theology in African American context*. St. Louis: Chalice Press.

Watts, Judy H. 2009. Building a new paradigm: Transdisciplinary research comes to the forefront. *Social Impact*, (Fall): 13–17. Brown School of Social Work, Washington University, St. Louis, MO.

Welch, Sharon D. 2000. *A feminist ethic of risk*, 2nd ed. Minneapolis: Fortress Press.

Wheeler, Barbara G., and Edward Farley (eds.). 1991. *Shifting boundaries: Contextual approaches to the structure of theological education*. Louisville: Westminster/John Knox Press.

Wilder, Amos Niven. 1976/2001. *Theopoetic: Theology and the religious imagination*. Lima: Academic Renewal Press.

Wolfteich, Claire E. (ed.). 2014. *Invitation to practical theology: Catholic voices and visions*. New York: Paulist Press.

Worden, J. William. 2009. *Grief counseling and grief therapy: A handbook for mental health practitioners*, 4th ed. New York: Springer.

Wright, Conrad. 1975/1989. *A stream of light: A short history of American Unitarianism*. Boston: Skinner House Books.

Wright, Conrad. 1989. *Walking together: Polity and participation in Unitarian Universalist Churches*. Boston: Skinner House Books.

Wyatt-Brown, Bertram. 1986. *Honor and violence in the old south*. New York: Oxford University Press.

Yoder, Carolyn. 2005. *The little book of trauma healing: When violence strikes and community security is threatened*. Intercourse: The Good Books.

# Index

A
Adams, James Luther, xvin9, 154, 186n24, 241n29, 243n37, 244n41, 284n16. *See also* covenantal theology; prophetic
Ammerman, Nancy, 33, 89, 120n8, 121n8, 137n91, 184n10, 198, 238n8, 243n37. *See also* lived religion; spiritual tribe
anthropology, xi, xv, 5, 25, 40, 43n9, 47n46, 93, 95, 110, 116–18, 123n22, 125, 143, 222, 275, 287n31
anti-oppression
  anti-oppression analysis, 57, 114
  anti-racism, 287n30
autoethnographic, xii. *See also* ethnography

B
Beste, Jennifer, 272, 273, 285n21, 285n22
  mediated grace, 273
bible
  Bible study, 199
  Ecclesiastes, 211, 217
  Ezekiel, 25, 26, 34
  Good Samaritan, 231, 251, 252
  historical approach, 24
  seven Principles of Peace, 57, 58, 184n6, 231

Note: Page number followed by 'n' refers to notes

Black Lives Matter (BLM), 2, 6, 85n27, 258
police violence, 2
body. *See also* feminism; Fulkerson, Mary McClintock; immanence; neuroaffective studies; queer; visceral
  embodied, 5, 11, 13–16, 21n29, 25–30, 32–4, 36, 37, 39–41, 43n8, 43n9, 56, 92–100, 103–5, 108, 109, 113, 116, 117, 119, 122n18, 127n43, 138n99, 144, 146–8, 150, 151, 160–2, 164, 165, 168, 170, 171, 182, 183, 188n34, 188n37, 189n39, 196–200, 202, 203, 206–8, 212–15, 218, 220, 221, 230, 233, 238n10, 239n14, 253, 258–61, 263, 269, 271–4, 276, 277, 279, 282n9, 290, 291
  enfleshed, 30, 91, 259, 272, 274
  enhormoned, 30, 91, 259, 272, 274
  en-neuroned, 30, 91, 213, 259, 272, 274
  limbic resonance, 95, 96, 223
  neuroaffective, 91, 93, 95, 117, 119, 213, 223, 259, 273
  neuroscience of corporeality, 116
  physiological, 93
  physiology, 95, 96
Scanlon, Michael J., 29, 43n9
border crossing. *See also* intersectionality; oppression; power analysis; queer
  borderlands, 52, 88, 194, 248–52, 290, 291
  borders, 12, 37, 167, 248, 290, 291
Brock, Rita Nakashima, 272, 284n19
  moral injury, 284n18

C
Centers for Disease Control and Prevention (CDC), 1, 16n1. *See also* Prothrow-Stith, Deborah; public health
Chopp, Rebecca S., 104, 105, 125n29, 128n49, 129n55, 130n55, 130n56, 131n58, 171, 189n40. *See also* poetics
climate change, 32, 35, 275, 276, 279, 292
Coates, Ta-Nehisi, 30–2
Collins, Randall, 34, 36, 46n31, 46n33, 46n36. *See also* interdisciplinary; sociology
continuing bonds theory. *See also* body; limbic resonance; neuroaffective studies
  bereavement, 97
  communal bond, 273
  limbic resonance, 95, 96, 223
  moral bond, 109, 143
  moral injury, 272
  phantom limbs, 97
  phantom presence, 97
  survivor's guilt, 272
Copeland, Shawn M., 30
correlation. *See also* interdisciplinary; metaphor
  embodied metaphorical correlational, 41, 91, 273
  interdisciplinary bridge tools, 41, 91, 104

Index 319

mutual critical correlational, 41
Poling, James N. and Donald
  E. Miller, 40, 48n51
covenantal theology, ix. *See also*
  Unitarian Universalist
  Association
congregational polity, 80, 256
critical race theory
  concealed story, 3, 4
  emerging or transformation story, 113
  resistance story, 18n10
  stock story, 18n10
culture. *See also* body; language;
  metaphor; poetics; worldsense;
  worldviews
  cultural, 5, 10, 11, 14, 24, 26, 32,
    56, 60, 79, 80, 82, 98–100,
    110, 111, 113, 117, 118,
    125n29, 131n58, 142, 194,
    195, 202, 221, 232, 235, 261,
    273, 277, 290
  dominant culture, x, 168, 221,
    235
  enculturated or encultured, 90, 91,
    97, 259, 272, 274
  paradigm shifts, 125n29, 258,
    259, 276, 291
  popular culture, 32, 38, 145
  ways of being, 101, 114, 143, 194,
    221, 237n2, 247, 274

D
dangerous memories, xi, 104, 105,
  236. *See also* metaphor; Metz,
  Johann Baptist; Welch, Sharon
disciplines. *See also* interdisciplinary;
  transdisciplinary

academic disciplines, 10, 12, 14,
  23–5, 28, 40, 93, 104, 114,
  213, 278, 287n31, 293n7
cross-disciplinary, 5
disciplinary boundaries, xii
multiple disciplines, 5
paradigm shifts, 114

E
ecological, ix, xiv, 14, 19n17, 93
ecological systems theory, 60
Epston, David, 112. *See also* narrative
  theory; power analysis
Estés, Clarissa Pinkola, 291, 293n7
ethical relations, 228. *See also*
  Unitarian Universalist
  Association
ethics, 110, 248, 276, 278, 292
ethnography, 15, 40. *See also*
  autoethnographic
ethnographic, 6, 8, 9, 12, 15, 16,
  20n21, 26, 45n20, 100, 167,
  184n16, 238n6, 275

F
feminism, 29, 33, 41, 43n11, 111,
  112, 122n19, 135n74, 237n4.
  See also body
patriarchy, 291
Fulkerson, Mary McClintock, 44n13,
  198, 238n6. *See also* place;
  visceral

G
Ganzevoort, R.Ruard, 19n16, 28, 33,
  37, 42n1, 43n7, 43n8, 45n25,

211, 240n20. *See also* lived
religion; narrative theory
Gerkin, Charles V. *See also* prophetic
pastoral care
Christian servanthood, 116
narrative image, 116
Graham, Larry Kent. *See also*
prophetic pastoral care
structural power, 116
systemic analysis, 116

H
healing. *See also* body; place; practices;
trauma
connection, 91, 103, 116, 161,
164, 165, 171, 180, 182, 197,
199, 207, 211, 234, 270
disability, 29, 272
disability theology or theory, 272
functionality and efficacy, 165
God, 56, 119, 161, 211, 212
holistic, 160, 161
integrative, 165
kaleidoscope, 42, 159
leadership role, 164, 228, 234
mediated grace, 273
movement, 157–9, 234, 283n11
normalizing, 160
pieces, 158, 159, 182
regaining control, 160
relational or relationships, 153,
182
relational sustenance, 229
scar, scar clan, scarred healer, 291,
293n7
shattering, 159
sustaining, 187n33

vulnerable communion, 272
wholeness, 156–63
wound, 116, 159
wounded healer, 164, 226, 233,
242n35, 293n7
wounded pieces, 159
Heimbrock, Hans-Günter, 37, 38,
40, 46n37, 47n46, 48n50,
138n99. *See also* lived religion;
metaphor; poetics
Herman, Judith, 78, 86n28, 88,
120n2, 122n15, 135n73. *See
also* trauma
homicide, vii, 7–9, 13, 17n1, 20n21,
53, 54, 62–4, 76, 82n2, 87, 97,
105, 106, 146, 157, 159, 162,
163, 166, 169, 171, 173,
187n33, 197, 201, 211, 215,
216, 234, 239n11, 239n14,
245n46, 260, 268. *See also*
trauma
hooks, bell, 61, 83n11, 114, 184n11
liberatory practice, 61

I
immanence. *See also* body; Johnson,
Mark ; Lakoff, George;
transcendence
energy, 38, 117, 118, 212, 259
God, 117
physicality, 212
intercultural, 16, 110–12, 114,
123n21, 195, 224, 229, 258,
261, 266, 269, 273, 274. *See
also* culture; metaphor;
oppression; power analysis
han, 261

interdisciplinary. *See also*
anthropology; lived religion;
social work; sociology;
transdisciplinary
clinical, 5, 261, 262
educational, 5, 55
health, 5, 55, 260–2
history, 40
human service, 16, 260–2
nursing, 117–18
pastoral, 5, 55, 260–2
philosophy, 30, 32
psychology, 40
religious, 94, 104
science, 41, 94
interdisciplinary bridge tools, 41, 104.
See also interdisciplinary;
metaphor; transdisciplinary
internal family systems theory (IFS).
See also correlation; culture;
interdisciplinary; metaphor;
oppression; power analysis;
spirituality
cultural burden, 99
eight C's of Self-Leadership, 119
legacy burden, 98, 99
multiplicity theory, 98, 134n72,
158, 159, 165, 175, 181
polarization, 221
Schwartz, Richard C., 98, 212,
241n27
Self energy, 119
systems theory, 158, 159, 165,
175, 181
intersectionality, 286n27, 290, 291.
See also border crossing; queer
intersectional, 2–4, 16, 275, 279,
290, 291

J
Janoff-Bulman, Ronnie, 86n30, 89,
120n3, 121n14, 122n15, 159.
See also trauma
Johnson, Mark, 28, 29, 36, 40, 41,
42n4, 42n6, 49n54, 92, 117,
138, 199, 220, 241n26. *See
also* body; Lakoff, George;
metaphor
Jordan, Judith V., 126n35, 126n36,
135n74, 136n80, 138n94, 175,
184n9, 185n17, 187n26,
187n28, 189n43, 238n9,
240n22, 281n4. *See also*
relational-cultural theory

L
Lakoff, George. *See also* Johnson,
Mark; metaphor
imaginative empathic projection,
117, 220
immanent, 117, 199
transcendent, 117
language. *See also* correlation;
metaphor; poetics
enlanguaged, 11, 26, 30, 33, 91,
259, 272, 274
han, 261
linguistic, 40, 273
translation, 12
liberation health theory. *See also*
culture; oppression; power
analysis
client as subject rather than object,
115
dominant ideological messages,
115

liberation health theory (*cont.*)
  dominant worldview discourse, 145, 159
  rescuing the historical memory of change, 115, 208
  triangulating the problem, 115
limbic resonance, 95, 96, 223. *See also* body; continuing bonds; trauma
lived religion, 4–7, 10, 14, 15, 25–8, 31–4, 37–41, 91–5, 97, 99, 100, 102, 104, 105, 111, 116, 117, 143, 145, 171, 183, 197, 211, 230, 270, 277, 282n9. *See also* Ammerman, McGuire, Meredith, Nancy; Ganzevoort, R.Ruard; Heimbrock, Hans-Günter; interdisciplinary; transdisciplinary

M
material religion, 100, 104, 127n42, 127n43, 131n58, 146, 185n19, 277. *See also* poetics; practices
material art, 137n91
McFague, Sallie, 48n50. *See also* metaphor
McGuire, Meredith, 38, 47n44, 102
meaning-making. *See also* healing; Johnson, Mark; poetics; practices; van der Kolk, Bessel
calling, 21n27, 24, 29, 56, 57, 66, 76, 99, 110, 128n49, 130n55, 134n71, 171, 198, 211, 215, 218, 231, 248, 252, 265, 267, 290

evil, 31, 153, 210–28, 232–3, 235, 236, 241n28, 244n44, 254, 257, 271
forgiveness, 55, 149, 201, 225, 227, 231, 252, 269–71
fullness of God's peace, 57, 232, 251
God, 12, 25, 43n9, 56, 57, 72, 73, 93, 117–19, 138n99, 153, 154, 161, 175, 201, 210–32, 240n18, 244n41, 252, 270, xivn6
han, 261
imagination, xii, 15, 25, 27, 28, 36, 41, 92, 100, 105, 130, 146, 277
imaginative, 25, 26, 41, 195, 220
othering, 221
polarization, 46n26, 221
religious liberal, ix, 66, 71–3, 78, 114, 165, 227, 241n28, 253
sacred, 26, 204, 266, 275
something more, 183, 225
theodicy, 88
memorial buttons, 52, 63, 152, 168, 171, 189n39, 215, 230, 236, 238n6. *See also* material religion; poetics; practices
metaphor. *See also* correlation; interdisciplinary; Johnson, Mark; Lakoff, George; meaning-making; Panksepp, Jack; poetics; transdisciplinary
embodied cognitive and affective root, 93
metaphoric, 16, 40, 41, 94, 95, 104, 105, 159, 214, 238n10, 260, 261

multivalent, 12, 41, 93, 104, 148, 214, 238n10
symbolic, 146
Metz, Johann Baptist, xi, 128n52. *See also* dangerous memories
Meyer, Birgit. *See also* new materialists
religious mediation, 277
sensational form, 277
Miller, Jean Baker, 112, 114, 126n35, 130n57, 131n57, 135n73. *See also* feminism; power analysis; relational-cultural theory
dominant and subordinate, 135
ministry
church, 9, 152, 176, 178, 180, 198, 201–4, 210, 214, 217, 218, 234
clergy or clergyperson, ix, 9, 51, 141, 202, 252, 280
community ministry, xiiin3, 23, 121n8, 254
ministry of presence, 153–5
religious institutions, 16, 39, 172, 176, 191n49, 221, 263–9
survivor ministries, 173, 202
trauma response ministry, 7–10, 180
urban ministry, xii, 53

N

narrative theory. *See also* body; meaning-making
alternative story or stories, 113, 114, 145, 153, 156
embodied hermeneutic, 25
hermeneutic, 26, 28, 273
storytelling rights, 112

textual, 25, 26, 32, 91
neuroaffective studies. *See also* body; continuing bonds; Panksepp, Jack; visceral
attachment studies, 95, 223
cognitive and affective spiritual experiences, 92, 93, 175, 212, 259, 282n9
empathic relationality, 117
limbic resonance, 95, 96, 223
New Materialists, 275, 277. *See also* material religion; Meyer, Birgit; poetics
Nhat Hanh, Thich, 93, 117, 124
normativity, 29, 40, 46n28, 142–3, 214, 247–8, 272, 274, 277. *See also* culture; oppression; power analysis
normative, xxi, 33, 39–41, 120, 142, 143, 157, 272, 275

O

oppression. *See also* critical race theory; feminism; intersectionality; normativity; power analysis
classism, 60, 261
colonialism, 27, 261, 276
historical structures, 6, 15, 41, 55, 90, 98, 117
LGBTQ, 289
marginalization, 143
microaggressions, 235
patriarchy, 291
racialized, 235
racism, 261
structural power, 98

oppression (cont.)
  whiteness, 195
  white supremacy, 31

P
Panksepp, Jack, 94, 124n25
paradigm shifts, 258, 259, 276
Parker, Rebecca, 272
pastoral, xi, xvn7, 5–7, 16, 18n15, 19n20, 20n21, 26, 29, 35, 38, 44n15, 48n50, 49n54, 55, 60, 64, 74, 76, 77, 79, 81, 93, 103, 104, 108, 110, 113, 116, 117, 121n13, 123n22, 125n29, 133n69, 133n70, 134n72, 137n92, 138n93, 138n99, 145, 150, 153–7, 159–2, 164, 165, 167, 168, 175, 176, 179–2, 184n13, 186n21, 188n36, 195, 198–201, 204, 210, 215, 216, 218, 220, 221, 226–8, 231–4, 236, 239n11, 239n16, 242n33, 242n35, 252, 253, 258–62, 273, 282n6, 282n9, 283n9, 283n11, 284n19, 285n20, 293n7. See also practices
pastoral prophetic, 5
Peace Institute. See also place; practices; Prothrow-Stith, Deborah; public health
advocacy skills, 60, 145
emotional literacy, 145, 183n6
healthy family, 199
holistic engagement, 259
Holistic Healing Center, 64, 146, 161, 185n16, 187n33
integrative learning, 263

Lesson One Company, 144
Louis D. Brown Peace Institute, xi, 6, 20n21, 194
memorial buttons, 63, 168, 170, 215, 230, 236
mission, 9, 54–7, 144, 211, 236, 249
Mothers Day Walk for Peace, 170, 175, 230, 236, 252
orders of funeral services, 63, 100, 168–9
Peaceville, 150, 151, 263
Peace Warriors, 9, 90, 167, 172, 259
Peacezone, 59, 83n7, 144, 250, 262
Peace Zones, 168, 249
safe boxes, 150
Sandplay or Sandtray Worldplay, 185n16
self-care, 166, 198, 261, 262
seven Principles of Peace, 57, 58, 231
sibling groups, 63
Survivor Leadership Academy, 60
survivor ministries, 202
Traveling memorial button project, 170
Tuesday Talks, 64, 90, 112
peacemakers, 54, 144, 175, 195, 211
peculiar, x, 63, 83n13, 160, 291. See also queer
performative, xi, 29, 101, 105, 109, 119, 132n61, 146–8, 171, 230, 236
political performative, xi
permanent Public Memorial, 107
phenomenology

phenomena, 37
phenomenological, 8, 9, 12, 13, 26, 40, 114, 119, 122n19, 167, 176, 214, 274
phenomenon, xi, 11, 14, 31, 37, 115, 119, 120n7, 127n41, 155, 167, 185n16, 230
Pineda-Madrid, Nancy, 272, 273, 285n21, 285n23
social-suffering hermeneutic, 273
Pink, Sarah, 20n21, 45n20, 124n23, 198, 237n5
emplaced, 45n20
place. *See also* Fulkerson, Mary McClintock; Pink, Sarah; space; spirituality
aura, 196–8, 215
building, 67, 208, 249, 250, 265
consistency, 197, 266
desecration,
embedded, 272
emplaced, 272
geographic or geography, 142
healing, 54, 55, 61, 106, 108, 153, 158, 160, 179, 196–9, 212, 219, 226, 234
localization, 266
peacefulness, 197
pews, 207
postmodern place theory, 198
re-sacralize, 203
sacralization, 196–202
safety, 79, 109, 196, 197, 199, 200
sanctuary, 61, 67, 109, 179, 208, 219
space, 67, 106, 109, 187n33, 196–202, 208, 212, 215, 218, 230, 234, 261

spatial, 198
stability, 197, 200
suburban, 250
urban, viii, 200, 250
poetics. *See also* body; Chopp, Rebecca S.; interdisciplinary; material religion; metaphor
material poetics, 107, 110, 273
poetic images, 144–56
poetic material art expressions, 144
religio/poetics, 104–8, 110, 132, 146–8, 168, 171, 183, 188n34, 198, 202, 204, 206–8, 215, 219, 224–7, 230, 239n14, 253, 257, 258, 260, 275
religio/socio, 151
socio/poetics, 104, 110, 132n65, 146, 147, 168, 171, 185n19, 215
theo/poetics or theopoetics, 104, 105, 109, 119, 128, 130n55, 130n57, 131n59, 132n59, 132n63, 171, 188n34
power analysis. *See also* critical race theory; feminism; normativity; oppression
accountability, 79, 80, 279
authorization, 209
colonialism, 27, 261, 276
cultural hegemony, 113, 235
dominant culture, 235
economic privilege, 235
funding, 268
governance, 180, 209
han, 261
historical structures, 111
infrastructure, 80
institutionalized power, 4, 5

power analysis (*cont.*)
  interpersonal, 5
  media, 110, 269
  normative or normativity, 39, 40, 142, 143, 272
  perpetrators, 252
  power and privilege, 51, 98, 110, 137n91, 143, 233–6
  power differentials, 14, 61, 137n84
  power relations, 26, 30, 34, 112, 229
  restorative justice, 252
  social-suffering hermeneutic, 273
  sociocultural, 111, 113, 269
  socioeconomic, 27, 98
  sociohistorical, 91, 259, 272, 274, 291
  stakeholders, 52
  structures of power, 36, 38, 259, 272
  whiteness, 143, 195
  white supremacy, 4, 31, 248, 286n25
practical theology, ix
practical theologian, x, 28
practical theological, 237n3, 272–3
practices and rituals. *See also* bible; Peace Institute; place; Tennessee Valley Unitarian Universalist Church (TVUUC); Unitarian Universalist Trauma Response Ministry (UUTRM)
  being church, 183, 234
  communal, 4, 5, 16, 26, 30, 33, 40, 88, 90, 100, 108, 144–6, 161, 163, 168, 180, 194, 218, 226, 229, 233, 258, 260–2
  credibility, 233
  curtain, 66
  ecumenical relationships, 180
  emergency preparedness, 81, 255, 268, 269
  Go-Bag, 268
  Good Samaritan, 252
  healthy family, 199
  holy humor, 224, 225, 228, 257
  interfaith relationships, 182
  kaleidoscope, 42, 159, 162, 200, 232
  leadership role, 164, 228, 234
  logistics, 179
  material testimony, 109, 167, 215
  memorial buttons, 152, 168, 171, 189n39, 215, 230, 236
  mindfulness, ix, 23, 119
  ministry of presence, 155
  Mothers Day Walk for Peace, 175, 230, 236, 252
  movement, xiiin5, 33, 100, 156, 157, 159, 160, 162, 180, 183, 211, 213, 215, 234
  normalcy, 163, 164, 219, 275
  normalizing, 160
  orders of funeral services, 100
  pastoral ear, 167
  pastoral prophetic, 5
  peace curriculums, 54, 62, 144, 145, 160
  Peace Zones, 168, 258
  placeholder, 154
  plaque, 226
  power point, 67, 115
  public practices or rituals, ix

religious practices or rituals, viii, 5, 14, 32, 228, 230
restorative justice, 54, 64, 233, 252, 271
sacred ambiguity, 181, 228, 253
sandplay, 100, 146, 150, 151, 168, 211, 213, 215, 230
Sandtray Worldplay, 185n16
sermons, 181, 225, 226
servanthood, 116, 234
seven Principles of Peace, 57
spiritual practices or rituals, ix, 4, 6, 32, 33, 39, 40, 44n16, 66, 88, 144, 194, 222
Standing on the Side of Love, 258
survivor ministries, 202
transforming pain and anger, 54–5
traveling button memorial project, 170, 236
yoga, 151
prophetic. *See also* practices
eschatological, 130, 148, 171, 218, 236
prophet, 11, 12
prophethood and priesthood, 154
prophetic social justice change, 161
soteriological, 233
testimony, 69, 103–5, 119, 128n43, 128n49, 131n58, 136n77, 146, 149, 167, 171, 198, 204, 207, 208, 253
prophetic pastoral care, 7, 19n20, 116, 117, 121n13, 138n93, 145, 150, 153, 161, 179, 183n1, 184n13, 218, 233, 236, 285n20. *See also* Gerkin, Charles V.; Graham, Larry Kent; practices

Prothrow-Stith, Deborah, 1, 16n1, 59, 82n1, 83n7, 83n8, 97, 126n33, 159, 183n3, 183n5, 187n32, 251. *See also* public health
psychoanalytic, 30, 38, 96, 97, 124n29, 125n29, 134n72, 238n10, 287n31
psychoanalysis, 112
psychodynamic, 110
public health, 2, 9, 11, 13, 19n17, 21n27, 59–62, 91, 96, 122n16, 144, 162, 172, 235, 251, 263, 269. *See also* Prothrow-Stith, Deborah
public health model, 59, 60, 251
public policy, 5, 60, 64, 250
public theology, xvn7, 44n15, 100, 188n34, 228. *See also* testimony
public theological, ix, 244n42

Q

queer. *See also* border crossing; intersectionality
queered, x
queerness, vii, 52, 290, 291

R

relational-cultural theory (RCT). *See also* interdisciplinary; Jordan, Judith V.; metaphor; Miller, Jean Baker; spirit; spirituality; Walker, Maureen
acute disconnection, 156
authenticity, 200, 220
central relational paradox, 150

relational-cultural theory (RCT) (*cont.*)
  condemned isolation, 117, 174
  controlling images, 113, 114, 135n74
  discrepant relational images, 113
  domination and subordination, 112
  five good things of connection, 116
  growth-fostering connection, 116
  mutual empathy, 174, 220
  mutual empowerment, 112, 117, 174
  mutuality, 112, 199, 258
  radical respect, 150
  relational images, 113, 116, 261
  strategies of connection, 116
  strategies of disconnection, 116
  traumatic disconnection, 116, 117
religions
  Buddhist or Buddhism, x, 93, 105, 119
  Christian or Christianity, x, xi, xivn6, 7, 29, 33, 93, 102, 104, 116, 117, 119, 127n42, 171, 211, 224, 230, 231, 243n37, 252, 270, 283n11, 283n33
  folklorist or folk religion, xi, 26, 121n13
  God, xivn6, 25, 34, 43n9, 48n50, 93, 117, 119, 138n99, 211, 213, 214, 224, 227, 230, 243n37, 252, 270
  Hindu or Hinduism, 119, 247
  humanist or humanism, x
  Jewish or Judaism, xi, 33, 93
  Methodist or Methodism, ix
  Muslim or Islam, 4
  ordinary theology, 33, 47n48
  popular religion, 26, 32, 34, 38, 40, 100, 127n42, 145
  Unitarian Universalist (UU) or Unitarian Universalism, xivn6, xvn7, 6, 7
resiliency
  resilience, 155, 156, 188n35, 208, 226, 253, 257, 260
  resilient, 166
restorative justice, 54, 64, 233, 252, 271
Reynolds, Thomas, 272, 285n20
  vulnerable communion, 272, 285n20

S
Santino, Jack, xi, xviin12, 128n43, 130n57, 132n61. *See also* spontaneous shrines
Scarry, Elaine, 29, 43n10, 271, 284n17. *See also* body; meaning-making; narrative
Schneiders, Sandra, 92, 123n20, 123n21. *See also* metaphor
secular, vii, ix, x, 6, 12, 13, 16, 23, 26, 33, 57, 60, 79, 119, 131n59, 172, 175, 178, 212, 225, 236, 248, 252, 262–3, 266, 269, 292
servitude, 56
  Christian servant, 56
social justice, ix, xvn7, 12, 34, 35, 55, 60, 66–8, 85n19, 103, 136n77, 137n82, 137n85, 149–51, 153, 161, 168, 171, 176, 184n8, 195, 201, 208,

219, 220, 232, 236, 243n37,
253, 254, 280
social sciences, x, 11, 24, 40, 41,
43n9, 94
social work, vii, ix, x, xiiin3, xiiin4, 7,
10, 11, 13, 20n21, 21n27, 23,
25, 32, 33, 45n20, 46n26, 51,
52, 55, 60, 87, 96, 110, 114,
115, 137n85, 137n86, 141,
184n8, 188n37, 229, 248,
282n9, 283n13, 287n31. *See
also* interdisciplinary; public
health; transdisciplinary
clinical social work, 52, 229
sociocultural
socioeconomic, 98
sociohistorical, viii, 91, 259, 274,
291
sociologist, 33, 271
sociology, 5, 31, 40, 46n31
space. *See also* place
desecration,
rededication, 67, 109, 202, 203,
207
re-sacralize, 203
sacralization, 196
spirit. *See also* body; continuing
bonds; immanence;
neuroaffective studies
embodied affective and cognitive,
119, 212, 259
metaphoric correlations, 33, 35,
93, 105, 117, 124n23, 125,
131n58, 159, 213, 238n10
translations for, 12
spirituality. *See also* body; healing;
immanence; metaphor; place;
transcendence

aura, 196–8, 215
faith, ix, x, 4, 24, 40, 66, 88, 175,
182, 211–15, 240n18, 251,
253, 283n10
revelation, 118
salvation, 234, 276
spiritual path, 24
spiritual tribe, 46n27, 89, 90, 92,
109, 112, 120n8, 121n8,
137n91, 153, 156, 182,
184n13, 198, 203, 208, 225,
226, 234, 243n37, 253, 260,
262, 291. *See also* Ammerman,
Nancy
sacred story, 89, 121n8, 208, 226,
234, 253
spontaneous shrines, xi, xviin12,
130n57. *See also* Santino, Jack
spontaneous street memorials, xi
suffering
evil, 236, 241n28, 257
flesh, 217, 272
God, 44n16, 57, 161, 211, 217,
236, 241n28
spirit, 161, 211, 217
survivors
Peace Warriors, 9, 90, 167, 172,
189n41, 259
sibling groups, 63
survivors as experts, 116, 141–92,
217, 234, 240n24, 258

T
Tennessee Valley Unitarian
Universalist Church (TVUUC).
See also practices; Unitarian
Universalist Association

(UUA); Unitarian Universalist
Trauma Response Ministry
(UUTRM)
All Souls Day, 260
being church, 182, 183, 234
building, 67, 68, 202, 204, 208
curtain, 66, 204, 239n14
God is love, 227
ministry of presence, 153–5
pastoral care office, 204
pastoral ear, 153, 154, 167
plaque, 70, 71, 115, 204, 206, 208, 226
power point, 67, 115
religious liberal, xvin9
sermons, 67, 181, 225–7
Standing on the Side of Love, 178
Welcoming Congregation, 69
testimony. *See also* narrative theory; prophetic; science; witness
confession or confessional, 104, 180, 215, 253
fierceness, 272
material testimony, 69, 109, 167, 208, 215
public testimony, 64, 146, 167–83, 215, 257, 263
Ricouer, Paul, 104, 128n49
survivor testimonies, 176
Thandeka, 30, 45n19, 125n29, 238n10
theological anthropology, 116. *See also* Unitarian Universalist Association
Bellah, Robert, 271
human nature, 125n29, 233
ontological individualism, 271

Tiffany, Daniel, 41, 48n52, 124n23. *See also* interdisciplinary; metaphor
transcendence, 38, 117, 118, 131n58, 199, 259, 282n9, 285n21. *See also* body; immanence; Lakoff, George
transdisciplinary, 6, 11, 16, 19n17, 21n27, 35, 42, 44n16, 45n21, 104, 105, 111, 258. *See also* culture; interdisciplinary; metaphor; public health
transformation
transformative, 13, 26, 105, 143, 145, 146, 149, 171, 173, 174, 183, 184n13, 204, 271
transforming, 18n10, 54, 55, 84n13, 88, 90, 144, 146, 150, 184n13, 195, 283n13
trauma. *See also* body; continuing bonds; interdisciplinary; meaning-making; poetics; van der Kolk, Bessel; visceral
climate change, 32, 35, 275
cultural trauma, 25
disassociation, 38, 87
historical trauma, 91, 98, 122n16
homicide, vii, 1, 7–9, 20n21, 54, 62–4, 76, 97, 105, 106, 146, 157, 159, 162, 163, 166, 171, 173, 187n33, 197, 211, 260, 268
limbic resonance, 95, 223
neuroaffective trauma studies, 91, 273
neurophysiological, 242n32, 261
police violence, 2, 30
posttraumatic growth, 89

resilience, 155, 156, 188n35, 208, 226, 253, 257, 260
unsayability, 162
vicarious growth, 89
vicarious trauma, 261, 262
violence, viii, xii, 2–5, 8, 23, 26, 27, 30, 31, 54, 60–3, 84n13, 90, 106, 111, 135, 168, 171, 174, 176, 191n50, 195, 218–20, 232, 235, 254, 256, 268, 269, 275, 284n19, 285n21, 291
violent trauma, viii, ix, xi, xii, 1–6, 10, 14, 23, 25–8, 31, 34, 35, 37–42, 61, 78, 89, 94, 98, 104, 111, 120, 137n91, 153, 154, 163, 174, 180, 195, 202, 208, 220, 225, 226, 230, 232, 254, 257, 259, 260, 266, 273, 291

U

Unitarian Universalist Association (UUA). *See also* covenantal theology; theological anthropology
living tradition sources, xvin8
principles and purposes, 72
Standing on the Side of Love, 178, 191n51
Unitarian Universalist Trauma Response Ministry (UUTRM). *See also* practices; Tennessee Valley Unitarian Universalist Church (TVUUC); Unitarian Universalist Association (UUA)

credibility, 76, 86n31, 154, 155, 233
emergency preparedness, 81, 255, 268, 269
Go-Bag, 268
Ground Zero or 9/11, 72
holy humor, 224, 228, 231, 257
ministry of presence, 153–5
mission, 74–6
sacred ambiguity, 181, 228, 253–7

V

Van der Kolk, Bessel, 26, 27, 38, 42n3, 47n43, 122n15, 122n17, 127n38, 186n20, 274, 286n26
Van der Port, Mattjis, 274, 286n28
visceral. *See also* body; Fulkerson, Mary McClintock
enlivened, 147, 230
Lamothe, Ryan, 38
limbic resonance, 95, 96, 223
Van der Kolk, Bessel, 38

W

Walker, Maureen, 114, 136n81, 137n84, 281n4. *See also* power analysis; relational-cultural theory
Welch, Sharon, xi, xviin12, 104, 128n52, 132n60, 245n48. *See also* dangerous memories
White, Michael, 112. *See also* narrative theory; power analysis
witness, xvn7, 10, 11, 39, 88, 104, 105, 109, 119, 128n43,

131n57, 147–9, 153, 168, 171, 172, 176, 178, 188n37, 196, 198, 206–8, 224, 230, 236, 258, 271, 290, 292. *See also* testimony

sacred witness, 148

worldsense, 91, 122. *See also* body; culture; metaphor

world/sense, 16, 21n26, 91, 98, 99, 104, 105, 113, 114, 119, 122n19, 123n19, 194, 195, 198, 214, 221, 232, 235, 247–87, 290–2

worldviews, x, 10–13, 24, 25, 33, 35, 37, 41, 79, 94, 143, 237n1, 244n44. *See also* body; culture; metaphor

world/view, 91, 98, 99, 104, 105, 113, 119, 194, 195, 213, 214, 221, 232, 259, 274, 275

The manufacturer's authorised representative in the EU is Springer Nature Customer Service Centre GmbH, Europaplatz 3, 69115 Heidelberg, Germany. If you have any concerns regarding our products, please contact ProductSafety@springernature.com

Printed and bound by CPI Group (UK) Ltd, Croydon, CR0 4YY
23/03/2026
02076739-0009